The Concept of Peace in the Bahá'í Faith

BY THE SAME AUTHOR

Diálogo de religiones, Camino de paz (Dialogue of Religions, a Pathway to Peace)
Hacia un discurso bahá'í (Towards a Bahá'í Discourse)

George Ronald Bahá'í Studies Series

The Concept of Peace in the Bahá'í Faith

Miguel Santesteban Gil

GR

GEORGE RONALD
OXFORD

George Ronald, Publisher
Oxford
www.grbooks.com

A catalogue record for this book is available from the British Library

ISBN 978-0-85398-650-8

Cover design: Steinergraphics.com

Contents

Preface and Acknowledgements vii
1 Introduction 1

PART I Bahá'u'lláh

2 Some Biographical Considerations 17
3 The Kingdom of God and the Abrogation of *jihád* 21
4 Bahá'u'lláh's Pronouncements on Peace 28
5 Conclusion 45

PART II 'Abdu'l-Bahá on Peace

6 The Convening of a Peace Conference 54
7 The 'Promulgation' of Universal Peace 62
8 The Role of America 69
9 Women and Peace 74
10 The Tablet to The Hague 77
11 Principled Action and the 'Twelve Principles' 86
12 Overcoming Violence and the Use of Force 96
13 Conclusion 99

PART III Shoghi Effendi: The Enlargement of the Peace Horizon

14 A New Sense of History 108
15 Shoghi Effendi on Peace 114
16 The Lesser Peace as a Process 119
17 The League of Nations and the United Nations 124
18 The Role of America 130
19 Peace-makers or Pacifists? 134
20 Conclusion 137

PART IV The Nature of Man in the Bahá'í Writings

21 A Spiritual Anthropology 143
22 Man's Dignity and Perfectibility 159

23 Violence and the Individual: The Power of Vain Imaginings and Idle Fancies 167
24 Conclusion 175

PART V A Framework for Peace

25 Bahá'í Morality 184
26 Spiritual Behaviour: Action as Service to Humanity 190
27 Divine Philosophy and Religious Unity 199
28 The Organic Analogy: Organic Unity and Unity in Diversity 209
29 Bahá'í Consultation 216
30 Towards the Most Great Peace 227

* * *

31 Summary and Conclusions 231

Bibliography 255
Notes and References 279
About the Author 335

Preface and Acknowledgements

This book analyses the concept of peace in the writings of Bahá'u'lláh, 'Abdu'l-Bahá and Shoghi Effendi. The general outline is divided into two distinct areas of interest. The first details Bahá'u'lláh, 'Abdu'l-Bahá and Shoghi Effendi's main statements connected with peace. This provides a basic timeline, as well as a more biographical sense of how the main sequence of Bahá'í peace-related ideas evolved with each succeeding interpretive authority. Bahá'u'lláh's abolition of *jihád* is thus given a prominent place as a first expression of the overarching principle of peace, ramifications of which were the principle of collective security, which comprised arbitration, disarming and demilitarization. Peace was further broadened by 'Abdu'l-Bahá as to encompass a full array of attending principles, and then resituated by Shoghi Effendi in historical perspective.

The second area tackles the question of peace from two major thematic angles: Bahá'í anthropology, and the Bahá'í ethos. Part IV shows that the Bahá'í conception of peace is anchored on a dynamic conception of human reality, one that reaffirms the dignity and perfectibility of man and postulates peace as a weaning out from atavistic forms of prejudice (*taqlíd*), vain imaginings (*awḥam*), and fanaticism (*ta'aṣṣub*). The repositioning of man in a middle point in the spiritual evolutionary scale is paired with a notion of true civilization as the recombination of materiality and spirituality. The resulting Bahá'í ethos (Part V) is then described as the creative tension between a maximum sense of autonomy and a full degree of responsiveness to societal needs. A number of privileged thematic expressions of this moderated ethos are examined, including the concepts of oneness of religion, organic unity and consultation. The open nature of the resulting approach is underlined by suggesting that the concept may move to a phase of increasing modelling.

This book has been some twenty years in the making. Its first general outline was already conceived in the early 1990s, but the project had to be postponed not once but several times due to major financial setbacks and, not the least, my resettlement in my country of birth for some eventful twelve years. Attempts at restarting the original project went no farther than the successful completion of the preliminary, prescribed doctoral courses at the Universidad Pública de Navarra and a first tentative draft made during the year when an allowance by the National Assembly of the Bahá'ís of Spain made it possible for me to set aside four days a week for the purpose. Alas, this came to nothing, as a move to Madrid meant that, because of the idiosyncrasies of the Spanish university system and the Bologna process, a new set of doctoral courses had to be undertaken. I was halfway through this process when it became clearer that the time had come for our family to move back to my adopted homeland, Australia. So, once more I found at La Trobe University not only a congenial place to bring the task to fruition but also a most supportive and understanding environment, represented first and foremost in the person of my supervisor Dr Greg Bailey, whose advice proved most helpful in directing my steps through the woods and thickets of academic work; and secondly, in its unique Humanities Faculty, which at the time provided ample and unrivalled room for the discussion and research of a vast tapestry of human concerns. The debt I contracted with my supervisor can hardly be repaid. His patience in waiting for the next instalments, as well as his brief comments, with a few question marks here and there, were enough to steer me in the right course.

I have a similar debt with May Hofman for her inestimable work in arranging the original dissertation into what I feel is now a far more cogent and readable whole. Except for the introduction, where an effort has been made to summarize things, the rest of the book remains essentially the same as the 2011 version. Readers will no doubt take note of the fact that a number of very valuable contributions bearing on peace from a Bahá'í perspective have been published since then. I believe all have their rightful place and can be read as part of a choral effort to pick up the waves of a powerful melody.

Needless to say, nothing of this would have been possible without the unfailing encouragement extended to me by my wife and my own children throughout all these years.

Miguel Santesteban Gil

A mi esposa, Elham
feliz y admirable

I
Introduction

Peace is a major defining theme in the writings of the Bahá'í Faith.[1] As such it ranks second only to 'unity',[2] of which it is said to be the outcome, and is often placed before justice, which in turn is conceived of as its true foundation.[3] As 'Abdu'l-Bahá was to put it:

> The fundamental truth of the Manifestations is peace. This underlies all religion, all justice. The divine purpose is that men should live in unity, concord and agreement and should love one another.[4]

As a major theme, peace is foundational to any Bahá'í elaboration on social issues. Doctrinal condensations by 'Abdu'l-Bahá, like the one that follows, have acted as more than just illustrations of a peace ideal:

> The divine religions were founded for the purpose of unifying humanity and establishing universal peace. Any movement which brings about peace and agreement in human society is truly a divine movement; any reform which causes people to come together under the shelter of the same tabernacle is surely animated by heavenly motives. At all times and in all ages of the world, religion has been a factor in cementing together the hearts of men and in uniting various and divergent creeds. It is the peace element in religion that blends mankind and makes for unity. Warfare has ever been the cause of separation, disunion and discord.[5]

In choosing the 'peace element' in the Bahá'í religion for this study my chief aim has been to highlight one element in the trilogy of unity, justice and peace that arguably sits at the core of Bahá'í beliefs. Taken as a whole, the trilogy has proven essential to an integrated understanding of other characteristic subsets of Bahá'í principles. How the three themes relate to each other, when they were first announced by any of the Bahá'í central figures, how they were theologically undergirded, under which circumstances or in response to which needs were formulated, and how these were articulated into a distinct framework remain largely matters for scholars to establish, yet worthy of attention in the light of the higher profile the Bahá'í religion is gaining worldwide. At any rate, the concepts of 'divine philosophy' and 'unity of conscience' mentioned by 'Abdu'l-Bahá in the context of the meeting between East and West (wisdom and rationality) and universal peace respectively, suggest the presence of a theological and metaphysical substratum that invites further explorations. The present work pursues the study and characterization through the relevant texts of Bahá'u'lláh, 'Abdu'l-Bahá, and Shoghi Effendi of just one aspect – that of peace – albeit one of the greatest significance.

By bringing the texts into sharper focus, rather than privileging the sociological or even the historical, it is hoped that the various ideological components of the concept of peace in the Bahá'í religion will be brought to sharper relief under a different light. It is not my aim to arrive at a doctrinal re-formulation, so much as to explore the logical, anthropological and ethical extensions of a key idea (or theme) as it moved from one stage to another in the development of a young religion heavily invested in the world.

Framed as a contribution to intellectual history, the question this study ultimately addresses amounts to this: what kind of peace, human nature and general morality did the key authors envisage when they made some of their weightiest proclamations on peace?

* * *

Over the last sixty years the Bahá'í Faith has been recognized as a world religious system[6] with a strong irenic imprint[7] and a cosmopolitan moral outlook in which peace, dialogue and non-confrontation act as buttresses of the core idea of unity. Yet, while it has been commonly acknowledged that peace is a major Bahá'í theme, few academic studies have set out to explore its implications. Back in 1993, in his overview of relevant citations contained in academic journals, Seena Fazel lamented:

> Surprisingly there is not even one paper on the Bahá'í approach to peace issues or international relations. This, of course, is not the state of affairs in the Bahá'í community where there are many conferences, publications and books exploring the Bahá'í approach to current social problems.[8]

While Fazel's contention was true, the overall explanations provided by Peter Smith in his earlier socio-historical analyses in *The Bábí and Bahá'í Religions*[9] had already shed new perspectives on the evolution of the Bábí and Bahá'í religions. Relying on the analytical category of 'motifs', Smith sought out to characterize the various stages in the historical sequence that both religions followed.[10] Smith had previously clarified and sharpened his use of the concept of dominant motifs in an erudite discussion of its applications in Peter Berger's doctoral dissertation and the two journal articles that followed in its trail, in which Berger expanded and refined his categories.[11] Smith's model furnished a different kind of periodization through a series of synchronic snapshots of the Bábí and Bahá'í communities, taken from the particular perspectives afforded by the selected motifs in question. Intended as sociological markers, these allowed the author to move with the subject matter while striking a middle ground between a text-based analysis and a phenomenological or sociological account of the movements.

Two of the categories in Smith's analysis are relevant with regard to purpose of the present study. One is the 'holy war and martyrdom' motif, especially significant for the Bábí phase, and the other is the 'social reformism' motif (modernization and the millennium), which would become relevant in the ensuing Bahá'í period (until 1921, and, arguably, until present). According to Smith the holy war motif, which in the Shí'i tradition necessarily blends with that of martyrdom, appears as important in the early recruitment and mobilization of Bábí adherents; yet Smith's account of this motif appears inconclusive, if not factually as well as doctrinally de-emphasized. The Bábí uprisings are in effect construed as instances of a defensive struggle (defensive *jihád*) and, by contrast, martyrdom is said to have remained even more important as evidence of the ultimate truth witnessed to by the Bábís. As for social reformism, according to Smith this motif was the second most dominant in the ensuing Bahá'í period. In it converged the millennial and alleged theocratic visions of the Báb, only now re-focused on the persons of Bahá'u'lláh and 'Abdu'l-Bahá, whose purpose was 'the unification and pacification of the whole world' through a programme of reforms on a universal scale – peace, arms reductions, one common language.[12] Such a programme was for the rulers of the world to carry out, but it was incumbent on the Bahá'ís themselves to set an example and attract others to their Cause, never through coercion, but through dialogue and persuasion. Smith illustrates the integrative approach of 'Abdu'l-Bahá by referring to His critique of the East and the West. The efforts of the secular authorities and those of the Bahá'í community would lead, in their own way, to the attainment of the Lesser Peace and ultimately the Most Great Peace.

No major revisitation of Bahá'í historical accounts occurred for a number of years until 1998, five years after Fazel's lamentation. Juan Ricardo Cole's study *Modernity and the Millenium* supplied a number of significant connections between Bahá'í doctrine and its historical milieu, demonstrating the relevance of Bahá'u'lláh's position in that context.[13] Conceived as a series of five case studies, the work offered a number of insights into an area of academic endeavour (modernity, globalization, and religion) which, as pointed out by Warburg, had been neglected considerably by scholars of religion.[14] The novelty in Cole's approach lies not so much in the fact that he locates the appearance of the Bahá'í religion in its own historical setting, an aspect that Amanat in his *Resurrection and Renewal* (published in 1989), and from a faith-based perspective Balyuzi in his *Bahá'u'lláh, the King of Glory* (first published in 1980) had already mapped, but rather in his use of the case study approach to illustrate the complex relationships between various emerging paradigms of modernity. As a result, political, social and cultural trends in the Ottoman and European spheres become alive and relevant to an understanding of Bahá'u'lláh's position, not simply as part of an elaborate background, but as integral and inseparable from it.

Key to an understanding of Cole's approach is his conceptualization of the nature of modernity (or rather modernities) as being far more pluralistic in scope than what has been envisaged from a monistic top-down western perspective.[15] This pluralism alone would be a disclaimer that the road to social paradise was already set once and for all in western cartography. The Bahá'í critique of the western template of modernization suggests that western ways, too, had to disentangle themselves from the associated evils of rampant nationalism, militarism, colonialism and imperialistic designs. Cole's study, which the monographies of Oliver Scharbrodt[16] and Necatí Alkan[17] have complemented and broadened, each in its own way, has shown that Enlightenment ideals were not unfamiliar to Bahá'u'lláh and 'Abdu'l-Bahá, Who might have come into contact with them through various sources. Thus, according to Cole, typical enlightened and liberal notions such as freedom of conscience, separation of Church and State, rule of law, democratic government, would have been adopted and adapted by Bahá'u'lláh and 'Abdu'l-Bahá from likely French sources, notably Saint Simonianism, either directly or most likely through their contacts with well-read and much travelled Ottoman figures. This adoption or adaptation remains somewhat speculative in the absence of more concrete evidence, but Cole is far from suggesting a wholesale migration of ideas, as made evident by his acknowledgement of the differences too.[18] In fact, he is more interested in noting that those ideas belong certainly in the *Zeitgeist* of the period.[19] The result is what Cole describes at key points in his narrative[20] as instances of 'utopian realism',[21] an oxymoron pointing to the fact that standard realist positions at the time may indeed have contained a number of largely untenable and eventually unworkable presuppositions; and vice versa, projects retrospectively catalogued as utopian can now be counterfactually argued as endowed with a potent streak of as yet unfulfilled realism.

Cole has also traced some of the fundamental elements in the approach to peace espoused by Bahá'u'lláh and 'Abdu'l-Bahá, suggesting, first, a possible connection with the Moghul Emperor Akbar, and second, with the ideas of the Enlightenment. In Cole's examination the grafting of western ideas appears to be especially attuned to the needs and possibilities current in the Ottoman Empire. In fact, as Cole indicates, Bahá'u'lláh's ideas went beyond what reformists such as the Young Ottomans would advocate, and, as in the case of 'Abdu'l-Bahá, more consistently and well before His time. While pointing generally to possible sources for some of Bahá'u'lláh's conceptions (the Enlightenment and the oeuvre of Saint-Simon and Enfantin),[22] Cole is particularly interested in pointing to their pertinence, their dynamic nature and the overall trend that they marked in the cosmopolitan environment that seemed to characterize the Ottoman elites at the time. Cole's work reflects in this sense a characteristic preoccupation in the field of cultural and postmodern studies to explore alternative worldviews from a critical and yet sympathetic perspective.

Finally, Cole notes that just as the *Tanẓimat* had laid the groundwork for the more ambitious reforms propounded by Bahá'u'lláh and the Young Ottomans, the collapse of the Ottoman Empire would have brought to the fore the relevance of the incipient system of collective security designed to settle the Crimean War. These likely influences allow Cole to posit the interaction between a series of currents of thought and historical pressures that would explain some of the similarities between Bahá'u'lláh's stand on peace and western approaches: hence both streams could be seen as providing a similar response to similar challenges.[23] In Cole's words, the Bahá'í community was to become the 'Middle East's first indigenous peace movement in the era of modernity, and one of the very few to become institutionalised over the long term'.[24]

For his part, and to some extent in response to Cole's methodological approach, Nader Saiedi[25] has reviewed the internal unity of Bahá'u'lláh's writings in the light of Bahá'u'lláh's proclaimed self-awareness as the divine theophanic figure or Manifestation of God (*maẓhar-i-ilahí*) announced by the Báb. A similar process has also been undertaken by Saiedi in his more recent *Gate of the Heart* (2008), the last chapter of which deals in greater detail with the Báb's concept of holy war, in direct response to MacEoin's exposition on the subject.[26] The substance of Saiedi's argument is that the Báb's revelation was indeed preparatory in character and gradual in that its own evolution moved from formally conforming to Islamic expectations to actually subverting their tenor in several fundamental ways: first, by making a number of harsh laws of his revelation enter into direct contradiction with others pointing to the exact opposite; second, by making the enforcement of those harsher laws conditional on His own sanction, or indeed the confirmation of 'Him Whom God shall make manifest', whose appearance was said to be imminent; third, by introducing conditions impossible of fulfilment; and fourth, by explicitly reinterpreting His own laws in ways that would render them unenforceable. Since not even the events of Ṭabarsí received such sanction, and the appearance of Him Whom God shall make manifest was consistently *also* foreseen as imminent, there is indeed no such chasm between alleged Bábí 'militancy' and Bahá'í 'quietism' (pacifism). Bahá'u'lláh would have thus consummated what in spirit was already contained in the revealed law of the Báb. Therefore, while the departure from Islam was indeed 'radical', the same can hardly be said from Bahá'u'lláh's superseding of the laws of the Báb, most of which had already undergone under the Báb's own hermeneutics the very process of spiritualization and mollification that MacEoin attributes to Bahá'u'lláh (and Bausani had already identified in his *Religion in Iran* as characteristic of the Báb's religion). In sum, the abrogation of the law of the sword was thus sweeping at a formal level, but very much in keeping with the trend marked by the Báb, and before Him by the Sufi reversal implied in the distinction between the Greater and the Lesser *jiháds*.

In stressing the cohesion of Bahá'u'lláh's approach, Saiedi has identified four hermeneutical 'principles' that, in his view, remained constant throughout the various phases in Bahá'u'lláh's lifetime. These principles would account for the internal unity of the stances Bahá'u'lláh adopted as he moved to proclaim his mission, and then establish his religion as a spiritual Dispensation endowed with the full attributes of a new Law. They are:

The prohibition or removal of the 'sword'
The principle of covenant
The universal revelation
The principle of heart

The prohibition of the 'sword' (paradigmatically represented by the abolition of *jihád*) was in fact the external expression of the primacy of the heart, that is, the prevalence of conscience over any forms of compulsion in faith matters. The abrogation of both holy war and ritual impurity, resulting from the authority of Bahá'u'lláh's new Covenant, thus came to symbolize the removal of two major obstacles to peaceful coexistence among the world's religions and their peoples.

* * *

The present analysis indeed makes it clear that Bahá'u'lláh's legislative activity was not limited to a purely religious context. The principle of collective security, as enunciated by Bahá'u'lláh in His public proclamations (1868–1873), seems to have implied not only the outlawing of interstate war but also the redirection of material and social pursuits towards the fleshing out of a world community. 'Just war' thinking, whether feeding on religious or secular grounds, or else on idealism or realism, was thus denied the sort of in-principle legitimacy it had enjoyed for centuries if not millennia. Instead, greater weight was accorded by Bahá'u'lláh to the collective interests of humanity than to national or communal interests. In this context, the distinction between the Lesser and the Most Great Peace, corresponding to two major stages in God's plan, was to operate as a correlate of the social distinction between the world at large and the people of Bahá, that is between those who had not yet recognized God's revelation for this Day and those, who having done so, accepted to abide by the provisions of the new living Covenant.

Similarly, in his Tablet to The Hague, 'Abdu'l-Bahá set forth an expanded definition of peace that, in addition to incorporating the principle of collective security and international arbitration, linked peace to a number of policies, attitudes and behaviours that ought to play a critical role in securing peace. It was also 'Abdu'l-Bahá Who established the theme of the Bahá'í Covenant firmly in the minds of the much-scattered Bahá'í community. But it fell upon Shoghi Effendi, 'Abdu'l-Bahá's grandson, to provide the Bahá'í community with a complete practical framework for the implementation and interpretation of these teachings; firstly by establishing the legal and spiritual bases of the Bahá'í community – or to be more precise, the 'Bahá'í Administrative Order'– and secondly by clarifying its complex relationships vis-à-vis a world that was neither condemned in its entirety nor accepted in its current form, hence neither world-rejecting nor *mondain*.

In this sequence the peace element seems to have emerged not so much as a set of clear-cut Bahá'í doctrinal positions, but rather as a dynamic focus of Bahá'í identity that evolved over time, with each change in the line of the interpretive authority introducing major emphases and amplifications in the overall paradigm. In this sense the Bahá'í 'idea' of peace appears defined not so much as a concept as an 'organic theme' connected to the example set by the central figures of the Bahá'í religion, particularly in the face of persecution, a theme whose expressions (for instance the 'amity meetings' promoted by the American believers in the 1920s and 1930s) cannot be dissociated from eschatological references to a world bound to become free from the scourge of war as it brings to fruition a divine civilization (i.e. God's Kingdom).

This substratum of ideas, set in the dynamic context of the advent of the Kingdom of God, is further clarified by some key doctrinal Bahá'í positions on *jihád*, collective security, *taqlíd*, and other sub-themes, the practical derivations of which will become more apparent after a closer examination of the Bahá'í view of man and the Bahá'í ethos. Indeed, while some fundamental preliminary conclusions can be drawn from the initial process of collating and regrouping some of Bahá'u'lláh's, 'Abdu'l-Bahá's and Shoghi Effendi's major references to peace and peace-related matters, these will not become definite unless they are read against the background provided by a survey, however cursory, of the Bahá'í view of human nature and the moral underpinnings that determine conduct in a social context. These two major areas are dealt with at some length in Parts IV and V.

* * *

References to the concept of 'idea', 'theme' and 'sub-themes' in previous paragraphs require some explanation. My own examination of the subject is framed in the tradition of intellectual history and the history of ideas, a field with a longstanding presence, whose key concepts owe much to the work and writings of Arthur Lovejoy, but which has also a firm rooting in the scholarly tradition of Jacob Burckhardt, Wilhem Dilthey and Johan Huizinga, through to Marc Bloch and Lucien Febvre. Some of the insights and corresponding analytical tools developed by Lovejoy are particularly apt for the purposes of my present thesis. This is so because the bulk of the present study, as in the case of many of Lovejoy's works, is based primordially on texts, whose logical inferences, implications and ramifications it seeks to clarify.

This privileging of texts is doubly important. Firstly, the Bahá'í writings, especially those that are accounted as authoritative, can be taken as providing a sufficient material basis to outline the contours and content of what is a crucial Bahá'í idea (that of peace). Secondly, a study of the texts is of primary importance to determine, through the analysis of the idea's key components (that is, the 'unit ideas'), the general sense that can be attributed to the idea *as a whole*. The chief purpose in this process, in substance, is none other than tracing the course of the unfolding idea of peace as adopted, invoked or logically implicit in Bahá'í scripture. More specifically, it is my intention to identify and discuss, rather than enumerate, the units or elementary components that combine into the idea, bestowing upon it a certain shape and resilience.

A further inspiration for this work has been found in the concept of 'themes' as developed by Edward Morris Opler. Conceived to serve the needs of his fellow anthropologists, it allows for greater flexibility in considering the ethical and socio-political ramifications of the theme of peace in the Bahá'í religion. Opler defines a theme as a 'postulate or position, declared or implied, and usually controlling behaviour or stimulating activity, which is tacitly approved or openly promoted in a society'. Themes do not present themselves in isolation or in a clear-cut manner:

> The activities, prohibitions of activities, or references which result from the acceptance of a theme are its *expressions*. Such expressions may be *formalized* or *unformalized*. *Limiting factors*, often the existence of other apposed or circumscribing themes and their extensions, control the number, force, and variety of a theme's expressions. The interplay of theme and *countertheme* is the key to the equilibrium achieved in a culture, and structure in culture is essentially their interrelation and balance.[27] *(Italics are mine to underline Opler's more technical usage.)*

Despite Lovejoy's much wider conception and preventions against over-specialization, the Lovejoyan 'idea' may tend in practice to be equated with a key word or with a verbal proposition and hence its 'meanings' might be logically derived through a process of skilful collating and contrasting of texts containing them. This kind of relative simplification is less likely in the Oplerian theme, which in a way is quite similar to the extended version of the programme propounded by Lovejoy.[28] The theme, in effect, can more properly be described as a complex idea (or even a 'motif' in the sense given to it by Smith), which is conveyed variously not just in discourse but in actual practice by way of other levels of expression such as rituals, gestures, legends, prohibitions, restrictions, art-crafts, etc. In Lovejoy, as pointed out by his critics and reviewers,[29] ideas may tend to have a life of their own ('they are the most migratory things') to the point where their genetic continuities become easily over-extended, much in the same way that general historians have tended to examine the past as already preformed in a concatenation of ever-receding pasts, or sociologists have found individual units framed within and replicating ever-larger units or contexts. This problem is more evidently brought to the fore when 'original' elements in the thought of an author are bypassed by ignoring their possible special role in the re-patterning of a whole conception, or by diluting them among a mass of analogous precedents or external influences, preferably of the material and political variety.[30]

In Opler, the theme is more laterally found in realms other than texts or oral traditions. Translated into patterns of behaviour or cultural activity, the theme may reappear in ways that bear only a limited relationship with the verbal theme; yet those patterns express it effectively.[31] This notwithstanding, the ideas of 'sub-themes', 'counter-themes' and 'limiting factors' advanced by Opler offer a number of possibilities, especially when considering facets of the main theme that would usually escape the attention of the historian of ideas, who may tend to over-rely on his or her texts. It is this criterion that has led me to the treatment of *taqlíd*, *ta'áṣṣub* and *awḥam* as sub-themes or controlling unit ideas in Part IV, and to the sub-themes of organic unity and consultation in Part V. The first set (*taqlíd*, *ta'áṣṣub* and *awḥam*) is discussed in the context of Bahá'í anthropology; they are the counter-themes of other themes that are given special prominence in the Bahá'í writings – the notion of perfection, refinement, dignity and exaltation, which in typical Bahá'í fashion are coeval with the mounting greatness of the present theophanic aeon. This portion of the study, in essence, links the idea-complex of peace with the Bahá'í theory of human nature.[32] The second set (organic unity and consultation) is the result of a widening of the same programme. Morality is seen here not in the developed form of 'ethics', but rather in its more prefigurative aspect of an *ethos*, a 'climate' in terms of Lovejoy, made up of a number of elements not typically associated with ethics. The selection in particular of the notions of organic unity and consultation is not accidental, but fundamental to our understanding of the evolving dynamics of the Bahá'í understanding of peace and its correlation with the notion of unity. As indicated, to the extent that a theme such as peace is operative through a number of sub-themes, expressions and even counter-themes, the theme itself does not need to be even spelled out for it to enjoy full currency.

Like Lovejoy, who thinks of unit ideas as being limited in number and deriving much of their meaning from the patterns and emphases they form,[33] Opler takes as a starting point that 'In every culture are found a *limited number* of dynamic affirmations, called themes, which control behaviour or stimulate activity' (emphasis added). This notion of a rather limited stock of unit ideas or of a 'limited number of dynamic affirmations'[34] may also have important consequences for an analysis of the continuities and discontinuities found in the general dynamic of religious movements. Just as a limited amount of genetic material may account for substantial changes in evolutionary terms, a few changes of emphasis, as indicated by Lovejoy and Opler, may result in fundamental changes in the overall feel and meaning of an entire system.

The result of this recombination is a more nuanced picture. Elements, that would otherwise have proved indefinable if only the main texts bearing on the *theme* peace were read as important, take on added prominence and gain natural admittance into the Bahá'í cohort of fundamental *expressions* supportive of peace. This is the case, for instance, of the Bahá'í critique of *taqlíd*, the importance of which clearly exceeds the narrow boundaries of technical discussions over *ijtihád* and *taqlíd* or those over innovation (*bida'*) and modernization (*tajaddud*, the adoption or borrowing of western technology and administrative practices).[35] As our discussion of the concept will attempt to show, the Bahá'í critique of *taqlíd* implies not only a reassertion of the dignity of men and women (there cannot be a relinquishment or vicarious exercise of the duty to know in matters of conscience and ethics), but also a parallel critique of the usurpation of that responsibility by the self-appointed elite of the *'ulamá*. Thus the Bahá'í critique of *taqlíd* entails, like Kant's *aude sapere*, not only a discarding of superstitions, but also an uncompromising denunciation of their religious custodians paralleled with a vigorous proclamation of faith in mankind's ability to exploit its endowments. Furthermore, the fact that the same concept of *taqlíd* is used in the plural by Bahá'u'lláh and 'Abdu'l-Bahá to refer to prejudices (*ta'aṣṣubat*) of nationality, culture, religion and race shows the seamless connection linking the kind of flawed, atavistic, received knowledge of religious and secular establishments with the attitudes and deeply rooted false moralities supporting them. Exposing prejudices for what they are is an operation calling for much more than a removal or replacement of falsehoods and half-truths. In fact, it is inseparable from a recasting of the social and institutional structures of knowledge and morality where they find expression.

Conversely, aspects emanating from Bahá'í statements that have captured Bahá'í imagination take on a different, though not necessarily more modest, place when situated in the overall framework. This is illustrated most conspicuously by the configuration of the pair 'Lesser Peace' and 'Most Great Peace', which in Bahá'í terms occupy almost polar positions in a peace continuum, the clarification of whose contours required the expanded view of sacred history supplied by Shoghi Effendi.

Otherwise expressed, this study is as much about what Bahá'u'lláh, 'Abdu'l-Bahá and Shoghi Effendi had to say about peace and its satellite expressions as it is about what they convey to us when interrogated from the thematic perspective of man's nature, and the characteristic configuration of the Bahá'í ethos.[36]

* * *

The structure of the present study reflects the approach so far described. The first three parts supply the basics of the Bahá'í teachings on peace in the writings of Bahá'u'lláh, 'Abdu'l-Bahá and Shoghi Effendi, while the remaining two look at the topic from an anthropological and moral perspective. The first three parts provide for a sense of the main ideas concerning peace as developed by the three authors. This has a number of advantages. First, the rough chronology that ensues from this presentation will help to avoid the pitfall of reading back to Bahá'u'lláh's time concepts and aspects of the doctrine which were first formulated or introduced by His successors. This has the added benefit of countering the often naïve impression of locating the 'meaning' of the 'creative word', once and for all, just in the text and context or even in the mind of the first author, rather than in the new relationship it brings about and its intended or 'unintended' consequences. Second, it may assist us in gathering a sense of where the main novelties and shifts of emphases are to be found with regard to peace, an important aspect if one is to establish some logical structure or dynamic from which further logical deductions might be derived.[37] Third, this convenient arrangement allows the reader to establish a healthy sense of distance between obvious meanings that were contemporary with the authors themselves, and those that belonged in the writings but need to be extracted from a logical process of deduction and analysis, examples of which are the importance that can be ascribed to the critical issue of *taqlíd* or to the Bahá'í concept of organic growth and unity.

Parts I and II can be taken as a summary review of positions concerning peace issues and allied matters as found in the writings of Bahá'u'lláh and 'Abdu'l-Bahá. Although some references to the personality of Bahá'u'lláh are made in connection with the shifting Bábí Movement, these are meant to provide a minimum context for His views. Part III looks in some detail at the writings of Shoghi Effendi concerning the place of peace in the new 'divine economy'. It should be noted that Shoghi Effendi acted less as a charismatic figure and much more as a trustee of Bahá'u'lláh and 'Abdu'l-Bahá's Wills and, thus, his life can be seen as a systematization of the work carried out by his predecessors. In the doctrinal field a considerable number of works by Shoghi Effendi were devoted to identifying the fundamentals of the Bahá'í Dispensation, as well as providing the Bahá'í community with a sense of mission in tune with his majestic perception of the unfolding of sacred history. The Bahá'í community was to be regarded as a conscious actor, contributing to the Major Plan of God and thus to the fulfilment of the eschatological promises portraying a world of peace and justice.

Taken together, the first three parts are of a fairly expository nature. They contain a representative selection of references, many of which appear to be rather straightforward and in need of little expansion in the way of historical interpretation or conceptualization. This notwithstanding, special attention has been paid to Bahá'u'lláh's abrogation of the Islamic law of *jihád*, an act whose significance needs to be reviewed not only in light of the evolution of this concept but also in conjunction with Bahá'u'lláh's position on state-led violence. Similarly, the attention paid to 'Abdu'l-Bahá's Tablet to The Hague and the concept of 'Bahá'í principles' is justified by the fact that its contents provided the first synthesis of Bahá'í thought on the subject of peace; a synthesis all the more significant since it was articulated in response to world concerns and was meant to set the tone for future Bahá'í stances.

Part IV examines the Bahá'í perspective on the nature of man. Neither the Enlightenment 'realist' assumption of a man driven by selfish but mutually beneficial urges, nor the 'idealized' image of a good savage brutalized in a disciplinary Hobbesian society, find echo in the Bahá'í writings. These appeal significantly to humanity's capacity to overcome man-made barriers by stressing the will-power and potentialities that lie hidden in both the mind and the heart of human beings.

Furthermore, this mobilizing rhetoric is given support by another important set of notions stressing human dignity. This can be appreciated by looking in some detail at the Bahá'í critique of blind following (*taqlíd*), vain imaginings (*awḥam*), and prejudices/fanaticism (*ta'aṣṣub*), which are considered to be sources of destructive power and thus major obstacles to the attainment of peace.

Part V takes a closer look at the Bahá'í ethos, its guiding principles and functioning, with particular attention to the concepts of religious unity, organic unity and consultation, the whole of which forms a consistent core of Bahá'í thought and practices with a definite bearing on the Bahá'í understanding of peace as a process reflecting mankind's ripeness and inner impetus in its approach towards God's Kingdom. The conclusion (Chapter 31) reviews and discusses the main findings while giving some suggestions for further research.

PART I

BAHÁ'U'LLÁH

> Praise be to God that thou hast attained! . . . Thou hast come to see a prisoner and an exile . . . We desire but the good of the world and happiness of the nations; yet they deem us a stirrer up of strife and sedition worthy of bondage and banishment . . . That all nations should become one in faith and all men as brothers; that the bonds of affection and unity between the sons of men should be strengthened; that diversity of religion should cease, and differences of race be annulled – what harm is there in this? . . . Yet so it shall be; these fruitless strifes, these ruinous wars shall pass away, and the 'Most Great Peace' shall come . . . Do not you in Europe need this also? Is not this that which Christ foretold? . . . Yet do we see your kings and rulers lavishing their treasures more freely on means for the destruction of the human race than on that which would conduce to the happiness of mankind . . . These strifes and this bloodshed and discord must cease, and all men be as one kindred and one family . . . Let not a man glory in this, that he loves his country; let him rather glory in this, that he loves his kind.[1]

Part I offers a cursory sketch of Bahá'u'lláh's life, then briefly conceptualizes His abrogation of the law of *jihád*, which sets the negative basis for His positive conception of peace, and finally discusses the principle of collective security in the context of the distinction between the Lesser and Most Great Peace. This latter distinction opened the possibility for a new chronology in the fulfilment of eschatological events and reflected a transitioning process from present conditions to a stage largely characterized by an increasing spiritualization of mankind and a parallel cosmopolitanism or, to be more precise, monoanthropism.

Bahá'u'lláh's conception of peace was the expected outcome of a world progressively freed from religiously or secularly-driven violence, moving – or rather maturing – by degrees towards unification ('one kindred and one "family"'). Peace was associated by Bahá'u'lláh with the dawning of God's Kingdom ('Is not this that which Christ foretold?'), whose promise and guarantees were all contained in the provisions of God's renewed covenant with mankind. Peace, in other words, was not a mere corollary of the new aeon, but, together with unity and justice, one of the pre-eminent hallmarks of Bahá'u'lláh's vision.

The outline of peace provided by Bahá'u'lláh was to find more elaborate details in the writings and allocutions of 'Abdu'l-Bahá (see Part II). Similarly, it was Shoghi Effendi's role to resituate the theme of peace in a properly historical and sociological perspective, thus furnishing Bahá'ís with much needed clarity as to the functions of the Bahá'í community vis-à-vis the world (see Part III). The combined pattern resulting from the piecing together of these elements, rather than the privileging of a single aspect, is what confers upon the Bahá'í view of peace some of its comprehensiveness and characteristic elusiveness. In Parts IV and V I will supplement this view by adding further insights into the Bahá'í concept of peace through a thematic appraisal of the place of the individual and the Bahá'í ethos in the general scheme of things, with special attention to their relevance to a Bahá'í conception of peace.

The texts used in Part I come from different sources, including, as in the quotation above, some reported statements regarded as particularly weighty and reliable. Excerpts from the writings and reported sayings of Bahá'u'lláh with direct relevancy to the matter of peace are brief and often appear to have been deliberately couched in terms of their special eschatological, prophetic and symbolic import. This stylistic feature confers on them a degree of solemnity but also renders them pregnant with allusions that transpositions into lay categories may easily neglect. Cole has a point when he remarks: 'Bahá'u'lláh's views were not expressed in reasoned treatises but in prophetic utterances and apocalyptic visions of a millenarian character.'[2] One is reminded of what S. Radhakrishnan had to say regarding the philosophy of Tagore: 'Rabindranath writes poetry, while this book [Radhakhrisnan's] is in prose.'[3]

Even considering the important advances already noted in the introduction and conspicuously illustrated by the works of Cole, Saiedi and others, restoring a sense of context to some of these statements is not always possible except in general and tentative ways. Much of their imputed significance may depend on theological analyses or assumptions rather than on purely empirical evidence, which at times may be scanty, despite micro-forensic efforts to magnify it. Conversely, the use of ideal-type constructs and their key categories may easily slip the researcher into a false sense of security in thinking that the dotted lines being followed have uncovered the true picture of 'what is going on here'. Moreover, the fact that biographical details about Bahá'u'lláh's life have to be reconstructed through fragmentary testimonies or recollections written down in chronicles well after the events, as is the case of *Nabíl's Narrative* or the spoken chronicles of relatives and followers,[4] needs to be taken with some caution. For the purposes of this book, most of the references to well-known episodes in Bahá'u'lláh's life such as His childhood experiences described in Chapter 2 can also be found in standard presentations of the same theme by Balyuzi, Buck, Cole, MacEoin or Saiedi.

2
Some Biographical Considerations

Bahá'u'lláh was born in Tehran in November 1817. His early years and youth were marked by the kind of education which was common to the offspring of the nobility. Although very little is known about His formative years, an episode Bahá'u'lláh witnessed in His childhood may constitute the first sign of His disaffection towards politics and power.[5] The story, as recounted by Bahá'u'lláh in the Lawḥ-i-Ra'ís, depicts the main scenes of the Sulṭán Salím puppet play – first a royal parade surrounded by pomp and majesty, followed by the lurid punishment inflicted on a thief, and, soon thereafter, by the monarch's review of his troops in readiness to quell a rebellion. Once the display was over, the inquisitive child asked about the contents of the box where the puppets had been put away. The impression left on Him is conveyed in these words:

> Ever since that day, all the trappings of the world have seemed in the eyes of this Youth akin to that same spectacle . . . How greatly I marvelled that men should pride themselves upon such vanities, whilst those possessed of insight, ere they witness any evidence of human glory, perceive with certainty the inevitability of its waning.[6]

Another event in Bahá'u'lláh's childhood illustrates even more forcefully His natural repulsion towards armed violence. The episode, as recounted by Bahá'u'lláh, shows Him deeply distressed in his youth while reading the story of the punishment meted out by the Prophet Muhammad to the Banú Qurayzah.[7] The episode can be regarded as all the more remarkable since it would again distance Bahá'u'lláh from the powerful undercurrents of anti-Jewish sentiment that historically have clustered around some of the foundational events in Islamic history such as this one.[8] Furthermore, Bahá'u'lláh's meekness of character would appear confirmed by His reported care for the poor and His refusal to follow in His father's footsteps when offered a high post in government.[9] In her recollections, Bahíyyih Khánum, Bahá'u'lláh's daughter, further refers to her parents' voluntary distancing from 'State functions, social ceremonies, and the luxurious habits of ordinary highly-placed and wealthy families'.[10]

His father, Mírzá Buzurg, a respected high-ranking officer (*vazír*) of noble lineage and a master calligrapher, served the Crown in several capacities. In 1835 the vazír suffered a spate of severe losses, including his dismissal from the governorship of Luristan and the legal misappropriation of most of his wealth.[11] Bahá'u'lláh's resulting dissatisfaction with the extreme volatility of Court politics would have been further confirmed by His personal experience when, as a follower of the Báb, He was not only a witness to the persecution of His coreligionists, but also suffered a crippling four-month incarceration in the notorious dungeon of Síyáh-Chál (the Black Pit) under charges of instigating a failed attempt on the life of the Shah.

Bahá'u'lláh had joined the ranks of the Bábí community at a very early stage, when He was barely 27 years of age. Although externally devoid of rank, His notable position within the Bábí community can be gauged retrospectively by the fact that the destinies of Babism were to be decided ultimately between Him and his half-brother.

Given the traditional differences between the religious establishment and the Iranian civil authorities, and the way these were played out in the form of mutual attempts at increasing or retaining their respective areas of influence, the Bábí challenge to the power wielded by the Muslim clergy may not have been received as an unwelcome event by the Court, provided it was kept within limits. Moreover, at those initial stages differences between the Báb and the Muslim community could still be construed principally as a further internal division amongst Shaykhí factions, Shaykhism remaining to all intents and purposes a somewhat controversial branch (school or *maktab*) within the confines of Twelver Shí'ism.[12] The gradual overtures and disclosures made by the Báb concerning His own status seem to have been measured to maintain and broaden this 'window of opportunity'. Difficulties in obtaining reliable reports from the provinces as well as some attraction to mysticism on the part of Muhammad Shah might have also played an important role in defusing harsher punitive action against the Bábís during the early period. In any case, it was not until the Conference at Badasht (1848) that the Bábí breakaway from Islam was broadcast publicly so as to reach a point of no return.

The attempt on the Shah's life in 1852, two years after the execution of the Báb, afforded what was probably the best opportunity for the Crown to dispose of Bahá'u'lláh and the last significant remnants of the Bábí community. A successful mediation by the Russian legation, however, and lack of incriminating evidence against Bahá'u'lláh allowed Him to move into exile,[13] thus putting behind Him the ordeal of his four-month incarceration in the awesome conditions of the Síyáh-Chál, the scars of which, including a failed attempt against His life by poisoning, would remain forever with Him.

More importantly, if Bahá'u'lláh's account is to be taken as an indication, the imprisonment at the Síyáh-Chál was fundamental in bringing about a new prophetic awareness. Certainly, it proved decisive in creating a fresh opening for the expectant Bábí community which, following the execution of the Báb was if anything more receptive to the coming of the *Man Yuẓhirúhu'lláh* (Him Whom

God Shall Make Manifest), the much awaited figure whose appearance in the near future was promised by the Báb.[14] Bahá'u'lláh's role during the ensuing years in Iraq can be seen in retrospect as one of preparing the Bábí community for His own proclamation.[15]

Just as the Banú Qurayzah episode was to influence his approach to other religious traditions, the experience of the Síyáh-Chál, in Bahá'u'lláh's own words, was to convince Him of the need for regenerating Babism from within:

> No pen can depict that place, nor any tongue describe its loathsome smell. Most of these men had neither clothes nor bedding to lie on. God alone knoweth what befell Us in that most foul-smelling and gloomy place!
>
> Day and night, while confined in that dungeon, We meditated upon the deeds, the condition, and the conduct of the Bábís, wondering what could have led a people so high-minded, so noble, and of such intelligence, to perpetrate such an audacious and outrageous act against the person of His Majesty. This Wronged One, thereupon, decided to arise, after His release from prison, and undertake, with the utmost vigour, the task of regenerating this people.
>
> One night, in a dream, these exalted words were heard on every side: 'Verily, We shall render Thee victorious by Thyself and by Thy Pen . . .'[16]

In Bahá'u'lláh's view the attempt on the Shah's life made by some recalcitrant Bábís was also a sign of the internal state of decomposition already eating away much of what was left of the Bábí community, hence His declared intention of reviving Babism. Yet, such regeneration was not to take place by relying on violent means, but rather on the strength of Bahá'u'lláh's own person and, most importantly, His pen.[17] This reliance on the power of the word, as against that of brute force, was to become a constant leitmotif in Bahá'u'lláh's writings for the rest of His prophetic ministry.

After the execution of the Báb and other outstanding Bábí personalities, no publicly recognized leaders were left in the Bábí community ready to assume unchallenged authority.[18] Mírzá Yaḥyá, Bahá'u'lláh's young half-brother, was the nominal figurehead, but according to most accounts unable to exert any effectual leadership.[19] Although Mírzá Yaḥyá followed His brother into exile to Baghdad,[20] at some early stage he made an attempt at asserting his own independent authority. Bahá'u'lláh's two-year retreat to the Kurdistan mountains (April 1854–March 1856) seems to have been motivated by His decision to avoid a direct confrontation and leave things to run their natural course. The account given by Bahíyyih Khánum, His daughter, of the attitude that prompted her father to abandon His family in Baghdad, again illustrates the peaceful inclination in Bahá'u'lláh's character:

> At length this state of affairs became very distasteful to my father, he being by nature a man of peace. Strife of any kind seemed to hurt him; more, however,

> because of the unhappiness which it brought upon others than because of the discomfort which it caused him. It was his habit, for the sake of peace and to quell strife, to take all the blame upon himself where possible, and to seek to pacify those in contention by his love.[21]

In the interim the vacuum thus created only served to compound the predicament of the beleaguered Bábí community of exiles residing in Baghdad.[22] Much of the effort made by Bahá'u'lláh during the second part of the Iraqi period can be seen in the light of his own prophetic self-awareness and the overall conditions encountered by what was a disbanded and demoralized Bábí community.

After Bahá'u'lláh's return from Sulaymaniyyih, His leadership became increasingly apparent. Paradoxically, it was this influence on the morale and the enhanced prestige of the Bábí community (which was now able to rally around a figure respected even by some of the leading Shí'i authorities at the *'Atabát*, the holy cities of Najaf and Karbila)[23] that was to trigger a further banishment. Although formally extended as an invitation to visit the Court in Istanbul, this measure was dictated by alarmist intelligence reporting Bahá'u'lláh's alleged preparations for an armed struggle in collusion with local tribal leaders.[24] Prior to His departure from the Iraqi capital, Bahá'u'lláh stayed for a brief period in the Garden of Riḍván, located in a river island in the outskirts of the city. The occasion assumed epochal proportions, for it was then, according to most accounts, that Bahá'u'lláh made a number of decisive pronouncements.

3

The Kingdom of God and the Abrogation of *jihád*

Bahá'u'lláh's forced exile to Istanbul effectively provides additional context for understanding the purport of two of his weightiest declarations made during the preceding Riḍván period of his Declaration (April 1863). The first concerns the abrogation of the institution of *jihád*; the second is an elaboration on the subject of suffering as exemplified by the prophet Job,[25] whose personification in Vaḥíd, the Bábí martyr of Nayríz, was intended to serve as a guide as to the impending dangers looming over the horizon for Bahá'u'lláh and his followers. By implication, both statements illustrate the nature and method of God's activity on this mortal plane.

The immediate context for the abrogation of *jihád* is perhaps better understood against the background of the Báb's own proclamation as the promised Qá'im, indefectibly concomitant, if not confused, with expectations about an imminent victory by sheer force. Prophecies attesting to the importance of the thirteenth century in the fulfilment of Islamic eschatology were not unknown to Muslims of various persuasions,[26] and likewise quasi-Messianic expectations were not uncommon to a number of revivalist movements, particularly throughout Muslim Africa.[27] In Iran many of these hopes, however, came to an abrupt end as soon as the Báb altered some of the rituals of Islam,[28] a major infringement that in the eyes of the population turned Him and His followers into renegades liable to the harshest forms of punishment, including the always profitable appropriation of *murtadd* (renegade) property. The resulting tensions seem to explain not only the excitement experienced by the Bábís in anticipation of a new Dispensation under the aegis of the Lord of the Time (a contest traditionally construed in terms of an apocalyptic clash between the forces of evil and good), but also their need to counter the attacks in the various episodes of armed confrontation that were to dot the fateful years between 1848 and 1852. While at least some Bábís may have entertained some reservations as to the moral nature of their armed confrontations, certainly these were not based on the kind of outright moral condemnation that was to characterize later Bahá'í doctrine. In his *Qayyúmu'l-Asmá'* the Báb had upheld and reviewed the doctrine of *jihád*. Accordingly, and since Islam was one of the religions of the Book, Muslims could not be targeted for offensive *jihád*.[29] Moreover, this was made conditional on the Báb's specific approval.[30] Interestingly no mention of *jihád* was made in his book of laws (*Bayán*). On this basis, and given that all the laws issued by the Báb were subject to final sanction by 'Him Whom God shall make manifest',[31] a situation of factual abeyance seems to have developed which equally applied to some of the more radical Bábí provisions, many of which, as pointed out by Saiedi, need to be considered in terms of the symbolic transformation operated by the Báb.[32]

If charges of apostasy were serious enough, the more generic one of rebelling or causing sedition (*fitnih*) entailed the most grievous and harshest penalties. Since the Bábís could not see themselves as rebels and much less as apostates of Islam, but rather as the agents of its fulfilment, it comes as no surprise that they would regard their own actions at Ṭabarsí, Zanján and Nayríz as heroic rehearsals of the Karbila passion, quite in conformity not only with the rules prevailing in their midst concerning defensive *jihád*[33] but also with the doctrine set forth by the Báb in His works. Moreover, such instances were so influential in uplifting the morale of the Bábís not because of their success (they all ended in massacres), but because they embodied what Ayoub has called 'redemptive suffering',[34] a radical form of bearing witness to the validity of one's claim before a disbelieving world. If Ṭáhirih's removal of the veil at a public male gathering of Bábís was already, by prevalent moral standards, an unthinkable act of immorality, the anomic behaviour of a few Bábís after the closing of the Bada<u>sh</u>t Conference was to cast a further layer of suspicion on the true intents and purposes of the community.[35] The fact that Bahá'u'lláh's life was endangered by these acts, as the Níyalá episode exposed, serves if anything to underscore the gravity of Bahá'u'lláh's pronouncements at a later period.

At any rate, however, the situation that these events portrayed was confusing enough to cast a shadow of doubt on the Bábís and their motives amongst the general populace and the authorities. The subsequent attempt on the Shah's life was to further compound this notoriety, adding fuel to the image of the Bábís as a radical group bent on destroying the Islamic *ummah*.[36]

Now, if there were any lingering hopes in the Bábí community of a quick and violent reversal in the fortunes of God's religion, in line with the literalist combative eschatology surrounding the appearance of Lord of the Time, these could no longer be justified in light of Bahá'u'lláh's Declaration at the Riḍván garden. This act divested such expectations of any content, thereby paving the way for a radical departure from previous conceptions. The preliminary work had already been undertaken by the Báb himself, and Bahá'u'lláh's *Kitáb-i-Íqán* had already disavowed any understanding of the Báb's mission (and of His seeming failure) in terms of a literalist interpretation of the eschatological signs accompanying His coming, including those portraying an Armageddon-like struggle.[37] What the Riḍván Declaration achieved was a complete shattering of any such expectations. Bahá'u'lláh's refusal to cast Himself in the light of a Prophet or an Imám Warrior, as well as His very utterances and writings on the occasion, contributed to dispel any misconceptions that could still colour the awaiting of the Supreme

Manifestation of God. Long-suffering and patience in the face of persecutions were the lot of the true followers of God's true religion.

In this context the abrogation of holy war was to serve a dual and somewhat paradoxical purpose: on the one hand it was a disclaimer of any seditious intentions (*fitnih*); but on the other hand, what more subversive act could then be imagined than wielding authority to cast aside one of the most powerful institutions in Islam? And yet the condemnation of *jihád* was in reality a highly symbolic expression of a much broader principle which Bahá'u'lláh was to repeatedly stress throughout His writings, namely that of shunning violence, contention and strife at all levels and in whichever forms they may present themselves. Bahá'u'lláh's disavowal of violence was thus unequivocal and left no further avenues for any Bábí recidivism. The following passage taken from the Lawḥ-i-Dunyá (circa 1891–92) is revealing:

> Strife and conflict [*nizá' va jidál*] befit the beasts of the wild. It was through the grace of God and with the aid of seemly words and praiseworthy deeds that the unsheathed swords of the Bábí community [*ḥizb-i-bábí*] were returned to their scabbards.[38]

Revealing because it proves that, whatever the claims made by the Báb and the immediate motives underlying the armed struggles at Ṭabarsí and Zanján, some members within the Bábí community, specially later Azalís, were nonetheless prone to take up arms or commit seditious acts that could in no way be endorsed by Bahá'u'lláh. In the same Tablet quoted above, the idea that violence, strife and mischief are not in keeping with the believers in God appears stressed several times. In this regard, the following statement can be taken as perhaps the most pregnant of all, for it clearly includes a strong repudiation of religious zealotry and fundamentalism, as typified by four characteristic behaviours depicted in an unmistakable progression:

> The unbelievers and the faithless have set their minds on four things: first, the shedding of blood; second, the burning of books; third, the shunning of the followers of other religions; fourth, the extermination of other communities and groups. Now however, through the strengthening grace and potency of the Word of God these four barriers have been demolished, *these clear injunctions have been obliterated from the Tablet* [*az lawḥ maḥv gashṯ*] *and brutal dispositions have been transmuted into spiritual attributes.*[39] (emphasis added)

The last two passages further confirm Bahá'u'lláh's approach. The transformation of the Bábí community was to be achieved through a new stress on its spiritual mission, and for this to occur the consciousness of the budding Bahá'í community had to gain a new impetus. Ideas commonly held in traditional Muslim society had to be definitely discarded to leave room for the new ones. Again in the Lawḥ-i-Dunyá, Bahá'u'lláh attached special importance to this reversal:

> The distinguishing feature that marketh the pre-eminent character of this Supreme Revelation consisteth in that We have, on the one hand, blotted out from the pages of God's holy Book [*az kitáb maḥí nimúdím*] whatsoever hath been the cause of strife, of malice and mischief amongst the children of men, and have, on the other, laid down the essential prerequisites of concord, understanding, of complete and enduring unity.[40]

Two main ideas conveyed in the above passage deserve further consideration. First, Bahá'u'lláh symbolically likened the act of blotting out (*maḥv*) a previous religious injunction (almost always a restrictive or negative one) to the removal of it from (the plane of) existence. The fact that this act would operate as a sort of complete erasure must be understood in two ways. Firstly, it is an act of God, which the Prophet limits himself to state as solemnly as possible. Secondly, it also makes God's will known in an act that becomes self-fulfilling. This way of accomplishing God's purpose can be identified in numerous such instances where Bahá'u'lláh seems to operate as a *rasúl,* a Messenger endowed with Moses-like authority.[41] Likewise, in the Tablet of Bis͟hárát Bahá'u'lláh announces formally that the first Glad-Tidings of the Mother Book (*ummu'l kitáb*) is 'that the law of holy war hath been blotted out from the Book'.[42] The act of 'blotting out' holy war thus takes on a special meaning in that it 'removes' prototypically – as it were – one of the leading causes of bloodshed in history.[43]

The second idea contained in the statement points already to unity as the overriding principle of the Bahá'í Revelation. This unity is achieved as a direct result of removing the root causes of conflict and is presented as the supreme aim of both religion and the individual's efforts. The new religion of God is defined then by implication in terms of its contribution to the establishment of unity and peace.[44] This same concept was to become the focus of 'Abdu'l-Bahá's treatise *The Secret of Divine Civilization.*

Significance of the abrogation of *jihád*

As noted above, the abrogation which took place in the Garden of Riḍván could be read as a disavowal before the civil and religious authorities, but in a more fundamental sense, it was intended to induce a change of heart in the Bábí community, which was its immediate if not sole addressee at the time. The laws of Islam and those of the Bayán had had their time; Bahá'u'lláh's task in the ensuing period of His proclamation was to recast the Bábí community from within, proclaim His mission to the world potentates, and to enact the laws and teachings of the new Dispensation, or render void those that were no longer conformable.[45]

According to Bahá'u'lláh, any vindication of truth no longer required combatting religious enemies by force (*jihád* of the sword); and it did not even need an active quest for sacrificial martyrdom, which at one stage was declared by Bahá'u'lláh secondary to teaching His Faith.[46] By suppressing *jihád* and reordering the place of martyrdom in the religious psyche of His followers, the underlying concept of 'exertion in the path of God' (*jihád*), which underpinned these two poles, was placed squarely on a new ecumenical relationship. Death, sacrificial (as in a martyr's death) or purgative (as in the defence of Islam by the sword) was no longer a defining element in Bahá'u'lláh's Revelation. Importantly, a similar transformation was to alter the relationship between the concepts of *ijtihád* (another word from the same root as *jihád*) and *taqlíd*, thus introducing a far greater alteration into the moral outlook of the Bahá'í community and its makeup.[47]

This realignment and spiritualization of deeply engrained religious and cultural institutions (*jihád* and martyrdom, *ijtihád*, *taqlíd*), often construed as essential to Islam, posed an additional, and in fact deeper, theoretical problem. What kind of authority could Bahá'u'lláh invoke to buttress His claims to Prophethood and hence His right to become, at the very least, the moral conscience of the monarchs to whom he addressed His summons during the Edirne and early 'Akká periods?[48] And more to the point, why would the Shah or the Sultan subscribe to His views, couched as they were in terms that unquestionably implied a higher authority than theirs?

In Naṣir-i-Dín Sháh's mind there could be no question that the abolition of *jihád* entailed a direct threat to His authority. As noted by Amanat, the Shah had attempted to style himself as the King of the Shí'i, much as the Sultan was the Caliph of the Sunni fold.[49] Just six years before Bahá'u'lláh's Riḍván Declaration, the Anglo-Persian war of 1856–57 following the short-lived capture of Herat by the Shah had been further fuelled by an officially endorsed call to *jihád* that scores of leading *mujtahids*[50] throughout the country proclaimed enthusiastically. The ensuing fiasco, resulting in the capture of Bushihr and the fall of Muhammara under British attack, probably served as fresh reminders of the previous debacle suffered by Fatḥ 'Alí Sháh in a similarly catastrophic *jihád* waged against the Russians. The humiliating and gruesome conditions of the Turkomanchy peace treaties in 1828, resulting in the loss of the Caucasian provinces and the no less onerous war reparations, could have alerted the young Shah to the dangers inherent in any military foray riveted with *jihadic* motifs.[51] Doubtless, these immediate precedents, furthermore set in the context of western imperialistic expansionism, coloured the perception of Bahá'u'lláh's abolition of *jihád*, investing them with a strong emotional and theological topicality.[52]

But, if we are to follow Balyuzi's account, even closer to Bahá'u'lláh's own experience were the moves by a number of Shí'i clerics in the '*Atabát* (the shrine cities in southern Iraq) in the months and years prior to Bahá'u'lláh's exile to Istanbul to have Him and the Iraqi Bábís eliminated by staging a holy war against Him.[53] The fact that these attempts failed to gain the endorsement of the leading clerics did not diminish the significance of the threat they posed.

Finally, the abrogation of *jihád* by Bahá'u'lláh was to serve as a disclaimer of any seditious intentions on His part, as much as a disavowal of the civil and religious authorities' right to wage war in the name of God or His hidden deputy. By extension, Bahá'u'lláh's legislative action was set in a context of religious renewal aimed at a further breakaway from Islam and Babism. The fact that unprovoked redemptive suffering was again repositioned by Bahá'u'lláh as key to God's method for His ultimate triumph represented a further confirmation that the divine call was averse to all forms of violence.

The abrogation of *jihád*, however, did not involve any devolution of authority, or a defaulting in favour of the state authorities – war after all had always remained an option within their grasp – but rather the elimination of religious motives as valid grounds for waging war. This precise rearrangement found its secular counterpart in Bahá'u'lláh's advocacy of a collective security regime, which was tantamount to a delegitimation of the undisputed monopoly of force exerted by the sovereign State. While not entirely eliminated, the use of force was now to be made compliant with a new moral and legal regime, the contents of which were stipulated in Bahá'u'lláh's letters to the kings and, finally, in the Kitáb-i-Aqdas (his Most Holy Book, or Book of Laws).[54] This regime made it conspicuously clear that none was to be exempted from the purview of the Law and God's justice, including kings, rulers and the learned. If sedition, particularly religiously motivated sedition, was repugnant, no less so was tyranny; if disorderly conduct was abhorrent, no less were abuses of power.

Condemnation of seditiousness and violence in general

In His letter to the Shah (dated circa March 1868), and in a clear reference to the Bábí attempt on the King's life, Bahá'u'lláh disclaimed not just any relationship between the notion of helping God to become victorious with any pretence to sedition (*fitnih*), but also any similar linkage between the attempt on the Shah's life and the true purport of the Bábí Revelation:

> Such is the true meaning of rendering assistance unto God. Sedition hath never been pleasing unto God, nor were the acts committed in the past by certain foolish ones acceptable in His sight. Know ye that to be killed in the path of His good pleasure is better for you than to kill.[55]

In stating these words Bahá'u'lláh was not speaking as an Islamic authority, but rather as a Lawgiver intent on bringing about a fundamental change in the nature and relationships obtaining between State and religion. Certainly, a balance had to be struck between state authorities and religious authority, as clearly pointed by Bahá'u'lláh in reference to Caesar's tribute, and to the hadith[56] claiming obedience to the Apostle and those in authority, by which:

> is meant primarily and more especially the Imams . . . Secondarily these words refer unto the kings and rulers – those through the brightness of whose justice the horizons of the world are resplendent and luminous.[57]

But while Bahá'u'lláh reaffirmed the autonomy of the lay powers He also boldly reasserted the authority of the Prophet and the Imam over that of kings and rulers, thus leaving no doubt as to the hierarchy of authority in which the Shah was to find his due place.[58] Even if the attribution of powers to the Imams (the legitimate successors of the Prophet Muhammad in the Shí'i tradition) was largely to be assumed ineffectual (i.e. in their absence),[59] that could hardly be applicable to the Báb or Bahá'u'lláh. Their respective claims – that of the Báb as the Qá'im, and that of Bahá'u'lláh as the Supreme Manifestation of God – allowed them to rearrange state affairs in their entirety, at least theoretically. Reassuring as Bahá'u'lláh's disclaimer of any power-seeking was, he nevertheless restated the basic preponderance of God's authority, implying in unambiguous terms that human authority has a derivative legitimacy. It is within the scope of such perspective that the daring tone of Bahá'u'lláh in some of His invectives against the Shah and the Sultan must have definitely struck a suspect chord. Furthermore, the encounter between Badí', Bahá'u'lláh's emissary to the Shah, and his cross-examining torturers, brought this tension to the fore in a most dramatic way: Badí'was repeatedly offered to save his life on condition that he would present Bahá'u'lláh's message not as a letter but rather as a petition,[60] not an academic distinction but rather a crucial one given its implied symbolism.[61]

4
Bahá'u'lláh's Pronouncements on Peace

Together with the provisions of the Aqdas, the letters that Bahá'u'lláh addressed to the kings and rulers of the time, both individually and collectively, contained His proclamation as God's Messenger and, more specifically, the counsels and admonitions that in various degrees distilled the essence of His legal and socio-political teachings. As noted by Stephen Lambden, the background to these letters is provided by an already well-established tradition in Islam of epistles allegedly sent by Jesus Christ (and more specifically by Muhammad) to the kings and rulers of the time.[62] It is this tradition that the Báb seems to have effectively followed as part of His proclamation in the first Sura of the *Qayyúmu'l-Asmá'* (Sura of the kings),[63] and that Bahá'u'lláh, as the newly found Joseph, resumed to its fullest form some twenty years later. In addition to this, Bahá'u'lláh's letters to the kings, and by extension the passages addressed to them in the Aqdas, do not seem to be modelled after the tradition of the Mirrors of Princes,[64] although parallels can be found, but, if anything, follow a pattern which combines Biblical and Quranic prophetic proclamation[65] with a clear self-perception of bringing about, albeit in a symbolic fashion, God's final judgement on earth.

The epistles were written throughout the climactic period of His exile in Edirne (December 1863) up to His incarceration in the prison city of 'Akká (August 1868). Those years were decisive on several counts. First, Bahá'u'lláh made public His status as a Manifestation of God, a step that precipitated His complete disassociation from His half-brother Mírzá Yaḥyá, who up until then had occupied a position as nominal leader of the Bábí community.[66] Bahá'u'lláh's declaration marked a turning point for the Bábí Azalís, thereby consummating the split and the beginning of the Bahá'í community as an independent religious body. Second, Bahá'u'lláh made a public presentation of His Messianic or theophanic status while seeking to persuade the Shah and the Sultan to redress their handling of state affairs. Both potentates were instructed to rearrange their rule in conformity with their duties and station. Moreover, in His letters to the rulers Bahá'u'lláh adopted a revelatory style, a blend of modest composure and apocalyptic overtones, indicative of His commanding authority. And finally, Bahá'u'lláh established, ostensibly in response to requests from different Bahá'í quarters (anxious to usher in the new Dispensation), the basic provisions which henceforth were to govern the conduct of the 'people of Bahá', through the *Kitáb-i-Aqdas* (circa 1872–73). Although the ensuing set of laws was disclosed quietly over time, its provisions re-enacted the Bábí breakaway with Islam, and provided the incipient Bahá'í community with a Qur'án or Bayán equivalent that set them apart from their contemporaries, and especially from the Muslim society from which a majority of Bahá'í adherents were drawn at the time. Interestingly, the *Kitáb-i-Aqdas* also included some important warnings to the emperors Francis Joseph of Austria and Wilhelm I of Prussia, as well as Bahá'u'lláh's summons to 'the Presidents of the Republics of the American continent', which in the aggregate summarized the tenor of His previous warnings issued to the secular authorities. In this way a clear link was established between Bahá'u'lláh's global mission as a proclaimer of God's Revelation, His 'prophecies' summoning humanity to God's remembrance, and the new Bahá'í canon enshrining the essentials of religious and social practice that the 'people of Bahá' was to embody. The all-embracing nature of the message conveyed in this way, as well as its legal ramifications, appeared summarized programmatically in the Aqdas' very invocation of God as the 'Supreme Ruler over all that hath been and all that is to be'.

The Lesser and the Most Great Peace

The implicit breakaway from Babism and Islam that these measures entailed was complete. Needless to say, it posed a formidable challenge to the Islamic authorities who, to the extent that they were able to infer the content of the new Revelation, were thus faced with an alternative new Sharia – in fact a new post-Muhammadan Covenant – many of whose precepts were specific reversals of Muslim customary practice and doctrine.

The notion implicit in the concept of 'Bahá'í law' was also altered in some fundamental ways which rendered useless the elaborate Shí'i system of jurisprudence, including the attendant professional class of *'ulamá*. Indeed, by suppressing the concomitant notion of *taqlíd* Bahá'u'lláh was to extend the capacity of *ijtihád* (free inquiry in matters of religion) to all classes of people, while letting the Book and its interpretive living extensions – 'Abdu'l-Bahá and Shoghi Effendi, now clear of reported traditions – speak for themselves.

This more egalitarian stand was consistently present across the range of Bahá'í doctrine that informed the abolition of holy war, as well as the abrogation of the concept of ritual impurity, and the call to consort freely with the followers of all religions.[67] And it was given further impetus through the notion of 'unity in rank and station', and the principle of *muvását* ('the freely chosen expending of one's substance', or voluntary sharing). The uprooting of *jihád* operated as a precondition for the establishment of tolerance and equality before the law among religious communities; it was also a severe blow to the Islamic Sharia, which could no longer find a justification for the enforcement of beliefs held by the *ummah* on the conscience of non-believers, including the forceful impositions of the customary injunction to enjoin the good and forbid evil (*amr bih ma'ruf va nahi az minkar*). Here an essential difference was to separate the Bahá'í conception of belief, as a matter that is decided in one's personal conscience, and the conception of 'shared belief',[68] implicit in Islamic practice, a point cogently conveyed by Bausani:

> The Truth (*ḥaqq*) of Islam is not chiefly a theoretical truth, but also and prevalently, law, customs felt as given by God, and obviously cannot be spread through personal persuasion, but only through the conquest of a region . . . Truth is not a theology, is not a knowledge that brings salvation to the single, but a true attitude or behaviour of an entire society (including therefore, amongst its essentials, canon law, customs and habits, even behaviour to be followed in a toilet). This cannot be taught personally, but only, more or less, violently imposed.[69]

That truth cannot be asserted violently is a fundamental tenet of Bahá'u'lláh that 'Abdu'l-Bahá conveyed in even more explicit terms:

> When Bahá'u'lláh appeared, He declared that the promulgation of the truth [*tablígh-i-amr*] by such means must on no account be allowed, even for the purposes of self-defence [*mudáfi'ih az khud*]. He abrogated the rule of the sword [*tashhír-i-shamshír*] and annulled the ordinance of 'Holy War' [*ḥukm-i-jihád*]. 'If ye be slain', said He, 'it is better for you than to slay.' It is through the firmness and assurance of the faithful that the Cause of the Lord must be diffused.[70]

Equally momentous was the attending abrogation of the notion of ritual impurity, which not only was to put a hold on legalistic religious-mindedness (and its corollary belief in the intrinsic value of ritual acts), but also to effectively terminate the derivative segregation of various categories of people (whether external, as between the various religious communities; or internal, as between men and women) and things (food and space restrictions):

> God hath, likewise, as a bounty from His presence, abolished the concept of 'uncleanness', whereby divers things and peoples have been held to be impure.[71]

Cole has pointed out that the Ottoman *Tanẓimát* (Reforms), starting with the 1839 imperial Edict of Gülhane, and culminating in the Nationality Law of 1869, constituted steps in that very direction, as they implied an end to discrimination on the grounds of religion and a means of equalizing non-Muslim subjects within Ottoman rule.[72] An important difference, however, is that Bahá'u'lláh's legislative measures were a challenge to the entire edifice of Islamic doctrine, yet grounded on the very authority that only, from the Muslim standpoint, a purely hypothetical commanding Prophet (*rasúl*) could wield.

Crucial as is this symbolic and explicit abrogation of the precepts of *jihád* and ritual impurity for a reordering of human affairs, the act of removing them was not by itself a guarantor of peace. A desacralization[73] of holy war, however welcome, was not synonymous with peace nor necessarily implied an absolute disaffirmation of war as an instrument of order; but certainly it divested it of one of its most powerful buttresses. In order to wipe out warfare from the world scene additional foundations were required. Bahá'u'lláh envisioned the scheme for this system in the form of a new universalistic polity unified through the binding force of a common religion for all humanity:

> That which the Lord hath ordained as the sovereign remedy and mightiest instrument for the healing of all the world is the union of all its peoples in one universal Cause, one common Faith. This can in no wise be achieved except through the power of a skilled, an all-powerful and inspired Physician.[74]

Unfortunately, mankind's 'failure' to recognize Bahá'u'lláh as God's Messenger, as symbolized paradigmatically by the refusal of the leading authorities to heed His message, meant that the materialization of this new system would need to take place through stages, mostly painfully. The distinction between the Lesser Peace and the Most Great Peace seems to reflect this chasm. Yet, peace – it is said – will eventually prevail as an inevitable outcome of humanity's fast approaching coming of age. Such was, according to 'Abdu'l-Bahá and Shoghi Effendi, Bahá'u'lláh's promise:

> The promise of the unification of the whole human race, of the inauguration of the Most Great Peace, of the unfoldment of a world civilization, had been incontestably given.[75]

As is the case, however, with many of the most solemn and far-reaching pronouncements made by Bahá'u'lláh, those in connection with peace were couched in particularly terse language.[76] One such declaration was the brief oral statement made in the course of His conversation with E.G. Browne, the eminent British scholar (the tenor of which is reproduced at the beginning of Part I). The encounter, which lasted no more than half an hour, took place on 15 April 1889, that is, three years before Bahá'u'lláh's decease and almost two decades after He had issued His letters to the world rulers. Shoghi Effendi avers that Browne's interviews were 'immortalized' by the Exile's historic declaration that 'these fruitless strifes, these ruinous wars shall pass away and the "Most Great Peace" shall come'.[77] Given that this is the only extant account of the few encounters known to have ever been held between Bahá'u'lláh and westerners, on that score alone it could be presumed to have a special solemn value of its own, a point that the reiteration of the topics covered in the ensuing two encounters seems to confirm. Bahá'u'lláh's words on that first meeting provided a summary of the Bahá'í viewpoint with regard to peace, the elements of which were stressed and partly elucidated by 'Abdu'l-Bahá, especially much later in the course of His journeys to the West.[78] Two days after this historic occasion, Browne was again received in audience for half an hour. The brief notes kept by the orientalist again bear witness to the centrality of the peace theme in Bahá'u'lláh's thinking:

> He again insisted very strongly on the necessity of unity and concord amongst the nations, and spoke of the *Sulḥ-i-Akbar* which will come soon . . . There must be one language and one writing . . . All nations must bind themselves to combine and put down any nation which attempts to disturb the general peace.
>
> Behá also spoke of the Bayt al-'Adl which, he said, is to settle all disputes. The members of this will be 'inspired' (*mulḥam*). *Jihád* is entirely forbidden in this *Ẓuhúr*.[79]

These two passages bring to the fore a terminological problem that by and large has gone unnoticed in Bahá'í literature. Although the Most Great Peace mentioned in them can be taken as the counterpart of its relatively minor correlate, namely the Lesser Peace,[80] it should be noted that the original writings of Bahá'u'lláh seem to establish a contrast between three categories or stages of peace (see Fig. 1).

In the translations of Shoghi Effendi, however, the distinction is somewhat blurred or rather simplified by the fact that *ṣulḥ-i-akbar* appears translated mainly as the 'Lesser Peace' (and, on at least two different occasions, as the 'Great Peace' and the 'Most Great Peace'), thus eventually reducing the distinction to the contrasting pair Lesser/Most Great Peace, with the intermediate stage (Greater Peace) virtually disappearing by assimilation to the lower end of the scale (i.e. Lesser Peace).

Figure 1: Peace (*ṣulḥ*)

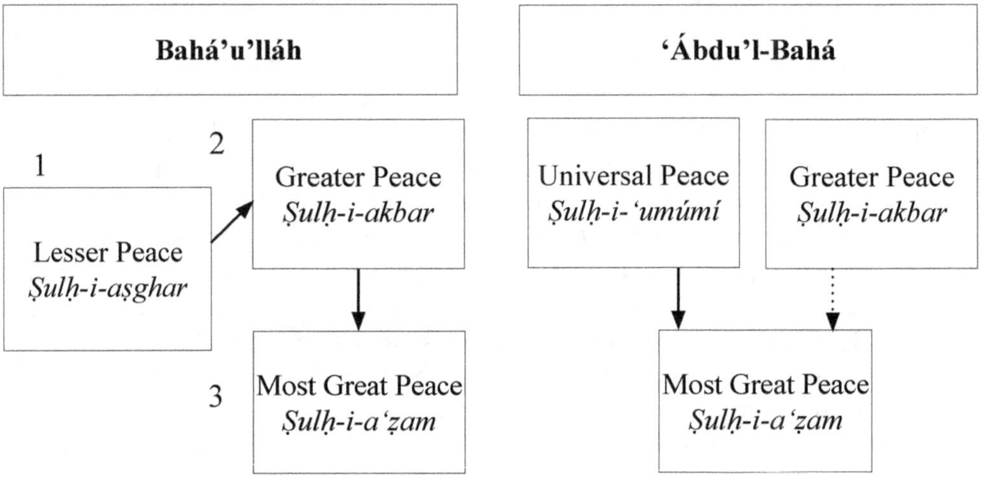

In the writings and talks of 'Abdu'l-Bahá the binary polarity *'umúmí/a'ẓam* is prevalent, with *ṣulḥ-i-'umúmí* retaining the combined characteristics of the pair *ṣulḥ-i-aṣghar* and *ṣulḥ-i-akbar*, although occurrences of the latter can also be found in contexts that render indistinguishable any difference between *'umúmí* and *akbar*.[81] A possible and so far only cogent explanation for the original tripartition of peace has been advanced by 'Alí Nakhjavání as follows:

> When one reads these carefully it becomes quite clear that whenever reference is made merely to the reduction of armaments, the need for consultation among nations, or the principle of collective security, Shoghi Effendi's translation is always the 'Lesser Peace'. However, when the context goes beyond political unification and deals with unity in all its aspects, including unity of race and of religion, the translation becomes the 'Most Great Peace'.[82]

As stated above, the very distinction between two kinds of peace appears to be an outcome of humanity's having rejected Bahá'u'lláh's message,[83] in effect forgoing the very possibility of achieving the Most Great Peace in a short period. This further explains why Bahá'u'lláh would speak of the Lesser Peace as an attainable substitute, understandably one whose main features, compared to those of the Most Great Peace, would have to be toned down accordingly:

> Your people are your treasures. Beware lest your rule violate the commandments of God, and ye deliver your wards to the hands of the robber. By them ye rule, by their means ye subsist, by their aid ye conquer. Yet, how disdainfully ye look upon them! How strange, how strange!
>
> Now that ye have refused the Most Great Peace [*ṣulḥ al-akbar*], hold ye fast unto this, the Lesser Peace [*ṣulḥ al-aṣghar*], that haply ye may in some degree better your own condition and that of your dependents.[84]

It is worth noting that Bahá'u'lláh links the 'postponement' of the Most Great Peace to the fact that the rulers of the world had violated God's commands by ignoring the rights of their peoples, the very ones who justify their existence as rulers. The Lesser Peace appears thereby as a second best alternative, but one which is fraught with some dangers, as suggested by the fact that it demands a 'holding fast'. This, however, does not preclude Bahá'u'lláh from proclaiming the Lesser Peace as one of His glad-tidings (circa 1885 or later):

> The sixth Glad-Tidings is the establishment of the Lesser Peace [*ṣulḥ al-aṣghar*], details of which have formerly been revealed from Our Most Exalted Pen. Great is the blessedness of him who upholdeth it and observeth whatsoever hath been ordained by God, the All-Knowing, the All-Wise.[85]

Not only the rulers of the world, but also the members of the Universal House of Justice (the supreme governing body of the Bahá'í Faith) are charged to take all necessary steps to bring forth the Lesser Peace (*ṣulḥ-i-akbar*, that is, the intermediate stage in the pacification process) as the previous and necessary step to the fulfilment of the Most Great Peace:

> It is incumbent upon the ministers of the House of Justice [*vuzaráy-i-baytu'l-'adl*] to promote the Lesser Peace [*ṣulḥ-i-akbar*] so that the people of the earth may be relieved from the burden of exorbitant expenditures. This matter is imperative and absolutely essential, inasmuch as hostilities and conflict lay at the root of affliction and calamity.[86]

Interestingly, it should be observed that the Lesser Peace referred to in this text is the *ṣulḥ-i-akbar* rather that the *ṣulḥ-i-aṣghar*, in what can be taken as indicative of a more significant role for the supreme Bahá'í body, particularly during the intermediate stage associated with the erection of a world-wide system of governance. If this tripartition and its relevant texts are to be taken as indicative, peace cannot be expected to be the result of a passive awaiting, but rather an outcome of a conscious process carried out by governments, nations and their peoples, not excluding the converging efforts made in this regard by Bahá'í institutions. At any rate, the distinction between the Lesser and the Most Great Peace seems to lie in the degree to which the peoples of the world and its governments espouse willingly and knowingly the principles set forth by Bahá'ú'lláh.

As for the origins of the distinction between the Lesser Peace and the Most Great Peace in Bahá'í thought, these remain largely unknown, although Burgel[87] and Cole[88] may be quite correct in pointing to the experiment by the Mughal Emperor Akbar (1542–1605) as an earlier example. Akbar had not only founded a House of Worship (*'ibádat-khánih*) as a meeting point for interreligious debates but had also instituted complementary measures of an ecumenical nature, including a decree establishing reason as the basis of religion and recognizing truth in all religions. It can be argued that these reforms might have been well known to Bahá'u'lláh and 'Abdu'l-Bahá, Who could have found further inspiration in the Akbarian expression *ṣulḥ-i-kull* (a general pacification), meaning a state of general toleration and acceptance of others that was deemed to be the lesser counterpart of the *muḥabbat-i-kull*, a state of universal fellowship among men.[89] Akbar had also abolished the poll tax and allowed Hindus to serve in the Administration in an effort to broaden the bases for peaceful coexistence in the Indian subcontinent. This measure could also have served as a significant precedent of the Ottoman *Tanẓimát* and Bahá'u'lláh's own abrogation of civil discrimination on the grounds of religion.

It is important to note that use of the word *ṣulḥ,* as in the expression *ṣulḥ al-aṣghar*, may suggest simply an agreement or a pact in the Quranic sense of the word (for instance when a dispute over property occurs).[90] But in the sense given under Ottoman rule – that is, 'a peace agreed upon by two governments' – it may also signify, as already noted, a process of transition and pacification towards a more definite and pervasive state of peace.[91] We may thus represent these meanings following a gradation (see Fig. 2):

Figure 2: General meanings of the word *ṣulḥ*

Ṣulḥ
Truce, armistice, pact, reconciliation, concord (the opposite of war) ↓
Peace agreement, as between two governments[92] ↓
Pacification, peacemaking, process of transition towards peace

Lewis notes that some Muslim authors were also to introduce a third category to the dichotomy *dár al-Islám* and *dár al-ḥarb,* namely that of the *dár aṣ-ṣulḥ* (not to be confused with that of *dár al-ímám*), meaning the dominion where other non-Muslim rulers could govern autonomously under the umbrella of a Muslim ruler. This distinction, together with the reciprocal nature of peace, seems to underline the intermediate, inconclusive and non-definitive state which is afforded by *ṣulḥ,* and it may explain why a distinction is made in Bahá'í terms between the Lesser Peace, defined basically as a 'political arrangement', and the Most Great Peace, which is linked not so much to mutual human agreements as to the fulfilment of mankind's Covenant with God and His realized sovereignty on earth through the establishment of His Kingdom.

The principle of collective security

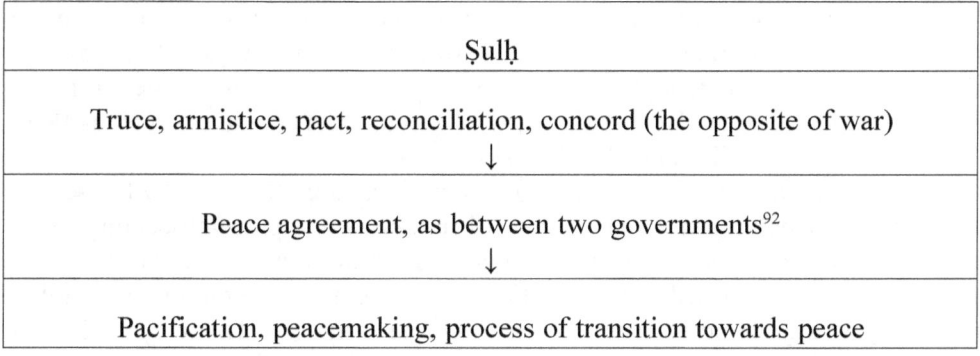

Although the texts already introduced are of considerable import, perhaps none is more so than the seminal statement where Bahá'u'lláh enunciates His version of the principle of collective security. The general tenor of Bahá'u'lláh's proposal for the unification of mankind, as noted by Cole, was not a novelty in Europe where the idea of a political peace through some federated pact had been in circulation for two centuries in various forms.[93] Already in the seventeenth century Jan Amos Comenius and Emeric Crucé had both articulated a number of ideas that doubtless laid the groundwork for many of the schemes that would ensue in the next centuries, including the push for an international auxiliary language, a universal system of education, and a collegiate system of decision-making that would replace autocratic power.[94] In his celebrated but hardly readable treatise on perpetual peace, the Abbé Saint-Pierre had already enunciated the basic tenets presiding over a confederation of European States aimed at superseding the Westphalian European balance of power.[95] In his view Europe had enjoyed a certain equilibrium, but this was essentially unstable and marred by a whirl of shifting allegiances. In order to achieve a lasting peace, States would perforce have to renounce wars of conquest, accepting the resolution of their differences by means of a Diet where they would be represented according to size and population. Each State would then be assigned a quota of armed forces for their own internal policing. In this way – so the theory goes – war would ebb away or be pushed to Europe's outer frontiers. Similar proposals were also circulated by other enlightened authors such as Penn, Rousseau, Bentham, Kant and Malinovskii.[96]

Building on the incipient tradition of toleration, supported now by the secular foundations of natural law and the law of nations, the eighteenth-century peace proposals were in effect meant to influence public discourse by laying the bases for a *vera pax* as opposed to the questionable peace achieved through the violent prevailing of a great power over other subordinated nations. This proposed peace would require some degree of intervention and enforcement from outside, although nothing akin to a world polity. Yet the system would have to be strong enough to satisfy the need for security among countries through the provision of guarantees, including mandatory arbitration via a special representative tribunal, and other enforcement measures. In these schemes peace was predicated on the assumption that war, in addition to being a destroyer of human nature and society (for human beings were thought to be reasonable and sociable), was also inimical to the truer interests of the State and its peoples. These interests could best be served through the promotion of commerce, trade and other exchanges which, by comparison, were considered inherently peaceful, a point that in true Mandevillian logic was to certify the replacement of war as an acceptable principle of international relations with the more amenable and productive 'hand of greed'. Seen from this perspective, the relationship between nations in a peaceful concert of federated European nations was no different from the relationship that obtains as between the State and its subjects.

Despite attempts to make these kinds of proposals appear enticingly practical, the peace 'project' genre was discontinued, partly as a result of its being subsumed within a broader reform literature, including international law tracts. After the Napoleonic wars, peace initiatives moved into the diplomatic phase of the Holy Alliance and the Quadruple Alliance, and the birth of the first Christian-inspired peace societies that in time would evolve into a very sizeable peace movement. By the middle of the nineteenth century peace congresses prospered, finding in the likes of Victor Hugo or Richard Cobden articulated exponents of the movement's more secularized pacifist ideals. A belief in the intrinsic value of commerce and communications to accomplish an important degree of understanding among the peoples of the world was by then common stock among enlightened and optimist liberal thinkers, convinced that perpetual peace would 'naturally' ensue from them.[97] The great 'universal' exhibitions held in Europe since the great 1851 London exhibition served as a showcase of industrialist societies, brimming with generic statements where words such as 'peace', 'free trade' and 'understanding among the peoples' of the world were almost interchangeable.[98] Some of these universal exhibitions resulted in international agreements on industrial property, intellectual property, weights and measures, and so on.[99] Standardization played a major role in securing those exchanges among the world's peoples. Bahá'u'lláh's push for an international language[100] and a common system of weights and measures can be seen in this light and, therefore, be regarded as quite in conformity with the *Zeitgeist*. What remains more difficult to determine is how and to what extent those ideas were given impetus by Bahá'u'lláh.

Cole has postulated the case of the Saint-Simonians as a likely focus for the propagation of some of these 'Utopian' ideas in the Mediterranean region, for instance through Enfantin and many of his followers, engineers from the Polytechnique, who believed that civil works such as the pan-European, pan-Asian and pan-African railroads or the projected Suez Canal could link the world, thereby bringing forth its unification.[101] In addition, Cole has surmised that the Crimean peace system went a step further in the implementation of some measures of international security, which undoubtedly were part of the background that Bahá'ú'lláh could have had in mind when He sketched His own plan.[102] The new state of affairs brought about by the Crimean War settlement did not only upset the arrangements laboriously created at the Congress of Vienna, but precipitated new climactic changes in the European balance of power leading to the reunification of Italy and Germany, and to further unrest in the emerging Balkan states. Another unforeseen consequence was the sea-change from defensive arrangements to an escalation of offensive preparations. Previous revolutionary wars gave way to a series of lethal clashes between the European powers. As a result, interstate warfare became again a normal recourse for the settling of disputes in international relations. Ever-increasing economic stakes and armed encounters between standing armies were to leave casualties equally measured, as in the Crimean War, in the hundreds of thousands.[103] In a critical assessment of the virtues and limitations of the system, Holsti asserts:

> The statesmen of the great powers created a static system for a world of change, an equilibrium of power that did not derive logically from their own diagnoses of the sources of international conflict (revolution), and a peace system that anticipated for the future little more than a recurrence of a problem that they had already resolved.[104]

Speaking to Browne in 1889, well after the Crimean War and the crushing experience of the Franco-Prussian war, Bahá'u'lláh had then good reason to believe that European powers, which had embarked on a wholesale arms race with devastating consequences for their peoples, stood in dire need of such a peace. The notion of collective security advocated by Bahá'u'lláh was however much broader than the peace arrangements customarily entered into by the European powers. In addition to requiring the participation of the great powers, its programme had to be world-embracing and much more ambitious than anything put to the test or publicized by earlier peace advocates, clearly moving beyond the international arbitration of disputes.

According to Rafael Calduch, the principle of collective security that emerged after World War I made it evident that the arms race had led the European powers to a level of confrontation that could only be averted if all countries were committed to the security of other countries as well. This admission, in turn, required that State-based security be replaced by positive cooperation in the fashioning of instruments capable of ensuring international security.[105] The previous balance of power system had resulted in a succession of alliances and counter-alliances which had proven simply unequal to the task of averting the dangers of war, much of it compounded by the twists of secret diplomacy, imperialistic ambitions and disparate nationalistic trends. While in the previous balance of power or concert 'system' war was an accepted means of settling differences or even consolidating a balance of power or status quo achieved in peacetime, in a system of collective security all recourse to force is outlawed, except when a collective response under stipulated conditions makes it necessary,[106] or a nation under attack has to use it as a means of 'last resort' in order to repel an aggression, pending action by the collective body.[107] In a system of collective security, confidence-building measures and cooperation are fostered in a way which previous arrangements would not seriously contemplate. The simplicity of the system is also one of its best known advantages, as most of its elements can be easily recognized.[108]

As noted by Claude Inis,[109] any such system requires the tacit recognition of a commonly shared human nature at the individual and societal levels (rationality and goodness of humanity), as well as the assumption that since peace is indivisible, any breach of the peace constitutes an attack on the whole. Hence the automatism of the responses the system must elicit regardless of the status of the aggressor (anonymity of the aggressor). The strength of the arrangement depends on its capacity to muster universal support, adopt clear and transparent mechanisms, and be seen as a fair and balanced system with no one-sided biases. In other words, it is not a unipolar peace imposed by the one dominant power or hegemon.

The basics of one such system can be identified in Bahá'u'lláh's main proposal for a peaceful agreement among nations, the bare outline of which was given in two texts. The first one is the Tablet to Queen Victoria (Lawḥ-i-Malikih, 1868, early 'Akká period) and a key passage of the Lawḥ-i-Maqṣúd, dated 20 January 1882.[110]

The Tablet to Queen Victoria contains in essence the most elementary aspects of the concept of collective security that were to be articulated in greater detail later. The first is a confirmation that the starting point of efforts towards peace is no longer the Most Great Peace but the Lesser Peace (a second best). The ethical horizon of perfect peace and composure was thereby removed from the realm of the immediately feasible to be replaced by a highly demanding but by comparison more modest utopia, of a world free from the most damaging effects of militarism. To this follows Bahá'u'lláh's invitation to disarm down to the level required for the maintenance of internal peace and order:

> O rulers of the earth! Be reconciled among yourselves, that ye may need no more armaments save in a measure to safeguard your territories and dominions. Beware lest ye disregard the counsel of the All-Knowing, the Faithful.[111]

The second idea is a more specific call to reconciliation and unity that specifies the need for all rulers to rise up in arms to overpower any aggressor.

> Be united, O kings of the earth, for thereby will the tempest of discord be stilled amongst you, and your peoples find rest, if ye be of them that comprehend. Should any one among you take up arms against another, rise ye all against him, for this is naught but manifest justice.[112]

The definition of this act as 'manifest justice' indicates that its execution is morally acceptable and should not be shunned on ethical grounds. Since this is an endorsement of a rather distant prospect, it becomes all the more revealing owing to the contrast it marks with the abolished *jihád* and anything that may fall short of the standard advocated by Bahá'u'lláh.

The last two points found a more detailed formulation in the Lawḥ-i-Maqṣúd written fourteen years later, and hence postdating the well-known passage by 'Abdu'l-Bahá in *The Secret of Divine Civilization* where reference is made in some more detail to the all-embracing assemblage of men proposed by Bahá'u'lláh. By comparison, Bahá'u'lláh's statement is also more succinct:[113]

> The Great Being, wishing to reveal the prerequisites of the peace and tranquillity [*sukún va ráḥat*] of the world and the advancement of its peoples hath written: The time must come when the imperative necessity for the holding of a vast, and all-embracing assemblage of men will be universally realized. The rulers and kings [*mulúk va saláṭín*] of the earth must needs attend it, and, participating in its deliberations, must consider such ways and means as will lay the foundations of the world's Great Peace amongst men [*ṣulḥ-i-akbar*]. Such a peace demandeth that the Great Powers [*duvval-i-'aẓímih*] should resolve, for the sake of the tranquillity of the peoples of the earth, to be fully reconciled among themselves. Should any king (*malikí*] take up arms against another, all should unitedly arise and prevent him. If this be done, the nations of the world will no longer require any armaments, except for the purpose of preserving the security of their realms and of maintaining internal order within their territories. This will ensure the peace and composure of every people, government and nation . . . The day is approaching when all the peoples of the world will have

> adopted one universal language and one common script . . . These things are obligatory and absolutely essential.[114]

Three interconnected principles can be distinguished in the above text:

- Peace is an outcome of joint multilateral and concerted efforts clearly exceeding military arrangements, for it includes the adoption of a universal language and one common script.
- It demands the enforcement of a system of collective security aimed at quelling aggression and establishing order. While this task must be accomplished primarily among the great powers of the world, its scope must be such that all 'the peoples of the earth' are clearly benefited.
- It entails a parallel and proportional resizing of arsenals down to a degree commensurate with internal security purposes. This latter exigency can be regarded in turn not just as an ultimate goal, but rather as a test and standard of the soundness of the system.

The peace conference envisaged by Bahá'u'lláh was 'universal' in scope and aimed at producing arms reductions to levels commensurate with internal policing. This gathering would eventuate at a time when its necessity would be realized as 'imperative', which is suggestive of a period of maturation (perhaps forced by circumstances) and of shared understanding in the international community. Furthermore, it is not a dynastic or purely diplomatic affair, but rather is intended to provide the means for, and lay the foundations of, a durable peace.

The attainment of peace is essentially the result of a consultative process. Cole has emphasized the 'idea of consultation in this context as synonymous with 'representative government'. In general, consultation (*mas<u>h</u>virat*) contrasts with absolutist or despotic ways of decision-making.[115] It is therefore through a broadening of freedom, or alternatively through a limitation of unipersonal rule, that consultation takes place, and this would imply a widening of the democratic nature of the peace conference advocated by Bahá'u'lláh. The fact that the assemblage is defined as 'all-embracing' and that it includes the powers of the 'earth' clearly suggests the universal scope of its arrangements, in marked contrast to the limited European concert which was in force at the time, or to the much older Kantian project for a perpetual peace, which the philosopher himself toned down considerably in his *Metaphysics of Morals*.

The universalistic outlook adopted by Bahá'u'lláh is not only underlined by the use of language, but also by the very nature of Bahá'u'lláh's previous addresses to the kings, presidents of the republics and religious authorities of the world, all of whom can be taken either singly or collectively as a representative cross-section of the organized powers at the time. Shoghi Effendi refers to these letters and addresses as amounting to a code of conduct in 'human and international relations'.[116] In this regard the important declaration addressed to the 'rulers of America and the Presidents of the Republic therein' in the Kitáb-i-Aqdas deserves special mention for its emphasis on combining justice with the fear of God:

> Bind ye the broken with the hands of justice [*'adl*], and crush the oppressor [*aẓ-ẓálim*] who flourisheth with the rod of the commandments of your Lord, the Ordainer, the All-Wise.[117]

The iteration of this idea in the exhortation to 'crush the oppressor' seems to be suggestive of a hitherto untried role for the American governments in the international scene, a point of considerable relevance for the expansion of the Bahá'í Faith and its vision of world affairs, as further elaborations by 'Abdu'l-Bahá and Shoghi Effendi made apparent at a later stage (see Chapters 8 and 18 on the role of America).

The 'vast and all-embracing assemblage of men' refers to a world peace arrangement where the great powers will have to assume the responsibility for settling their own disputes as well as for creating a system of collective security whereby aggression against another nation is not only outlawed but vigorously repelled by an alliance of international forces. On the basis of this arrangement, existing armed forces will be reduced and reassigned an internal or defensive role. This, as implied elsewhere, will render the creation of expanding arsenals redundant:

> O Rulers of the earth! Be reconciled among yourselves, that ye may need no more armaments save in a measure to safeguard your territories and dominions. Beware lest ye disregard the counsel of the All-Knowing, the Faithful.[118]

Likewise, Bahá'u'lláh exhorted the kings to reduce the size of these arsenals:

> Compose your differences and reduce your armaments, that the burden of your expenditures may be lightened, and that your minds and hearts may be tranquillized.[119]

Discussions should not be intended to bring about just a new *status quo* or a mere balance of power, as was the characteristic of the various failed systems of checks and balances developed among European nations. Rather, in addition to securing frontiers and bringing about a system of retaliation/sanctions against offending or aggressor nations, they should be centred on the needs of the age. In other words, the future agreements shall formulate the new goals for mankind, based on an understanding of the needs they purport to satisfy. This is a recurrent theme in the writings of Bahá'u'lláh, as evinced in the following passage:

> Every age has its own problem, and every soul its particular aspiration. The remedy the world needeth in its present-day afflictions can never be the same as that which a subsequent age may require. Be anxiously concerned with the needs of the age ye live in, and centre your deliberations on its exigencies and requirements.[120]

This point was made even more explicitly in Bahá'u'lláh's exhortation to Queen Victoria and the British members of Parliament to uphold and consider the needs of mankind rather than their own more parochial concerns. Accordingly, the object of the deliberations is not to be exclusively confined to military security issues or dependent on keeping a given *status quo*. The adoption of a universal language, whose enforcement is considered 'absolutely essential', can be counted as part of the concerns which should feature prominently in the global agenda. Elsewhere, Bahá'u'lláh refers to the holding of a special congress of 'men of understanding and erudition', reminiscent in several respects of Kant's endorsement of the role he envisaged for the 'philosophers',[121] who by acting in this capacity would considerably lend support to the promotion of world peace:

> It is incumbent upon all nations to appoint some men of understanding and erudition to convene a gathering and through joint consultation choose one language from among the varied existing languages, or create a new one, to be taught to the children in all the schools of the world.[122]

By linking peace to an enforceable system of security, supplemented by world-building measures of trust, peace is no longer viewed in terms of mere absence of conflict, or as an intermittent period of calm between wars, nor as a felicitous interposition of Providence in an otherwise anarchical world of sovereign States. By squarely stating the core content of the Lesser Peace Bahá'u'lláh seemed to have brushed aside the fatalistic or realistic views of human nature that turn alleged descriptions of a state of affairs into political prescriptions. Human behaviour, embodied typically by rulers, is not presented as a fully autonomous area that remains out of bounds or is unanswerable to any overarching moral principles, particularly in the international sphere. Whereas Kant viewed Nature, or alternatively moral legislative reason, as guiding human impulses in a process of self-clarification,[123] Bahá'u'lláh subordinated those impulses to compliance with God's commandments. This naturally suggests that politics, national or international, must be subjected at any rate to standards which at heart are of a spiritual nature; thus the international realm is not a field where the laws of nature (i.e. war) inhere, but on the contrary, a domain which needs to be shaped by adherence to an even higher sense of law and justice.

The balance of power system introduced by the treaties of Vienna and Paris, it should be noted, was not incompatible with military escalation, wars by proxy, and limited warfare, with all the more reason if these only involved a sharing in the spoils of non-European nations, a fact of which Bahá'u'lláh, an Iranian exile living as a prisoner under Ottoman rule, could not help but be painfully aware. At variance with it, the system of collective security advocated by Bahá'u'lláh appears to be geared not only towards a massive reduction of military expenditure, significant as this was, but also to a reversal of the nature and purpose of military might, a hope equally cherished by 'Abdu'l-Bahá:[124]

> We cherish the hope that through the earnest endeavours of such as are the exponents of the power of God – exalted be His glory – the weapons of war throughout the world may be converted into instruments of reconstruction and that strife and conflict may be removed from the midst of men.[125]

While in Clausewitzian thinking war was understood as subservient to politics, an idea heavily indebted to the Enlightenment as it implied the taming of violence under the rule of reason (or rather calculus),[126] war nevertheless still remained at the core of a world of conflictual relationships between States. In contrast, Bahá'u'lláh's brief exposé pointed in the direction of a new social dynamics of what, for lack of a better word, might be termed humanitarianism or monoanthropism: the cosmopolitan ethos of a world ecumene. States, societies and their individuals would have to move towards a demilitarized civilian culture in an effort that would require the support of subsidiary principles and norms, and an ethics positively aligned with the prosecution of such a general goal. Quite naturally, this thinking assumed a reversal of commonly held notions about human nature and the status of interstate relationships. Bahá'u'lláh seems to have linked the subverting of prevailing notions of order and governance to the realization of the Kingdom of God, implying that the powerful and the mighty will be overpowered by the meek through the power of truth alone. The eschatological theme underlying this perspective – the inheritance of the earth by the weak – appears associated with the realization of Bahá'u'lláh's 'wondrous system' and with the 'mystery of the great Reversal in the sign of the Sovereign'.[127]

An important element in this vision of peace is that Bahá'u'lláh seems to have consistently refused to see the nation-state as the ultimate agent in world affairs. For as long as the needs and rightful concerns of the whole of humanity remained unaddressed, the State system was declared defective and lacking implicitly in full legitimacy. Bahá'u'lláh had significantly defined the earth, not its various sections, as one country or fatherland (*waṭan*); and mankind as its 'people' (*ahl*, citizens).[128] The system envisaged by Bahá'u'lláh, as made plain to Browne, entailed the acknowledgement of the essential oneness of mankind and a cosmopolitan form of loyalty transcending the narrow limits imposed by the concept of national sovereignty. At variance with Kant or Paine, but yet deferring to the republican ethos, Bahá'u'lláh was careful to point out that the republican form of government, while indicative of humanity's coming of age, was not meant to be the only form of government for all nations.[129] In fact, a monarchical system was preferable, although obviously one endowed with the advantages of a parliamentary system such as the one prevailing in Great Britain at the time. The combination of the benefits of a democratic monarchic system and the urge to embrace a world perspective in the consideration of human affairs was epitomized in Bahá'u'lláh's address to Queen Victoria:

> We have also heard that thou hast entrusted the reins of counsel into the hands of the representatives of the people. Thou, indeed, hast done well, for thereby the foundations of the edifice of thine affairs will be strengthened, and the hearts of all that are beneath thy shadow, whether high or low, will be tranquillized. It behoveth them, however, to be trustworthy among His servants, and to regard themselves as the representatives of all that dwell on earth.[130]

At a basic level the solution to world problems requires the activity of a new consciousness of solidarity and reciprocity in human relations. The new definition of man given by Bahá'u'lláh clearly incorporated into its terms this broader sense of unity:

> That one indeed is a man who, today, dedicateth himself to the service of the entire human race. The Great Being saith: Blessed and happy is he that ariseth to promote the best interests of the peoples and kindreds of the earth. In another passage He hath proclaimed: It is not for him to pride himself who loveth his own country, but rather for him who loveth the whole world. The earth is but one country, and mankind its citizens.[131]

Peace, then, can be properly established only if society at large engages in peace-making, and rulers are obliged to abide by its code of conduct:

> We have enjoined upon *all mankind* to establish the Most Great Peace [*ṣulḥ-i-akbar*] the surest of all means for the protection of humanity. The sovereigns of the world should with *one accord*, hold fast thereunto, for this is the supreme instrument that can ensure the security and welfare of *all the peoples and nations.*[132] (emphasis added)

5
Conclusion

As we survey the life and writings of Bahá'u'lláh there emerges a composite picture of His approach to peace. Rather than a systematized body of thought, what we find is an interaction between biography and the awareness brought about by the totalizing experience of the new aeon. The biographical element complements and clarifies the scriptural; and vice versa, the writing explains key aspects of the biography. This interplay applies quite conspicuously to the origins of Bahá'u'lláh's obliteration of *jihád* (the Arabic word sometimes crudely translated as 'holy war', short for 'struggle in the path of God'), an act which at once would disclose Bahá'u'lláh's claimed status as the Revealer of God's Word and His willingness to effect a complete change in the nature of religion and the place of force in its propagation. In the Islamic world, peace (*salám, ṣulḥ*) and *jihád* could simply not be separated. *Jihád* was ultimately the way to secure the final triumph of God over the unbelievers and only this triumph could result in a fully peaceful society. *Jihád* was also expressive of the inconclusiveness of the status quo in a world deeply divided into different religious communities with which conflict and ultimately war could be expected. As a mental category, the 'house of war' (*dar-al ḥarb*), the realm where war is legitimate, was perhaps not much different from the state of nature and the state of anarchy posited by European philosophers as the normal state prevailing within and between societies where human beings or their authorities are left to their own devices. Even in its spiritualized Sufí forms, the inner struggle of *jihád* could not nullify the external struggle. Not unlike the imperial *pax Romana,* or their modern equivalents the *pax Britannica* or the *pax Americana*, the Islamic peace was conceived in over-realistic terms as the unavoidable result of a violent process of pacification, implying a direct confrontation with unbelief. By abrogating *jihád* Bahá'u'lláh thus gave peace again a different salience. By disentangling it from the usual religious and moral justifications of 'just war thinking' (and its jihadic equivalents), and reframing it as an outcome of collective security, the Bahá'í peace could no longer be understood as forced 'pacification', but rather had to be reinterpreted in the positive terms of reciprocal guarantees under strict and mutually agreed conditions among deliberating nations.

Bahá'u'lláh's injunctions to His followers not to engage in violent action, and His emphasis on the spiritual content of His message, were clearly designed to dissociate His doctrine from jihadic or war-like precedents. His own life and writings exemplified this trend and further linked it to a distinct lifestyle characterized by its being inwardly and outwardly devoid of violent traits. The mystic strand, so characteristic of Bahá'u'lláh's Iraqi period, was thus recast and incorporated into the body of the new Revelation, thereby infusing it with a powerful underpinning that in previous Dispensations had only uneasily coexisted with mainstream religion.

Bahá'u'lláh's most significant texts situated peace in the context of eschatological and prophetic fulfilment, or alternatively as a result of God's law-giving activity.[133] God's sovereignty was not to be understood as the triumph by the sword of a Qá'im or Mahdí figure, but, quite the contrary, as the achievement of the meek and humble over the powerful, of the Word of God and the sheer power of example over the forces of the world, all of which were said to be exemplified by Bahá'u'lláh Himself and His followers. Bahá'u'lláh's vindication of the example set by the martyrs and champions of the Báb's Faith was equally given a new focus under this light. His own authority as the Manifestation of God on earth was asserted through His own discourse, which assumed the bearings of a fully-fledged Revelation deriving legitimacy from its claim to being the fulfilment of previous Dispensations. An important implication of the abrogation of *jihád* was the cancellation of all theologically derived doctrines justifying the existence of an underlying state of war, violence, alienation or suspicion among believing and unbelieving nations. Bahá'u'lláh's activity was soon accompanied by a full proclamation addressed to the potentates of the world.

The subsequent issuance of the Aqdas helped to establish the legal framework of Bahá'u'lláh's covenant with His followers and the whole of humanity. This legal framework was cast in such a way as to mitigate the harshness of previous religious laws (including those of the Bayán), emphasize purity of motive (in keeping with the Bayán), shun all forms of hypocrisy and regulate the relationships between the sections of mankind. In this way the abolition of ritual impurity and the command to His followers to freely associate with the followers of other religions would stand as fundamental reversals of customary practices standing in the way of a civil yet God-minded society.

In His assumed role as a Prophet of God and a royal counsellor, Bahá'u'lláh approached the rulers and sovereigns of His time, counselling them to exert moderation and to be responsible for the welfare of their subjects, a major function for which they were made fully accountable. The basic distinction established by Bahá'u'lláh between the Lesser Peace, the Greater Peace and the Most Great Peace also cleared the way for an understanding of peace as the result of a gradual, yet decisive, enterprise that demanded, *inter alia*, agreement among rulers and the implementation of a sound system of collective security, a bare outline of which was presented by Bahá'u'lláh to the potentates of the world. The rule of (divine) law in effect made it imperative for the powers of the world to conduct their affairs in accordance with an agreed measure of collective action to repel aggression. The

Lesser Peace would thus mark the beginning of a process of pacification (*ṣulḥ*) that, in the fullness of time, would lead to the unification of the world under one common faith.

The system of collective security propounded by Bahá'u'lláh implied not only arms reductions but also a consultative process on the main issues confronting humanity as a whole. The realization of this goal made it all the more necessary to identify global needs as well as to adopt a new loyalty towards humanity. Bahá'u'lláh saw mankind as a whole entity that, as it was coming of age,[134] would reach increasing levels of unity, all as a direct result of God's creative influence. This readiness, which was precipitated by the appearance of God's new Revelation, was discernible through some signs foreboding not only the rapid maturation of humanity as a unified body, but also pointing to the nature and character of Bahá'u'lláh's own new world order.

Briefly stated, the system of collective security required that the great powers agreed on repelling aggressor nations unitedly, but this had to be coupled with the adoption of such measures (for instance disarmament, or the selection or creation of an international auxiliary language) as would ensure its effective implementation. The task was not entirely left to the devices of the powerful, but actually enjoined upon all mankind, a point which shows clear connections with 'Abdu'l-Bahá's exhortations to establish a peace constituency through the cultivation and reinforcement of public opinion.

Ultimately, however, it is clear that Bahá'u'lláh identified unity in one common faith as the main means for remedying the 'ailing body' of humanity.[135] For this to happen efforts would have to be made by the Bahá'ís themselves. It is significant that Bahá'u'lláh charged the ministers of the House of Justice (the Universal House of Justice) 'to promote the Lesser Peace so that the people of the earth be relieved from the burden of exorbitant expenditures'.[136] These efforts would of necessity have to combine with the initiatives taken up by governments and other leaders, including religious dignitaries:

> Our hope is that the world's religious leaders and the rulers thereof will unitedly arise for the reformation of this age and the rehabilitation of its fortunes. Let them, after meditating on its needs, take counsel together and, through anxious and full deliberation, administer to a diseased and sorely-afflicted world the remedy it requires.[137]

PART II

‘ABDU’L-BAHÁ ON PEACE

> Quench ye the fires of war, lift high the banners of peace, work for the oneness of humankind and remember that religion is the channel of love unto all peoples.[1]

> There are many kinds of war and conflict going on, political war, commercial war, patriotic and racial war; this is the very civilization of war.[2]

'Abdu'l-Bahá was appointed by Bahá'u'lláh 'Centre of the Covenant' (*Markaz-i-Mitháq*)[3] of the new Dispensation and the only authoritative interpreter of His Father's intent. His words, therefore, are regarded by Bahá'ís as an extension of Bahá'u'lláh's will and hence equally binding.[4] There is still no comprehensive biography of 'Abdu'l-Bahá. The existing biographies by Faydí[5] and Balyuzi[6] and the two extensive chapters that Shoghi Effendi devoted to His ministry in *God Passes By* offer uneven coverage which can be partly offset by the extant memoirs of some of His secretaries, attendants, visitors and Bahá'í pilgrims, all of which contain valuable references to His daily routine and activities.[7] Important details on His engagements with officials, intellectuals and public figures have also been provided by Alkan, Balyuzi, Cole, Day, Egea, Hogenson, Hollinger, Momen, Redman, Scharbrodt and Stockman, all of which depict an 'Abdu'l-Bahá well aware of the social, political and religious circumstances of His time and well connected with key political figures.

'Abdu'l-Bahá's major works are few in number and have all been translated into English since an early date. Of particular interest to the present study are *The Secret of Divine Civilization* (1875), the Tablet to The Hague (1919), the conversations he held between 1904 and 1906 with the American Bahá'í Laura Clifford Barney compiled under the title *Some Answered Questions* (1908), and the speeches and addresses delivered in the course of His trips throughout the West (1910–1913). The initial anonymous character of the first work was unveiled at a later date. The fact that it is ostensibly concerned with the proposals for the regeneration of Iran raises important questions as to how the book can be back-read and reworked as a Bahá'í contribution in terms of the East/West polarity, past and present. As indicated in the introduction, the texts of 'Abdu'l-Bahá's speeches delivered in the West have been handed down in the form of notes, rather than as direct translations from the Persian transcriptions, which may not exist. This makes the language in some English texts less dependable and the status of the content more reliably classed as 'reported speech'. The Tablet to The Hague presents no such textual difficulties as it summarizes in a straightforward manner the Bahá'í proposal for peace, clearly linking Bahá'u'lláh's stance to the post-war order of the day, which is critically assessed as bound to fail pending the adoption of fundamental reforms at the international level. A cursory reading of 'Abdu'l-Bahá's correspondence further corroborates, almost to the point of exhaustion, the importance that he attached to the efforts that 'day and night' Bahá'ís had to make in order to embody Bahá'u'lláh's entreaties. To lead an exemplary life devoid of any of the traits of partiality, rancour or enmity that had beset the world for endless generations was in itself a fundamental contribution to the peace and composure of the world, a point repeatedly stressed by Shoghi Effendi.[8]

Since His incarceration in 'Akká in 1868 until 1908, 'Abdu'l-Bahá lived officially as a prisoner of the Ottoman empire. Although His freedom was at times severely restricted and His life endangered,[9] His work at the helm of the nascent Bahá'í community proceeded uninterruptedly.[10] Following His release in 1908 in the wake of the Young Turks Revolution, 'Abdu'l-Bahá embarked on a physically gruelling journey that attracted the attention of the press and large audiences in Egypt, Europe and North America.[11] Throughout His voyages 'Abdu'l-Bahá articulated a message where unity, peace and the coming of the Kingdom figured prominently as the axis around which other Bahá'í tenets hinged.[12] 'Abdu'l-Bahá, often depicted by the western press as an 'Apostle of peace' calling for the reconciliation of humanity, pointed to the emergence of a small yet vibrant community of Bahá'ís who, throughout the Middle East, were effectively working towards the realization of Bahá'u'lláh's ideals, thus providing a new pattern that could be adopted as a worldwide model, a concept that He was to highlight often as a proof that peace and reconciliation were possible, and that Shoghi Effendi would further enlarge by characterizing the Bahá'í community as providing the pattern and a last refuge for a 'long-afflicted humanity'.[13]

'Abdu'l-Bahá's references to the concepts of peace and arbitration reinforced the underlying notion that peace had to be worked out in a comprehensive manner, so that international agreements would need to address some of the burning issues of the day such as the settlement of frontier disputes between countries (a major *casus belli* in international affairs), the adoption of an auxiliary international language and, perhaps more compellingly, the need for a reconciliation between the followers of all religions. He also laid considerable stress on the notion that the system of collective security would have to be supported by a ratification process, doubtless aimed at lending it democratic legitimacy and popular support. 'Abdu'l-Bahá was careful to point out that peace implied much more than a removal of 'war causes' or the attainment of political goals, however important. In this connection, His reference to the concept of 'unity of conscience' and to some of the basic Bahá'í tenets as integral to the contents of peace show that His conception was clearly more in the order of what Galtung terms 'positive' peace.[14] In addition, Abdu'l-Bahá's critique of the concept of 'struggle for existence' demonstrated His awareness of the dangers implicit in the blunt adaptation of Darwinian ideas to social theory and practice, which he counterbalanced by stressing the neat superiority of the forces of cooperation and reciprocity. Materialist theories of a Superman were discarded as divisive 'superstitions', no different from the kind of mistaken beliefs in imaginary Messiahs upheld by Jews, Christians or Muslims.[15]

Similarly, 'Abdu'l-Bahá's receptiveness to the plight of women and His conscious linking of women's advancement with the furtherance of the cause of peace attest to the scope and articulation of His thinking, a point that is discussed at length with regard to the internal structure that can be perceived in His summaries of Bahá'í teachings (principles). In Parts IV and V I will examine some of the underpinnings of these general ideas, showing in greater detail how man's nature, as an individual or as a collective, is conceived in the Bahá'í writings.

6
The Convening of a Peace Conference

One of 'Abdu'l-Bahá's earliest works, *The Secret of Divine Civilization*,[16] written around 1875 and published anonymously in 1882 in Bombay, can be regarded as His first major elaboration on the question of peace. The treatise is all the more remarkable given its contemporaneity with Bahá'u'lláh's letters to the kings and its precedence in time with regard to the Lawḥ-i-Maqṣúd (1882), whose text it closely parallels. This is true in two critical ways. First, the book as a whole is a reflection on the constructive forces of civilization – wisdom, reason, a higher sense of morality – as measured in terms of their contribution to the prosperity, peace and ethical development of Iran. This is contrasted with those forces which negate any material progress (the *'ulamá*), or else excuse their own misuse in the name of culture or in adulation of brute force (western powers). True civilization, explains 'Abdu'l-Bahá, can only qualify as such if it contributes to the elimination of war by extricating itself from its internal logic of self-destruction. In fact, Abdu'l-Bahá states elsewhere, 'civilization is conjoined with barbarism. Progress and barbarism go hand in hand, unless material civilization be confirmed by Divine Guidance [*hidáyat-i-kubrá*]'.[17] For, and this is at the crux of the book, a deeper spiritual and ethical restraint is required for civilization to stave off the diversion of its potentialities towards war designs and the bolstering of ever-improved weaponry. Without those restraints, which religion provides, and as warned by Bahá'u'lláh: 'carried to excess, civilization will prove as prolific a source of evil as it had been of goodness when kept within the restraints of moderation'.[18]

These warnings were not intended in a purely generic way. Bahá'u'lláh Himself would attest to future developments such as the creation and manipulation of lightning-like devices, whose contamination, if unleashed, could prove lethal for the entire earth.

> Strange and astonishing things exist in the earth but they are hidden from the minds and the understanding of men. These things are capable of changing the whole atmosphere of the earth and their contamination would prove lethal. Great God! We have observed an amazing thing. Lightning or a force similar to it is controlled by an operator and moveth at his command.[19]

A clear reference by 'Abdu'l-Bahá to this passage was set in the context of His brief courtesy call upon Viscount Arakawa, Japan's Ambassador to Madrid, while the Viscount and his wife were staying in Paris in 1912. After mentioning the need to work for 'the abolition of war', 'improving conditions of life for the worker', the 'necessity of educating girls and boys equally', and advising that 'Religion must never be used as a tool by party politicians', 'Abdu'l-Bahá had this to say in connection to science and religion:

> Speaking of religion and science, the two great wings with which the bird of human kind is able to soar, He said: 'Scientific discoveries have increased material civilization. There is in existence a stupendous force, as yet, happily undiscovered by man. Let us supplicate God, the Beloved, that this force be not discovered by science until spiritual civilization shall dominate the human mind. In the hands of men of lower nature, this power would be able to destroy the whole earth.'[20]

But at the same time these admonitions were not intended to please the ears of the *'ulamá* by a xenophobic denouncing of the West and its contraptions. For applied in reverse, the same formula made it imperative for the learned elite to reform itself from its sectarianism and dreams of "enforcing the good" by the sword:

> In this way the primary purpose in revealing the Divine Law [*sh͟arí'iy-i-muqaddasih*] – which is to bring about happiness in the after life and civilization [*tamaddun-i-dunyaví*] and the refinement of character [*tahd͟híb-i-ak͟hláq*] in this – will be realized. As for the sword [*bih ḍarb-i-sayf*], it will only produce a man who is outwardly a believer, and inwardly a traitor and apostate.[21]

Secondly, the overall theme in *The Secret of Divine Civilization* explains the presence in the book of two uneven but significant passages regarding peace and the conduct of war. The first passage has usually attracted much attention and has been quoted extensively in general introductions to the Bahá'í religion and further elaborations on peace. This has tended to occur to the detriment of the part that it plays in the context of the book's much broader discussion, namely the role of religion in the gradual civilizing of humanity and the acceptability of cultural and technical borrowings. The universal peace proposed by 'Abdu'l-Bahá in this passage becomes a true mark of civilization, at variance with the peaceful protestations made by the great militarized European powers, which, while certainly acknowledged as materially advanced, in the following sections are depicted as morally 'uncivilized'.[22] The contrast is further completed with parallel criticisms of the Iranian Muslim clergy and its retrograde understandings of the nature of material and spiritual advancement. The passage reads as follows:

> True civilization [*tamaddun-i-ḥaqíqí*] will unfurl its banner in the midmost heart of civilization whenever a certain number of its distinguished and high-

> minded sovereigns [*mulúk-i-buzurgvár*] – the shining exemplars of devotion and determination – shall, for the good and happiness of all mankind [*'umúm-i-bashar*], arise, with firm resolve and clear vision, to establish the Cause of Universal Peace [*ṣulḥ-i-'umúmí*]. They must make the Cause of Peace the object of general consultation [*mashvirat*], and seek by every means in their power to establish a Union of the nations of the world [*'aqd-i-anjuman-i-duvval-i-'álam*]. They must conclude a binding treaty [*mu'áhidiy-i-qavíyyih*] and establish a covenant [*mitháq*], the provisions of which shall be sound, inviolable and definite. They must proclaim [*i'lán*] it to the world and obtain from it the sanction [*ittifáq*] of all the human race.[23]

'Abdu'l-Bahá contemplates the possibility for such a peace conference to be convened under the initiative of a few, albeit influential, heads of state, but not one unilaterally convened, as would be the case with Nicholas II's hosting of the Hague Conferences.[24] The gathering itself must be a 'Peace Conference', based on general consultation, and directed towards the founding of a 'Union of the nations of the world'. The wording of the peace treaty and constitution of the international union must be 'sound, inviolable and definite'. In addition, 'Abdu'l-Bahá foresees an unspecified mechanism of ratification by 'all the human race' (perhaps by referendum or by parliamentary approval). In this way full legitimacy would be obtained. This latter provision confirms a preoccupation with peace being attained and given real support through democratic participation or representation. 'Abdu'l-Bahá makes it also clear that the whole undertaking, regarded as 'the source of the peace [*ásáyish*] and well-being of all the world', will have to be seen as 'sacred [*muqaddas*] by all that dwell on earth', adding that 'all the forces of humanity must be mobilized to ensure the stability and permanence of this Most Great Covenant [*'aḥd-i-a'ẓam*]'.[25]

Regarding the specific issues to be pursued by the assembly, 'Abdu'l-Bahá states:

> In this all-embracing Pact [*mu'áhidiy-i-'umúmíyyih*] the limits and frontiers [*ḥudúd va thughúr*] of each and every nation should be clearly fixed, the principles underlying the relations of governments towards one another definitely laid down, and all international agreements and obligations [*munásibát-i-dawlatíyyih va ravábiṭ va ḍavábiṭ-i-mábayn-i-hiyy'at-i-ḥukúmátíyy-i-basháríyyih*] ascertained. In like manner, the size of the armaments (*quvviy-i-ḥarbí*) of every government should be strictly limited, for if the preparations for war and the military forces of any nation should be allowed to increase, they will arouse the suspicion of others.[26]

These major tasks – arms reduction, delimitation of frontiers, and the establishment of a union of the world's governments (*anjuman-i-duvval-i-'álam*) on a firm basis of international agreements – are regarded as absolutely imperative.

The above provisions contain, therefore, and perhaps more clearly, the foundations of a system of international cooperation based on the preponderance of international law, respect for its freely covenanted provisions, and a powerful (albeit unspecified) system of peace enforcement and trust-building supported by armament reductions. Arsenals will need to be curtailed to such an extent that the remaining weaponry will be confined to 'the purposes of internal security [*tá'mín-i-mamlikat*], the correction of criminal and disorderly elements and the prevention of local disturbances'.[27] As indicated, another significant aspect has to do with the firmness and guarantees of the Pact. As 'Abdu'l-Bahá states:

> The fundamental principle underlying this solemn Pact [*aṣl-i-mabnáy-i-ín 'aḥd*] should be so fixed that if any government later violate any one of its provisions, all the governments on earth should arise to reduce it to utter submission [*iḍmiḥlál*, perhaps better translated as 'overthrow'], nay the human race as a whole should resolve, with every power at its disposal, to destroy [*bi kamál-i-quvvat bar tadmír-i-ín ḥukúmat*] that government.[28]

There is no further elaboration on what the expression 'to destroy that government' might entail in terms of both military and non-military measures, but the text seems to clearly imply regime change as a result of a panoply of sanctions. Under the strict conditions envisaged in such a pact the use of force and enforcement measures could no longer be considered morally abhorrent.

The second relevant, and much less quoted text, in *The Secret of Divine Civilization* bears relation to the reasons that may justify the use of force. At first a superficial reading of it might excuse finding in it a justification even for expansionist wars, provided that their animating purpose is sufficiently altruistic.[29] This more belligerent reading may appear all the more logical since 'Abdu'l-Bahá argues in the same book for a complete reform of the entire State apparatus, including an overhaul of the military along modern lines:

> If, for example, a high-minded sovereign marshals his troops *to block the onset of the insurgent and the aggressor* ['*adúíy-i-bághíy-i-ṭáqí*, lit. a rebellious and tyrannical enemy] or again, if he takes the field and distinguishes himself in a struggle *to unify a divided state and people* [*hiyy'at va mamálik-i-mutishatatíiy-i-parákandih*] if, in brief, he is waging war [*muḥáribiash*] for a righteous purpose, then this seeming wrath is mercy itself, and this apparent tyranny the very substance of justice and this warfare the cornerstone of peace. Today, the task befitting great rulers is to establish universal peace [*ṣulḥ-i-'umúmí*], for in this lies the freedom [*ázádí*] of all peoples.[30] (emphasis added)

The text can be taken at first as an endorsement of cases that in a western context would fall under either the 'just war' or even 'internal policing' categories, but hardly as an endorsement of imperialistic or colonialist designs, which the book clearly condemns by implication.[31] A closer examination shows that, in the first instance (*to block the onset of the insurgent and the aggressor*), what seems to be implied is a recognition of the right of a country to defend itself against insurgency and to repel aggression. In the second instance (*to unify a divided state and people*) the idea seems to fit more clearly situations of civil or internecine war where, as put by 'Abdu'l-Bahá, the use of force may be equally justified as a means for unification or pacification. 'Abdu'l-Bahá does not give examples that could illustrate any of these instances, but it may not be unwarranted to surmise that he may have had in mind cases such as the still fresh American civil war[32] or even the reunification of Italy. It could also be argued that the modern so-called 'right to intervene' or the invocation of a 'duty of care' obligation (in humanitarian crises) with its corollary use of force may find some support here.[33] At any rate, however, even if the scope of interventions contemplated by 'Abdu'l-Bahá were to be enlarged, it would be difficult to disconnect such cases from the internal logic underpinning them in terms of their place within the book and the broader context of 'Abdu'l-Bahá's statements on war and peace. In reality, 'Abdu'l-Bahá is careful to qualify this second statement by observing in the following lines that yet 'the task befitting great rulers is to establish universal peace (*ṣulḥ-i-'umúmí*), for in this lies the freedom of all peoples', which can be taken as a cross-reference to His previous elaboration on the subject in that same work. This qualification makes it clear that, whatever the interim situations of more or less legitimate warfare that might take place, ultimately only a collective system of security such as the one outlined in the preceding pages of *The Secret of Divine Civilization* has the potential to provide a secure basis for peaceful coexistence. This understanding is consistent with 'Abdu'l-Bahá's often expressed view that world peace is a multilateral affair, which, by implication, also means that in the absence of an effective collective arrangement, intermediate stages may obtain. In his introduction to the Bahá'í religion, Esslemont identifies this paragraph as likely applicable to a transition period in international relations (but note the important qualification of military actions as being framed in the context of 'in the cause of international justice, unity and peace' and the 'may be' that follows):

> During the period of transition from the old state of international anarchy to the new state of international solidarity aggressive wars will still be possible, and in these circumstances, military or other coercive action in the cause of international justice, unity and peace may be a positive duty.[34]

Other statements by 'Abdu'l-Bahá would further reinforce the notion that war in general – that is, the use of force for purposes other than those contemplated in a collective security regime – is to be discounted as contrary to morality. This is true even of class struggles:

> Fighting, and the employment of force, *even for the right cause*, will not bring about good results. The oppressed who have right on their side, must not

take that right by force; the evil would continue. Hearts must be changed.[35] (emphasis added)

Thus both the outlawing of war as a legitimate 'last resort' available in the settling of disputes between nations (a remedy which lies at the heart of just war theory), and the linking of a war-free condition to the realization of freedom, demand the implementation of a solidaristic system of defence and security whereby authority and legitimacy are vested not in one particular nation or hegemon, but in the full body of nations.

An interesting point that deserves being mentioned in passing is that in the above texts, as well as in the overwhelming majority of subsequent passages, the expression 'universal peace' used by 'Abdu'l-Bahá is conveyed by the Persian and Arabic phrase *ṣulḥ-i-'umúmí*. The word *'umúmí*, usually also rendered as 'public', 'general', 'universal' or 'common'[36] is clearly unproblematic and is intended to specify the scope of the peace under consideration, not a limited truce or an intermission between wars, but rather a peace aimed at achieving the status of abiding permanence among nations. This is the peace that according to 'Abdu'l-Bahá had been proclaimed by His Father while imprisoned in 'Akká, some fifty years before.[37] While Bahá'u'lláh's *ṣulḥ-i-akbar* contrasts necessarily with *ṣulḥ-i-a'ẓam* (in the pair *a'ẓam/akbar*, most great/greater, *a'ẓam* always carries a sense of excellence and superiority over *akbar*), here the notion stands by itself and does not evoke any counterpart, whether inferior or superior. In this sense *ṣulḥ-i-'umúmí* can be taken as a more secular standard expression referring to a peace resulting from the transactions and understandings arrived at by the powers that be. This, however, does not mean that in 'Abdu'l-Bahá's writings references to the Most Great Peace (*ṣulḥ-i-akbar*) are not to be found. Such instances, although fewer in number, show that the contrast between *ṣulḥ-i-'umúmí* and *ṣulḥ-i-akbar/a'ẓam* cannot be discounted. In addition, it must be borne in mind that very often 'Abdu'l-Bahá uses the word *ṣulḥ* in combination with such words as *ṣaláḥ* or *ráḥatí* (usually translated as 'well-being' or 'comfort'), *á<u>sh</u>tí* (the original Persian word for 'peace' and 'reconciliation'), *árámi<u>sh</u>* (tranquillity, quiet), and *salám* (Arabic for peace), which in some cases appears to have been employed as a synonymous alternate of *ṣulḥ* as in the expression *salam-i-'ám* (general peace).[38]

A further twist is found when English Bahá'í texts based on notes collated from 'Abdu'l-Bahá's speeches are compared with the extant Persian transcripts. Thus, the phrase or concept of 'arbitration' (as in 'international arbitration') is often the result of a meaning expansion introduced by the interpreter or collator which, however warranted in the context of the time, seems to have the paradoxical effect of restricting the wider nature of the divine policy (*síyasat-i-iláhíyih*) with regard to peace. For instance, the sentence 'Bahá'u'lláh declared the Most Great Peace and International arbitration' corresponds to a simpler and, in fact stronger, 'Bahá'u'lláh established the foundations of universal peace' (*Ḥaḍrat-i-Bahá'u'lláh asás-i-ṣulḥ-i-'umúmí nihád*).[39] While the idiom of 'international arbitration' may have been 'implicit' in contemporary notions of 'universal' or 'international peace', arbitration itself is just but one important component of the Great Tribunal proposed by Bahá'u'lláh and 'Abdu'l-Bahá.

The ideas hitherto examined were restated by 'Abdu'l-Bahá in 1911, almost three decades later, pointing out again the features which an International Court would have to meet, and assuring His listeners that this would come to pass as predicted by Bahá'u'lláh.[40] Eight years later, in the Tablet to The Hague (1919), 'Abdu'l-Bahá, gave an outline of how this 'Supreme Tribunal' would need to be formed. The contents of this latter tract provided greater detail, implying even more forcefully a permanent setting endowed with judicial and legislative powers far beyond anything that might have been attempted by the Tsar in the previous Hague peace initiatives, or with the bungled birth of the League of Nations:

> This would be the highest *court of appeal*, and the *parliament of man* so long dreamed of by poets and idealists would be realized. Its accomplishment would be more far-reaching than the Hague tribunal.[41] (emphasis added)

Speaking of the Hague Conferences held in 1899 and 1907, 'Abdu'l-Bahá had expressed quite critical remarks of the intentions and purposes guiding the most powerful nations, including Russia itself. Their gathering – he said – was comparable to a meeting of wine sellers keen on discussing the evils of wine. The analogy was clarified by stating:

> Nations who are constantly thinking either of worldly conquest, the expansion of their own dominion or waging war upon their contemporaries, send ministers and representatives to the congress of The Hague to discuss the problem of universal peace and legislate regulations for the prevention of war![42]

In contrast, and according to 'Abdu'l-Bahá, His Father's plan was:

> And His [Bahá'u'lláh's] plan is this: that the national assemblies [*majális-i-millí*] of each country and nation – that is to say parliaments [*párlamánt*] – should elect two or three persons who are the choicest men of that nation, and are well informed concerning international laws and the relationships between governments and aware of the essential needs of the world of humanity in this day ([*bar ikhtiáját-i-dhurúríyiy-i-'álam-i-insání dar in áyyám váqíf*]. The number of these representatives should be in proportion to the number of inhabitants of that country. The election of these souls who are chosen by the national assembly, that is, the parliament, must be confirmed by the upper house, the congress and the cabinet and also by the president or monarch so these persons may be the elected ones of all the nations and the government. From among these people the members of the Supreme Tribunal [*maḥkamiy-i-kubrá*][43] will be elected, and all mankind will thus have a share therein, for every one of these delegates is

> fully representative of his nation. When the Supreme Tribunal gives a ruling on any international question, either unanimously or by majority rule, there will no longer be any pretext for the plaintiff or ground of objection for the defendant. In case any of the governments or nations, in the execution of the irrefutable decision of the Supreme Tribunal, be negligent or dilatory, the rest of the nations will rise up against it, because all the governments and nations of the world are the supporters of this Supreme Tribunal.[44]

Here the stress is on the procedures to be followed by State members to make their elected delegates fully representative not just of governments, but also of the entire nation via parliamentary and presidential ratification, a cautious addition which may have been spurred by disappointment at the American withdrawal from the League of Nations. Interestingly, 'Abdu'l-Bahá indicates that the number of representatives should be proportional to the number of inhabitants. The emphasis on following this particular and lengthy course seems focused on addressing the main shortcomings affecting the League of Nations and the previous Hague conferences. From the make-up suggested by 'Abdu'l-Bahá it seems that two different institutions are envisaged. One would be formed by the elected representatives of all countries (i.e. the Union of the Nations or the 'interparliamentary body composed of delegates from all the nations of the world'[45]), while the second, itself an emanation of the legislative, would be the Tribunal or Court proper,[46] and would be empowered to decide in all matters duly referred to it for adjudication.

> To remedy this condition there must be universal peace. To bring this about, a Supreme Tribunal must be established, representative of all governments and peoples; questions both national and international must be referred thereto, and all must carry out the decrees of this Tribunal. Should any government or people disobey, let the whole world arise against that government or people.[47]

It is worth noting that the above reference to questions of national import being referred to the Supreme Tribunal for decision may be taken as a clear sign that some areas of internal sovereignty are expressly not excluded from the purview of the international community.

7
The 'Promulgation' of Universal Peace

Shortly after His release from home imprisonment, 'Abdu'l-Bahá travelled extensively throughout Europe and North America on a mission which was often described as one of peace and love. A considerable number of articles published at the time in the media referred to 'Abdu'l-Bahá as a 'prophet' or 'apostle' of peace, including summaries of His talks and interviews on the subject.[48] One of His main reasons for travelling to America was to accept the invitation extended to 'Abdu'l-Bahá by several peace organizations:

> I have come to visit the peace societies of America because the fundamental principles of our Cause are universal peace and the promotion of the basic oneness and truth of all the divine religions. Differences between religions are due to misunderstanding and imitation. If these imitations were to be eliminated, all religions would be united.[49]

Peace could be realized 'through the attraction and support of world public opinion',[50] and doubtless access to the press and to large audiences offered ample opportunity for a more systematic and open presentation of the main Bahá'í tenets. As expected, the high ideals of unity and peace featured prominently in most of 'Abdu'l-Bahá's talks. It seems, however, that for a vast majority of 'Abdu'l-Bahá's listeners those ideals were filtered through the somewhat pervasive individualistic thinking that typified religious and social minds at the time.[51] In practice, this meant that 'Abdu'l-Bahá's message was experienced by many as a source of personal hope, a 'proclamation' whose real scope and consequences could be but dimly fathomed. Peace and its necessary constituents had been 'promulgated'; that in itself was enough. Bahá'ís had only to concern themselves with sharing the 'glad tidings', acting as if already all the promises of God's Kingdom had come or were about, at long last, to come to fruition. Taken in isolation, letters such as the one addressed by 'Abdu'l-Bahá to an individual believer might have contributed to create this impression of imminent or even instant fulfilment:

> Ere long, however, shall the power of heaven, the dominion of the Holy Spirit, hoist on the high summits the banners of love and peace, and there above the

castles of majesty and might shall those banners wave in the rushing winds that blow out the tender mercy of God.[52]

The proclamation of the 'Great Announcement'[53] was accompanied by the announcement of the advent of God's Kingdom. The identification of God's sovereignty with the renewal brought about by the Universal Manifestation of God (i.e. Bahá'u'lláh) had already been made patently clear by 'Abdu'l-Bahá, for instance in His interpretation of Revelation 11:15 in connection with the words uttered by the seventh angel:

> It will be announced that this day is the day of the advent of the Lord of Hosts [*Rabb-i-Junúd*], and this Dispensation the merciful Dispensation of the Divine providence. It has been promised and recorded in all the Sacred Books and Scriptures that in the Day of God His divine and spiritual sovereignty [*ṣalṭanat-i-iláhí*] will be established, the world will be renewed . . . war, dissension, strife, and contention [*jang va jidál va nizá' va fisád*] will vanish; truthfulness, uprightness, peace, and godliness will prevail; love, concord, and union will encompass the world; and God will rule forevermore – that is, a spiritual and everlasting sovereignty will be established.[54]

Confirming Bahá'u'lláh's word regarding the establishment of His faith by virtue of the power of His utterance, 'Abdu'l-Bahá had further stated that the Universal Manifestation of God:

> will subdue the world through a spiritual power [*bi quvvay-i-ruḥáníyyih*], not through war and strife [*bi jang va jidál*]; He will array the world with peace and harmony [*ṣulḥ va salám*], not with swords and spears[*sayf va sunán*]. He will establish this divine sovereignty through genuine love [*bih muḥibat-i-ṣaḥíḥih*], not through military might [*quvvat-i-ḥarbíyih*].[55]

The twentieth century was extolled by 'Abdu'l-Bahá as the 'century of light', the greatness of which could be witnessed at every turn in the physical and spiritual domains.[56] This 'optimistic' message was nevertheless offset by 'Abdu'l-Bahá's warnings of impending catastrophes. The 'century of light' remained ignorant of the true source of its radiance,[57] unaware of the many dangers looming on the horizon, possessed of a false sense of self-confidence which ultimately would bring more tragedy upon itself:

> Notwithstanding this, the world of humanity doth not take warning, nor doth it awake from the slumber of heedlessness. Man is still causing differences, quarrels and strife in order to marshal the cohorts of war and, with his legions, rush into the field of bloodshed and slaughter.[58]

Both aspects, the celebration of the 'new day' and the warnings regarding fresh calamities, combined to give a complex picture, neither complacent with the order of the day nor completely removed from its hopes.

A similar blend of prophetic fulfilment and ominous warnings surrounded 'Abdu'l-Bahá's references to the Jews. During His American journey 'Abdu'l-Bahá, Who had previously clearly anticipated the formation of the Jewish State in fulfilment of biblical prophecies,[59] still had stern words for the Jews who were reluctant to accept Jesus's manifestation, thus forfeiting the opportunity of averting a forthcoming and even greater wave of persecution at the hand of Christians in Europe.[60] And the same 'Abdu'l-Bahá Who was to celebrate many technical advancements as signs of mankind's newly-found prowess (to be sure, all made possible through the bestowals from on high),[61] was none the less highly critical of the direction technical civilization was heading for.[62]

This difficult balance may help us to understand the extent to which 'Abdu'l-Bahá's presentation of the Bahá'í tenets was permeated by a compelling, if not overwhelming, sense of religious duty. Peace was not thought to be easily achievable,[63] nor idealized to the point where nothing else seemed relevant, nor for that matter conceived of as intrinsically incompatible with the use of legitimate force, provided that force was representative of mankind and made subservient to justice.[64] To be sure, the long road to peace was marked with immense obstacles; but peace was within reach if all nations committed their utmost to the implementation of a sound system of collective security backed up by other supportive measures:

> A few, unaware of the power latent in human endeavour, consider this matter as highly impracticable, nay even beyond the scope of man's utmost efforts. Such is not the case, however. On the contrary, thanks to the unfailing grace of God, the loving-kindness of his favoured ones, the unrivalled endeavours of wise and capable souls, and the thoughts and ideas of the peerless leaders of this age, nothing whatsoever can be regarded as unattainable.[65]

The need for peace was in proportion to the increasing risk of mass destruction, hence 'Abdu'l-Bahá's urgency:

> The time is ripe. It is time for the abolition of warfare, the unification of nations and governments. It is time for love. It is time for cementing together the East and the West.[66]

The process whereby peace was to be brought about could be delayed only at mankind's own peril. Already, by the time 'Abdu'l-Bahá was visiting America it was too late for an imminent war of incalculable proportions to be averted. Europe was in 'Abdu'l-Bahá's words a 'powder keg' awaiting just a tiny spark for it to kindle the flame of war, dragging along the rest of the world into its deadly vortex.[67]

In fact, the great conflagration that was World War I had been repeatedly and most emphatically predicted by 'Abdu'l-Bahá on account of the state of affairs prevailing in Europe at the time (particularly in the Balkans).[68] There was nothing of a prophecy in such a dire prediction; if anything, it was a foregone conclusion.[69] So much so that, upon returning to the Holy Land from His western tours, 'Abdu'l-Bahá made the required provisions to cultivate and irrigate swathes of land that proved vital in palliating the famine that ensued in the wake of the conflagration when scarcities hit hard on Haifa and 'Akká's populations.[70] War preparations in the agitated first days of August 1914 in the Haifa area were described by 'Abdu'l-Bahá in the most sombre terms, further witnessing to the wrongfulness of an 'Illusion' which after replacing 'reality' was to turn Europe into a bloodbath, the outcome of which, as borne out by previous wars, would have no real victors.[71] As already seen, identical self-assurance would inspire 'Abdu'l-Bahá to portend the inevitability of a second world conflagration while the ink of the Versailles Treaty was still fresh.

Material causes of the impending war were all too clear to 'Abdu'l-Bahá's mind. The exponential growth registered in the hoarding and development of lethal weapons was in itself conducive to war, the whole of Europe had become 'an armed camp': 'These warlike preparations will necessarily culminate in a great war. The very armaments themselves are productive of war. This great arsenal must go ablaze.'[72] The arms race had been described by 'Abdu'l-Bahá at various occasions in dramatic language, leaving no doubt as to the sentiment they evoked in Him. The following words (circa 1875) are already paradigmatic:

> Each day they [the European nations] invent a new bomb or explosive and then the governments must abandon their obsolete arms and begin producing the new, since the old weapons cannot hold their own against the new. For example at this writing, in the year 1292 A.H. [1875 AD] they have invented a new rifle in Germany and a bronze cannon in Austria, which have greater firepower than the Martini-Henry rifle and the Krupp cannon, are more rapid in their effects and more efficient in annihilating humankind. The staggering cost of it all must be borne by the hapless masses.[73]

The 'science of killing' had been perfected to a point where it bore no resemblance to whatever had transpired in the past in the way of warfare:

> So perfected has the science of killing become and so efficient the means and instruments of its accomplishment that a whole nation can be obliterated in a short time. Therefore, comparison with the methods and results of ancient warfare is out of the question.[74]

The very logic of creation of new weapons meant that all avenues would be exhausted in order to conceive new killing devices. Speaking while en route to

New York aboard the *Cedric* 'Abdu'l-Bahá had explained that the air would not be spared and that future developments in warfare would turn the existing implements into mere playthings:

> Those who have provided the means for transporting arms and ammunition and the instruments of wars and massacres will do so in the air. There will come to exist such instruments as to cause all the means of destruction in the past to be looked as children's playthings.[75]

The folly of war was exposed in detail. Reporting a conversation with the German consul, 'Abdu'l-Bahá expounded how his Excellency and those in the gathering concurred that increases and improvements in military power (*quvviy-i-ḥarbíyih*) were tantamount to progress (*taraqíyyát*). But 'Abdu'l-Bahá retorted that, by resorting to its instrumentality, people would become quiet and overly silenced, while a permanent state of war (*ḥarb-i-dá'imí*) would unfold covertly.[76] Standards to measure suffering were unfortunately biased along nationalistic lines. The death toll sustained in a train accident could cause a public outcry, yet the deaths of thousands in Tripoli were met almost with indifference, lamented 'Abdu'l-Bahá.[77] Generals and warriors, whose sole merit was to have killed thousands of men, were hailed as heroes, while the single murderer was condemned to capital punishment:

> Man needlessly kills a thousand fellow creatures, becomes a hero and is glorified through centuries of posterity. A great city is destroyed in one day by a commanding general. How ignorant, how inconsistent is humankind! If a man slays another man, we brand him as a murderer and criminal and sentence him to capital punishment, but if he kills one hundred thousand men, he is a military genius, a great celebrity, a Napoleon idolized by his nation. If a man steals one dollar, he is called a thief and put into prison; if he rapes and pillages an innocent country by military invasion, he is crowned a hero. How ignorant is humankind![78]

Wars were entered into for the most specious excuses or motives. 'Abdu'l-Bahá enumerates a number of them: 'At one time the pretext for war has been religion, at another time patriotism,[79] racial prejudice,[80] national politics, territorial conquest or commercial expansion' or the combinations thereof.[81] But, in the end, it is 'self-interest', rather than the customarily alleged pretexts, which motivates this kind of behaviour. 'Do not listen to anything that is prejudiced, for self interest prompts men to be prejudiced,'[82] is the advice of 'Abdu'l-Bahá, and its effects are all the more destructive, for prejudices blind and desensitize humankind to the follies of war and its carnage:

> Self interest is at the bottom of every war. The moral effect of the expenditures of these colossal sums of money for military purposes is just as deteriorating

> as the actual war and its train of dreadful carnage and horrors. The ideal and artistic forces of the contending parties become barbaric and bestial, the spiritual powers are stunted and the laws of divine civilization are disregarded. Such a financial drain ossifies the veins and muscles of the body politic, and congeals the delicate sensibilities of the spirit.[83]

It is this process of desensitization that explains the paradox of the excitement in the preparations for war, even the zealous enthusiasm (*ghayrat*) witnessed in the masses of young volunteers joining the contending armies, mixed with the fear.[84]

The pursuit of self-interest (*khud-parastí*, lit. self-adoration) is contrasted with the adoration of God or service to the common weal (*manfi'at-i-'umúmí*).[85] It does not take much reading between the lines for even today's readers to bring to mind examples of inequality from the following description:

> Thus you can observe, on the one hand, a single person who has amassed a fortune, made an entire country his personal dominion [*áqlímírá mustimarrih*], acquired immense wealth, and secured an unceasing flow of gains and profits, and, on the other, a hundred thousand helpless souls – weak, powerless, and wanting even a mouthful of bread. Here is neither equality here nor benevolence. Observe how, as a result, general peace and happiness have become so wanting, and the welfare of humanity so undermined, that the lives of a vast multitude have been rendered fruitless! For all the wealth, power, commerce, and industry are concentrated in the hands of a few individuals, while all others toil under the burden of endless hardships and difficulties, are bereft of advantages and benefits, and remain deprived of comforts and peace.[86]

Disarmament was an imperative need, not only because of the obvious dangers posed by armament, but also because of the heavy burden that the arms race was placing on the citizens through exorbitant taxation:

> One of these ills is the people's restlessness and discontent under the yoke of the war expenditures of the world's governments. What the people earn through hard labour is extorted from them by the governments and spent for purposes of war. And every day they increase these expenditures. Thus the burden on men becomes more and more severe. This is one of the great ills of the day.[87]

In the last analysis, concluded 'Abdu'l-Bahá, peace would be brought about not so much as a result of a sudden change of heart in mankind, but as an outcome of the impracticability of keeping pace with the ever-increasing costs of war:

> The nations will be forced to come to peace and to agree to the abolition of war. The awful burdens of taxation for war purposes will get beyond human endurance.[88]

This did not mean that global disarmament was to be undertaken unilaterally. To think of that possibility was not realistic. Universal peace would have to be reached through multilateral and simultaneous disarmament rather than appeasement, neutrality or a unilateral renunciation of war:

> No nation can follow a peace policy while its neighbour remains warlike. There is no justice in that. Nobody would dream of suggesting that the peace of the world could be brought about by any such line of action. It is to be brought about by a general and comprehensive agreement, and in no other way.[89]

A remarkable example of how the principle of collective security could have worked in retrospect can be seen in the detailed counterfactual response given by 'Abdu'l-Bahá to a group of westerners visiting Him in Palestine before World War I. These visitors – Youness Afroukhteh reports – were eager to learn whether the Russo-Japanese war (1905) would eventually lead to a world conflagration in their own lifetime and which side would prevail. 'Abdu'l-Bahá gave assurances that such a confrontation would materialize, but declined to answer the second question. The attention was then shifted to whether the Russo-Japanese war could have been averted, a query probably meant to cast some doubt on the workability of a peaceful resolution. At that point 'Abdu'l-Bahá launched on a detailed explanation in the affirmative. Indeed it would have been quite befitting for the main mover of the Peace Hague Conferences to lead by example. Russia – explained 'Abdu'l-Bahá – could have attempted a temporary retreat. This would have allowed her to muster the support of a number of powers in order to issue an ultimatum for a ceasefire. The account was illustrated with a map showing Russia's frontiers and a full description of its naval capabilities. 'Then He elaborated on the design and execution of a comprehensive peace plan.'[90]

Whatever the means through which it was to come about, peace was more than a necessity and a moral imperative: it was a certainty. Bahá'u'lláh had made that specific promise:

> Universal peace is assured by Bahá'u'lláh as a fundamental accomplishment of the religion of God – that peace shall prevail among nations, governments and peoples, among religions, races and all conditions of mankind. This is one of the special characteristics of the Word of God revealed in this Manifestation.[91]

And on yet another occasion 'Abdu'l-Bahá had this to say regarding the hoisting of the 'standard of the Most Great Peace':

> This has come to pass. The powers of earth cannot withstand the privileges and bestowals which God had ordained for this great and glorious century. It is a need and exigency of the time. Man can withstand anything except that which is divinely intended and indicated for the age and its requirements.[92]

8
The Role of America

On His own admission 'Abdu'l-Bahá had come to America to meet with the 'standard bearers of international conciliation and agreement'.[93] He was not alone in expressing this hope as, soon after his departure, the famous poet Rabindranath Tagore reached American soil anxious to spread his message of *visva-bharati* (all India).[94] Bahá'í individuals were at the time involved in the peace movement. According to Hollinger, some of the wealthy New England Bahá'ís had established contacts with other New England peace activists very early in the century.[95] Not surprisingly, 'Abdu'l-Bahá met with the most prominent figures in the American peace movement at two major peace gatherings, the first time at a special reception held in His honour by the New York Peace Society,[96] whose work had found in the steel magnate Andrew Carnegie a keen benefactor, and the other at the Lake Mohonk Conference,[97] whose founder and president, Albert Smiley, a Quaker, had in 1911 invited 'Abdu'l-Bahá to address the gathering.[98]

These two societies, arguably the peak peace bodies at the time, had been able to capitalize on a sea change that occurred around 1905 in American perceptions on peace and the more confident role of the United States in the wider concert of nations. As a result, peace had gained stronger acceptance not only among the general public, but also among major political figures, businessmen and professionals. This new respectability was supported by ampler material means (some of them supplied by well-known magnates), and the broader approaches brought to bear by the new professional cadres of lawyers, industrialists, businessmen and journalists who soon were to overshadow the old philanthropical elites made up by prominent religious figures and proponents of abolitionism. 'Abdu'l-Bahá was clearly aware of the difference between the old utopian approaches to peace and the fresh perspectives brought into the movement by the new peace advocates. In 1915 'Abdu'l-Bahá wrote to Andrew Carnegie: 'A number of souls who were doctrinaires and unpractical thinkers worked for the realization of this most exalted aim and good cause, but they were doomed to failure.'[99] But peace was not necessarily the dominant concern in the minds of its new proponents and was often associated with the achievement of a state of non-war by means of arbitration, commerce, new open diplomacy (instead of Europe's failed model), federalism, and an internationalism based on the extension to all countries of democracy and the rule of law. Efforts in this arena were considerable at the time, as illustrated by the work of the American Society of International Law (established in 1906). It was at the invitation of this institution, for instance, that the Italian Senator Professor Pasquale Fiore had also boarded the *Cedric* at the same time that 'Abdu'l-Bahá did.[100] Also worth noting were other important encounters held between 'Abdu'l-Bahá and other renowned figures and peace activists such as philanthropist Jane Addams, later to become a Nobel laureate,[101] David Starr Jordan, president of Stanford University,[102] or the industrialist Maxim Hudson, the inventor of the smokeless gunpowder and author of *Defenseless America*.

In particular, the spirited discussion between 'Abdu'l-Bahá and Hudson merits a cursory review as both interlocutors were characteristically true to their respective visions and missions. This outstanding exchange was doubtless representative of the hundreds of engagements that occupied 'Abdu'l-Bahá's daily schedule during His journey throughout North America. Hudson, the inventor, comes across as the outspoken American genius who combines some of the raw ideas of the *zeitgeist* with an almost naïve faith in the possibilities of modern technology and commerce to reduce casualties or replace war altogether. 'Abdu'l-Bahá, cordial but uncompromising in His friendly approach, concludes by inviting His interlocutor to turn his talents to the pursuit of peace. The tenor of the conversation, preserved for posterity by Howard MacNutt, an early American believer, reproduces the excitement that 'Abdu'l-Bahá's arrival caused amongst curious Americans. Present in the room was also W. H. Short, the Vice-secretary of the American Peace Society who previously had this to say in his conversation with 'Abdu'l-Bahá: 'Our press is not the reflector of foreign news. Our people travel in distant countries; but few important and influential foreigners come to visit us.'[103]

Hudson commenced by asking whether there should be an international policing or else whether nations would be required to disarm and eliminate their navies. 'Abdu'l-Bahá responded by indicating that 'everything that prevents war is good'. Hudson, perhaps unprepared for such broad answer, changed tack, now hinting at war as a universal phenomenon; after all had not Jesus come to make war and was not war that which made Caesar great? 'Abdu'l-Bahá retorted by suggesting that given that after six thousand years the destructive effects of war were now plain for all to see, perhaps it was time to experiment with peace for a while. Hudson added then a new twist to his argument by suggesting that commerce had replaced warfare: 'Business is war, cruel, merciless.' To which 'Abdu'l-Bahá agreed, adding that 'war is not limited to one cause. There are many kinds of war and conflict going on, political war, commercial war, patriotic and racial war; this is the very civilization of war.' Another question was put to 'Abdu'l-Bahá as to whether 'the next great national war' was necessary. 'Abdu'l-Bahá suggested that all efforts had to be made to prevent it from happening. Hudson seemed to concur, but his approach to the question (exemplified in a possible clash with Japan) was that commerce would make it unprofitable: 'We don't want to kill good customers . . . We make more money by being peaceful, so long as the other fellow keeps quiet and sticks to business.' His own contribution to peace, he added without a cringe in reference to his own efforts, would consist in making 'war so expensive that the nations could not afford to fight and therefore would agree to maintain peace'. 'Abdu'l-Bahá's more detailed comment to this was an elaboration on the woes of war, which were all magnified by technical prowess. In contrast with the past, it was presently possible to have as many as one hundred thousand victims in one single day and still the course of the war would remain undecided. 'The first consequences are grievous enough, but the after-results are even more deplorable,' added 'Abdu'l-Bahá. And he further illustrated this with a description of the dire consequences to which the humble *fellahin* of Egypt would be exposed in the event of a hypothetical war. Perhaps dissatisfied with this argument, Hudson made the point that 'fewer are killed in modern engagements than in the battles of ancient times; the range is longer and the action less deadly.' 'Abdu'l-Bahá counter-instanced, pointing out the recent war between Russia and Japan. At this point Hudson laid emphasis on the alleged fact that more people were dying of preventable accidents in a year than as a result of war, to which 'Abdu'l-Bahá then signified that, if that was the case, 'war is the most preventable accident'. Undaunted by this, Hudson went back to his previous premise detailing the lesser number of casualties caused by the machine gun compared to the short sword. 'Abdu'l-Bahá retorted, signalling the deadly effects of shelling compared to the wars between the Persians and the Romans. Hudson insisted on the smaller lethal capabilities of modern ordnance, which he even took the trouble of sketching in a diagram. 'Abdu'l-Bahá brought the argument to a conclusion by pointing out that human energies had to be diverted to other more creative purposes:

> The greatest intelligence of man is being expended in the direction of killing his fellowman. The discovery of high explosives, perfecting of death dealing weapons of war, the science of military attack, all this is a wonderful manifestation of human intelligence; but it is in the wrong direction. You are a celebrated inventor and scientific expert whose energies and faculties are employed in the production of means for human destruction. Your name has become famous in the science of war. Now you have the opportunity of becoming doubly famous. You must practice the science of peace. You must expend your energies and intelligence in a contrary direction. You must discover the means of peace; invent guns of love which shall shake the foundations of humanity. The guns you are now building cause the death of man; you must build guns which will be the cause of life to humanity.[104]

In effect, the arrival of 'Abdu'l-Bahá on the North American continent and His own personal call raised the issue of peace into prominence among the small Bahá'í community, and acted as a catalyst for their increasingly concerted efforts deployed in this field. Throughout His American tour 'Abdu'l-Bahá alluded on numerous occasions to America's role in facilitating the attainment of universal peace. In most cases this was expressed as a hope rather than as an assurance; in others it definitely had the ringing sound of a foregone conclusion. America had been found to be 'vast and progressive, the government just and equitable, the nation noble and independent'.[105] On account of its many capabilities – its freedom, its democracy and its civilization – America was certainly in a unique and enviable position to raise the banner of universal peace:

> because I find the American nation so capable of achievement and this government the fairest of western governments, its institutions superior to others, my wish and hope is that the banner of international reconciliation may first be raised on that continent and the Standard of the Most Great Peace be unfurled here.[106]

But there was a more pragmatic reason for America being singled out for that position of prominence. 'Abdu'l-Bahá thought that if the American government was to pursue peace policies, its motives for doing so would not be found as objectionable. If other countries such as Russia, Britain, or France were to take the initiative, there could be grounds to suspect ulterior motives. In contrast, America had, 'strictly speaking, no colonies to protect' and, therefore, it would prove difficult for other nations to allege self-interest on the part of the Americans and in this way oppose joining in the peace process.[107] The hope of 'Abdu'l-Bahá, as conveyed to *The San Francisco Chronicle* on 4 October 1912, was that the United States would take the lead in the promotion of international peace inasmuch as other nations were not as well positioned to take up the challenge:

> Other peoples of the world have to contend with international difficulties. First, the nations are rivals with each other so far as commercial advantages are concerned. Second, they are thinking of the nation self-aggrandizement. Third, they are thinking of planting new colonies. Therefore, it is difficult for them to step into this field, to uphold international peace, because they are contending, warlike, victory-loving people. They cannot be instrumental in promulgating international peace.[108]

The Bengali poet Rabindranath Tagore had in 1913 something very similar to say; after His first sejourn in the United States he concluded:

> I have an impression that America has a great mission in the history of Western civilization, for it is rich enough not to concern itself in the greedy exploitation of weaker nations. Its hands are free and perhaps it will hold up the torch of freedom before the world.[109]

This way of reasoning was remarkably attuned to the ideals expressed by the American progressivists that later on President Wilson would take on board to justify America's participation in the Great War, the same war ironically that in his re-election campaign of 1916 he had committed himself to keeping at bay under the slogan 'he kept us out of war'.[110] Speaking at Stanford University 'Abdu'l-Bahá expressed His wish for California to become the focal point of that process whereby peace would irradiate to other American states, and from there to the rest of the world.[111] However, if 'Abdu'l-Bahá's hopes were to stand a chance, strenuous exertions had to be made. Upon returning from His western tours 'Abdu'l-Bahá expressed His ardent hope that the well-wishers of mankind and peace proponents could create an extraordinary movement as well as arranging major conferences to be attended by influential personalities. Fifty years ago – he added – peace advocacy would have met with derision, but now everyone was in agreement that the issue of universal peace was the spirit of the age.[112] Yet, volition and action were required to translate peace from the realms of words to that of reality. In addition, peace advocacy would have to follow a greater agenda. President Taft's peaceful agreements with other nations, valuable as they were, had to be extended to all other countries as envisaged by Bahá'u'lláh:

> But when we have the *interparliamentary body* composed of delegates from all the nations of the world and devoted to the maintenance of agreement and goodwill, the utopian dream of sages and poets, the *parliament of man*, will be realized.[113] (emphasis added)

President Woodrow Wilson's attempt to secure peace was particularly praiseworthy. According to 'Abdu'l-Bahá most of the famous fourteen principles constituting the so-called 'Wilson doctrine' could also be found in the Bahá'í teachings; for which reason it was hoped that his work would be confirmed.[114]

9
Women and Peace

Another point which 'Abdu'l-Bahá underscored during His visit to the West was women's contribution to the cause of universal peace. 'Abdu'l-Bahá's admiration for the position attained by women in western countries was indeed heartfelt. In His own words, this was 'the age of woman'.[115] 'Abdu'l-Bahá, Who had met some conspicuous western women of the time, amongst them the suffragettes Emmeline Pankhurst and Charlotte Despard, had a message for them of encouragement seasoned with a call to exercise moderation.[116] Ṭáhirih, the famous Bábí heroine and poetess, was often presented by 'Abdu'l-Bahá as the standard bearer of women's rights for self-emancipation in the Islamic world: 'Qurratu'l-'Ayn was really the liberator of all Persian women.'[117] Her action at removing her veil both before[118] and at the historic Bábí Conference of Badasht had symbolically marked the complete secession of Babism from Islam, and more specifically from Islamic law, and in the process the equality between both sexes.[119] According to 'Abdu'l-Bahá women should occupy the exalted position to which they were entitled in the Bahá'í Dispensation:

> In this Revelation of Bahá'u'lláh, the women go neck and neck with the men. In no movement will they be left behind. Their rights with men are equal in degree. They will enter all the administrative branches of politics. They will attain in all such a degree as will be considered the very highest station of the world of humanity and will take part in all affairs. Rest ye assured. Do not look upon the present conditions.[120]

That this was certain to happen rested on Bahá'u'lláh's authority: 'For His Holiness Bahá'u'lláh Hath willed it so!'[121] Furthermore, the example set by Ṭáhirih and other remarkable Bahá'í women in the East and the West was meant to serve as a source of encouragement to other women who were to follow in their footsteps.[122] In reality, all that was needed was for women to be brought up in the same manner as men, following an identical curriculum,[123] and endeavouring to prove themselves equal to men.[124] Such an effort on their part was all the more necessary because sooner or later women would have to come to the fore to do their fair share: 'Fit yourselves for responsibility, you will inevitably have it thrust upon you.'[125]

In 'Abdu'l-Bahá's view, and as matter of course, women were spiritually equal to men: 'The one whose heart is purest, whose deeds are most perfect, is acceptable to God, male or female.'[126] Women had been handicapped for no other reason than their being considered inferior to men. History, however, had shown what remarkable achievements some women had been able to accomplish when the right opportunities presented themselves,[127] thereby proving that, contrary to common assumptions, they were not inherently inferior to men. Nor was it true that women were in any sense naturally inferior to men on account of certain physical characteristics such as a smaller brain or the like.[128] When given the opportunity for acquiring education – concluded 'Abdu'l-Bahá – 'they have shown equal capacity with men'.[129] Far from what was believed since time immemorial, women were as capable as men, and the reason for the non-actualization of their potential was indeed a function of male dominance rather than a sign of inferiority:

> The world in the past has been ruled by force, and man has dominated over woman by reason of his more forceful and aggressive qualities both of body and mind. But the balance is already shifting; force is losing its dominance, and mental alertness, intuition, and the spiritual qualities of love and service, in which woman is strong, are gaining ascendancy. Hence the new age will be an age less masculine and more permeated with the feminine ideals, or, to speak more exactly, will be an age in which the masculine and feminine elements of civilization will be more evenly balanced.[130]

'Abdu'l-Bahá went even further. Women were men's equals except for some features in which they clearly excelled over their counterparts: 'In some respects woman is superior to man. She is more tender-hearted, more receptive, her intuition more intense.'[131] Hence, it was in the interest of humanity as a whole for women to be raised to their true position in society. 'Abdu'l-Bahá would often use analogies when referring to this matter. Men and women were individuals, 'just as the waves of the sea are innumerable and different, but the reality of the sea is one'.[132] More frequently, mankind was likened to a bird whose two wings needed to be equally developed for it to soar into the heaven of attainment:

> Until womankind reaches the same degree as man, until she enjoys the same arena of activity, extraordinary attainment for humanity will not be realized; humanity cannot wing its way to heights of real attainment. When the two wings or parts become equivalent in strength, enjoying the same prerogatives, the flight of man will be exceedingly lofty and extraordinary.[133]

It is in this light that 'Abdu'l-Bahá spoke in glowing terms of the role of women in spreading peace:

> War and its ravages have blighted the world; the education of woman will be a mighty step toward its abolition and ending, for she will use her whole influence against war. Woman rears the child and educates the youth to maturity. She will refuse to give her sons for sacrifice upon the field of battle. In truth, she will be the greatest factor in establishing universal peace and international arbitration. Assuredly woman will abolish warfare among mankind.[134]

How women would become instrumental in establishing peace was never set out in detail. From 'Abdu'l-Bahá's statements it is clear that women were thought of as being biologically and emotionally 'naturally' disinclined to sacrifice their own offspring for the sake of violently settling disputes.[135] This may explain the correlation that 'Abdu'l-Bahá established between the question of universal suffrage and the establishment of peace, as women would not allow the fruits of their labours to be immolated in the battlefields, 'no matter what cause'.[136] 'Abdu'l-Bahá expected that the granting of universal suffrage would lend women a strong leverage that they could use toward the abolition of war, as confirmed by the following reasoning:

> [M]others will not sanction war nor be satisfied with it. So it will come to pass that when women participate fully and equally in the affairs of the world, when they enter confidently and capably the great arena of laws and politics, war will cease; for woman will be the obstacle and hindrance to it. This is true and without doubt.[137]

10
The Tablet to The Hague

While the outline given in Chapter 6 summarizes the 'political' approach to peace through the principle of collective security, 'Abdu'l-Bahá's Tablet (or Epistle) to The Hague substantiates other important elements that constitute the global Bahá'í approach to peace building. It can be regarded as a comprehensive and clear 'position statement' on the subject, and as such would provide an unambiguous precedent of the statements that Shoghi Effendi and the Bahá'í International Community were to issue on the subject at a later date. Being the only scriptural Bahá'í text exclusively concerned with the issue of peace, its significance is enhanced by the fact that it helped successive generations of Bahá'ís to frame their understanding of the 'Bahá'í principles' in the context of their contribution to peace, a point that will inform my discussion in Chapter 11.

Dated 17 December 1919, the Tablet was written in reply to a letter addressed to 'Abdu'l-Bahá by the Executive Committee of the Central Organization for a Durable Peace.[138] The original was hand-delivered by Aḥmad Yazdání and Ibn-i-Aṣdaq. The assessment it distils is no longer the hopeful one expressed by 'Abdu'l-Bahá in January that same year to the effect that the end of the war would 'at least lead to the preliminaries of universal peace, just as it is plainly foretold in the blessed Tablets'.[139] The contents of 'Abdu'l-Bahá's message must be placed against the immediate political background of the negotiations which led to the Versailles Peace Treaty, negotiations which Keynes described most poignantly at that time in his *The Economic Consequences of the Peace.*[140] The following is an outline of the Tablet:

Greetings

I Introduction

1. Contrast between war and peace
2. Peace, mankind's goal
3. Unity of conscience, the fundamental requirement

II Main body

A Teachings of Bahá'u'lláh:

1. Universal peace
2. Independent investigation of truth
3. Oneness of the world of humanity
4. Religion must be the cause of love and unity
5. Religion must agree with science
6. Abolition of prejudices (religious, patriotic and political ones)
7. Adoption of one international language
8. Equality of men and women
9. Voluntary sharing
10. Freedom from the world of nature
11. Law and religion, the safeguards of mankind
12. Material civilization must be accompanied by divine civilization
13. Promotion of education
14. Justice must prevail

B Other considerations:

15. Any approach to peace must be conceived within a framework of principles such as those outlined above
16. The scope of the peace envisaged must be such as to embrace the noblest aspirations of different religions and political parties (liberals, socialists), in keeping with present world conditions
17. The League of Nations will not accomplish its own ends. Nothing short of a Supreme Tribunal such as the one proposed by Bahá'u'lláh can succeed in bringing about international peace
18. The example set by the Persian Bahá'i Community sets a model worthy of consideration
19. Readers, however, are warned of the existence of individuals who present Bahá'u'lláh's teachings as their own.

III Conclusion

'Abdu'l-Bahá opens His address with a salutation to the members of the Executive Committee of the Central Organization for a Durable Peace. He refers to them as the 'pioneers among the well-wishers of the world of humanity', praising their work as a service 'to the world of humanity'. After this a description of war and peace follows:

> This recent war [World War I] has proved to the world and the people that war is destruction while universal peace is construction; war is death while peace is life; war is rapacity and bloodthirstiness while peace is beneficence and humaneness; war is an appurtenance of the world of nature while peace is of the foundation of the religion of God; war is the destroyer of the edifice of mankind while peace is the everlasting life of the world of humanity; war is like a devouring wolf while peace is like the angels of heaven; war is the struggle for existence while peace is mutual aid and co-operation among the peoples of the world and the cause of the good-pleasure of the True One in the heavenly realm.[141]

Characteristic of 'Abdu'l-Bahá, this text is based on the alternation of contrasting pairs arranged according to parallelism. The reiteration of contrasts underlines two fundamental ideas. Firstly, war and peace are incompatible because they belong to worlds apart, namely the world of nature and the spiritual realm. It is interesting to note at this point that 'Abdu'l-Bahá reasons by analogy that war is a prolongation of the natural state. Secondly (and this is an obvious though necessary conclusion), peace needs to be positively characterized in terms of mutual aid and cooperation, and war in terms of the struggle for existence (*manázi'iy-i-baqá*). Use of this latter concept shows 'Abdu'l-Bahá's awareness of the social consequences that the Darwinian concept entailed,[142] especially bearing in mind that theorists indulging in this concept tended to overlook the power of education, a point made in one of His American speeches:

> In the world of nature we behold the living organisms in a ceaseless struggle for existence. Everywhere we are confronted by evidences of the physical survival of the fittest. This is the very source of error and misapprehension in the opinions and theories of men who fail to realize that the world of nature is inherently defective in cause and outcome and that the defects therein must be removed by education.[143]

Warfare could then be seen as an outdated extension of the struggle which human beings necessarily had to fight against wild animals, rather than as a necessary expression of the same principle, only transposed into the human realm.[144] The idea had already developed in one of His previous talks given in London:

> In the days of old an instinct for warfare was developed in the struggle with wild animals; this is no longer necessary; nay, rather, co-operation and mutual understanding are seen to produce the greatest welfare of mankind. Enmity is now the result of prejudice only.[145]

An even more powerful expression of this idea had been conveyed in North America by explicitly inviting His audience to unlearn war and to divert humanity's creative energies to the pursuit of the 'blessed arts of peace', extending them the benefit of at least an opportunity to be tried:

> What human powers and forces have been employed in the prosecution of war and applied to inhuman purposes of battle and bloodshed? In this most radiant century it has become necessary to divert these energies and utilize them in other directions, to seek the new path of fellowship and unity, *to unlearn the science of war and devote supreme human forces to the blessed arts of peace.* After long trial and experience we are convinced of the harmful and satanic outcomes of dissension; now we must seek after means by which the benefits of agreement and concord may be enjoyed. When such means are found, we must give them a trial.[146] (emphasis added)

'Abdu'l-Bahá moves on in the Tablet to The Hague to explain that 'there is no more important matter in the world than that of universal peace'.[147] This was one of the lessons to be drawn from the sufferings of the previous world conflagration. While 'Abdu'l-Bahá had been an outspoken exponent of the cause of peace in European countries during the pre-war period, it was in the United States and Canada that His speeches took on a more dramatic and yet more hopeful tone. Thus, in a talk given in California in October 1912, he had insisted on the importance of peace:

> The issue of paramount importance in the world today is international peace. The European continent is like an arsenal, a storehouse of explosives ready for ignition, one spark will set the whole of Europe aflame, particularly at this time when the Balkan question is before the world. Even now war is raging furiously in some places, the blood of innocent people is being shed, children are made captive, women are left without support, and homes are being destroyed. Therefore, the greatest need in the world today is international peace. The time is ripe. It is time for the abolition of warfare, the unification of nations and governments. It is the time for love. It is time for cementing the East and the West.[148]

Whatever the significance of peace as a single, discrete and urgent issue in mankind's agenda – warned 'Abdu'l-Bahá – peace will remain unattainable unless unity of conscience (*vaḥdat-i-vujdán*) is established. This important concept, which is introduced in the epistle as a corrective to a narrow view of peace, also gives substantial content to the idea of the affirmative role that religion may play by infusing meaning into that consciousness:

> But the wise souls who are aware of the essential relationships emanating from the realities of things [*bar ravábiṭ-i-ḍurúríyyih kih monba'i͟th az ḥaqáyiq-i-as͟hiást*] consider that one single matter [*masa'iliy-i-váḥidih*] cannot, by itself, influence the human reality as it ought and should, for until the minds of men become united, no important matter can be accomplished. At present universal

> peace [*ṣulḥ-i-'umúmí*] is a matter of great importance, but unity of conscience [*vaḥdat-i-vujdán*] is essential, so that the foundation of this matter may become secure, its establishment firm and its edifice strong.[149]

'Unity of conscience' would refer to that vantage position from which the facets of a whole, along with its corresponding web of relationships, can be placed into perspective. Peace efforts should be many-sided rather than restricted to the old view of peace as an outcome of diplomatic or military negotiations between sovereign nations, which in fact amounted to little more than an 'armed peace'.[150] A global policy transcending the limitations imposed by nationalism and other prejudices of various kinds had to be brought to bear on the matter of peace for this to eventuate on a firmer basis. Moreover, such peace should embrace not just political aims but also consider the aspirations of all religions and communities, for:

> If the question of peace is restricted to universal peace alone [*agar masa'ilih munḥaṣir dar ṣulḥ-i-'umúmí bás͟had*], the remarkable results which are expected and desired will not be attained. The scope of universal peace must be such that all the communities and religions may find their highest wish realized in it.[151]

The above statement could also be taken as setting a clearer distinction between the yet limited peace usually referred to as 'lasting' or 'universal', and the far more substantive peace resulting from a resolution of mankind's more besetting problems as well as its social, cultural and spiritual needs. The above qualification is by no means the only powerful instance where 'Abdu'l-Bahá makes it abundantly clear that for peace to become firmly entrenched a variety of perspectives needs to inform the efforts of the peace advocates:

> The world of humanity . . . will not be transformed into the heavenly paradise through the promotion of one, single principle. Every progressive principle which is the cause of the advancement of the world of humanity is like a simple element. A simple element does not produce a composite life. But when the elements are associated together then a being is brought into existence.[152]

As seen in Part IV, all reality can be regarded as a web of integrated and mutually interdependent parts. While acting on one section of it would influence the rest, a major change would normally require intervention on a number of interrelated parts. Once this general principle of inclusiveness is established, 'Abdu'l-Bahá provides a summary of Bahá'u'lláh's teachings. In doing so He brings into relief two important aspects. One, that Bahá'u'lláh dealt with the matter of universal peace in several letters addressed to the kings of the world at a time when he was a prisoner of one of His addressees. Second, that Bahá'u'lláh established peace 'among His friends [Bahá'ís] in the Orient'.[153] In other words, 'Abdu'l-Bahá was not putting forward just His own ideas, but acting as a spokes-person for the followers of Bahá'u'lláh who had embraced these ideals in many practical ways.

Most of the teachings mentioned in the Tablet to The Hague reproduce what 'Abdu'l-Bahá had already presented in the course of His journeys throughout the West. It is important to note here that these were to figure prominently among the most significant ones usually mentioned by Bahá'ís. Even so, it would be misleading to draw any firm conclusion from the number and the order in which they are introduced.

The first among the teachings listed is 'universal peace' (*ṣulḥ-i-'umúmí*). In this connection 'Abdu'l-Bahá refers to the Bahá'í gatherings in which peoples of different origins and beliefs used to see themselves as part of 'one nation, one teaching, one pathway, one order, for the teachings of Bahá'u'lláh were not limited to the establishment of universal peace', adding that they 'embraced many teachings which *supplemented and supported* that of universal peace'[154] (emphasis added).

Next, mention is made of the principle of free and independent investigation of truth (*taḥarríy-i-ḥaqíqat*), which occupies a central position. In numerous instances, it is placed among the first three principles in any enumeration. Explanations on this fundamental tenet revolve around a thematic cluster made up of the following ideas: truth/reality is one; allegiance to mere 'imitations' or dogmas without personal realization is in itself divisive; truth/reality alone can be conducive to genuine unity. At heart – declares 'Abdu'l-Bahá – all religions agree on these premises inasmuch as they share in the same source of truth. Yet, according to 'Abdu'l-Bahá, this is the first time in which an injunction to investigate truth has been made an integral and explicit part of any religion.[155]

'Abdu'l-Bahá further adds that religious, political, economic and patriotic prejudices (*ta'aṣṣub*) must be abandoned. Mankind, being one, cannot be rescued from nature except through the relinquishment of prejudices and the acquisition of the morals of the Kingdom (*akhláq-i-malakútí*). Prejudices together with 'blind imitations' (*taqálíd*) and 'vain imaginings' (*awḥám, zunún*) are perhaps the most serious obstacles standing in the path towards peace, for they 'strike at the very root of human life; one and all they beget bloodshed, and the ruination of the world', so much so that their existence is coterminous with 'continuous and fearsome wars'.[156]

Next in the Tablet to The Hague, 'Abdu'l-Bahá gives a description of some of the prejudices which stand contrary to reason. He invites the reader to consider all peoples and nations as branches, fruits and blossoms from the tree of Adam.[157] Patriotic prejudices are originated in 'absolute ignorance'. No frontier or boundaries have been set up by God. Those divisions are man-made and have no permanent status in God's eyes. If 'this conception of patriotism' is allowed to follow its own course, confined to its own limited circle –'Abdu'l-Bahá warns –'it will be the primary cause of the world's destruction'.[158] What is befitting is to regard the whole earth as one's fatherland, rather than placing an exclusive attachment on one's country of birth. Besides, considered from another perspective, it would be quite improper to value so highly what ultimately is to become 'our eternal tomb'.[159]

Political prejudice is the last prejudice mentioned by 'Abdu'l-Bahá and appears contrasted negatively with God's policy, the latter being described as 'greater than human policy' and applicable to all individuals alike.[160]

'Abdu'l-Bahá moves on to explain that a universal language must be adopted and widely spread so as to remove misunderstandings between the peoples. Similarly, men and women need to be regarded as equal, or, to use an analogy, as the two wings of a flying bird, for: 'Not until the world of women becomes equal to the world of men in the acquisition of virtues and perfections, can success and prosperity be attained as they ought to be.'[161]

'Abdu'l-Bahá presents voluntary sharing (*muvását*) as another teaching of Bahá'u'lláh in direct contraposition to economic equality enforced by coercion (*jabr*, legally or otherwise). The example set by the Persian Bahá'ís in sharing their properties is extolled as being far more meritorious.

Freedom (*ḥurríyat*) is next described by 'Abdu'l-Bahá as freedom from the 'captivity of the world of nature', i.e., from those animalistic features which turn the struggle for existence into a principle governing social life. According to 'Abdu'l-Bahá, the very notion of 'struggle for existence' (*manázi'iy-i-baqá*) is 'the fountain-head of all calamities and is the supreme affliction'.[162] The importance of this distinction rests on the clear polarity between the concept of freedom and its counterpart, the notion of 'struggle for existence'. Freedom takes here the form of liberation from material concerns and wants (a concept close to the traditional way of regarding material pursuits as attachment or enslavement), yet infused with a critical sense pointing to a positive characterization through cooperation and justice.

Accordingly, 'Abdu'l-Bahá describes social life as governed by two kinds of law. One is the law that punishes the criminal, and the other is the law that 'prevents both the manifest and the concealed crime'. Both are defined as safeguards against wrongdoing, but only God's religion is presented as the 'ideal safeguard' without which no permanent order can be achieved.[163] 'Abdu'l-Bahá clarifies that by 'religion' is meant that which is 'ascertained by investigation and not that which is based on mere imitation'.[164] Closely connected with this is 'Abdu'l-Bahá's ensuing characterization of material and divine civilization. The contrast between the two is fundamental, in that material civilization, indispensable though it might be, cannot be counted as complete unless accompanied and perfected by divine civilization.[165]

'Abdu'l-Bahá concludes His listing of Bahá'u'lláh's teachings by referring to the need for providing instruction in the sciences to every child. So important is this principle that, should the parents be presented with the dilemma of not being able to give their offspring an education, preference should be given to girls in the family.

After His brief presentation of some other relevant Bahá'í principles 'Abdu'l-Bahá then explains that if these are not added to any discussion on peace, its feasibility will become doubtful.

> These manifold principles, which constitute the greatest basis for the felicity of mankind and are of the bounties of the Merciful, must be added to the matter of universal peace and combined with it, so that results may accrue. Otherwise the realization of universal peace by itself in the world of mankind is difficult . . . If the question is restricted to universal peace alone, the remarkable results which are expected and desired will not be attained.[166]

'Abdu'l-Bahá presents then the teachings of Bahá'u'lláh as being endowed with the capacity to satisfy mankind's aspirations, all the more so since His teachings, at variance with the teachings of other political and religious formations, are in conformity with the requirements of the time, free from imitations and from the burdens of the past. Neither the 'party of freedom' (*millali kih arizúy-i-ḥúrríyyat nimáyand,* i.e. the liberal parties), nor the 'party of equality' (*hizb-i-musávát,* i.e. the socialist parties), nor any other parties for that matter, are in a position to embody mankind's highest aims. Answering the claims by the liberals, 'Abdu'l-Bahá further remarks that the kind of freedom which is acceptable is the 'moderate freedom' (*húrríyyat-i-mu'tadilih*) that 'guarantees the well-being of mankind and maintains and preserves the universal relations'. And answering the claims by the socialists, 'Abdu'l-Bahá confines Himself to commenting that 'their solutions are not practicable'.[167]

Stress on the notion of all-inclusiveness and practicability allows 'Abdu'l-Bahá to return to the main topic, concluding that the League of Nations cannot bring about universal peace as it was intended. However, a Supreme Tribunal (*maḥkamiy-i-kubrá*) similar to the one envisaged by Bahá'u'lláh, that is, one with executive powers[168] and based on a proportional and officially sanctioned system of representativeness, would indeed lay the foundations for universal peace:

> . . . although the League of Nations has been brought into existence, yet it is incapable of establishing universal peace. But the Supreme Tribunal which Bahá'u'lláh has described will fulfil this sacred task with the utmost might and power.[169]

The League of Nations and World War II

In 1920 a Bahá'í believer wrote to 'Abdu'l-Bahá once again concerning a meeting of the same Executive Committee of the Central Organization for a Durable Peace, to which the letter to The Hague had been addressed the previous year. In His reply 'Abdu'l-Bahá commented that the Committee in question 'is not what it is reputed to be' and 'is unable to arrange affairs in the manner which is befitting and necessary'. 'Abdu'l-Bahá requested the recipient of His letter to convey to the Committee's members that, prior to the war, The Hague had already been the venue for another mighty conference presided over by no less a person than the Tsar, yet no result whatsoever stemmed from that gathering. 'Abdu'l-Bahá then asked the following question:

> Now how will it be? For in the future another war, fiercer than the last, will assuredly break out; verily of this there is no doubt. What can The Hague meeting do?[170]

Despite these ominous remarks, 'Abdu'l-Bahá still counsels His addressee to 'express the greatest love and kindness, and leave them to their own affairs'.[171]

The significance of this letter is threefold. First, it leaves no doubt as to the separate and distinct nature of the Bahá'í approach to peace. The efforts of The Hague Committee are praised, but, short of helping to meet the necessary requirements, as explained by 'Abdu'l-Bahá, it is concluded that they would fail to leave any enduring impression. Not only will the efforts of a clique of well-wishers be doomed to failure, but also those of the same nations which signed the Versailles Treaty in the vain hope of putting an end to all wars. Secondly, the letter reveals once again the holistic and internationalist nature of the Bahá'í perspective on the matter of peace.

It should be noted that 'Abdu'l-Bahá reaffirms His position by declaring with remarkable conviction that yet another greater conflagration will break out. Shoghi Effendi has left us a poignant description of how this failure was regretted by 'Abdu'l-Bahá at the time, closer to His last years:

> How serenely, yet powerfully, He stressed the cruel deception which a Pact, hailed by peoples and nations as the embodiment of triumphant justice and the unfailing instrument of an abiding peace, held in store for an unrepentant humanity. 'Peace, Peace,' how often we heard Him remark, 'the lips of potentates and peoples unceasingly proclaim, whereas the fire of unquenched hatreds still smoulders in their hearts.' How often we heard Him raise His voice, whilst the tumult of triumphant enthusiasm was still at its height and long before the faintest misgivings could have been felt or expressed, confidently declaring that the Document, extolled as the Charter of a liberated humanity, contained within it seeds of such bitter deception as would further enslave the world.[172]

This was not the only letter on record portending such events. Elsewhere Shoghi Effendi quotes the contents of a letter written by 'Abdu'l-Bahá shortly after World War I portraying the future scenarios of confrontation:

> The ills from which the world now suffers . . . will multiply; the gloom which envelops it will deepen. The Balkans will remain discontented. Its restlessness will increase. The vanquished powers will continue to agitate. They will resort to every measure that may rekindle the flame of war. Movements, newly born and world-wide in their range, will exert their utmost effort for the advancement of their designs. The Movement of the Left will acquire great importance. Its influence will spread.[173]

11
Principled Action and the 'Twelve Principles'

The Tablet to The Hague was instrumental in providing Bahá'ís not only with a handy summary of the essentials of their doctrine, but also with a framework that would enable them to relate Bahá'í principles (*ta'alímát*, perhaps better translated as teachings or tenets) to the pressing needs of the time and in so doing form an explicit conception of their own place in society as contributors of a model experience. Moreover, the Tablet moved away from a narrow treatment of the question of peace by inviting its addressees (Nobel nominees) to consider the interconnectedness of peace by referring to the need for a unity of conscience. Peace, and by default war, had to be seen in the light of a series of outcomes failing which no security or safety would be achieved.

Most of the principles listed by 'Abdu'l-Bahá in the Tablet were familiar to His western audience. The word 'principles', in the sense of a set of doctrinal formulations regarded as central to their Faith, was used in a number of early introductions to the Bahá'í Faith.[174] At some point in time, and probably due to mnemonic and symbolic reasons, the number of principles was reduced to twelve. Prior to 1911 short lists of Bahá'í 'verities' had already been compiled by western Bahá'ís in an effort to sum up the essentials of their Faith.[175] Yet it was not until 'Abdu'l-Bahá's travels throughout the West that western Bahá'ís became familiar with a number of summary expositions that ever since then have been taken as standard presentations of Bahá'í doctrine. Thus, in an address delivered in November 1912 'Abdu'l-Bahá listed thirteen such teachings, including, significantly, the concept of 'universal peace'. A pamphlet by Mason Remey published about 1917 entitled 'Some Vital Bahá'í Principles' listed exactly twelve principles. The Tablet to The Hague also included a similar number of principles, including, like the previous ones, universal peace. Although 'Abdu'l-Bahá was careful to point out that the teachings of Bahá'u'lláh were 'boundless and without end in their far-reaching benefit to mankind',[176] the list was sufficiently comprehensive and seemed to have been adopted soon as a convenient tool for 'proclamation' purposes and as a model *summa* of Bahá'í beliefs. The roundness and religious connotations of the figure, including the fact that its items squared with previous records of Bahá'í teachings, made the list especially popular with Bahá'ís. A majority of western Bahá'ís were attracted to the new religion through these modern ten-commandment-like

Table 1: Lists of Bahá'í principles

'Abdu'l-Bahá[177] (November 1912)	Mason Remey[178] (1917)	'Abdu'l-Bahá[179] (1918)	Shoghi Effendi[180] (1944)
1. The oneness of the world of humanity 2. The protection and guidance of the Holy Spirit 3. The foundation of all religion is one 4. Religion must be the cause of unity 5. Religion must be in accord with science and reason 6. Independent investigation of truth 7. Equality between men and women 8. The abandoning of all prejudices among mankind 9. Universal peace 10. Universal education 11. A universal language 12. Solution of the economic problem 13. An international tribunal	1. The Oneness of the world of humanity 2. Independent investigation of truth 3. The Foundation of All religion is one 4. Religion must be the Cause of Unity among mankind 5. Religion must be in accord with science and reason 6. The equality of men and women 7. The abolition of all prejudices of whatever nature 8. Universal peace 9. All mankind should partake of knowledge and education 10. The solution of the economic question 11. Universal language 12. A universal tribunal	1. Universal peace 2. Independent investigation of truth 3. Oneness of the world of humanity 4. Religion must be the cause of love and unity 5. Religion must agree with science 6. Abolition of prejudices (religious, patriotic and political ones) 7. Adoption of one international language 8. Equality of men and women 9. Voluntary sharing 10. Freedom from the world of nature 11. Law and religion, the safeguards of mankind 12. Material civilization must be accompanied by divine civilization 13. Promotion of education 14. Justice must prevail	1. The independent search after truth, unfettered by superstition or tradition; 2. the oneness of the entire human race, the pivotal principle and fundamental doctrine of the Faith; 3. the basic unity of all religions; 4. the condemnation of all forms of prejudice, whether religious, racial, class or national; 5. the harmony which must exist between religion and science; 6. the equality of men and women, the two wings on which the bird of human kind is able to soar; 7. the introduction of compulsory education; 8. the adoption of a universal auxiliary language; 9. the abolition of the extremes of wealth and poverty; 10. the institution of a world tribunal for the adjudication of disputes between nations; 11. the exaltation of work, performed in the spirit of service, to the rank of worship; 12. the glorification of justice as the ruling principle in human society, 13. and of religion as a bulwark for the protection of all peoples and nations; 14. and the establishment of a permanent and universal peace as the supreme goal of all mankind

principles. Overall, they furnished the basis for most public talks and discussions at informal gatherings ('firesides') offered by local Bahá'ís and travelling teachers, and further expanded into full chapters or sections of general introductions to the Bahá'í Faith.[181] The 'twelve principles' provided a useful starting point from which it was easier to move on to explain the history of the Bahá'í Faith – a religious history by all counts – as well as the basics of the Bahá'í Administrative Order with its own set of specific principles.[182] A number of Bahá'í introductory works arranged their contents doubtless influenced by the tripartition suggested here (history, teachings, administration).[183]

While the actual number of principles and the specifics about them were hardly an issue among Bahá'ís, the symbolism of the figure and a general conviction that in a fundamental way they enshrined the core of Bahá'í doctrine were not without some consequences. By identifying a workable number of tenets Bahá'ís were able not only to memorize the gist of the Bahá'í message, but also to have a handy creed equivalent of their own to which they could refer back in their presentations and discussions of their Faith. At the same time, however, by encapsulating Bahá'í doctrine within the confines of a limited list, other principles and doctrinal aspects could see their importance diminished or sidelined in the eyes of the Bahá'ís.[184] Moreover, since the enumeration was taken for granted, no particular effort was made to see how the principles would interrelate nor in what sense they could be further elaborated into a more developed programme of Bahá'í action.[185]

The use of such a succinct listing posed in addition a challenge of a semantic nature. In limiting the list of main teachings down to a set of twelve, and in calling them 'principles', the impression was perhaps erroneously conveyed that the Bahá'í message was to a great extent a social creed based on a limited supply of what to many appeared as utopian ideals. To be sure, while some of the teachings could be articulated as 'principles', in the sense of 'a comprehensive and fundamental law, doctrine, or assumption',[186] others did not clearly fit such a definition and, in the prevailing climate of conflicting ideologies, could lay themselves open to various criticisms.[187]

True, the twelve principles seemed to have distilled the essence of the Bahá'í contribution to the solving of society's most intractable problems, but it was far from clear how the new message would effect change in the world as a result. Although this was not what Bahá'ís could learn from the sophisticated writings of Shoghi Effendi and other works,[188] some inertia in the established communities, largely dependent on the self-evidence of these sets of principles, invested them with a disproportionate currency as the fundamental expression of the Bahá'í message.[189]

Interestingly, the order and even the wording in which Bahá'í principles were given were subjected by successive Bahá'í generations to rearrangements, doubtless in an effort to adapt their meaning to changing realities. Lack of an officially established set of principles or a common rendering of them facilitated the introduction of new more idiomatic renditions, sometimes incurring an anachronistic back-reading of their originals. As a handy set of Bahá'í fundamentals, and despite the difficulties involved in an over-reliance on their self-explanatory character, the twelve principles were representative of the spiritual, moral and social philosophy contained in the Bahá'í writings.

But as important as the principles themselves, if not more, was the considerable stress laid by 'Abdu'l-Bahá from the outset on the need to 'recombine' them with peace (defined in narrow terms as absence of war) in order to arrive at a durable basis for international reconciliation, one that was meant to be far more 'encompassing' than the peace intermissions achieved through the unstable balance of the power system.

This holistic approach provided for an expanded concept of security, linking as it did issues of general humanitarian import (such as universal education, equality between men and women, harmony between science and religion, and the eradication of prejudices), with the instituting of world reforms such as the creation of a 'supreme world tribunal' or the 'institution of a universal auxiliary language'. Furthermore, the emphasis on the eradication of prejudices and on the need to overcome man-made barriers of all kinds, including 'unbridled nationalism', racism, class struggles, and all forms of particularism pointed clearly in the direction of a spiritual movement with a broad cosmopolitan outlook premised on the assertion of the oneness of humanity and religion. This latter aspect added a sharper progressive edge to the Bahá'í movement which Shoghi Effendi was keen to see maintained and reinforced:

> It should also be borne in mind that the machinery of the Cause has been so fashioned, that whatever is deemed necessary to incorporate into it in order to keep it in the forefront of all progressive movements, can, according to the provisions made by Bahá'u'lláh, be safely embodied therein.[190]

This cosmopolitan outlook was further supported by a strong appeal to investigate truth independently, a principle often cited first in the Bahá'í writings because of its value as a hermeneutical key to the other Bahá'í tenets. In true enlightened fashion, no liberation from the fetters of the past was deemed possible without it:

> The first [principle/teaching] is the independent investigation of truth; for blind imitation of the past will stunt the mind. But once every soul inquireth into truth, society will be freed from the darkness of continually repeating the past.[191]

Although the grouping of the Bahá'í principles given below (see Fig. 3) is tentative, this reordering shows how some missions and issues usually listed as part of the twelve principles may be understood to evolve from and relate to a core of foundational principles. The applied ethics implicit in the Bahá'í global agenda for peace may be said to stem from a combination of columns two and three, which stand supported by the spiritual or metaphysical convictions described in the first column.[192] The concept of 'unity of conscience' mentioned in the Tablet to The Hague is placed at the top, even taking precedence over 'search after truth', to denote more clearly its overarching epistemological value in that it posits a dynamic interconnection between the various orders of life (metaphysical, gnoseological, practical), as well as a basic reliable correspondence between knowledge and the undivided truth/reality (often expressed as 'reality is one').[193]

As a corollary of this process, peace moves from various avenues to ever higher degrees of integration and universalization. Thus, the principle of universal education is emphasized (in bold in Fig. 3) to indicate more clearly that the perfectibility of man depends in large measure upon the extent to which the whole set of principles inform Bahá'í educational practices. As a matter of principle, a Bahá'í-inspired pedagogical practice, for instance, would require not only the extension of education to all segments of mankind, even a preference to reach women, but also the conscious implementation of a pedagogy of both minors and adults that effectively counters prejudices, promotes the use of the scientific method and advances the interests of humanity by blending the ideals of the East and the West, and creates the pattern of a 'divine philosophy' whereby the attainment of peace is given a strong focus. The whole system presupposes interdependence of personal, collective, national and international phenomena:

> Study the sciences, acquire more and more knowledge. Assuredly one may learn to the end of one's life! Use your knowledge always for the benefit of others; so may war cease on the face of this beautiful earth, and a glorious edifice of peace and concord be raised. Strive that your high ideals may be realized in the Kingdom of God on earth, as they will be in Heaven.[194]

Bahá'í principles and the varieties of unity

The above considerations concerning Bahá'í principles can be further expanded by relating their contents to two texts of comparable significance in Bahá'í thought, namely the 'Seven Candles of Unity', where as many forms of unity are summarily identified by 'Abdu'l-Bahá, and the Tablet of Unity (Lawḥ-i-Ittiḥád), in which Bahá'u'lláh briefly describes a number of unities or unions, some of which have since then deeply influenced Bahá'í thinking and practice (see Table 2). 'Abdu'l-Bahá's text merits being quoted in full (emphasis added):

> Behold how its light is now dawning upon the world's darkened horizon. The first candle is *unity in the political realm*, the early glimmerings of which can now be discerned. The second candle is *unity of thought in world undertakings*, the consummation of which will erelong be witnessed. The third candle is *unity in freedom* which will surely come to pass. The fourth candle is *unity in religion* which is the corner-stone of the foundation itself, and which, by the power of God, will be revealed in all its splendour. The fifth candle is the *unity of nations*

Figure 3: A representation of some basic Bahá'í principles

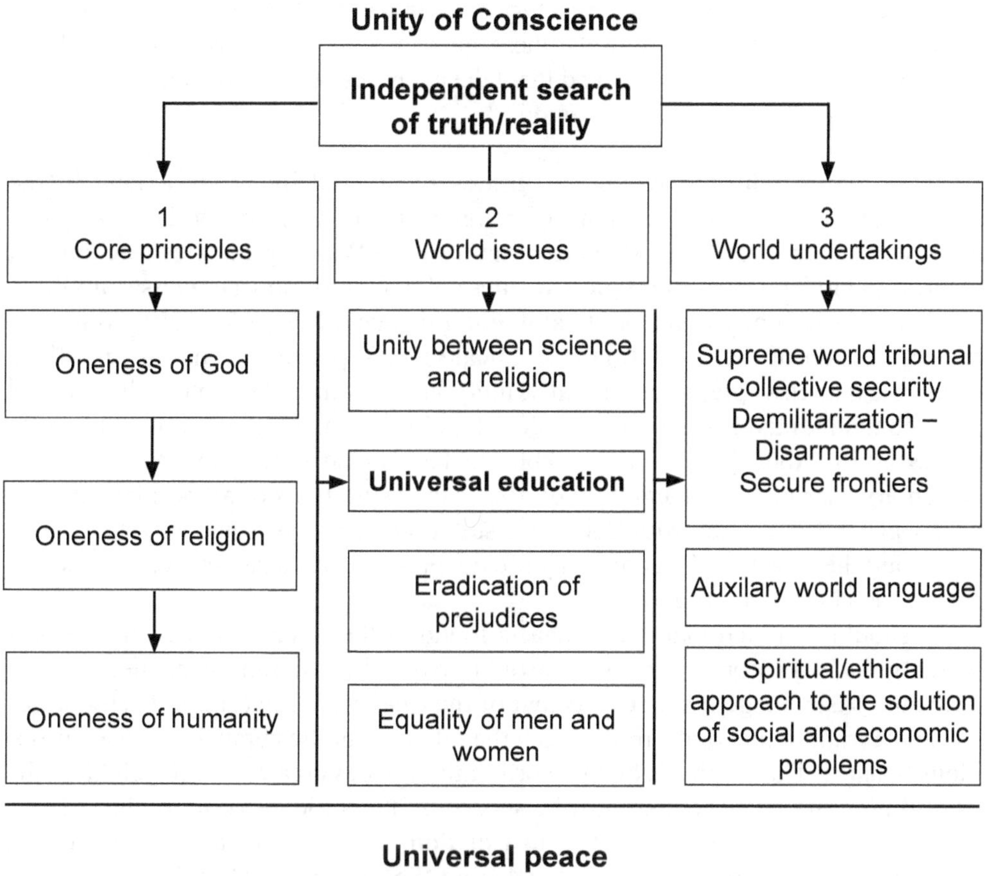

> – a unity which in this century will be securely established, causing all the peoples of the world to regard themselves as citizens of one common fatherland. The sixth candle is *unity of races*, making of all that dwell on earth peoples and kindreds of one race. The seventh candle is *unity of language*, i.e., the choice of a universal tongue in which all peoples will be instructed and converse. Each and every one of these will inevitably come to pass, inasmuch as the power of the Kingdom of God will aid and assist in their realization.[195]

'Unity of thought in world undertakings' seems to correlate directly with 'unity of conscience' – which, as already seen, is mentioned at the beginning of the Tablet to The Hague – as well as with 'Abdu'l-Bahá's proposal advanced in *The Secret of Divine Civilization* advocating the articulation of an informed public opinion,[196] an idea again expressed in His travels throughout North America:

> Today questions of the utmost importance are facing humanity, questions peculiar to this radiant century. In former centuries there was not even mention of them. Inasmuch as this is the century of illumination, the century of humanity, the century of divine bestowals, these questions are being presented for the expression of public opinion, and in all the countries of the world, discussion is taking place looking to their solution.[197]

At least four among the remaining unities mentioned by 'Abdu'l-Bahá in the Seven Candles of Unity (i.e. unity of religion, nations and races, language) can be taken as correlates or good approximates of the Bahá'í principles/teachings of oneness of God, oneness of religion, oneness of humanity, and a universal auxiliary language. As for unity in the political world, this may be regarded partly as a positive expression of the intimation to eradicate racial, patriotic, religious, political, economic and class prejudices. Finally, unity in freedom, although usually omitted from contemporary listings of the 'ideal type' of the twelve principles' is partly expressed by 'Abdu'l-Bahá in His Tablet to The Hague as 'freedom from nature', 'voluntary sharing' and integration of ideals and aspirations of all political parties. It may also be connected with Bahá'í consultation. While the standard Bahá'í principles and the Seven Candles of Unity are not entirely interchangeable, they clearly share much common ground.

It should be noted that the emphasis found in the Seven Candles on the very word 'unity' takes on a significance of its own. As a luminescent metaphor of unity, the basic image it suggests is that of the trunk of a tree (unity of religion) or a candelabrum (a menorah) from which the other six unities branch off in a harmonious balance. The emphasis on the word 'unity' places greater moral weight on the overall unifying purpose that must be served by the varieties of unity thus identified. None of them are to be taken in isolation; all are necessary, and none, not even 'unity of religion', can be isolated from the rest, although unlike the others, it has a truncal nature. This same interconnectedness is illustrated by the principle of the 'oneness of humanity', which, briefly stated, implies that the human race *is* one and *must*, accordingly, form a unit *despite* obvious differences of colour, ethnic origin, culture, class, sex, or religion. 'Abdu'l-Bahá specifically applies the image of the tree in order to describe the concept:

> A fundamental teaching of Bahá'u'lláh is the oneness of the world of humanity. Addressing mankind, He says, 'Ye are all leaves of one tree and the fruits of one branch.' By this it is meant that the world of humanity is like a tree, the nations or peoples are the different limbs or branches of that tree, and the individual human creatures are as the fruits and blossoms thereof. In this way Bahá'u'lláh expressed the oneness of humankind . . .[198]

The idea is reinforced by explaining that, at variance with other historical religions, the Faith of Bahá'u'lláh does not draw a dividing line on the basis of faith (believers vs. non-believers), stressing that this is a specific Bahá'í teaching and that all must see themselves as 'submerged . . . in the sea of divine generosity'. This idea connects logically with Bahá'u'lláh's 'unity of the souls':

> . . . whereas in all religious teachings of the past the human world has been represented as divided into two parts: one known as the people of the Book of God, or the pure tree, and the other the people of infidelity and error, or the evil tree. The former were considered as belonging to the faithful, and the others to the hosts of the irreligious and infidel – one part of humanity the recipients of divine mercy, and the other the object of the wrath of their Creator. Bahá'u'lláh removed this by proclaiming the oneness of the world of humanity, and this principle is specialized in His teachings, for He has submerged all mankind in the sea of divine generosity. Some are asleep; they need to be awakened. Some are ailing; they need to be healed. Some are immature as children; they need to be trained. But all are recipients of the bounty and bestowals of God.[199]

Table 2: Varieties of unity

'Abdu'l-Bahá (*Seven Candles of Unity*)	**Bahá'u'lláh** (*Lawḥ-i-Ittiḥád*)[200]	**Other forms of unity**
1. Unity in the political realm *vaḥdat-i-síyásat*	Unity in religion *ittiḥád dar dín*	Unity of conscience *vaḥdat-i-vujdán*
2. Unity of thought in world undertakings *vaḥdat-i-árá dar 'umúr 'aẓímih*	Unity of speech *ittiḥád dar qawl*	Unity in diversity
3. Unity in freedom *vaḥdat-i-ázadí*	Unity of action *ittiḥád-i-a'mál*	Organic unity
4. Unity in religion *vaḥdat-i-dín*	Unity of rank and station *ittiḥád-i-maqám*	Unity of existence *waḥdat al-wujud*[201]
5. Unity of nations *vaḥdat-i-vaṭan*	Unity of wealth *ittiḥád-i-amvál*	Unity of action[202]
6. Unity of races *vaḥdat-i-jins*	Unity of souls *ittiḥád-i-nufus*	
7. Unity of language *vaḥdat-i-lisán*	Oneness of God *tawḥíd*	

The assertion of the oneness of mankind embraces not so much an 'ideal' as a factual reality – however counterfactual it may appear – from which a moral imperative is derived. Oneness, in this context, far from implying sameness – that is, the elimination of sub-identities – points to a harmonizing of these in the light of their underlying unity. Put differently, the unity principle holds whenever the sum of the differences does not detract but rather adds to the strength of the universal principle.[203] Seen in this light, a typical Bahá'í ideal such as the 'eradication of prejudices' reads as an ethical and logical derivation of the principle of the oneness of humanity, and, as such, calls for a fundamental change in one's opinions, perceptions and behaviours with regard to deeply entrenched ideas or misconceptions that at any rate are no longer in keeping with reality. By 'eradication' of prejudices is not meant suppression of a given identity but its regularization in the face of a higher order of reality. Thus when Shoghi Effendi qualified 'Nationalism, Racialism and Communism' as 'triple gods'[204] he was not just singling out Nazi or communistic regimes for criticism, but in fact was extending his critique to the entire fabric of the western systems, most of which was built on an uncritical acceptance of the supremacy of one particular nation, race, or class over their counterparts. The same line of reasoning explains why Shoghi Effendi would consider the principle of national sovereignty as a 'fetish'.[205]

The varieties of unity identified by 'Abdu'l-Bahá in the 'Seven Candles' contrast with those given by Bahá'u'lláh in His *Lawḥ-i-Ittiḥád* ('Akká period) where except for 'unity in religion' all other unities bear no direct relation with 'Abdu'l-Bahá's text. A possible reason for this marked difference can be attributed to the fact that the themes elaborated upon in this Tablet address more specifically issues of unity within the Bahá'í community, partly because the letter was addressed to a wealthy Bahá'í who had been put to the test by the Azalís while he was living in Qazvin. Like 'Abdu'l-Bahá in His Tablet to The Hague, Bahá'u'lláh declares that the subject cannot be exhausted in a few sentences, and that other forms of unity may also have to be considered, thus reinforcing the open-endedness of the whole. Unity in religion is introduced in the first place as most conducive to the triumph of any faith. This assertion implies that religious divisions along sectarian lines bring defeat in their wake: 'togetherness is the mystic sword of God' (*ijtimá' sayf-i-ma'anavíy-i-ilahí ast*). Next Bahá'u'lláh mentions unity of speech, which illustrates both the need for a coherent discourse among believers, and a consideration for self-restraint in light of the primacy of deeds over words. Unity of deeds is illustrated as the overcoming of the major divisions brought about by wrangling over insignificant ritual matters. Likewise, particularly in reference to arrangements within the Bahá'í community, Bahá'u'lláh describes unity of ranks and station, and unity of wealth and souls, as being paramount in bringing about a transformation unlike anything experienced in the past. With regard to the former Bahá'u'lláh confirms that there is no denying that human beings can be more or less exalted (different or unequal); yet He lays the emphasis on the principle that to consider oneself 'more learned, more favoured, more accomplished, more righteous or more exalted is a mighty error and sin'. As for the principle of unity of wealth and of souls, Bahá'u'lláh makes a distinction between equality (*musávát*), which is defined in terms of just and generous treatment of one's fellow human beings, and *muvását* (rendered variously as beneficence, philanthropy or altruism), which elevates the stakes by implying complete sacrifice of one's substance in that preference is accorded to others over oneself to the point that no avarice is left in one's soul.[206]

In closing. Bahá'u'lláh urges His followers to 'meditate upon God and in particular upon the Unity of God' (*tawḥíd-i-ilahí*), yet cautioning them not to act 'like unto the peoples before you who spoke the words but remained bereft of their meaning, being worshippers of names and devotees of idols'. This intimation, framed in the context of loyalty to God versus idolatry, summarizes in a sense the spirit of the Tablet: a separation between spiritual meaning and form is analogous to the separation that originates sectarian divisions, contradictory discourses, or differences over ritual practices, as well as hierarchical, social and human cleavages. This sense is further reinforced elsewhere by Bahá'u'lláh as follows:

> Beware, O believers in the Unity of God (*tawḥíd*), lest ye be tempted to make any distinction between any of the Manifestations of His Cause, or to discriminate against the signs that have accompanied and proclaimed their Revelation. This indeed is the true meaning of Divine Unity, if ye be of them that apprehend and believe this truth.[207]

The unities set forth in the Tablet of Unity can be considered to have had a lasting effect on the ethical and institutional development of the Bahá'í community, especially noticeable in the priority accorded to deeds versus words, the minimization of rituals, the absence of priestly and professional missionaries, and the collegiate nature of the administrative institutions, all of which have remained powerful motifs up to the present. Less evident, but equally influential, 'unity of wealth' was stressed by 'Abdu'l-Bahá as part of the Bahá'í moderate solution to economic problems and was linked, first, to the conscious steps taken in the implementation of the Law of *ḥuqúqu'lláh* through 'voluntary sharing' (*muvását*, 'the freely-chosen expending of one's substance'),[208] and second to the social and economic projects that since the early beginnings appeared associated with the institution of the Mas͟hriqu'l-Ad͟hkár.

12
Overcoming Violence and the Use of Force

According to 'Abdu'l-Bahá, moral choices are not thrust upon human beings by external influences in a deterministic or fatalistic way. The individual is not completely at the mercy of social influences, nor entirely dependent on inherited traits or other characteristics acquired at birth. Within the confines dictated by birth, fortune, upbringing and the like, all persons are fundamentally free to discriminate good from evil and responsible for the consequences of their moral choices.[209] Their ethical horizon is illumined by both reason (*'aql*), which establishes the wrongness of such acts as 'murder, theft, treachery, falsehood, hypocrisy and iniquity',[210] and revealed law (*Sharí'a*), which adds a supplementary dimension by establishing a higher degree of morality, as illustrated by Christ's command to return good for evil.[211] While good deeds are praiseworthy, for them to be acceptable and complete from a religious standpoint, they need to be informed by the knowledge and love of God:

> In the world today we meet with souls who sincerely desire the good of all people, who do all that lies in their power to assist the poor and succour the oppressed [*mu'ávinat-i-maẓlúm va i'ánat-i-fuqará*], and who are devoted to universal peace and well-being [*maftún-i-ṣulḥ va ásáyish-i-'úmúmí*]. Yet, however perfect they may be from this perspective, they remain deprived of the knowledge [*'irfán*] and love [*muḥibbat*] of God and, as such, are imperfect.[212]

The reason for this sober assessment of rational morality is in the main attributable to two facts: first, rational morality is nevertheless deeply indebted to the spiritual and moral teachings of the Prophets, which provide a supportive moral substratum that often goes unrecognized:

> There are some who imagine that an innate sense of human dignity will prevent man from committing evil actions and insure his spiritual and material perfection. That is, that an individual who is characterized with natural intelligence, high resolve, and a driving zeal, will, without any consideration for the severe punishments consequent on evil acts, or for the great rewards of righteousness, instinctively refrain from inflicting harm on his fellow men and

> will hunger and thirst to do good. And yet, if we ponder the lessons of history it will become evident that this very sense of honour and dignity is itself one of the bounties deriving from the instructions of the Prophets of God.[213]

Second, since rational morality tends to be minimalist, it progresses at a very slow pace, whereas religion 'produces all human virtues, and it is these virtues which are the bright candles of civilization'.[214]

> If we undertook to spread such morals and manners merely by means of knowledge and learning, a thousand years would pass and still they would not have been achieved among the masses.[215]

A problem, however, arises from the coexistence of two principles (punishment and pardon) that can be grossly ascribed to secular and religious moralities respectively. 'Abdu'l-Bahá expounds that both reason and revelation confirm that no individual has a right to take revenge (*intiqám*), for 'vengeance appeases the anger (*tashfí*) of the heart by opposing one evil to another'. According to 'Abdu'l-Bahá forgiveness (*'afv*) and compassion are attitudes that must govern relationships between individuals:

> We must look upon our enemies with a sin-covering eye and act with justice when confronted with any injustice whatsoever, forgive all, consider the whole of humanity as our own family, the whole earth as our own country, be sympathetic with all suffering, nurse the sick, offer a shelter to the exiled, help the poor and those in need, dress all wounds and share the happiness of each one. Be compassionate, so that your actions will shine like unto the light streaming forth from the lamp.[216]

But personal forgiveness in the face of an aggression becomes injustice when it leads to inaction and actual violation of the rights of others. 'Abdu'l-Bahá illustrates this point by recalling the rightful rejection of Attila and by explaining that He Himself would restrain the hand of an armed man who attacks his interlocutor.[217] For society has a right to protect the rights of individuals against aggression, otherwise no community would be able to survive. Punishments administered by society do not stem from anger, but from a need to extend protection to all its members. Social existence is founded on justice (*'adl*), not forgiveness, adds 'Abdu'l-Bahá[218] in a sentence that restates Bahá'u'lláh's axiom 'that which traineth the world is Justice, for it is upheld by two pillars, reward and punishment'.[219]

On the other hand, even if punishment may have a pre-emptive and shielding effect against crime, it cannot be relied upon as the chief means to protect society. Efforts by the public – explains 'Abdu'l-Bahá – need to be transformed so that the prevention of crime rather than its punishment is made the focus of attention. To counter lack of morals and the ensuing criminality with over-legislation and other repressive measures will not do, however, because these methods have in themselves a demoralizing if not perverse effect on society:

> The body politic is engaged day and night in devising penal laws and in providing for ways and means of punishment. It builds prisons, acquires chains and fetters, and ordains places of exile and banishment, of torment and hardship, seeking thereby to reform the criminal, whereas in reality this only brings about the degradation of morals [*sabab-i-taḍíí'y-i-akhláq*] and the subversion of character [*tabdíl-i-aḥvál*] . . . At the present time the contrary prevails: the body politic is ever seeking to strengthen penal laws and securing means of punishment, instruments of death and chastisement, and places of imprisonment and exile, and then waiting for crimes to be committed. This has a most detrimental effect [*bisíár sú'i tá'thír*].[220]

Regardless, therefore, of whether society is prepared – as it should be – to punish the actual commission of crimes, a point that 'Abdu'l-Bahá stresses by indicating that some people will do harm for the sake of it, or even for their own merriment, the key issue is to create social and personal conditions that positively prevent crime:

> The body politic should instead strive night and day, bending every effort to ensure that souls are properly educated, that they progress day by day, that they advance in science and learning, that they acquire praiseworthy virtues and laudable manners, and that they forsake violent behaviour, so that crimes might never occur.[221]

As in most of the enlightened programmes, education becomes then the central piece of all Bahá'í reforms, whether they are aimed at changing social and economic conditions, uplifting the moral tone in the community, promoting self-improvement, or preventing criminality by eradicating squalor and poverty. Yet, the type of education advocated is one that seeks to build rational and spiritual morality into the fabric of society, not one that dispenses with any of the two or favours one at the expense of the other.

13
Conclusion

Building on the foundations already set by Bahá'u'lláh, 'Abdu'l-Bahá stressed the importance of attaining peace through the concerted efforts of all nations. Seen from this perspective, universal peace entailed both the institutionalizing of international law and the creation *eo ipso* of a commanding and permanent mechanism for the enforcement of collective security arrangements. Such mechanism was to be made up of both a legislative and a judicial branch, together with an implicit and perhaps suffused executive power, but at any rate much stronger than the one afforded by the League of Nations, whose failure was given out by 'Abdu'l-Bahá as a *fait accompli* from inception.[222] The comprehensiveness of the peace congress was stressed by underlining the importance of its being as fully representative of humanity as possible, a feature which the ratification process of the treaties envisaged by 'Abdu'l-Bahá was to solemnify.

The Secret of Divine Civilization, 'Abdu'l-Bahá's first text dealing with the matter of peace, was ostensibly set in the context of a scheme for a renewal of Persia and also, by natural extension, other Muslim societies.[223] But its proposals transcended these more proximate circumstances by relating the overall discussion to the fundamental role of religion in the civilizing of man, a question which 'Abdu'l-Bahá sought to clarify by also calling into question the concept of civilization prevalent in western societies. Universal peace was not an adjunct of material civilization, but in truth its ultimate test and sure outcome. This broader contextualization of peace, apparent in the amount of attention that 'Abdu'l-Bahá devoted to the subject in *The Secret of Divine Civilization*, mapped thereby a far wider territory of reforms (moral, spiritual, economic) that were conducive to peace.

As further conveyed by 'Abdu'l-Bahá throughout His western tours and in the Tablet to The Hague, universal peace entailed a reformulation of human standards that, premised on the oneness of mankind, necessitated a far greater degree of intellectual consistency than hitherto attained in the political, economic, social, cultural, religious and educational arenas. Ideologies, and their respective policies, based on incompatible notions such as 'struggle for existence', or the glorification of one's nation, culture or religion, had in consequence to be counteracted by an equally powerful cultivation of the 'blessed arts of peace'. This conception was otherwise expressed through a wide variety of metaphors and expressions alluding to the scope and breath of the new world undertakings to be adopted under its banner (see Part V). The bold references to the role of a non-isolationist America in the establishment of peace and the significance of women as peace agents, together with the forebodings of a second world war, and a no less ominous impending persecution of Jews on a European scale, completed in its broad lines 'Abdu'l-Bahá's holistic view of the war–peace equation. In sum, peace was presented by 'Abdu'l-Bahá as stemming from a moral and spiritual impetus – the realization of mankind's unity – that would then branch out in various directions embracing the whole panoply of social, moral, political and spiritual reforms.

'Abdu'l-Bahá's Tablet to The Hague condensed effectively the main elements of this broader vision. Peace, here positively contrasted with the evils of war, was not to be understood as mere absence of violence, but rather as a broad category that conceptually came to light through 'unity of conscience'. This latter concept called for a deeper understanding of the issues and principles that would lead to such outcomes as peace and security. Unity of conscience implied a shared realization as regards the needs and necessary connections emanating from the reality of things, including social reality. From this perspective science and religion were intimately connected in bringing about such realization, the reason being that the perception of reality and the ability to shape it hinge to a large extent on scientific, ethical and spiritual presuppositions. Otherwise expressed, reality, from a human point of view, has inescapably a physical as well as moral and metaphysical structure. Just as in the realm of religion 'Abdu'l-Bahá would posit the need to identify the common ground that underpins all existing religions, as a way to overcome religious prejudices and problems arising from religious fanaticism, similarly in the scientific domain there is also no less a need to redirect technological advances to uses worthy of the station of man (that is, beyond satisfying material wants or avoiding the forging of war implements) such as the uplifting and expansion of mankind's conscience.[224]

Paramount among the major principles stemming from this conscious realization are, according to 'Abdu'l-Bahá, the recognition of the oneness of mankind and the principle of free and independent investigation of truth. Religious unity is also regarded as fundamental, but it must be applied to a religion capable of withstanding the test of science, otherwise it would not become a vehicle for the unification of mankind. On this sure basis the elimination of all other forms of prejudice will be accelerated by extending education to all, women and men alike, as well as by adopting measures such as an international auxiliary language, and finally – but most importantly – by focusing on the implementation of a peace plan of collective security duly sanctioned by the totality of the peoples of the world. This plan – warned 'Abdu'l-Bahá – could not be met by following the single-minded approach of the collectivists, whose policies are doomed to failure because they are based on coercion; nor could it be achieved by stressing unrestricted freedom, as the liberals would have it, because if carried to its natural conclusion this kind of freedom would upset human relationships.

Indeed, the very concept of 'struggle for existence', denounced by 'Abdu'l-Bahá as the 'fountain head of all calamities', appeared as a major barrier whose removal from people's hearts and minds was imperative for the attainment of peace. 'Abdu'l-Bahá's profound dislike for this notion, or His considerations on the demoralizing and counter-productive effect of the treatment of criminals – criticized for its punitive and predatory biases – reflected an underlying optimistic view of human nature. This sense was further reinforced by repeated invitations to see human life in continuity with the life of the Kingdom, in clear contrast with existentialist or materialist views that would negate the immortality of the soul and hence the promises of an after-life, a view which 'Abdu'l-Bahá considered destructive of society's foundations. References to the Bahá'í experience in Iran served as an index of what could be reasonably expected, if a spiritual culture was to find its way.

Importantly, it would readily be noticed that 'Abdu'l-Bahá's position on peace, whether in His public addresses in the United States or in His correspondence and conversations, was in sympathy with the chief preoccupations shared among peace organizations at the time. Peace activism in America was mainstream, but programmes towards its realization were not, ranging from temperance campaigns to the fourteen points proposed by the hopeful Woodrow Wilson. 'Abdu'l-Bahá's proposals were characterized by their comprehensiveness, including an emphasis not only on collective security and a strengthening of international law at the top, but also on a broadening of the base and scope of peace efforts. More significantly, 'Abdu'l-Bahá made it clear that such an enterprise necessitated an iron-clad determination and a stronger understanding of how humanity's needs interrelate in various spheres, shifting in time and emphasis. He further encapsulated this programme in the context of a meeting of the East and the West, which in His vision were bound to interact and bring about a new civilization.

The notion of diverting human ingenuity from warmongering to the expansion of the 'blessed arts of peace' was still an undeveloped concept when 'Abdu'l-Bahá asserted it as a necessary antidote to warfare. Not only did racialism, imperialistic expansionism, class struggles, sex discrimination and a plethora of other expressions of social malaise tend to hold sway at the time, they also dictated the very way any countering of their effects could even be contemplated from a theoretical and practical standpoint even by the most forward-thinking minds at the time. Complete lines of peace reasoning, carefully constructed during the previous four centuries (linking peace to international arbitration, the abolition of slavery, commerce, collective security, arms reductions, cultural exchanges, and so on) tended to be refuted by the bare facts of life, which voluntaristic philosophies and ideologies of various supremacies could reassert in their own self-confirmatory and violent way. 'Abdu'l-Bahá inverted the view and placed the onus of proof on the other side.

PART III

SHOGHI EFFENDI: THE ENLARGEMENT OF THE PEACE HORIZON

> His mission [Bahá'u'lláh's] is to proclaim that the ages of the infancy and of the childhood of the human race are past, that the convulsions associated with the present stage of its adolescence are slowly and painfully preparing it to attain the stage of manhood, and are heralding the approach of that Age of Ages when swords will be beaten into plowshares, when the Kingdom promised by Jesus Christ will have been established, and the peace of the planet definitely and permanently ensured.[1]

From 1921 until Shoghi Effendi's death in 1957, the Bahá'í community experienced its transformation from a loosely held ensemble of followers residing in a few scattered countries into a widely and firmly knit international body. Such mutation was largely the result of Shoghi Effendi's strenuous efforts to endow the community with a sound structural basis, a working plan for its expansion, a doctrinal corpus and a sound conscience of its mission and place in history,[2] all of which were areas intimately interconnected.[3]

Shoghi Effendi was born in 'Akká, Palestine, on 1 March 1897. He was the grandson of 'Abdu'l-Bahá 'Abbás, and the great-grandson of Bahá'u'lláh. In him converged both Bahá'u'lláh's and the Báb's prophetic and noble lineages.[4] Shoghi Effendi's first and foremost education was provided by his own family environment, which revolved around the outstanding figure of his Grandfather. It was in those surroundings where Shoghi Effendi learned his prayers, memorized Bahá'u'lláh's words, and later on served his Grandfather as a personal secretary and as an English interpreter and translator. Persian, Arabic and to a lesser extent Turkish being the languages spoken in the household, would have come naturally to him. French and English were acquired as part of Shoghi Effendi's formal studies, first at the Jesuit Collège des Frères in Haifa, then at a Catholic school in Beirut, and later at the Syrian Protestant College in Beirut which would in time become the American College, from which he received his Bachelor of Arts in 1918.[5]

Shoghi Effendi's life as a boy and youth was not an easy one. The long separation from his Grandfather during the latter's European and American voyages was a blow to him.[6] Likewise, general living conditions during the Great War were marked by severe famines, political instability and, not the least, Jamal Pasha's renewed death threats made on 'Abdu'l-Bahá and His household.[7] This situation was further compounded by the opposition from within, which prevented closer contact between Shoghi Effendi and his Grandfather.[8]

In the summer of 1920 Shoghi Effendi arrived in England in order to gain admittance to Balliol College, Oxford. There he would study politics and economics, and equip himself with the mastery of the English language as would allow him to render greater services to his Grandfather.[9] Significantly, in a letter addressed to a friend while in Oxford he wrote:

> My hope is that I may speedily acquire the best that this country and this society have to offer and then return to my home and recast the truths of the Faith in a new form, and thus serve the Holy Threshold.[10]

His education at Oxford, however, came to an abrupt end barely a year later, on 29 November 1921, when a cable sent from Haifa broke the news of the passing of 'Abdu'l-Bahá. Upon arrival in Haifa, Shoghi Effendi read the Will and Testament of 'Abdu'l-Bahá (which was addressed to him), only to learn then of his appointment as Guardian of the Faith, interpreter of the divine words and permanent head of the future Universal House of Justice.[11]

Although it is perhaps no exaggeration to say that Shoghi Effendi never recovered from the devastating news of his Grandfather's death, his appointment as head of the Bahá'í community when he was barely twenty-four years old did nothing but aggravate the unmistakable agony of those fateful days of distress and separation.[12] In his ensuing efforts as Guardian of the Bahá'í Faith, 'peace' could again be recognized as a critical theme; but its salient features were now more clearly linked to a very long-term view of history. This, in turn, was supported by an enlarged perception of the overall role of revelation and the place that the work to be carried out by the Bahá'ís was to occupy in the great scheme of things.

A note of caution needs to be added here with regards to the scholarly status of some of Shoghi Effendi´s works. The overwhelming majority of these were written in English, when he was already acting in his official capacity as head of the Bahá'í community and interpreter of the Bahá'í writings, and hence can be considered as directly relevant to the discharge of his office. His leadership and directions, together with his function as translator/interpreter of a considerable number of key Bahá'í texts, resulted in an intricate interrelationship between his more temporal functions and those that required of him to produce enduring guidance. Doctrinal aspects, and questions of fundamental import ('fundamental verities') were conveyed in some lengthy letters, or simply marked through emphasis and explicit references suggestive of their significance, yet avoiding any formalization. A grey area in this sense relates to his wide-ranging conception of history and the degree to which its broad outlines, let alone specifics, need to be taken as more or less normative guidelines, whether they refer to past or future developments. This may affect the reading of some of his major works, chiefly *God Passes By*, *The Promised Day Is Come* and *The Unfoldment of World Civilization*, but it may also extend to other works. In general, it is quite clear that Shoghi Effendi had a non-dogmatic conception of truth, and that a rigid prescriptive understanding of the general dynamics of historical processes, and even the formation of the Bahá'í system, would be inimical to its intent and contrary to its method, which (as will be shown) relied on a number of categories believed to be universal as well as certain analogues and metaphors that acted as basic signposts or foci capable of generating useful working hypotheses.

A degree of relative incompleteness and tentativeness in the whole of Shoghi

Effendi's production was therefore necessitated by an acknowledgement and indeed an openness to the contingent character of human achievements. Even a major historical work such as *God Passes By* needs to be treated less as a scholarly account of historical facts – certainly the addition of an apparatus would have rendered the task impossible and turned the work into something else – than as a comprehensive survey of the 'outstanding events of the century':

> It is not my purpose – nor does the occasion demand it, – to write a detailed history of the last hundred years of the Bahá'í Faith, nor do I intend to trace the origins of so tremendous a Movement, or to portray the conditions under which it was born, or to examine the character of the religion from which it has sprung, or to arrive at an estimate of the effects which its impact upon the fortunes of mankind has produced. I shall rather content myself with a review of the salient features of its birth and rise, as well as of the initial stages in the establishment of its administrative institutions – institutions which must be regarded as the nucleus and herald of that World Order that must incarnate the soul, execute the laws, and fulfil the purpose of the Faith of God in this day.[13]

Seen from this perspective, the important aspect to retain in our survey of Shoghi Effendi's work is not whether matters of historical detail can be verified from independent sources other than those regarded as official, but rather the significance that he attached to those facts and how these were linked or subordinated to a higher conception. In the following chapters I will explore these features and their connections with the view of history and the perceived roles of the Bahá'í community in its maturation towards peace.

14
A New Sense of History

> The present is always unimportant, but we must make our present so filled with mighty, altruistic deeds as to assume significant weight and momentous importance in the future. A shallow present will surely be followed by a superficial future.[14]

In Shoghi Effendi's view a turning point in humanity's life could be dated with great accuracy. It was on 23 May 1844 that a young merchant of Shiraz, Muḥammad-'Alí, the Báb, presented Himself to Mullá Ḥusayn Bús͟hrú'í, a leading disciple of the late Siyyid Káẓim Ras͟htí,[15] as the Báb to the Twelfth Imám.[16] It was on that same day that 'Abdu'l-Bahá, the future Centre of the Bahá'í Covenant, was born.[17] On that fateful day history had found a new hinge. A millennium had elapsed from the disappearance of the Hidden Imám, and it was then that the apocalyptic year 1260 AH was taking its course.[18] Furthermore, a series of edicts issued by the Ottoman Empire authorized the resettlement of the Jewish people back in their former homeland. No other twist of dates than this could bring closer Jewish, Christian and Muslim eschatologies to a crossroads. Hence 23 May 1844 was to mark the 'opening of the most glorious epoch in the greatest cycle which the spiritual history of mankind has yet witnessed'.[19]

According to Shoghi Effendi, the significance of this 'Day' was not to be inferred simply from claims to biblical or qur'ánic fulfilment. The historical events associated with its origins, explained Shoghi Effendi, bore 'the most outstanding features of what the world will come to recognize as the *greatest drama in the world's spiritual history'* (emphasis added).[20] History would have to be entirely rewritten in the light of these unique events[21] and it would fall upon future Bahá'í historians to trace the influence of God's creative word in the shaping of a new world which still remained uninformed of the new theophany. Mankind could well continue opposing and delaying the emergence of God's new world order; but, at variance with the past, this opposition was not to succeed. For this was the time when the day was not to be followed by night;[22] the day when 'valleys' and 'mountains' had been levelled.[23]

While the world was proceeding in its own way towards its destiny, the Bahá'í community was finding itself in the midst of a road whose milestones were still unclear to the vast majority of its members. Shoghi Effendi took it upon himself to explain from his vantage position what those milestones had been, and where the Bahá'í community was standing *vis-á-vis* the world.[24] To a great extent Shoghi Effendi's ministry can be seen in this light. His only book proper, *God Passes By,* which traces the history of the first century of the Bahá'í Faith from its inception until 1944, was written in an effort to condense the totality of the salient features which could be discerned during that period.[25] Likewise, Shoghi Effendi's translation of the first part of *Nabíl's Narrative*, itself a tribute to the figure of the Báb, was a historical piece of literature intended to equip western believers with a reinforced sense of belonging and a deeper sense of their already splendid history.[26]

Other works by Shoghi Effendi, notably his lengthy 'letters' grouped under the generic title *The World Order of Bahá'u'lláh,* were marked by a similar urge to provide the Bahá'ís with a deeper historical and spiritual perspective. While 'The Dispensation of Bahá'u'lláh' clarified the relationship between the central figures of the Faith, and presented the Bahá'í Administrative Order as a natural consequence of Bahá'u'lláh's and 'Abdu'l-Bahá's injunctions, other letters such as 'The Goal of a New World Order' and 'The Unfoldment of World Civilization' neatly defined the Bahá'í position with regard to the world and its older sister faiths, the latter work offering a vast panorama of future trends.[27] In these letters history, contrary to the prevalent practice, was not read through the lens of a privileged nation or civilization, but rather as the gradual progression of a humanity moving from various stages of political unity (clan, tribe, city state) and relative maturity (infancy, adolescence, coming of age). Religions, as explained by 'Abdu'l-Bahá, came in cycles, with each 'Dispensation' representing stages in a progression from Adam to its consummation in the Revelation of Bahá'u'lláh, whose advent marked the beginning of a new cycle. With the appearance of the Supreme Manifestation (*ẓuhúr-i-kullí*), the world is thus poised to attain to maturity (*ẓuhúr-i-ú sabab-i-bulúgh-i-'álam gardad*).[28] The oft-used metaphor to represent this process (that of an embryo moving through various developmental phases) had a long and highly symbolic story and had been used by Siyyid Káẓim,[29] Bahá'u'lláh,[30] and 'Abdu'l-Bahá.[31] This would illustrate the transitioning of the 'entire human race' from an embryonic or adolescent stage to a new stage: the new cycle of fulfilment inaugurated by the Báb, one characterized by an acceleration of unprecedented development and knowledge, as 'Abdu'l-Bahá stated:

> In this present cycle there will be an evolution in civilization unparalleled in the history of the world. *The world of humanity has, heretofore, been in the stage of infancy; now it is approaching maturity.* Just as the individual human organism, having attained the period of maturity, reaches its fullest degree of physical strength and ripened intellectual faculties so that in one year of this ripened period there is witnessed an unprecedented measure of development, likewise the world of humanity in this cycle of its completeness and consummation will realize an immeasurable upward progress, and that power of accomplishment

> whereof each individual human reality is the depository of God – that outworking Universal Spirit – like the intellectual faculty, will reveal itself in infinite degrees of perfection.[32] (emphasis added)

The present period in human history was often compared with the latter period of the Roman Empire. Shoghi Effendi, an admirer of Gibbon's *The Decline and Fall of the Roman Empire*,[33] recognized and traced broad parallels between the two periods. The beginnings of Christianity, in particular, offered the Bahá'í observer a similar pattern of experience from which important lessons could be drawn. In the following passage this reasoning can be readily appreciated:

> Does not the history of primitive Christianity and of the rise of Islám, each in its own way, offer a striking parallel to this strange phenomenon the beginnings of which we are now witnessing in this, the first century of the Bahá'í Era? Has not the Divine Impulse which gave birth to each of these great religions, through the operation of those forces which the irresistible growth of the Faith itself has released, to seek away from the land of its birth and in more propitious climes a ready field and a more adequate medium for the incarnation of its spirit and the propagation of its cause? Have not the Asiatic churches of Jerusalem, of Antioch and of Alexandria, consisting chiefly of those Jewish converts, *whose character and temperament incline them to sympathize with the traditional ceremonies of the Mosaic Dispensation, been forced as they steadily declined to recognize the growing ascendancy of their Greek and Roman brethren*?[34] (emphasis added)

Any western Bahá'í sufficiently aware of Christian history would have certainly felt encouraged by the implications of this parallelism, and there is no doubt that Shoghi Effendi used these obvious inferences not only to foster a spirit of emulation between western and eastern Bahá'ís, but also to point out in a subtle way the need for correctives in the way both of them were embodying their beliefs in actual practice.

The emergence of Christianity precisely at a time when the Roman Empire was headed for its collapse was again illustrative of what could be expected of present times. At least in one important sense, the parallel entailed a serious warning about the imminence of a catastrophe analogous to the one which swept aside the colossal structures of the Roman Empire:

> Are we, the privileged custodians of a priceless Faith, called upon to witness a cataclysmical change, politically as fundamental and spiritually as beneficent as that which precipitated the fall of the Roman Empire in the West?[35]

This warning was repeated on several occasions prior to World War II and thereafter. In reality – as Shoghi Effendi was careful to point out – the whole process of 'sudden' transformation witnessed by humanity was nothing but the result of

Bahá'u'lláh's full disclosure in His proclamation to the kings and rulers, which was to be followed by the dramatic fall of all but one of the imperial dynasties thus addressed.[36]

In Shoghi Effendi's view, the Bahá'í Faith had experienced a transformation after having cast away the rigid mould of Babism and then moved until reaching the contemporary phase of systematization and universal application:

> We perceive a no less apparent evolution in the scope of its teachings, at first designedly rigid, complex and severe, subsequently recast, expanded, and liberalized under the succeeding Dispensation, later expounded, reaffirmed and amplified by an appointed Interpreter, and lastly systematized and universally applied to both individuals and institutions.[37]

This process was largely matched by the passing of a series of ages. While the 'heroic' or 'apostolic' age was already gone, the Bahá'í community was standing at the beginning of a transitional period known as the 'formative age', itself made up of different successive stages which would gradually lead to the promised Golden Age. This transition, whatever its importance, could not possibly compare in intensity with the outpourings of revelation and the pregnant sacrifices of its thousands of martyrs.

Although the hiatus between the heroic age and the formative age was not intended to be a radical one,[38] nevertheless, Shoghi Effendi was acutely aware that after the passing of 'Abdu'l-Bahá an entire period of Bahá'í history had come to a close. No conceivable substitution was possible for this personal bond with the 'central figures' of the Faith. From then onwards the heroic age was a period to look back on for inspiration and to spur emulation:

> Now, if ever, is the time to emulate the example of these heroes, saints and martyrs . . . No more befitting tribute can be paid to the memory of these luminous souls, by those who carry the torch of Divine Guidance after them, than by a corresponding manifestation of solidarity, self-abnegation, zeal and devotion.[39]

And again, the transitional age could not compare with the glory of the Golden Age, a period which would be characterized by the allegiance of the majority of the peoples of the world to the Faith of Bahá'u'lláh, thus fulfilling the prophecies of former religions. In this way, Shoghi Effendi was able to design a temporal frame whereby the Bahá'ís could identify more clearly their mission and be more apt at identifying their duties:

> Pending the establishment of the Universal House of Justice, whose function it is to lay more definitely the broad lines that must guide the future activities and administration of the Movement, *it is clearly our duty to strive to obtain as clear*

> *a view as possible of the manner in which to conduct the affairs of the Cause,* and then arise with single mindedness and determination to adopt and maintain it in all our activities and labours.[40] (emphasis added)

While outstanding parallels with former religions could be found in the inception and evolution of the Bahá'í Dispensation, the salient features of the new religion were conceived as simply 'unique'. Shoghi Effendi outlined some of these fundamental differences in the course of his works[41] and for similar reasons he repeatedly encouraged western Bahá'ís to become familiar with Islam.[42] Shoghi Effendi seems to have been fully appreciative that in drawing parallels and comparisons with 'former religions', the entire exercise of searching for similarities and differences, commonalities and original features could be misconstrued for an attempt at belittling those religions. He insistently disclaimed entertaining such intentions;[43] but at the same time was apprised that Bahá'ís were in dire need of understanding where they stood, as well as the nature of the obstacles they were likely to face. Therefore, it was all the more necessary to assist in the transformation of the Bahá'í experience into a repository of consolidated knowledge. Thus, there appears to be no randomness about the fact that one of the first undertakings carried out under the direct instructions of Shoghi Effendi was the publication of the *Bahá'í Year Book*.[44]

Other devices were also employed. Nothing may perhaps better describe Shoghi Effendi's eagerness to enhance the historical consciousness of Bahá'í believers than his constant allusions to the 'synchronization' of events. The following piece of advice given in 1936 by Shoghi Effendi to the North American Bahá'í community is particularly illustrative as it condenses a number of the essential aspects of the Bahá'í unfolding of history and its ultimate peaceful outcome:

> Far from yielding in their resolve, far from growing oblivious of their task, they [the believers] should, at no time, however much buffeted by circumstances, forget that the synchronization of such world-shaking crises with the progressive unfoldment and fruition of their divinely appointed task is itself the work of Providence, the design of an inscrutable Wisdom, and the purpose of an all-compelling Will, a Will that directs and controls, in its own mysterious way, both the fortunes of the Faith and the destinies of men. *Such simultaneous processes of rise and of fall, of integration and of disintegration, of order and chaos, with their continuous and reciprocal reactions on each other, are but aspects of a greater Plan*, one and indivisible, whose Source is God, whose author is Bahá'u'lláh, the theater of whose operations is the entire planet, *and whose ultimate objectives are the unity of the human race and the peace of all mankind.*[45] (emphasis added)

Most of the National Plans he carefully arranged for implementation by the few National Spiritual Assemblies existing at the time were conceived so as to coincide with some historic event, be it an anniversary, the inception of some work in the Holy Places (Haifa and 'Akká), or a special intercontinental conference, and the like.[46] In all of these instances, the 'synchronizing' of events seems to have been both a means to deepen the sense of vision of the Bahá'ís, and an expression of the orderly yet multifarious projection of God's Will. In most cases it is evident that a symbolical connection with the central figures of the Faith was construed to be the animating force behind Bahá'í undertakings,[47] a connection made obvious in the very way the 'world administrative centre' and the 'world spiritual centre' were to interact at the holiest of Bahá'í Holy Places,[48] the orienting pole to which some Bahá'í prayers were to be directed.[49] Furthermore, the entire experience of the Bahá'í pilgrimage was arranged by Shoghi Effendi in such a manner as to enhance the intimate connection with the central figures of the Bahá'í Faith and their visible stamp, as evinced by the expansion of their message throughout the world.[50]

Even the divinely-appointed institutions would derive inspiration from the sacrificial ground in which the sacred remains of the Central Figures were laid to rest. Shoghi Effendi meticulously designed the Holy Places and the adjoining sites for the future administrative buildings so as to remind the Bahá'í believers of the fundamental analogies and correspondences that were to be found in the Bahá'í Faith. While the remains of the Báb constituted the 'heart and centre of the world',[51] the administrative sites had been arranged in perfect symmetry along an arc crowned at the top by the seat of the Universal House of Justice,[52] the whole arc centring around a hub of small monuments containing the resting-places of the Holy Family, and linked to the Shrine of the Báb through a series of landscaped paths. The whole setting was surrounded by monumental gardens and bathed in light at night,[53] all facing the distant Shrine of Bahá'u'lláh. Sacred space and sacred history were thus fused into the new Zion, the one spot whence the new law and the new justice, as had been said, would emerge.

15
Shoghi Effendi on Peace

'Pattern and order were innate' in Shoghi Effendi.[54] This brief sentence provides a key to apprehend his characteristic approach not just to landscaping in the most arid and improbable conditions, but also to social and religious evolution. Most of the 'patterns' so identified by Shoghi Effendi were numerous, simple and based on some fundamental schemata. The organic analogy is perhaps the most pervasive of these; but others such as the binary system of identities and polarities,[55] or the concept of 'manifestation' as the expression of God's will in the course of history, are also fundamental. Yet, no single pattern nor theme can be said to enjoy pre-eminence, except perhaps for the very notion of unity, peace and justice.[56]

In Shoghi Effendi's works peace is treated as an essential feature of the Bahá'í economy, which bears little comparison with other peace proposals and solutions, for the 'Bahá'í programme' is supported by God's will:

> To disregard the *Bahá'í solution* for world peace is to build on foundations of sand. To accept and apply it is to make peace not a mere dream, or an ideal, but a living reality (. . .) The *Bahá'í peace programme* is, indeed, not only one way of attaining that goal. It is not even relatively the best. It is, in the last resort, the sole effective instrument for the *establishment of the reign of peace in this world.* This attitude does not involve any total repudiation of other solutions offered by various philanthropists. It merely shows their inadequacy compared to the Divine Plan for the unification of the world.[57] (emphasis added)

The 'Bahá'í solution' alluded to by Shoghi Effendi is an implicit reference to the main ideas and promises conveyed already by Bahá'u'lláh and 'Abdu'l-Bahá, which Shoghi Effendi obviously felt he had no need to restate: 'The promise of the unification of the whole human race, of the inauguration of the Most Great Peace, of the unfoldment of a world civilization, had been incontestably given.'[58] But how this peace would fit into the general pattern of unfolding events leading towards the unification of mankind was something that warranted further elucidations, which Shoghi Effendi set out to do in the course of his correspondence with the Bahá'í world at large.

In general terms, peace is presented by Shoghi Effendi as part of a long-term process comprising several epochs and phases. Both the Lesser Peace and the Most Great Peace describe two crucial junctures in the 'unfolding' of mankind's spiritual history/destiny. While the Lesser Peace can be 'dated' with some precision, the Most Great Peace, which encompasses and transcends both the Lesser and the Greater Peace, is described in its essential features but with no specific references as to the time when it will eventuate; its dawning, however, is traceable to the foundations already laid out by President Woodrow Wilson:

> The ideals that fired the imagination of America's tragically unappreciated President, whose high endeavours, however much nullified by a visionless generation, 'Abdu'l-Bahá, through His own pen, acclaimed as signalizing the dawn of the Most Great Peace, though now lying in the dust, bitterly reproach a heedless generation for having so cruelly abandoned them.[59]

In order to understand how these two modalities of peace are meant to work in a Bahá'í economy, a few words must be said about the role that the concept of synchronization plays in its dynamics.[60] As already seen, synchronization brings to the fore a relationship between events which to the outward eye appear unrelated. This connection might be deliberate, as in Shoghi Effendi's carefully designed plans, where rhythm and timing combine with each other as counterparts of sacred events (such as anniversaries);[61] or else it is an inherent feature that the careful observer may discover beneath the surface of otherwise disparate events.[62] Whether prescriptive or descriptive, conscious or unconscious, this synchronizing is but a part of a more fundamental process whereby the will of God interplays with mankind through the intermediary of His Manifestations.

In historical terms this unfolding of events resembles more a drama of epic proportions than an orderly display of the enlightened and liberal notions of Progress; it is more reminiscent of the Hegelian intertwining of the thesis and its antithesis, or of the Marxian advance through the surfacing of contradictions:

> A titanic, a spiritual struggle, unparalleled in its magnitude yet unspeakably glorious in its ultimate consequences, is being waged as a result of these opposing tendencies, in this age of transition through which the organized community of the followers of Bahá'u'lláh and mankind as a whole are passing.[63]

Here impersonal forces such as materialism, individualism, collectivism, racism, national prejudice, and several others are matched by other counterforces such as the thrust for unity, the quest for God, and love for peace.[64] But the theatre of operations where these forces clash is not impersonal. The world rulers, the States and nations of the world, the established religions, and the Bahá'í community, all have an important part to play in this stage of dramatic if not tragic proportions.[65] Opportunities are taken or lost,[66] challenges can be met, progress can be retarded, calamities may occur.[67] An iron will, a righteous mind, unparalleled sacrifices, sustained and coordinated efforts, unity of action, all these and much more are elements deemed necessary to reverse the trend marked by the centrifugal forces operating in the world.[68] 'No sacrifice can be deemed too great.'[69] The following statement by Shoghi Effendi illustrates some of the above aspects while pointing to the central idea of two divergent processes:

> The record of the Bahá'í community since inception of the Formative Age conclusively demonstrates that accomplishment of signal acts accompanied, or followed upon, periods of acute distress in European and American contemporary history.[70]

At variance with the delirium of war and violent exaltation, which were rife among the George Sorels and Ernst Jüngers[71] of the interwar period, and in contrast with the so-called realistic tradition that saw and sees warfare as a necessary expedient in the anarchic interaction between states, warfare and the havoc it wreaks on all human affairs were not regarded by Shoghi Effendi as a civilizing force or a legitimate medium for the attainment of state goals, but quite on the contrary were portrayed as the defeat of true civilization, the result of pride and absence of spirituality.

William II of Germany, the prototype of the late nineteenth-century tyrant monarch, for instance, is described by Shoghi Effendi as a hypocrite 'temperamentally dictatorial, politically inexperienced, militarily aggressive, religiously insincere' who 'posed as the apostle of European peace, yet actually insisted on "the mailed fist" and "the shining armour"'. His pride was largely responsible for his downfall: 'War indeed became a religion of his country, and by enlarging the scope of his multifarious activities, he proceeded to prepare the way for that final catastrophe that was to dethrone him and his dynasty.'[72] Comparable descriptions were attached by Shoghi Effendi to other European rulers. The downfall of Napoleon III, the recipient of two of Bahá'u'lláh's most celebrated Tablets, and of Francis Joseph, Emperor of Austria, were seen in a similar light.[73] World War II in particular represented in Shoghi Effendi's view the collapse and impotence of a 'so-called Christian civilization'.[74]

In this dialectic nothing was considered conclusive except God's promises and warnings. The Lesser Peace and the Most Great Peace appeared as two major promises made by Bahá'u'lláh. Yet they did not describe two single events, but a sequence of them, or to be more precise, a synchronized whole. This can be seen characteristically in a most illuminating reference to the Lesser Peace and the Most Great Peace contained in a passage where Shoghi Effendi expatiates on the significance of the Bahá'í Archives on the arc of buildings on Mount Carmel as a repository of sacred memory. The raising of this edifice is seen as a prelude to the erection of other administrative seats, the completion of which will mark 'the culmination of the development of a world-wide divinely-appointed Administrative Order'. Shoghi Effendi further adds:

> This vast and irresistible process, unexampled in the spiritual history of mankind, and which will *synchronize* with two no less significant developments – the establishment of the Lesser Peace and the evolution of Bahá'í national and local institutions – the one outside and the other within the Bahá'í world – will attain its final consummation, in the Golden Age of the Faith, through the raising of the standard of the Most Great Peace, and the emergence, in the plenitude of its power and glory, of the focal Centre of the agencies constituting the World Order of Bahá'u'lláh. The final establishment of this seat of the future Bahá'í World Commonwealth will signalize at once the proclamation of the sovereignty of the Founder of our Faith and the advent of the Kingdom of the Father, repeatedly lauded and promised by Jesus Christ.[75] (emphasis added)

In other words, the raising of the Bahá'í administrative seats is simultaneous with two other processes, namely the Lesser Peace and the maturation of the national and local institutions of the Bahá'í community. Although Shoghi Effendi was careful not to point out a causal connection between these three processes, the correlation cannot be said to be merely coincidental either. That there was a certain yet intricate (if not mysterious) relationship between progress at the Bahá'í World Centre and progress in the rest of the Bahá'í world could not be doubted.[76] Shoghi Effendi was undeniably aware of the role of the future Universal House of Justice in the promotion of the Lesser Peace (*ṣulḥ-i-akbar*), which task had been entrusted by Bahá'u'lláh to its members. In the aggregate, however, the Lesser Peace was to be fundamentally attributable to the concerted efforts of mankind.[77]

The completion of the Bahá'í institutional framework would mark then the culmination of the Administrative Order. But this, as can be gathered from the rest of the above passage, will only be but a preliminary step to yet another stage which is typified by the following traits: 'the raising [in due time] of the standard of the Most Great Peace', and the emergence 'of the focal Centre of the agencies constituting the World Order of Bahá'u'lláh'.

Moreover, this important passage establishes a clear distinction between the Bahá'í Administrative Order and the World Order of Bahá'u'lláh. The former, although in embryonic form, is already active and visible in the world, while the latter is the 'consummation' of a wider and complex progression of disintegration and convergence with the world at large. It is also fair to say that the Administrative Order is the World Order of Bahá'u'lláh in an embryonic form.[78]

The two aspects – i.e. the raising of the standard of the Most Great Peace and the emergence of the 'focal Centre'– are set to happen sometime during the Golden Age of the Bahá'í Faith. The 'focal Centre' is defined as the 'seat of the future Bahá'í World Commonwealth',[79] and its establishment signals the 'kingdom of the Father'. Thus the main elements characteristic of the Bahá'í Revelation, 'whose mission is none other but the achievement of this organic and spiritual unity of the whole body of the nations', are significantly enumerated by Shoghi Effendi and are said to 'synchronize with the initial stages in the unfoldment of the Golden Age of the Bahá'í Era'. They are as follows:

- the emergence of a world community
- the consciousness of world citizenship
- the founding of a world civilization and culture[80]

Shoghi Effendi would explain three years later, before World War II broke out, that out of the world catastrophe would emerge the

> consciousness of world citizenship . . . a consciousness that can alone provide an adequate basis for the organization of world unity, on which a lasting world peace must necessarily depend, the peace itself inaugurating in turn that world civilization which will mark the coming of age of the entire human race.[81]

In turn, the World Order of Bahá'u'lláh will:

> in the course of successive Dispensations of the Bahá'í cycle, yield its fairest fruit through the birth and flowering of a civilization, divinely inspired, unique in its features, world-embracing in its scope, and fundamentally spiritual in its character – a civilization destined as it unfolds to derive its initial impulse from the spirit animating the very institutions which, in their embryonic state, are now stirring in the womb of the present Formative Age of the Faith.[82]

In this broad picture a divine or spiritual civilization appears to be the finest and ultimate result of the processes set in motion through the agency of the new Bahá'í Dispensation. Just as the individual reaches maturity after a series of stages, likewise humanity is to find itself in a position when it will have attained an equivalent degree of consummation.[83] The overall impression this picture conveys is one of a monumental display of evolutionary stages unfolding through intermittent crises which, as a result of humanity's coming of age, challenge human beings to ever higher levels of excellence.[84] Peace is not here an event, but the expression of the fullness achieved in the overall process of mankind's maturation.

16
The Lesser Peace as a Process

As already seen, Shoghi Effendi's aim was not so much to give a full view of events, and much less an infallible forecast, as that of providing a sense of direction. The identification of future trends, supported by a sense of their sacred underpinnings, was essential to the nascent Bahá'í community. From these hints the followers of Bahá'u'lláh could then derive not only a sense of mission but also a historical awareness of the patterns defining the evolution and scope of Bahá'í activities. In this monumental view of history, peace could no longer be conceived as a sudden datable event, but rather as a process, operating, as everything in God's creation, by degrees: 'The kingdom of peace, salvation, uprightness and reconciliation is founded in the Invisible World, and it will by degrees become manifest and apparent through the power of the Word of God!'[85]

When describing the likely long-term destiny of humankind some degree of generality was quite naturally in the nature of things. What is surprising in Shoghi Effendi's addresses is the amount of detail that can be found in the description of the 'short term'.[86] For instance, in the following passage, dated June 1947, Shoghi Effendi describes the basic features accompanying the Lesser Peace:

> During this the Formative Age of the Faith, and in the course of present and succeeding epochs, the last crowning stage in the erection of the framework of the Administrative Order of the Faith of Bahá'u'lláh – the election of the Universal House of Justice – will have been completed, the Kitáb-i-Aqdas, the Mother-Book of His Revelation, will have been codified and its laws promulgated, the Lesser Peace will have been established, the unity of mankind will have been achieved and its maturity attained, the Plan conceived by 'Abdu'l-Bahá will have been executed, the emancipation of the Faith from the fetters of orthodoxy will have been effected, and its independent religious status will have been universally recognized, whilst in the course of the Golden Age . . .[87]

Of the above distinguishing features, some have already taken place. The election of the Universal House of Justice took place in 1963, a date anticipated by Shoghi Effendi and seen as related to the fulfilment of Daniel's prophecy.[88] The codification of the Kitáb-i-Aqdas was completed in 1973, and the book itself published in its English version in 1992. By that same date the last territories mentioned by 'Abdu'l-Bahá and Shoghi Effendi in their plans had finally been opened to the new Faith.[89] The 'emancipation' of the Bahá'í Faith from 'orthodoxy' and the recognition of its independent status have been increasingly acknowledged by religious and political bodies,[90] although religious freedom for Bahá'ís remains yet precarious in a significant number of countries, not least in Iran.

Shoghi Effendi also provided some descriptions of the pattern which the Bahá'í Administrative Order would follow. Taken as a whole, they clearly point to a process whereby the world will be welded into a single entity, leaving aside the 'fetish' of national sovereignty.[91] At the same time the Bahá'í Administrative Order is seen as gathering strength in the face of increasing opposition.[92] The Lesser Peace, therefore, represents a stage at which the political unification of the world is a tangible reality synchronizing with the maturation of the Bahá'í Administrative Order. The difference between the Lesser and the Most Great Peace appears clearly set out:

> With reference to the question you have asked concerning the time and means through which the Lesser and Most Great Peace, referred to by Bahá'u'lláh, will be established, following the coming World War: Your view that the Lesser Peace will come about through the political efforts of the states and nations of the world, and independently of any direct Bahá'í plan or effort, and the Most Great Peace be established through the instrumentality of the believers, and by the direct operation of the laws and principles revealed by Bahá'u'lláh and the functioning of the Universal House of Justice as the supreme organ of the Bahá'í superstate – your view on this subject is quite correct and in full accord with the pronouncements of the Guardian as embodied in 'The Unfoldment of World Civilization'.[93]

Ordeals and the Lesser Peace

A few words are in order to clarify the dating and speculation in Bahá'í circles about the turn of the second millennium of the Christian era as marking a decisive transition in the unfolding of the Lesser Peace. The popular Bahá'í notion that the Lesser Peace was to take place by the end of the twentieth century had been fuelled by a number of correlates. Initially the concept of the Lesser Peace appeared linked with 'Abdu'l-Bahá's vision of the 'seven candles of unity' (see Chapter 11 above); and, secondly, with Bahá'u'lláh's warning over the imminence of a sudden calamity.

The basis for the first linkage can be found in 'Abdu'l-Bahá's statement that the unity of nations (*vaḥdat-i-vaṭán*) 'will be securely established' in the present century (twentieth), 'causing all the people of the world to regard themselves as peoples of one common fatherland'.[94] However, since according to 'Abdu'l-Bahá 'unity in the political realm' (*vaḥdat-i-síasíyat*) had started but to glimmer at the time, the whole issue became marred by some degree of confusion as to the implications of these two categories of 'unity' (that is, unity among nations and political unity). In this connection, Shoghi Effendi explained that the 'candles of unity' referred to would not necessarily appear in the order given, and that 'unity in the political realm' (i.e. unity between states) should indeed be distinguished from the 'unity of nations' (i.e. unity between the peoples of the world):

> The first [unity in the political realm] is a unity which politically independent and sovereign states achieve among themselves; while the second [unity of nations] is one which is brought about between nations, the difference between a state and a nation being that the former, as you know, is a political entity without necessarily being homogeneous in race, whereas the second implies national as well as political homogeneity.[95]

Since popular attention in the Bahá'í world was often focused on identifying the Lesser Peace with either of these 'unities' to the exclusion of the other, and thinking of it as an event rather than as a process, sight was lost of the other synchronizing elements enumerated elsewhere by Shoghi Effendi (see above), all of which are indicative of a gradual approaching or perfecting of the Lesser Peace (a peace process which combines features of both the *ṣulḥ-i-aṣghar* and the *ṣulḥ-i-akbar*), and one possibly accelerated by a combination of catastrophic upheavals whose early manifestations could be seen in the turmoil of the great European wars, but a process none the less. While in London 'Abdu'l-Bahá had already given a response to the vexing question:

> 'By what process', continued the questioner, 'will this peace on earth be established? Will it come at once after a universal declaration of the Truth?'
>
> 'No, it will come about gradually,' said 'Abdu'l-Bahá. 'A plant that grows too quickly lasts but a short time. You are my family' and he looked about with a smile, 'my new children! If a family lives in unison, great results are obtained. Widen the circle; when a city lives in intimate accord greater results will follow, and a continent that is fully united will likewise unite all other continents. Then will be the time of the greatest results, for all the inhabitants of the earth belong to one native land.[96]

Moreover, the urge to reformulate the Lesser Peace in terms of a particular time-frame (year 1963, 2000)[97] or a modality of 'unity' clouded the obvious fact that the Lesser Peace had in time to give way to the Most Great Peace in what, once again, had been unmistakably defined as a concatenation of events and processes leading to the formation of a spiritual world civilization.

As for the idea that the Lesser Peace will be precipitated by, or rather will post-date, a great catastrophe,[98] this was linked to a number of dire 'predictions', some of which were in fact more suggestive of a downward spiralling culminating in one single catastrophic collapse than of an interplay of forces and counter-forces:

> The world is in travail, and its agitation waxeth day by day. Its face is turned towards waywardness and unbelief. Such shall be its plight, that to disclose it now would not be meet and seemly. Its perversity will long continue. And when the appointed hour is come, there shall suddenly appear that which shall cause the limbs of mankind to quake. Then, and only then, will the Divine Standard be unfurled, and the Nightingale of Paradise warble its melody.[99]

The sombre panorama thus described was further reinforced by similar references, like this one significantly addressed by Bahá'u'lláh to the 'peoples of the world':

> Know, verily, that an unforeseen calamity followeth you, and grievous retribution awaiteth you. Think not that which ye have committed hath been effaced in My sight. By My beauty! All your doings hath My pen graven with open characters upon tablets of chrysolite.[100]

Thus by combining the image of a 'fiery ordeal' (a 'world catastrophe', an 'unforeseen calamity' that 'shall cause the limbs of mankind to quake') with the unfurling of the Divine Standard and the eventuation of the Lesser Peace (understood as political unity), considerable attention was diverted to speculation on the dating and the consequent deciphering of the 'calamity' in question, all to the detriment of other key aspects pointing not so much to a date or dates, but to a convergence of both destructive and constructive elements in the unfolding civilizational process. Already in 1948, in a letter to the American Bahá'í community, Shoghi Effendi could lay stress on the nadir/zenith metaphor:

> The champion builders of Bahá'u'lláh's rising World Order must scale nobler heights of heroism as humanity plunges into greater depths of despair, degradation, dissension and distress. Let them forge ahead into the future serenely confident that the hour of their mightiest exertions and the supreme opportunity for their greatest exploits must coincide with the apocalyptic upheaval marking the lowest ebb in mankind's fast-declining fortunes.[101]

Not surprisingly, some Bahá'ís must have felt serious doubts at the time as to the soundness of following human pursuits that in the face of an impending 'apocalyptic upheaval' must have been seen as rather banal. The following response from Shoghi Effendi, dated 1949, was most probably intended to allay those sentiments:

> He advised you to go ahead and plan your college education. We have no indication of exactly what nature the apocalyptic upheaval will be: it might be another war . . . but as students of our Bahá'í writings it is clear that the longer

> the 'Divine Physician' (i.e. Bahá'u'lláh) is withheld from healing the ill of the world, the more severe will be the crisis, and the more terrible the sufferings of the patient.[102]

The pattern described by Shoghi Effendi is thus less one of a once-and-for-all calamitous, yet felicitous, transformation[103] than the outcome of a complex interaction of intermittent crises and victories, peaks and troughs, setbacks and leaps forward, disintegration and unification, divine intermissions and providential intervention. Awareness as to this pattern, as indicated by Peter Smith, was used to spur Bahá'ís to redouble their commitment to carry out their part and 'share' in the divine work that they, and only they, could carry forward.[104] This is again exemplified in the mollified reference to a 'world catastrophe' employed by the Hands of the Cause in a message dated September 1958:

> The need of our fellowmen to hear the Glad-Tidings of Bahá'u'lláh is greater than ever. The doors to pioneering, to the construction of the Mother Temples called for in the Ten Year Plan, to the founding of Bahá'í schools, to the dissemination of our literature, to the erection of our administrative institutions, still stand open. Before some world catastrophe closes them devastatingly, albeit temporarily, in our faces, let us not waste one precious moment![105]

To be sure, profound changes had to necessarily occur to release the potentialities of the new eon, some of them as formidable – and as ample in their scope – as those that led to the downfall of the Roman Empire, the birth of the Islamic civilization, or the welding together of the Great Republic of the North. The following text, dated in 1931, illustrates this perspective:

> That the forces of a world catastrophe can alone precipitate such a new phase of human thought is, alas, becoming increasingly apparent. That nothing short of the fire of a severe ordeal, unparalleled in its intensity, can fuse and weld the discordant entities that constitute the elements of present day civilization, into the integral components of the world commonwealth of the future, is a truth which future events will increasingly demonstrate.[106]

But, on the whole, the general pattern was one of a movement towards embracing, even if reluctantly, Bahá'u'lláh's principles. An active awaiting of the fulfilment of Bahá'u'lláh's promises was clearly incompatible with a pious passive stance or with the pinning of hopes on a sudden reversal of human fortunes, be it revolutionary or apocalyptical in nature. This being the case, it was only natural that Bahá'ís would further ponder what role the League of Nations and its successor could play in the deployment of the fledging structures envisioned by Bahá'u'lláh and 'Abdu'l-Bahá as part of that peace process.

17
The League of Nations and the United Nations

Since the Lesser Peace was mostly defined in terms of a political unification, entailing a degree of union between the world's constituent nations, it seems pertinent to review how Shoghi Effendi outlined this course. As already stated, Shoghi Effendi's view of history was that of a progressive, slow and painful unfolding of mankind's potentialities through a process of successive 'incorporations', which, similar to the process of progressive revelation, appear to be intimately interlocked:

> Just as the organic evolution of mankind has been slow and gradual, and involved successively the unification of the family, the tribe, the city-state, and the nation, so has the light vouchsafed by the Revelation of God, at various stages in the evolution of religion, and reflected in the successive Dispensations of the past, been slow and progressive.[107]

While, contemplated from this vantage point, the general orientation of history towards its promised destiny was therefore not in doubt, resistance to it and the refusal to give up the fetish of national sovereignty could be regarded as major causes of mankind's present suffering. In 1936 Shoghi Effendi wrote:

> Unification of the whole of mankind is the hall-mark of the stage which human society is now approaching. Unity of family, of tribe, of city-state, and nation have been successively attempted and fully established. World unity is the goal towards which a harassed humanity is striving. Nation-building has come to an end. The anarchy inherent in state sovereignty is moving towards a climax. A world, growing to maturity, must abandon this fetish, recognize the oneness and wholeness of human relationships, and establish once for all the machinery that can best incarnate this fundamental principle of its life.[108]

The above text seems to take up 'Abdu'l-Bahá's idea of 'collective centres' (*jahat-i-jámi'ih)* a step further in that it lays unprecedented stress on the shallowness of national sovereignty.[109] To be sure, all collective centres have a positive role to play in their own degree and level. 'Abdu'l-Bahá enumerates some of these:

> In the contingent world there are many collective centres which are conducive to association and unity between the children of men. For example, patriotism (*vaṭaníyat*) is a collective centre; nationalism (*millíyat*) is a collective centre; identity of interests (*ittiḥád-i-manáfi'*) is a collective centre; political alliance (*vaḥdat-i-síyásíyih*) is a collective centre; the union of ideals (*vaḥdat-i-afkár*) is a collective centre . . .[110]

But the positive result of these centres is effective only to the extent that they allow for the operation of the Collective Centre of the Kingdom. This, being eternal, is said to embody 'the institutions and divine teachings', and is inclusive of 'other collective centres'. It is this supreme collective centre that 'establishes relationship between the East and the West, organizes the oneness of the world of humanity, and destroys the foundation of differences'.[111] By analogy, the family, the tribe, the city-state and the nation represent successive collective centres that must now give way to the next and much overdue phase of instituting a supranational identity.

Shoghi Effendi takes this as a given, making no attempt at describing how each of those former embodiments of unity had 'evolved' into yet more complex forms of social organization. A rudiment of such an explanation can be found with regard to the latter phase, which is to take nation-statehood into a world federation. Thus, Shoghi Effendi links the development of 'nationhood' as one of the 'distinguishing characteristics of the Muḥammadan Dispensation, in the course of which the nations and races of the world, and particularly in Europe and America, were unified and achieved political independence'.[112] This view was elaborated upon in a letter where mention is made of the Islamic tradition calling for love of one's country as an element of faith:

> In the 'Gleanings', page 95 (third printing Jan. 1943) Bahá'u'lláh says: – 'Of old it has been revealed: Love of one's country is an element of the Faith of God!' Here Bahá'u'lláh is quoting not the Qur'án but an Islamic tradition, and it is this statement which the Guardian has used as the basis of his argument in the 'Promised Day' that nationhood grew out of the direct influence of Muḥammad's teachings, and was one of the great contributions to mankind's evolution of Islam. The building up of nations came after Muḥammad, and was a step forward in the direction of a unified world which the teachings of Bahá'u'lláh has [sic] provided for.[113]

But nation-building as a principle of international relationships had ceased being the decisive constructive factor in mankind's evolution. Quite on the contrary, resistance to some form of supra-nationality (and eventually a super-state), particularly on the basis of the nation's inalienable sovereignty, was repudiated by Shoghi Effendi in most emphatic terms, as seen in the two key sentences: 'The anarchy inherent in state sovereignty is moving towards a climax. A world, growing to maturity, must abandon this fetish . . .'[114] In consequence, the fundamental principle governing modern life was the 'oneness and wholeness of human relationships'.[115] For this reason it was all the more necessary to establish some 'machinery' conformable to that recognition. To do otherwise was tantamount to mankind's inflicting upon itself all the rigours of a useless discipline with none of its former advantages.[116] The League of Nations was in this regard an important step:

> Though the great out-cry raised by post-war nationalism is growing louder and more insistent every day, the League of Nations is as yet in its embryonic state, and the storm clouds that are gathering may for a time totally eclipse its powers and obliterate its machinery, yet the direction in which the institution itself is operating is most significant.[117]

The League of Nations was to be regarded as the precursor of the World Tribunal foreshadowed by Bahá'u'lláh.[118] However, from the outset this great institution lacked many of the features that could have enabled it to become an effective arbitrator,[119] such as its lack of universality: 'The League of Nations, its opponents will observe, still lacks the universality which is the prerequisite of abiding success in the efficacious settlement of international disputes.'[120] Moreover, the League of Nations was framed in a political context, the Treaty of Versailles, which by imposing terms of 'monstrous' severity on Germany, left open too many wounds to be healed in the normal course of time.[121]

In 1924 France pressed for the signing of a Protocol for the peaceful solution of international conflicts. England endorsed it at the League's Council; but a month later, following a disputed election campaign, this same decision was revoked by the newly elected conservative government. In 1927, when the optimism of the Locarno spirit was still very much alive, the 'inevitability' of 'yet another deadly encounter' was obvious to Shoghi Effendi.[122] Renewed attempts were made by France and the United States to provide for a more consistent mechanism of enforcing sanctions, yet the 'universal pact of non-aggression' met with disappointment. Shoghi Effendi's criticism about the League of Nations was then unambiguous:

> Observe the fierce and as yet unsilenced dispute which the proposal for the introduction of a binding and universal pact of non-aggression among the nations of Europe has aroused among the avowed supporters of the League of Nations – a League so auspiciously welcomed for the ideal that prompted its birth, yet now so utterly inadequate in the actual principles that underlie its present-day structure and working. And yet in the outcry raised by post-war nationalism in blindly defending and upholding the unfettered supremacy of its own sovereignty, and in repudiating unreservedly the conception of a world super-state, can we not discern the re-enactment only on a larger scale of the dramatic struggles that heralded the birth of the reconstructed and unified nations of the West?[123]

In March 1936, while deploring the defection of the United States, Germany and Japan, which had rendered the League of Nations totally ineffective, and in view of the measures adopted against Germany and Italy, Shoghi Effendi was prompted to welcome the decision to impose sanctions, stating that:

> so important a decision marks one of the most distinctive milestones on the long and arduous road that must lead it to its goal, the stage at which the *oneness of the whole body of nations will be made the ruling principle of international life*.[124] (emphasis added)

Shoghi Effendi considered that the principle of collective security outlined by Bahá'u'lláh had for the first time in history been upheld. More than fifty nations had unequivocally condemned the actions of one of the major European powers (i.e. Italy), imposed sanctions against the aggressor, and to some extent succeeded in carrying out their decisions:

> For the first time in the history of humanity the system of collective security, foreshadowed by Bahá'u'lláh and explained by 'Abdu'l-Bahá, has been seriously envisaged, discussed and tested. For the first time in history it has been officially recognized and publicly stated that for this system of collective security to be effectively established strength and elasticity are both essential – strength involving the use of an adequate force to ensure the efficacy of the proposed system, and elasticity to enable the machinery that has been devised to meet the legitimate needs and aspirations of its aggrieved upholders. For the first time in human history tentative efforts have been exerted by the nations of the world to assume collective responsibility, and to supplement their verbal pledges by actual preparation for collective action. And again, for the first time in history, a movement of public opinion has manifested itself in support of the verdict which the leaders and representatives of nations have pronounced, and for securing collective action in pursuance of such a decision.[125]

Despite this signal precedent for greater things to come, Shoghi Effendi had no delusions as to the likely outcome of these efforts. His sober appraisal of its shortcomings and the overall trend towards greater disorder leaves no room for doubting what his assessment of the situation was:

> This historic step, however, is but a faint glimmer in the darkness that envelops an agitated humanity. It may well prove to be no more than a flash, a fugitive gleam, in the midst of an ever-deepening confusion. The process of disintegration must inexorably continue, and its corrosive influence must penetrate deeper and deeper into the very core of a crumbling age. Much suffering will be required ere the contending nations, creeds, classes and races of mankind are fused in the crucible of universal affliction, and are forged by the fires of a fierce

> ordeal into one organic commonwealth, one vast, unified, and harmoniously functioning system. Adversities unimaginably appalling, undreamed of crises and upheavals, war, famine, and pestilence, might well combine to engrave in the soul of an unheeding generation those truths and principles which it has disdained to recognize and follow. A paralysis more painful than any it has yet experienced must creep over and further afflict the fabric of a broken society ere it can be rebuilt and regenerated.[126]

Five years later, in 1941 the opening page of *The Promised Day Is Come* was a summary of all the above, only now the description, of apocalyptic overtones, referred to contemporary events.

On the whole Shoghi Effendi's views remained unchanged after World War II.[127] The United Nations system brought about chiefly by the victors was positively valued by Shoghi Effendi, but not so much for its intrinsic merits as for the trend the new institution was marking and the opportunities it could afford the Bahá'í community. References to the United Nations were even scantier than those dealing with its predecessor, and were mostly concerned either with the tightening of ties between the Bahá'í International Community and the United Nations, or with the ascending role of the United States in international affairs. The fact that humanity seemed to have taken no stock of the lessons drawn by World War II was no obstacle for Bahá'ís throwing their weight in support of the newly born institution. From a very early date, in effect, Bahá'í delegations participated in several regional non-governmental conferences.[128] The Bahá'í International Community was accorded consultative status,[129] and concerted plans were adopted in order to secure protection for the Bahá'ís in Iran and other countries through the United Nations. The increasingly important contribution of the Bahá'í International Community to the United Nations was to result in the submission of statements to its various bodies. The first in this series with a significant impact was 'A Bahá'í Declaration of Human Obligations and Rights' presented to the first session of the United Nations Commission on Human Rights. Its opening paragraph delineated an argument for human rights and obligations based on the recognition of a divine 'endowment' (*amánat*), a concept with deep rooting in Bahá'í metaphysics and resonances in numerous texts, not the least the invocation paragraph of the *Secret of Divine Civilization*:

> The source of human rights is the endowment of qualities, virtues and powers which God has bestowed upon mankind without discrimination of sex, race, creed or nation. To fulfil the possibilities of this divine endowment is the purpose of human existence.[130]

But no statement was perhaps more illustrative in this sense than the 1955 proposal by the Bahá'í International Community, which envisaged important amendments to some key articles in the UN Charter, amounting to a complete overhaul of the

Security Council (suppression of the veto power, reduction of its membership), and a democratization of the General Assembly through the introduction of a corrective principle of proportionality according to population. The International Court of Justice was to be given authority to extend its jurisdiction to all legal interstate disputes, while the Military Staff Committee would become answerable to a revamped nine-member Security Council.[131] Being a proposal contemporary with Shoghi Effendi, it can be confidently expected that its tenor was given his full approval.

In this connection the Palestinian issue had also important implications for the Bahá'í community. During World War II Palestine had been under constant threat. The balance between the Jewish and Arab populations was shifting, and alliances with the European contending parties created an unstable state of affairs. The Battle of Alamein made it possible for Palestine to remain under the former British protectorate, thus averting the serious dangers hanging over the Bahá'í sites.[132] Later, a Special United Nations Committee, to which Shoghi Effendi made a submission, gave due recognition to the international and religious character of the Bahá'í Holy Places and its administrative centre.[133] This major step, although not unprecedented,[134] consolidated a pattern of constructive relationships with UN authorities upon which Shoghi Effendi laid great emphasis. In line with these efforts, in 1952, Shoghi Effendi included the strengthening of bonds with the United Nations as one of the major goals of the Ten Year Crusade (1953–1963).[135] To some extent the consolidation of the Administrative Centre of the Bahá'í Faith in the Holy Land, the strengthening of ties with the United Nations, and the emergence of the State of Israel were all part of a synchronized process.[136]

18
The Role of America

As seen previously, 'Abdu'l-Bahá entertained great hopes for the North American continent and its role as the standard bearer of the Lesser Peace. Shoghi Effendi did nothing but confirm them. A brief mention in *God Passes By*, for instance, refers to Bahá'u'lláh's 'significant summons to the Chief Magistrates of the New World, forerunner of the Mission with which the North American continent was to be later invested'.[137] A clear distinction, however, was made between the American people as a whole and the North American Bahá'í community. In a letter dated June 1947 Shoghi Effendi referred once again to the existence of two processes. On the one hand, the American Bahá'í community – he said – was the chief executor of 'Abdu'l-Bahá's plan as contained in the *Tablets of the Divine Plan,* a series of letters instructing the North American believers to spread the Bahá'í message throughout the continent, and from there to the rest of the world.[138] The American Bahá'ís were made thereby responsible for the dissemination and consolidation of the entire Bahá'í administrative system,[139] a mission that was to be crowned with the 'world establishment of the Cause of Bahá'u'lláh' in 1963, and was to continue in successive epochs.[140]

As for the United States, its coming of age was a direct consequence of its involvement in World War I and the subsequent formulation of Wilson's fourteen points.[141] The withdrawal from the League of Nations was its 'first setback'[142]; but the outbreak of World War II re-established links between the American continent and the Old World. The process:

> was further reinforced through the declaration embodied in the Atlantic Charter . . . It assumed a definite outline through the birth of the United Nations at the San Francisco Conference. It acquired significance through the choice of the City of the Covenant [New York] itself as the seat of the newly born organization . . . as well as through the submission to the General Assembly of the United Nations of the thorny and challenging problem of the Holy Land, the spiritual as well as the administrative centre of the World Faith of Bahá'u'lláh.[143]

Shoghi Effendi completed this panorama with a sober description of what was to follow:

> It [the process] must, however long and tortuous the way, lead, through a series of victories and reverses, to political unification of the Eastern and Western Hemispheres, to the emergence of a world government and the establishment of the Lesser Peace, as foretold by Bahá'u'lláh and foreshadowed by the Prophet Isaiah. It must, in the end, culminate in the unfurling of the banner of the Most Great Peace, in the Golden Age of the Dispensation of Bahá'u'lláh.[144]

On the basis of the expansion of the North American Bahá'í Community and that of the American nation, Shoghi Effendi drew a series of parallels. But his words were not aimed at creating a false sense of nationalistic pride.[145] Indeed the road which was to lead America to its destiny was 'long, thorny and tortuous', as pointed out in 1947:

> The impact of various forces upon the structure and polity of that nation will be tremendous. Tribulations, on a scale unprecedented in its history, and calculated to purge its institutions, to purify the hearts of its people, to fuse its constituent elements, and to weld it into one entity with its sister nations in both hemispheres, are inevitable.[146]

The participation of the United States of America in the First and Second World Wars was characteristically appraised by Shoghi Effendi as having

> redressed the balance, saved mankind the horrors of devastation and bloodshed involved in the prolongation of hostilities, and decisively contributed, in the course of the latter conflict, to the overthrow of the exponents of ideologies fundamentally at variance with the universal tenets of our Faith.[147]

The United States had not only provided assistance at these crucial junctures, it had also contributed other elements which, from a Bahá'í point of view, were worth being imitated and required further enhancement. Notably, the principle of federalism,[148],responsible for the effective union of the states, could well be applied to international relationships on a larger scale. But it rested on the American nation whether she was:

> prepared to play a preponderating role, as foretold by 'Abdu'l-Bahá, in the hoisting of the standard of the Lesser Peace, in the unification of mankind, and in the establishment of a world federal government on this planet.[149]

Writing in 1936, Shoghi Effendi described the earth as transformed into an 'armed camp'; ominous threats were looming on the horizon and America was ever closer to being caught in its ordeals. Shoghi Effendi's hope was that, unlike the events following World War I, those following the next war would see America seizing its opportunity 'to bring the full weight of its influence to bear upon the gigantic problems that such an ordeal must leave in its wake':

> Then, and only then, will the American nation, molded and purified in the crucible of a common war, inured to its rigours, and disciplined by its lessons, be in a position to raise its voice in the councils of the nations, itself lay the corner-stone of a universal and enduring peace, proclaim the solidarity, the unity, and maturity of mankind, and assist in the establishment of the promised reign of righteousness on earth. Then, and only then, will the American nation, while the community of the American believers within its heart is consummating its divinely appointed mission, be able to fulfil the unspeakably glorious destiny ordained for it by the Almighty, and immortally enshrined in the writings of 'Abdu'l-Bahá. Then, and only then, will the American nation accomplish 'that which will adorn the pages of history', 'become the envy of the world and be blest in both the East and the West'.[150]

Yet, to succeed in such an enterprise the North American nation had to overcome several major challenges confronting it. One was the temptation of retreating into isolationist positions, the much lamented price for which had been the abandonment of the Wilsonian ideal and the consequent doom of the League of Nations.[151] The American paradox was that in a world already contracted 'into a neighbourhood', where oceans had 'shrinked into channels', there was no retreat for the Great Republic of the West:

> The world is contracting into a neighbourhood. America, willingly or unwillingly, must face and grapple with this new situation. For purposes of national security, let alone any humanitarian motive, she must assume the obligations imposed by this newly created neighbourhood. Paradoxical as it may seem, her only hope of extricating herself from the perils gathering around her is to become entangled in that very web of international association which the Hand of an inscrutable Providence is weaving. 'Abdu'l-Bahá's counsel to a highly placed official in its government comes to mind, with peculiar appropriateness and force. 'You can best serve your country if you strive, in your capacity as a citizen of the world, to assist in the eventual application of the principle of federalism, underlying the government of your own country, to the relationships now existing between the peoples and nations of the world.'[152]

The United States would have to come to terms with its own international stature and assume a preponderating role 'for purposes of national security, let alone any humanitarian motive'. Yet, for this to be really meaningful, a truly internationalist outlook had to inform its policies. The notion of extending the principle of federalism to world relations, as conveyed by Shoghi Effendi, inexorably implied the admission on the part of the greatest world power of a yet greater and nobler loyalty to humanity, and a matching disposition to shape the instruments that would progressively weld together a new community of nations. If the 'beacon [isolationist]-crusader [commitment to international affairs]' metaphor used by

Kissinger serves as a guide,[153] it is clear that the advice given by Shoghi Effendi transcended in many ways the idealist 'crusader' role, in as much as the Bahá'í emphasis not only situated the interest of the whole of mankind first, but also saw a future beyond, though not incompatible with, the sovereign state. Writing in 1954, an already disappointed Shoghi Effendi described the ills of American society without mincing his words:

> The woes and tribulations which threaten it are partly avoidable, but mostly inevitable and God-sent, for by reason of them a government and people clinging tenaciously to the obsolescent doctrine of absolute sovereignty and upholding a political system, manifestly at variance with the needs of a world already contracted into a neighbourhood and crying out for unity, will find itself purged of its anachronistic conceptions . . .[154]

A second major problem, racism, was particularly abhorrent in Shoghi Effendi's eyes. 'A revolutionary change in the concept and attitude of the average white American towards his Negro fellow citizen' was sorely needed.[155] If this threat was not properly handled – was his warning – there would be extremely serious consequences for the American social fabric.[156] Bahá'ís were called upon to do their utmost to uproot any trace of racial prejudice from their own ranks and to conduct themselves in society accordingly. A typical Bahá'í institutional answer to this challenge was the world unity meetings.[157]

19

Peace-makers or Pacifists?

As the Bahá'í Administrative Order was gaining a firm footing in Iran and in the North American continent, matters pertaining to private conduct or in connection with the work of the Bahá'ís in society necessitated further clarification. Were Bahá'ís allowed to become conscientious objectors? Was the Bahá'í community a pacifist movement? Could Bahá'ís carry arms and retaliate in self-defence? Were Bahá'ís allowed to join the pro-constitutionalist Iranian forces? The latter question could be answered by a direct appeal to the principle of obedience to one's government, which, though grounded on the provisions of the Kitáb-i-Aqdas ('Take heed not to stir up mischief in the land after it hath been set in order'),[158] 'Abdu'l-Bahá had articulated conclusively in His treatise on politics (*Risáliy-i-Síyasíyyih*). As for the issue of self-defence and the carrying of arms, again the provisions of the Aqdas required no special elaboration. Moreover, the tradition of non-retaliatory responses in Iran, where the martyr spirit of resignation was alive, and the example set by 'Abdu'l-Bahá in the Holy Land enduring at times most precarious conditions, were sufficient guidelines.

However, when these elements were combined with the Bahá'í stand on military service and the ethics of not killing, the matter required a careful reassessment of the place of personal conscience with regards to the principle of compliance with the law and loyalty to one's faith. Perceptions among the American Bahá'ís on peace had been shaped as much by their socio-political circumstances as by the prophetic words of 'Abdu'l-Bahá during His visit when the inevitability of a great war was presented as a foregone conclusion and the addresses given at the peace societies in New York and Lake Mohonk were still fresh in the minds of His Bahá'í audience. Bahá'ís were also familiar with the non-retaliatory system advocated for the treatment of criminals, and the need to avoid violent behaviour when confronted with aggression.[159] The North American tour of 'Abdu'l-Bahá had acted as a catalyst for peace awareness. For all this, however, the nascent North American community was almost entirely on its own when faced with the quandary of deciding its 'involvement' in the war effort. Cut off from contact with 'Abdu'l-Bahá and caught up in the dilemma of supporting the war, the American Bahá'í community stressed obedience to government, yet vacillated in its position from a pro-war stand (after all that was the war to end all wars), to withdrawing its endorsement.[160] This issue became somewhat of a controversial matter. Bahá'ís had been quite active in their advocacy of peace and, when World War I broke out, of a mediated peace. America's coming into play in 1917 divided the peace movement and cast a shadow of suspicion on peace activists, including Bahá'ís, who were now subject to investigation by the Justice Department even well after the war. The word 'pacifist' soon gained an unpleasant ring.[161] At the root of this dilemma was the fact that much stress had been placed on two principles: loyalty to one's government, and non-involvement in politics.[162] Ideally both were fully compatible, but in war situations the tension between the two was brought to its very limits and further compounded by the moral issue of the taking of life. Moreover, a shift of positions, from upholding a pacifist stance to supporting America's going to war, although a coherent move reflecting obedience to the government, was such as to raise suspicions anyway from both sides of the equation.

Furthermore, at variance with other Christian-based denominations, the American Bahá'ís did not share in the strong non-conformist tradition of anti-statism and anti-Church sentiments. Instead, they relied on a self-image conveying the distinct impression that Bahá'ís were basically a movement of law-abiding citizens concerned with spiritual and humanitarian matters, but lacking the more radical stand of Quakers, Jehovah's Witnesses and other religious denominations which did not accept middle-ground positions. In a state of war, such differences, however apparent, tended to be blurred or simply appeared to be immaterial to outside observers. Doubtless, with this background in mind Shoghi Effendi clarified the issue of military service by establishing a clear dividing line. In countries which provided for the possibility of exemption from military service, Bahá'ís were counselled to avail themselves of this avenue. Failing this, they were advised to request serving in a non-combatant capacity.[163] The justification for this general stand had much more to do with the lack of an 'International Police Force' than with a compromise between personal conscience and obedience to one's government. Here again the Bahá'í position appeared distinctive:

> As there is neither an International Force nor any immediate prospect of one coming into being, the Bahá'ís should continue to apply, *under all circumstances,* for exemption from any military duties that necessitate the taking of life.[164] (emphasis added)

But even this alignment could be potentially seen as a threat to the stability of a given country, particularly in emergency or war situations. Beyond this there was no middle term, as stated by Shoghi Effendi in a cablegram:

> No change whatsoever in status of Bahá'ís in relation to active military duty. No compromise of spiritual principles of Faith possible however tense the situation, however aroused public opinion.[165]

The provisional character of the Bahá'í stand, pending the creation of an International Force, was a clear indication that the main objection was not so much to the use of force by the authorities, but to lack of collective security arrangements that would provide minimum ethical standards for the use of force. Implicit in this was a deeper philosophical divide between 'extreme pacifists' and Bahá'ís:

> Extreme pacifists are thus very close to the anarchists, in the sense that both of these groups lay an undue emphasis on the rights and merits of the individual. The Bahá'í conception of social life is essentially based on the subordination of the individual will to that of society. It neither suppresses the individual nor does it exalt him to the point of making him an anti-social creature, a menace to society.[166]

Congruous with this view was also the idea that peace could not be achieved by the mere radiation of peace thoughts. In a letter written on behalf of Shoghi Effendi this point was made equally apparent:

> I might add that he does not believe any radiations of thought or healing, from any group, is going to bring peace. Prayer, no doubt, will help the world, but what it needs is to accept Bahá'u'lláh's system so as to build up the World Order on a new foundation, a divine foundation![167]

Similarly, Bahá'ís were given general guidelines as to whether they could carry arms. This practice was not permissible except in very exceptional circumstances, for instance when living in remote areas lacking police protection, or the like.[168] Bahá'í children, so often an easy target of public abuse and bashings, particularly in Iran and Middle Eastern countries, were encouraged to avoid adopting measures of 'active self-defence', but not to the extent of passively accepting their own vilification.[169] Similarly, the Bahá'í community as a whole was to articulate progressively strategies to defend itself from persecution. A present development in that direction and in the context of responses to persecution in Iran or to calamitous events, man-made or otherwise, has been the framing of the concept of 'constructive resilience'. This concept is described by Karlberg as 'pioneering a radical new model of social change – entirely non-adversarial in nature – that appears initially to be viable even in the face of violent oppression'.[170]

20
Conclusion

Shoghi Effendi's life work was devoted to the task of shaping the Bahá'í community into a worldwide, well established religion. Through a series of carefully designed plans, supported by a strong Iranian following and led by a hyperactive North American Bahá'í community of scarcely two thousand followers, local and national Bahá'í communities sprang into existence all over the world. This missionary enterprise, regarded as the implementation of the main 'charters'[171] of the Bahá'í revelation, was aimed at laying out the foundations of the Universal House of Justice, whose election was to culminate the main framework of the Bahá'í Administrative Order.

In his capacity as expounder of the Bahá'í teachings Shoghi Effendi clarified the meaning of the 'administrative machinery'; he pointed out the interdependent nature binding the spiritual and administrative work; and presented an authorized interpretation of the teachings of Bahá'u'lláh and their significance vis-á-vis the world and its history. All this, in its turn, involved an immense amount of effort in several directions, especially in providing general guidance, securing the Bahá'í Holy Places, planning the spread and consolidation of the community, and translating. Shoghi Effendi's vision of history as a drama staged in successive epochs, and marked by an alternation of crises and victories leading to the promised Golden Age, was the basic pattern that Bahá'ís could identify in the unfolding of sacred history. Religions, or rather the revelations brought by God's Messengers, had been preparing humanity through stages for a climax at a time where it would reach maturity and be able to recognize itself as one. The Lesser Peace, as an expression of the underlying oneness of mankind, was identified as a process that would gradually move humanity from endorsing the fetish of national sovereignty to a unified transnational polity. This process was not an outcome of Bahá'í activity, but it would synchronize with the maturation of their international, national and local institutions. Peace would not be easily attainable, however. If religious history was an index to go by, only through ordeals and strenuous collective efforts would humanity adopt the decisions required to embody its supranational character. Historical parallels showed that adaptation to new realities was often precipitated by corresponding convulsions, out of necessity rather than as a result of virtue. Even a third apocalyptic upheaval was not an improbable prospect in view of the shortcomings attending the creation of the new post-war order.[172] The Most Great Peace appeared as an inchoate but rather distant prospect set to coincide with the spiritualization of the world and the constitution of a Bahá'í Commonwealth of Nations.

In the process, related issues of great significance were clarified by Shoghi Effendi. The role of America was once again reasserted with sharper and more powerful statements which, while contradicting much of the long-held doctrine of the manifest destiny, yet confirmed the aptness of the American nation, itself a model for the reunification of mankind under a federal system, to lead the way of a desperate world. Likewise, the Bahá'í position with regard to contentious issues such as conscription, self-defence and the carrying of arms were equally elucidated in ways which placed the Bahá'í community in a position clearly distinct from 'pacifism' or from mere compliance with or subservience to state rules.

Shoghi Effendi was weary of attempts by Bahá'ís to leave the Bahá'í work undone for the sake of joining many other worthy causes.[173] A convergence of efforts was ultimately possible, but in the interim Bahá'ís had the major duty of rearing the seed of Bahá'u'lláh's embryonic order, which, as a working model, contained much of what the world would need to assimilate in order to transform itself into a peaceful world society. The transitional stages which the Bahá'í community would undergo through a series of well designed plans offered a sharp contrast with the major disruptions that the broader society would perforce experience.[174] This was not to mean, however, that there were no connections between the two processes. Bahá'ís did not live in an isolated environment, nor were they exempt from the tests and trials afflicting their fellowmen, as the very course of 'crisis and victory', and learning through 'trial and error' was to underscore. The increasing imbrication between the Bahá'í community and the world at large suggested that at one point the parallel processes would make contact, intersecting more frequently and in increasingly more fruitful ways. The synchronizing of events inside and outside the Bahá'í community, with the Lesser Peace going side by side with the very maturation of the Bahá'í Administrative Order, exemplifies more clearly how this complex dialectics would in the end lead to a more extensive overlapping between the two.

PART IV

THE NATURE OF MAN IN THE BAHÁ'Í WRITINGS

> Endeavour, ceaseless endeavour, is required. Nothing short of an indomitable determination can possibly achieve it. Many a cause which past ages have regarded as purely visionary, yet in this day has become most easy and practicable.[1]

As implied in the aforementioned words, the achievement of the international collective security system outlined by Bahá'u'lláh, 'Abdu'l-Bahá and Shoghi Effendi was construed as belonging in the category of visionary 'world undertakings'[2] that humanity would ultimately have to embrace, however reluctantly. The conquering of universal peace was elevated in the mind and words of 'Abdu'l-Bahá to the status of the one defining element of the twentieth century, 'the crying need of the time'. Just as the nineteenth century had witnessed a colossal struggle for freedom, peace had to become the 'predominating problem':

> Every century holds the solution of one predominating problem . . . In the past century the most important question that occupied the mind of man was the establishment of political freedom, and this aim was more or less broadcast. But in this luminous century the greatest bestowal of the world of humanity is universal peace.[3]

Yet the attainment and prosecution of collective security was, as explained in previous chapters, but one fundamental element within the scope of a wider synchronous 'peace process' (*ṣulḥ*) including such key developments as women's full incorporation into world affairs, the universalization of education, a more proactive and genuinely multi-lateralist America, the gradual reconciliation of religions, and a balanced view of the relationship between science and religion. The magnitude of the peace thus contemplated was linked with the eschatological promises of a world filled with knowledge where irreconcilable opposites were at long last overcome or harmonized (swords into ploughshares).

While titanic human efforts are recognized as necessary if this vision is to come to fruition, the enabling energies required for this colossal transformation are to be found in the largely ignored potentialities of the new Covenant. For, in essence, the kernel of this mysterious evolution of mankind through successive Dispensations is of a mystic type, with ramifications extending far and wide; an evolution in which revelation plays a sun-like, logocentric function of saturation whereby the Word of God imparts life to a 'new garden':

> Verily, all created things were immersed in the sea of purification when, on that first day of Riḍvan, We shed upon the whole of creation the splendours of Our most excellent Names and Our most exalted Attributes.[4]

Long-lasting peace, in the end, is not only a property of the true sovereignty that God wields over humanity, or otherwise expresses the fulfilment of His eschatological promises, but is also an effect of the 'purification' and 'renewal' whereby human beings are empowered to look afresh at the fabric of reality without being subjected to the tyranny of the past and its obsolete views. At an elementary level this transformation must take effect in the heart of the individual and then be reaffirmed as a societal given. War and anarchy, long held as the default realities, need to be counteracted by a reaffirmation of peace and order as the normative starting points. But if this process of spiritual globalization is to succeed an explanation must be advanced as to how individuals, being what they are, or have been historically, can overcome violence, conflicts and war. After all, 'Abdu'l-Bahá had clearly indicated that 'peace (*ṣulḥ va salám*) must first be established among individuals (*afrád-i-insání*), until it leadeth in the end to peace among nations (*ṣulḥ-i-'umúmí*)'.[5]

In the following sections an attempt will be made at exploring the Bahá'í view of man, his twofold – or threefold – nature, as well as two major subthemes, namely man's dignity and perfectibility. The resulting 'image', to use Waltz's language,[6] reveals a clear contrast with the static view of man in which variations such as war and peace, aggression or peaceful behaviour, are posited as historical constants that can at most be managed or controlled through an array of external means. It also contrasts with other religious views which situate the approaching of the kingdom and its peace in either a continually receding future, or more squarely in the afterlife. In the Bahá'í view human nature is seen not as an admixture or a given of bad and good, but as a relational *faciendum*, an unfolding reality which, like society, has the capacity to evolve into a more polished mirroring of its original God-given models. This capacity to acquire virtues and perfections, which extends to all created things without exception, is what may in the end transform the individual both in her inner and outer being giving rise in the process to a divine civilization. Thus, the internal peace of the person, like her salvation, is incomplete without the peace and orderly life of the social milieu, a point most conspicuously made by Bahá'u'lláh when he declared the need to move towards a salvation of mankind.[7]

For the purposes of this presentation preferential attention will be given to the writings of Bahá'u'lláh and the writings and talks of 'Abdu'l-Bahá, particularly with regard to the root causes of violence, which in Bahá'í terms appear closely linked to the operation of a series of counter-themes, namely 'prejudices', 'blind imitations' and 'vain imaginings'. These considerations will clear the way for the next chapter, in which an attempt will be made to identify the main features of the Bahá'í ethos.

21
A Spiritual Anthropology

The study of the place of man in the universe requires both a cosmology (or at least an implicit view or theory about the general order of all things, i.e. nature, the universe) and an anthropology (an implicit assumption about the place man occupies in that order). The following excerpt from the writings of Bahá'u'lláh provides a suitable starting point for a presentation addressing both aspects:

> Whatsoever in the contingent world (*rutbiy-i-mumkin*) can either be expressed or apprehended, can never transgress the limits which, by its inherent nature, have been imposed upon it (*maḥdúd ast bi ḥudúdát-i-imkáníyyih*). God, alone, transcendeth such limitations.[8]

Here a contrast is established between divinity and the world of creation at large. While God remains free from all contingencies, being 'alone' and 'without partners' in his unicity, every created thing is subject to limits that shape them. The fact that human knowledge and its corresponding expressions are by their very nature limited is also underscored. This contrast is radical to the extent that it prevents believers from conceiving of God's essence after man's own image, in other words, in anthropomorphic terms.[9]

As noted by Mircea Eliade, traditional religious images of the world share in the belief that physical reality is 'animated'. All things, including raw matter such as dust, rocks and pebbles, are meaningful and have a life of their own because they are rooted in some degree of the transcendent reality (divine spirit, grace, will of God)[10] which makes them inherently good and powerful. While distinct from God, nature is not separable from Him, as the following explanation by Bahá'u'lláh makes obvious:

> Nature in its essence is the embodiment of My Name, the Maker, the Creator. Its manifestations are diversified by varying causes, and in its diversity there are signs (*áyát*) for men of discernment. Nature is God's Will (*irádat*) and its expression (*ẓuhúr*) in and throughout the contingent world.[11]

Not only is the diversity of God's work inherent in the 'varying causes' which appear in it, it is also a source of 'signs' which 'men of discernment' must learn to recognize. Bahá'u'lláh stresses the bond between this diversity and the Creator by identifying nature with the Will of God and its expression in the contingent world:

> a world which is adorned with the splendours of the Ancient of Days, yet is being renewed and regenerated at all times. Immeasurably exalted is the God of Wisdom Who hath raised this sublime structure.[12]

The continuous renewal which takes place in the world describes the way nature manifests itself to the human observer, who, in contemplating the world as a 'book', reads out what 'the Fashioner, the All-Informed, hath inscribed therein'.[13] Interestingly, reading of the Book of creation in this fashion confers upon the 'reader' the capacity to 'become independent of every eloquent expounder'.[14] For the Word of God is the cause of everything in existence:

> The world of existence came into being through the heat generated from the interaction between the active force (*fá'il*) and that which is its recipient (*manfa'il*). These two are the same, yet they are different . . . Such as communicate the generating influence and such as receive its impact are indeed created through the irresistible Word (*kalíma*) of God which is the Cause of the entire creation, while all else besides His Word are but the creatures and the effects thereof.[15]

This conception of nature as a 'text' framed by the creative Word of God,[16] and set in motion by a continuous heat-generating process, suggests more clearly the notion of a world under constant re-creation and care rather than an autonomous entity with an existence of its own. Bahá'u'lláh alludes explicitly to this view, stating:

> Those who have rejected God and firmly cling to Nature as it is in itself are, verily, bereft of knowledge and wisdom.[17]

In reality, Nature cannot be seen 'as it is in itself' because the root principle of everything in existence is spiritual. From the perspective delineated by Bahá'u'lláh and 'Abdu'l-Bahá, the contingent world appears ordered into levels or degrees (*marátib*) of existence, each order being a dim reflection of what follows next in a higher level of existence. According to 'Abdu'l-Bahá:

> The worlds of God are in perfect harmony and correspondence one with another. Each world in this limitless universe is, as it were, a mirror reflecting the history and nature of all the rest. The physical universe is, likewise, in perfect correspondence with the spiritual or divine realm. The world of matter is an outer expression or facsimile of the inner kingdom of spirit. The world of minds corresponds with the world of hearts.[18]

By emphasizing, however, the singleness of God and the pervasiveness of His presence or influence everywhere, the Bahá'í doctrine of divine unity avoids any ascription of divinity to the creatures themselves after the pantheistic fashion:

> He is really a believer in the Unity of God (*tawḥíd*) who recognizeth in each and every created thing the sign of the revelation of Him Who is the Eternal Truth, and not he who maintaineth that the creature is indistinguishable from the Creator (*khalqrá Ḥaqq dánand*).[19]

To express belief in God is in most cases an explicit recognition of this truth,[20] while adoration is the state of servitude implied by such recognition. A human being is, therefore and above all, a 'creature' who tries to live within the confines and in accordance with such a consciousness, as a servant of God and humanity, for adoration towards God, as 'Abdu'l-Bahá writes, does not become effective except in ministering to His servants.[21] Any attribution of merit on the part of human beings is only possible to the extent that human actions are governed by and reflective of the 'tie of servitude':

> The tie of servitude established between the worshipper and the adored One, between the creature and the Creator, should in itself be regarded as a token of His gracious favour unto men, and not as an indication of any merit they may possess. To this testifieth every true and discerning believer.[22]

But how can this consciousness be secured in man? Human beings are not born wise and aware of their surroundings. The Bahá'í writings address this question by stating that man is endowed with a power – the gift of understanding (*'áql, khirád*)[23] – which can be put to good use because all created things, in reality, can be apprehended through the forms or signs shaping them. As 'Abdu'l-Bahá states:

> For every thing, however, God has created a sign and symbol (*'alá'im va áthárí*), and established standards and tests (*mihakk va imtahán*) by which it may be known.[24]

According to Bahá'u'lláh all things are but signs:

> He hath entrusted every created thing with a sign of His knowledge (*áyiy-i-'irfán-i-khudrá*), so that none of His creatures may be deprived of its share in expressing, each according to its capacity and rank (*miqdárih va marátibih*), this knowledge.[25]

Even the minutest formations on earth are endowed with sun-like powers, how much more so the human reality, which embraces all the attributes and perfections of the realms below:

> How resplendent the luminaries of knowledge that shine in an atom, and how vast the oceans of wisdom that surge within a drop! To a supreme degree is this true of man, who, among all created things, hath been invested with the robe of such gifts, and hath been singled out for the glory of such distinction.[26]

But things are not indexes of a greater or deeper reality in an all too evident manner. It is in their innermost heart that things become evidences pointing to God's names and attributes. While God 'knoweth all things', 'mortal man is prone to err, and is ignorant of the mysteries that lie enfolded within him'.[27] In the *Kitáb-i-Íqán* Bahá'u'lláh states:

> all things, in their inmost reality, testify to the revelation of the names and attributes of God (*asmá' va ṣifát-i-ilahíyyih*) within them. Each according to its capacity (*isti'idád-i-khud*), indicateth, and is expressive of, the knowledge of God (*ma'arifat-i-ilaḥíyyih*).[28]

The idea that things are endowed with a 'given' capacity and a corresponding 'rank' and limits indicates that reality is not an amorphous mass in a state of chaos, but an organic, moving whole, the constituents of which are ordered according to degrees and capacities.[29] It is this concept of movement which explains the need for a religious renewal,[30] or justifies showing respect for the body of the deceased in the form of interment, for the 'degradation' of the body must also be part of the entire natural process of decay and renewal.[31] The entire creation appears thus not only as an orderly sequence of states of being (stations, degrees, stages, planes, *maqámát, maráḥil, rutb, marátib)*, but also, as described by Aristotle,[32] as an interlinked chain or series of stages and kingdoms, leading towards spirituality, and as such propelled by an internal movement which is consubstantial with nature, for 'all created things are in motion'.[33] Also:

> This material world has an outward appearance, as it has also an inner reality. All created things are interlinked in a chain leading to spirituality and ultimately ending in abstract realities. I hope that these spiritual links will become stronger day by day and that this communication of hearts, which is termed inspiration, will continue. When this connection exists, bodily separation is not important; this condition is beyond the world of words and above all description.[34]

Furthermore, reality can also be said to consist of interconnected worlds which share in the same traits and display analogous forms resulting in a harmonious whole. The infinite array of forms that nature displays is held together by virtue of the connections and interactions binding all phenomena, be they large or small: 'As one's vision is broadened and the matter observed carefully, it will be made certain that every reality is but an essential requisite of other realities.'[35] This world of nature, moulded by 'interaction, cooperation and interrelation amongst beings',[36] is certainly a larger, subtler, more resilient and an even kinder reality than the reduced feral world of species that feed on each other, often proposed as a valid analogue of the human kingdom. Seen from this perspective, each world appears less as a self-contained unit than as a summary of the other worlds. The same relationship which obtains between the various physical realms is also applicable to physical matter and to the 'divine realm'.

The human body provides a stock analogy to illustrate the fact that different degrees are to be found in all the living expressions:

> Consider your own selves. Your nails and eyes are both parts of your bodies. Do ye regard them of equal rank and value (*rutbih va yik shán*)? If ye say, yea; say, then: ye have indeed charged with imposture the Lord, my God, the All-Glorious, inasmuch as ye pare the one, and cherish the other as dearly as your own life.[37]

Man's trust consists precisely in conducting his life accordingly. In this regard Bahá'u'lláh observes:

> To transgress the limits of one's own rank and station (*tajávuz az rutbih va maqám*) is, in no wise, permissible. The integrity of every rank and station must needs be preserved. By this is meant that every created thing should be viewed in the light of the station it hath been ordained to occupy.[38]

Preservation of things is made synonymous with having due regard for their intimate essence as made apparent by their corresponding position in the hierarchy of beings. Recognition of the existence of degrees is not merely then a classificatory device whereby things can be placed within relatively fixed confines. It is not, at any rate, an excuse for ascribing special authority, power or wealth to any such degrees, many of which are purely accidental:[39]

> Ever since the seeking of preference and distinction came into play, the world hath been laid waste. It hath become desolate . . . Indeed, man is noble, inasmuch as each one is a repository of the signs of God. Nevertheless to regard oneself as superior in knowledge, learning or virtue, or to exalt oneself or seek preference, is a grievous transgression.[40]

The resulting 'equality' is not only based on a pronounced ethics of service, but perhaps more importantly on an understanding of the spiritual nature of humans. This awareness transcends worldly limitations by casting them under a different light ('On this plane the highest heavens are neither opposed to, nor distinguished from, the lowly earth, for this is the realm of divine favours, not the arena of worldly contraries')[41], or see them as either surmountable through education, or of little or no account in the general scheme of things.

In reality, recognition of the existence of limits makes it possible for human beings to organize and make sense of their own experience. Their very perception is based on their capacity to recognize the shapes and contours of existing things. This seems to be implied in Bahá'u'lláh's repeated calls upon every created thing to 'recognize its capacity and limitations'.[42] But at the same time, this exercise in 'recognition' can be seen as a preliminary step to a transcending of the world of contrasting forms. The affirmation of diversity is then followed by a further recognition of the underlying unity that informs the varying realities. The Bahá'í writings insist on this double perspective:

> As to thy question whether the physical world is subject to any limitations, know thou that the comprehension of this matter dependeth upon the observer himself. In one sense, it is limited; in another, it is exalted beyond all limitations.[43]

Recognition of limits and condition is also a description of the course which the human soul must take in its journey from this world of earth and water to the realm of the spirit:

> The wisdom of the appearance of the spirit (*rúḥ*) in the body (*jasad*) is this: The human spirit is a divine trust (*vadí'iy-i-raḥmání*) which must traverse every degree, for traversing and passing through the degrees of existence (*marátib-i-vujúd*) is the means of its acquiring perfections (*kamalát*).[44]

Acquiring perfections is the ultimate goal of all forms of existence, and particularly of human beings, who by birth (that is, by virtue of what they essentially are) aspire to perfection and achieve true happiness only when they abide by it:

> As for the spiritual perfections they are man's birthright and belong to him alone of all creation. Man is, in reality, a spiritual being, and only when he lives in the spirit is he truly happy.[45]

The passage from one stage to another within one's own plane of existence is part of the process of spiritual evolution or inner perfecting which is so characteristic of all the worlds of God:

> [T]he growth and development of all beings proceeds by gradual degrees (*bi tadríj ast*). This is the universal and divinely ordained law (*qánún-i-kullíy-i-ilahí*) and the natural order (*naẓm-i-ṭabí'í*) . . . All beings, whether universal or particular, were created perfect and complete from the beginning. The most one can say is that their perfections only become apparent gradually. The law of God (*qánún-i-ilahí*) is one; the evolution of existence (*taraqíyyát-i-vujúdí*) is one; the divine order (*niẓam-i-ilahí*) is one. All beings great and small are subject to one law and one order. Every seed has, from the beginning, all the perfections of the plant.[46]

Man's three natures

But, if this is so, it seems appropriate to consider at which point human beings set out on their personal journey. In connection with this 'Abdu'l-Bahá explains that the human reality has two natures and both summarize or collapse various degrees;[47] one is the animal nature, in which all the perfections and attributes inherent in the mineral, vegetable and animal kingdoms are enfolded. This realm is related to the *animal soul,* understood as the 'animating' power which sustains all the bodily functions, urges and psycho-biological drives.

The second nature is properly speaking the human nature, and it is at this 'point' or 'realm' that human beings may initiate their particular journey towards God. Shoghi Effendi further clarifies that the 'consciousness of self in man is a gradual process, and does not start at a definite point. It grows in him in this world and continues to do so in the future spiritual world'.[48] The animating power empowering this nature is the 'soul' or *human spirit,* and the rational power or mind constitutes man's most distinguishing faculty, thanks to which man can rule over other creatures. This realm is intermediary in the sense that it is empowered to apply itself exclusively to the contingent world, or else can be illumined by the lights of God in order to become a mirrored image of the Kingdom of God (that is, the spiritual realm), which is man's third nature.

Therefore, it is peculiar to a human being that he or she should live in a dual tension. As 'Abdu'l-Bahá states:

> . . . man is the noblest of all existing things (*ashraf-i-mujúdát*).
>
> Man is the ultimate degree of materiality, and the beginning of spirituality (*dar niháyat-i-rutbiy-i-jismáníyyat ast va bidáyyat-i-rúḥáníyyát*); that is, he is at the end of imperfection and the beginning of perfection. He is at the furthermost degree of darkness and the beginning of the light. That is why the station of man is said to be the end of night and the beginning of day, meaning that he encompasses all the degrees of imperfection and that he potentially possesses all the degrees of perfection. He has both an animal side and an angelic side . . .[49]

On the basis of this distinction, it would be true to say either that man has two natures, or alternatively three natures,[50] depending on whether the animal and human natures are counted as separated or not, as opposed to the spiritual reality:

> Yet there is a third reality in man, the spiritual reality. Through its medium one discovers spiritual revelations, a celestial faculty which is infinite as regards the intellectual as well as physical realms. That power is conferred upon man through the breath of the Holy Spirit. It is an eternal reality, an indestructible reality, a reality belonging to the divine, supernatural kingdom; a reality whereby the world is illumined, a reality which grants unto man eternal life. This third, spiritual

> reality it is which discovers past events and looks along the vistas of the future. It is the ray of the Sun of Reality. The spiritual world is enlightened through it, the whole of the Kingdom is being illumined by it. It enjoys the world of beatitude, a world which had no beginning and which shall have no end.[51]

References to 'two' or 'three' natures can be justified by a shift of perspective along these lines. Thus, the word 'soul' (*nafs, rúḥ*) can be used indistinctly in references to the 'animal soul' or to the 'rational soul'. Reliance on the context for clarification of the intended meaning makes it sometimes difficult for the reader to identify the referent. In this regard 'Abdu'l-Bahá explains:

> The human spirit, which distinguishes man from the animal is the rational soul, and these two terms – the human spirit and the rational soul (*ruḥ-i-insání va nafs-i-nátiqih*) – designate one and the same thing.[52]

In other instances references are quite clear and reflect the three layers which form a human identity:

> The soul is a link between the body and the spirit. It receives bounties and virtues from the spirit and gives them to the body just as the outward senses carry to the inward senses what they receive from the outer world in order that it may remain deposited in the memory and may be made serviceable by man through his power.[53]

Man, then, appears as a bifrontal reality, halfway between the animal and the angelic, the accidental and the essential, in agreement with the principle 'the outward is the expression of the inward: The earthly realm is the mirror of the heavenly Kingdom, and the material world is in accordance with the spiritual world.'[54] The difference between man and the animal is that man has been empowered to consciously realize and voluntarily reflect God's image in himself:

> The human kingdom is replete with the perfections of all the kingdoms below it with the addition of powers peculiar to man alone. Man is, therefore, superior to all the creatures below him, the loftiest and most glorious being of creation. Man is the microcosm; and the infinite universe, the macrocosm. The mysteries of the greater world, or macrocosm, are expressed or revealed in the lesser world, the microcosm.[55]

Compared to other species man definitely enjoys a wider scope for expansion. Endowed with a powerful mind, he can 'transgress' the laws of nature, placing them to his personal advantage. But, here again, the notion of limit is applicable, not only in a moral and social sense, but also with regard to the possibilities of the human mind itself:

> It is through the power of the soul that the mind comprehendeth, imagineth and exerteth its influence, whilst the soul is a power that is free. The mind comprehendeth the abstract by the aid of the concrete, but the soul hath limitless manifestations of its own. The mind is circumscribed, the soul limitless. It is by the aid of such senses as those of sight, hearing, taste, smell and touch, that the mind comprehendeth, whereas the soul is free from all agencies.[56]

The human mind is unable to go beyond the knowledge of things. Its reflexivity can be multiplied ad infinitum, but left to its own devices cannot escape the limits imposed by the ephemeral. For it to reach scientific truths it must proceed by means of a lengthy, costly and sometimes unrewarding process of inquiry. This kind of knowledge is speculative, reflexive, and mental. The outward 'formal' or 'figural' knowledge (*'ilm-i-ṣúrí*) thereby attained is 'quite limited, as it is conditioned upon acquisition and attainment'.[57] Moreover, scientific knowledge is also subject to the law of change that defines life in this world:

> nothing is fixed, nothing final; everything is continually changing because human reason is progressing along new roads of investigation and arriving at new conclusions every day. In the future much that is announced and accepted as true now will be rejected and disproved. And so it will continue ad infinitum.[58]

The scientific method cannot operate otherwise. Scientists work on the basis of assumptions and hypotheses which if proven incorrect are readily dismissed:

> Unquestionably this will not satisfy men of science, for when they find premise or conclusion contrary to present standards of proof and without real foundation, they reject that which has been formerly accepted as standard and correct and move forward from new foundations.[59]

Other references to an intuitive way of knowing, which is the preserve of the Manifestations of God and His Chosen Ones, and one transcending the limits of cumulative knowledge acquired through reasoning, are equally consistent in pointing to the need to combine mental or rational knowledge with spiritual knowledge:

> Science does not know; but the Manifestation makes discoveries with the power of the Spirit. For instance: a philosopher with induction finds out a way. But the Prophet discerns with sight. A blind man has to find his way with a stick from point to point; so a philosopher through arguments from premises goes to conclusions, and not by sight. But the Manifestations see with their inner eye (own eye); they do not go from premises to conclusions. The prophets see many things with their inner eye. They do not need to go by discoveries. The scientist with induction is like a blind man who cannot see two steps ahead of him. The prophet sees a long distance.[60]

This is not to say that discursive knowledge is unnecessary, but to point to its inadequacy to account for all phenomena, and much less to furnish by itself a sufficient basis for a peaceful and durable order:

> The spirit of man is not illumined and quickened through material sources. It is not resuscitated by investigating phenomena of the world of matter . . . Material development may be likened to the glass of a lamp whereas divine virtues and spiritual susceptibilities are the light within the glass.[61]

Thus, only a combination of spiritual awareness and material as well as scientific attainment can succeed in bringing about a world free from the evils of the past.

'Abdu'l-Bahá, in addition, sets an important distinction between material progress and spiritual progress. The first 'is from one degree of perfection to another', whereas the second 'does not evolve from degree to degree as a law – it only evolves nearer to God, by the Mercy and Bounty of God'.[62] This distinction is further reinforced by the following statement:

> In the world of spirit there is no retrogression. The world of mortality is a world of contradictions, of opposites; motion being compulsory everything must either go forward or retreat. In the world of spirit there is no retreat possible, all movement is bound to be towards a perfect state. 'Progress' is the expression of spirit in the world of matter. The intelligence of man, his reasoning powers, his knowledge, his scientific achievements, all these being manifestations of the spirit, partake of the inevitable law of spiritual progress and are, therefore, of necessity, immortal.[63]

The world of opposites is marked by oscillations; progress tends to be countered by retreat. Yet in the world of spirit there can only be movement towards perfection. The above distinction is further reflected in the contrast between human and divine civilization. To the extent to which scientific knowledge is a reflection of divine knowledge it also moves towards perfection. There is, however, an important distinction between faith and knowledge attained through reason:

> For faith (*ímán*), which is life eternal, is a token of grace (*faḍl*) and not the result of justice (*'adl*). The flame of the fire of love, in this world of earth and water, burns by the power of attraction and not through human effort and striving, although through the latter one may indeed acquire knowledge (*iṭṭilá'*), learning (*'ilm*), and other perfections. It is the light of the divine Beauty, then, that must stir up and move the spirit through its attractive power.[64]

Similar occurrences of texts instancing this principle – that spiritual discoveries work in a different, unconventional way – have also important applications in social arrangements and the shaping of general attitudes. For instance, with regard to deniers of religion (atheists), 'Abdu'l-Bahá comments: 'You must be tolerant and patient, because the station of sight is a station of bounty; it is not based on capacity. They must be educated.'[65]

Human spirit and divine spirit

> Know that spirit in general is divided into five sorts – the vegetable spirit, the animal spirit, the human spirit, *the spirit of faith, and the divine spirit of sanctity*.[66] (emphasis added)

While the human spirit is common to all human beings, regardless of their rank and position in society, the 'divine spirit' is specific to those 'chosen' or 'born to the spirit'. Although use of the term 'spirit' may lead to some imprecision, it helps to underscore the unity of principle underlying the different manifestations of being:

> . . . all phenomena are realized through the divine bounty, and the explanation of true pantheistic statement and principle is that the phenomena of the universe find realization through the one power animating and dominating all things; and all things are but manifestations of its energy and bounty. The virtue of being and existence is through no other agency. Therefore, in the words of Bahá'u'lláh. the first teaching is the oneness of the world of humanity.[67]

The 'divine spirit', as opposed to the human spirit, is also termed 'spirit of faith' (*rúḥ-i-ímání*), 'heavenly spirit' (*rúḥ-i-ásmání*), 'bounty of God' (*fayḍ-i-raḥmání*).[68] Devoid of this spirit of faith the human spirit would remain ignorant of the divine attributes it contains. Deprived of the breath of the Holy Spirit the celestial part of the human spirit would become atrophied, thus paving the way to the promptings of human desires.

'Abdu'l-Bahá draws a further parallel. The mind, although not located in one single part of the human body, has a connection with the brain. 'So it is with the Kingdom (*malakút ham chinín ast*). Likewise, love has no place, but it is connected with the heart. And in the same way, the Kingdom has no place, but it is connected with the human reality.'[69] The world of the Kingdom, then, transcends the limitations of the human world. Man can reach its heights by becoming spiritual, an operation which, as already established, implies an overcoming of his lower nature. The balance between both poles is much more a matter of proportion and equilibrium than one of deprivation and exclusion, for:

> the inner reality of man is a demarcation line between the shadow and the light, a place where the two seas meet; it is the lowest point on the arc of descent, and therefore it is capable of gaining all the grades above.[70]

Interestingly, as underscored by 'Abdu'l-Bahá, the higher the realm the stronger and subtler become the relationships obtaining between its elements:

> In surveying the vast range of creation thou shalt perceive that the higher a kingdom of created things is on the arc of ascent, the more conspicuous are the signs and evidences of the truth that co-operation and reciprocity at the level of a higher order are greater than those that exist at the level of a lower order.[71]

Yet the language of exclusion and negation is overtly used to depict what in this journey is or must be 'left behind'. Those human beings who appreciate the contingent character of their own undertakings, who refuse, out of love for God, to identify themselves with their own works, will burn 'to ashes the harvest of reason'.[72] The pilgrimage towards God must of necessity lead the seeker to:

> turn away from imitation (*taqlíd*), which is following the traces of their forefathers; and shut the door of friendship and enmity (*dústí va dushmaní*) upon all the people of the earth.[73]

This process needs to be carried out to its limit so that things may be judged not for what they are in themselves, but for what they have 'in common' with God: 'In every face, he seeketh the beauty of the Friend.'[74] This paradox, this denial of enmity and friendliness, which is finally superseded by unconditional true (detached, disinterested) love and a meeting in unity illustrates the non-dualistic character of this spiritual perspective. In order to become celestial man must be in a state of spiritual awakening. He must be patient rather than passive.[75] In other words, he must be actively receptive, or to use the contrast between dream and wakefulness: vigilant. '[M]an must seek capacity and develop readiness'.[76] The reason is simple:

> It [divine bounty] is moving, circulating and becomes effective wherever capacity is developed to receive it. In every station there is a specialized capacity.[77]

To achieve this state of full receptivity man has to become impervious to the influence of 'vain imaginings' and 'worldly affections'.[78] By suppressing or rather cancelling this continuous flow of 'temptations' emerging from his lower nature, man starts to develop a taste for the spiritual peace he is longing for:

> Unless the heart be filled with longing, the favours of the Lord will not be evident. Unless a perfect melody be sung, the ears of the hearers will not be attracted.[79]

According to Bahá'u'lláh, nothing short of a burning desire for liberation can quench the fire of passion or extinguish the promptings of idle fancies. By making room for the descent of the divine spirit, the human soul is thus enabled to reach a state of peace and composure, as well as acquire intuitive knowledge (*'ilm-i-vujudí*).[80] 'Abdu'l-Bahá's words are expressive:

> The heart's ambitions should ascend to a more glorious goal, mental activity should rise to higher levels! Men should hold in their souls the vision of celestial perfection, and there prepare a dwelling-place for the inexhaustible bounty of the Divine Spirit.[81]

This second faculty born in man may be called the faculty of inner vision[82] and correlates to the 'divine intellectual power':

> This divine intellectual power (*quvviy-i-'aqlíyiy-i-iláhíyyih*) is confined to the holy Manifestations and the Daysprings of prophethood. A ray of this light falls upon the mirrors of the hearts of the righteous, that they may also receive, through the holy Manifestations, a share and benefit of this power.[83]

By means of the faculty of inner vision and through the agency of the divine spirit the human heart receives the ray of the Divine Light. For it is the heart that adheres to either of the two kinds of knowledge, the knowledge of God, or satanic knowledge;[84] that assents to the 'world' or renounces it. In the end, an election must be made, as it is not possible for the heart to remain divided against itself. In this regard, man is seen as being able to transform himself, passing from the state of virtuality to the state of realization, from seed to fruit, from bird attached to earth to bird soaring to the heavens of God. The heart, in so far as the centre of man, is the one organ that ensures that human perception is possible. When man attunes his heart to the remembrance of God, unity of purpose, action and thought comes naturally:

> So complete must be thy consecration, that every trace of worldly desire will be washed from thine heart. This is the meaning of true unity (*ín ast maqám-i-tawḥíd-i-ḥaqíqí*).[85]

When such a remembrance is fixed in one's heart, all things are sifted from their accidental traits and come to be seen under a new light. Here 'Abdu'l-Bahá's saying may be applied:

> When you love a member of your family or a compatriot, let it be with a ray of the Infinite Love! Let it be in God, and for God![86]

It is this love, and the accompanying capacities that come with it, that provides human beings with the power to transcend the divisiveness that would otherwise appear attached to a fragmentary this-worldly perspective.

In the words of 'Abdu'l-Bahá there are two kinds of light. One is the 'light of the intellect' (i.e. the mind in so far as the supreme faculty of the rational soul), 'the highest light that exists, for it is born of the Light Divine'. But it is only the second, the Divine Light, 'that can give us sight for the invisible things', that 'shows to the eyes of our spirits all that exists in God's Kingdom and causes the realities of things to be made visible'. 'Abdu'l-Bahá adds: 'By the help of this effulgent Light all the spiritual interpretation of the Holy Writings has been made plain.'[87] Although there is a sharp contrast between the ranges of both 'lights', the light of the intellect, that is, the rational soul, is nevertheless 'born of the Light Divine'. It is for this reason that there exists a fundamental analogy between rational discoveries and spiritual understanding (*edrák-i-rawḥání, elhám-i-raḥmání*):

> These true disclosures which conform to reality are similar to visions – which consist in spiritual understanding, heavenly inspiration, and the close communion of human spirits – and thus the recipient will say that he saw, or said, or heard such a thing.[88]

With the coming of each new prophetic Dispensation, and, particularly, with the advent of Bahá'u'lláh, the world of thought and knowledge is said to be experiencing a complete revolution. Mankind's receptivity has been increased through the spiritual education imparted by God's Messengers:

> He must also impart spiritual education (*tarbíyyat-i-rawḥáníyyih*), so that minds may apprehend the metaphysical world (*'alam-i-mávará'*), breathe the sanctified breaths of the Holy Spirit, and enter into relationship with the Concourse on high . . .[89]

Left to its own devices, humanity is incapable of making this possible:

> It is clear, however, that mere human power is incapable of fulfilling this great office, and that the results of human thought alone cannot secure such bounties.[90]

The 'spirit of faith' in reality belongs to the kingdom of God, whereas the human mind and the powers of the animal soul are of the kingdom of creation. As long as man is not 'touched' by the divine spirit he has no access to the divine reality:

> For this, other faculties are required, other senses: should such powers become available to him, then could a human being receive some knowledge of that world; otherwise, never.[91]

The attainment of the spirit of faith, as stated before, does not depend on the refinement of the mind. 'Entrance into the Kingdom is through the love of God,'[92] and love cannot be imposed, but rather follows its own logic and dynamics. For the realm of the kingdom is also the realm of absolute freedom, where 'merit and capacity are not to be considered'.[93] God's kingdom shuns the laws of necessity that typify the world of creation. The surrender of one's will to God entails the recognition of one's powerlessness and poverty. According to Bahá'u'lláh:

> This confession of helplessness which mature contemplation must eventually impel every mind to make is in itself the acme of human understanding, and marketh the culmination of man's development.[94]

Acceptance of this essential limitation is not meant to quash the responsible exercise of the human intellectual and sensorial powers, but to redirect them – in line with this admission – towards the attainment of inspiration and true knowledge from the spiritual Source. The criterion for measuring human knowledge is then not so much the extent of one's science,[95] but its unselfish application and, more importantly, its self-regulation in recognition of the existence of a higher purpose. Otherwise, human knowledge becomes an end in itself leading to a mere restatement of multiplicity, as implied by Bahá'u'lláh's reference to the saying: 'Knowledge is one point, which the foolish have multiplied.'[96] This view is not limited typically to theological and metaphysical hair-splitting of the kind often censured by Bahá'u'lláh, but it is made co-extensive to all forms of human knowledge, including the western traditions of materialistic thought, both ancient and contemporary:

> When the eyes of the people of the East were captivated by the arts and wonders of the West, they roved distraught in the wilderness of material causes, oblivious of the One Who is the Causer of Causes, and the Sustainer thereof, while such men as were the source and the wellspring of Wisdom never denied the moving Impulse behind these causes, nor the Creator or the Origin thereof.[97]

And 'Abdu'l-Bahá adds that any of the established means of acquiring knowledge is incomplete if taken in isolation from the rest. Thus, the four accepted means for acquiring knowledge (that is knowledge through the senses [*ḥiss*], by reasoning [*'aql*], by tradition [*naql*], and through the Grace of Holy Spirit or inspiration [*fayḍ-i-Rúḥu'l-Quds*])[98] cannot be entirely relied upon. Sensory perception is manifestly prone to illusion and miscalculations. Reasoning and traditional knowledge are basically dependent upon the same source, namely the human mind, from which often conflicting results are derived. Only the fourth method[99] can guarantee some measure of certainty:

> But the grace of the Holy Spirit is the true criterion regarding which there is no doubt or uncertainty. That grace consists in the confirmations of the Holy Spirit which are vouchsafed to man and through which certitude is attained.[100]

Yet, 'Abdu'l-Bahá cautions against a radical separation between the three first methods (two, if rational and 'traditional' or 'transmitted' knowledge are blended into one) and the fourth one. In actual fact, great care should be taken not to lay claim to exclusiveness for the inspirational method, which can also prove most defective when inspirations are prompted by man's lower nature.[101] That is why ideally the truth of a matter must be established through a combination of the four criteria, in other words, through an integration of the four dimensions:

> [A] statement presented to the mind accompanied by proofs which the senses can perceive to be correct, which the faculty of reason can accept, which is in accord with traditional authority and sanctioned by the prompting of the heart, can be adjudged and relied upon as perfectly correct.[102]

This integrative method of approaching the truth of any matter has undeniably important ramifications in the context of Bahá'í consultation and decision-making, as it legitimizes both the insights and perceptions obtained through the processes of experimentation, critical inquiry and logical reasoning, on the one hand, and those derived from revelation (or its interpretation) and the contemplation of divine realities, on the other.

22
Human Dignity and Perfectibility

Human nobility is proven not simply by restating the centrality of man in the context of God's creation, a point which helps to create a positive contrast with the wild world of nature, but rather by demonstrating the capacity of mankind to unburden itself from the yoke of its lower nature. This nobility is then characterized by the capacity of men and women to perfect themselves, attracting the divine blessings and instancing counterexamples that prove the opposite of what would commonly be expected if the laws of the world would apply: 'Pay ye no heed to aversion and rejection, to disdain, hostility, injustice: act ye in the opposite way.'[103] The very energies so often invested in the destruction of other fellowmen must be diverted to constructive purposes worthy of man's station; the science of war must be unlearned and then leave way to the 'blessed arts of peace'.[104]

The Bahá'í notion of man's nobility implicit in this state of magnanimity is linked to a vision of mankind intimately bound up with the realization of God's will and the mirroring of the Kingdom in human reality.[105] In Bahá'í terms, the realization of God's will is indicated both by the alleged excellence of the new religious Dispensation and by its concomitant regeneration, or rather 're-creation', of a new race of men and women[106] free from the kind of attachments that have perpetuated endless cycles of violence. As for the mirroring of the Kingdom, this activity points in the direction of a divine civilization fully informed by the standards of the new Dispensation. In this sense, the reaffirming of mankind's nobility takes on a parallel note of eschatological fulfilment, both elements (nobility and fulfilment) being coextensive. The following can be taken as a representative statement touching on various aspects of this question:

> The All-Merciful hath conferred upon man the faculty of vision, and endowed him with the power of hearing. Some have described him as the 'lesser world', *when, in reality, he should be regarded as the 'greater world'*. The potentialities inherent in the station of man, the full measure of his destiny on earth, *the innate excellence of his reality, must all be manifested in this promised Day of God.*[107] (emphasis added)

The dignity of man becomes here an expression of the capacity to rise above the 'natural' plane, out of one's own free will, in order to distinguish oneself from others, to conquer one's passions, to acquire excellence and to be at one with oneself and one's Maker. In a characteristic Bahá'í way, the usual perspective (man being in the Platonic tradition the microcosm), is elevated metaphorically to the position of 'macrocosm', a change of perspective justified by the fact that all 'innate excellence' seems bound to become manifest in this the Day of God. This representation of man as the noblest being in creation implies first and foremost the capacity to transcend violence, contention and strife, i.e. the instinctual world of opposites, fragmentation and contradictions that man needs to leave behind. Bahá'u'lláh links clearly the abolition of the causes of dissension – which was His first action at the Garden of Riḍván – with the basic theme of human dignity and the enabling role of education:

> Whatsoever hath led the children of men to shun one another, and hath caused dissensions and divisions amongst them, hath, through the revelation of these words, been nullified and abolished. From the heaven of God's Will, and for the purpose of ennobling the world of being and of elevating the minds and souls of men, hath been sent down that which is the most effective instrument for the education of the whole human race.[108]

The Manifestations of God, as educators of mankind, train the human realities so that they may excel themselves in the path of service. Education, spiritual and material, is a formidable means for the improvement of mankind. This enlightened theme appears uppermost in the concerns of Bahá'u'lláh and 'Abdu'l-Bahá:

> Man is the supreme Talisman (*insán ṭilism a'ẓam ast*). Lack of a proper education hath, however, deprived him of that which he doth inherently possess. Through a word proceeding out of the mouth of God he was called into being; by one word more he was guided to recognize the Source of his education; by yet another word his station and destiny (*marátib va maqámátis<u>h</u>*) were safeguarded. The Great Being saith: Regard man as a mine rich in gems of inestimable value (*ma'adan kih dáráy-i-aḥjár-i-karimih ast*). Education (*tarbíyat*) can, alone, cause it to reveal its treasures, and enable mankind to benefit therefrom. If any man were to meditate on that which the Scriptures, sent down from the heaven of God's holy Will, have revealed, he would readily recognize that their purpose is that all men shall be regarded as one soul, so that the seal bearing the words 'The Kingdom shall be God's' may be stamped on every heart, and the light of Divine bounty, of grace, and mercy may envelop all mankind.[109]

This seminal text in Bahá'í pedagogical thinking can be regarded as a reaffirmation of the inherent worth of human beings, and a stimulant for promoting education as a means to actualize it. It is also a confirmation of the link between recognition of the divine Source and the safeguarding (salvation) of man, and finally a reference to the overall purpose of human existence, 'that all men shall be regarded as one soul', a point which transcends or rather transforms notions of equality by pitching them at a deeper level of moral and metaphysical reality. Interestingly it is this realization that is depicted as bearing the true marks of God's kingdom. The implicit assumption in the above passage is that for education to be complete, effective and stable, it needs to be reinforced by a consciousness of its spiritual foundations. Failing this, education, like freedom or civilization, will be carried to extremes, thus ceasing to be of benefit: 'However much men of understanding may favourably regard them,' warns Bahá'u'lláh, 'they will, if carried to excess, exercise a pernicious influence upon men.'[110] This same admonition appears reformulated in yet another Tablet ironically targeting excess of civilization as a flagellum wreaking havoc on the very focal points of civilization itself, namely its cities:

> The civilization, so often vaunted by the learned exponents of arts and sciences, will, if allowed to overleap the bounds of moderation, bring great evil upon men. Thus warneth you He Who is the All-Knowing. If carried to excess, civilization will prove as prolific a source of evil as it had been of goodness when kept within the restraints of moderation. Meditate on this, O people, and be not of them that wander distraught in the wilderness of error. The day is approaching when its flame will devour the cities, when the Tongue of Grandeur will proclaim: 'The Kingdom is God's, the Almighty, the All-Praised!'[111]

While man is seen as 'essentially' a noble creature endowed with manifold gifts, these can nevertheless be diverted towards the wrong ends.[112] Hence, in addition to proclaiming the excellence and nobility of human beings, itself a powerful motivating factor, stress must also be laid on the need to display behaviours that are commensurate with man's higher calling. The role of the Manifestations of God is to train the realities of men accordingly. Similarly, the role of the 'learned and worldly-wise men of this age' (*'ulamáy-i-'aṣr*) consists in allowing 'mankind to inhale the fragrance of fellowship and love', signifying that in doing so:

> every understanding heart (*nufús-i-'árafih*) would apprehend the meaning of true liberty, and discover the secret of undisturbed peace (*ráḥat*) and absolute composure (*asáyi<u>sh</u>*). Were the earth to attain this station and be illumined with its light it could then be truly said of it: 'Thou shall see in it no hollows or rising hills.'[113]

The responsibility of the learned is couched in terms suggestive of the need for concentrating on whatever may increase fellowship and love among the generality of mankind. In fact, a Bahá'í definition of the learned class and the role of the intelligentsia would need to take into account this foremost task of establishing peace and fellowship as central to their own self-understanding as a class of people. Thus the harmonizing of otherwise clashing poles (liberty and peace/ composure) is seen as the culmination or realization of the apocalyptic dream of a world secure and peaceful, where war and contention cease to hold their sway. Education undoubtedly plays here not just a levelling role; it is an empowering tool that supplies human beings with the proper arena for the deployment of their noblest endeavours.

From a Bahá'í standpoint, then, a transformed human personality and a new satisfying social framework become a realistic prospect because, taking aside the eschatological promises of ultimate realization, human reality is not seen as marred by a doctrine of a 'fallen nature',[114] nor by a naturalistic view of society whereby men are irrevocably bound to use violence against each other, nor by the Islamic notion of *taqlíd*, which ascribes human beings (and their behaviours) into two separate categories, namely the learned and the untutored class. And while humanity is not perceived in terms of metaphysical or moral pessimism, there is little room in the Bahá'í view for the kind of optimism that enlightened and liberal authors posited by appealing to an eventual mysterious harmonization of selfish motives with appeals to an omnipresent goodness in man, much less for the kind of social Darwinism that 'Abdu'l-Bahá repudiated by condemning the notion of struggle for existence as the 'fountain-head of all calamities' and 'the supreme affliction'.[115]

Certainly, a reification of evil in the form of Satan or the like is no longer needed nor justified:

> No sooner, however, did a quarrel break out between Adam and Satan than they were, one and all, banished from the Garden, and this was meant as a warning to the human race, a means of telling humankind that dissension – even with the Devil – is the way to bitter loss. This is why, in our illumined age, God teacheth that conflicts and disputes are not allowable, not even with Satan himself.[116]

Analogues of this position in Bahá'í thought and practice are pervasive. Thus, Bahá'ís are exhorted to avoid entering into controversies, disputes and the like,[117] a fact with serious implications in Bahá'í consultation, implying as it does a self-disciplining of the right to self-expression. Another instance is furnished by the well-known Bahá'í saying (from reported words of 'Abdu'l-Bahá): 'if religion becomes the source of antagonism and strife, the absence of religion is to be preferred',[118] a stance originally meant to defeat dogmatic tendencies and sectarianism,[119] and which is supported by the fundamental Bahá'í distinction between authoritative and personal interpretation in Bahá'í exegesis.

But neither the elaboration of a counterfeit sense of optimism nor a naturalistic acceptance of predatory notions of human nature are possible, two extreme positions in fact intimately connected. The Bahá'í principle of 'free and independent search after truth' should prevent this not so much by establishing, through a method of rational inquiry, what truth is, but rather by liberating the mind from self-imposed blinkers in the form of a false conscience. For, standing in the way of mankind's dignity is, as Kant would put it, its voluntary relinquishment of its own endowments in deferment to established or received views. This attitude may occur as a by-product or ignorance, but also as a result of different power and knowledge relationships. It is those relationships and the false conscience they create that the Bahá'í critique of *taqlíd* addresses with recurrent emphasis.

The path to peace: Overcoming *taqlíd* (blind imitation)

In Islamic thought the term *taqlíd* usually is described as unreasoning acceptance of settled doctrine. The word is often used in contrast with its correlative opposite *ijmá'* (consensus), construed as the exercise of independent reasoning. Now, since the positive exercise of *ijmá'* in a community of believers leads to and is epitomized by the consensus of its leading scholars, *ijmá'* is often understood as the agreement reached in the process of history by such community of *'ulamá*.[120]

In Islam the holding of doctrinal opinions and their public discussion was made the preserve of those well acquainted with the subtleties of the law. The discussion and elucidation of theological and legal questions was declared beyond the ken of ordinary men. In a sense, therefore, *taqlíd* was the normal course open to laymen who lacked the time, resources or talents to initiate themselves into the deeper study of those questions that go beyond the fundamentals of religion (*uṣúl ad-dín*).[121] It should be noted that from the standpoint of the Sharia, human actions can be classified as being either obligatory (*farḍ*), strongly recommended (*mandúb*), allowed (*mubáḥ*), strongly discouraged (*makrúh*), or forbidden (*harám*).[122] Establishing the differences between these areas was one of the main concerns of the *'ulamá* and formed the basis of Islamic legalism. Being alert to the importance of observing these aspects and keeping them alive in daily practice, particularly noticing the significance of the grey areas, was the main obligation of laymen.

Yet, to the extent to which *ijmá'* became a crystallization of positions, carrying authority over the Muslim community, *taqlíd* was better contrasted with *ijtihád*, which is the exercise of independent reason proper:[123]

> The classical meaning of *ijtihád*, as found with some minor variations in the technical dictionaries and handbooks on legal methodology, is exerting one's effort in order to derive from the bases of the law (*adlillah*) an opinion concerning a legal rule. Its complement is *taqlíd*, by which term is understood 'accepting an opinion concerning a legal rule without knowledge of its bases'.[124]

In Sunni Islam a distinction was made between the founders of the four legal schools of jurisprudence – who were considered absolute *mujtahid*s – and those who by following their principles in such matters were to be regarded as secondary *mujtahids*. In Shí'i Islam a *mujtahid* (one who exercises *ijtihád*) is the Muslim authority whose training and proven capacity, as endorsed by a special license, enables him to issue binding legal opinions on legal matters by means of *fatwas*.[125] In Sunni Islam *ijtihád* was confined historically to the period when the four legal schools of jurisprudence evolved, after which time the door of *ijtihád* was considered to be closed. Since then, Muslim scholars could not rely on their own independent reasoning, and were forced to model their decisions on the authority of the *ijmá'*. Therefore, rather than *mujtahids* (exercisers) they are *muqalids* (imitators).[126]

Although *taqlíd* is forbidden in the Qur'án, this prohibition is regarded as confined to the essentials of religion. Hence Shí'i laymen are referred for the most part of their private dealings and ritual practices to the authority of a *mujtahid*, whose role and authorized opinions, being of an exemplary nature, call for imitation. Leading *mujtahids* have a following of their own, becoming on that basis referents and models worthy of emulation (*marja'at-i-taqlíd*). Those who follow a *marja'at taqlíd* are called *muqallid*; and the following of a qualified living *mujtahid* is *taqlíd*. Since lay people are to follow the example set by living *mujtahids*, a generational and personal bond between exponents of Islamic law and their constituencies is assured. Given the tendency for families of jurisprudents to carry on the traditions and office of their illustrious ancestors, a dynastic element is also ingrained in the system. Management by these *mujtahids* of bequeathed endowments provides additionally a basis for their own economic independence, one that continues to this day.

Open criticisms of the doctrine of *taqlíd* were not uncommon in the medieval period, but resurfaced strongly during the eighteenth and nineteenth centuries coinciding with the birth of modern fundamentalist Islamic movements. As noted by Peters:

> John Voll has applied the term fundamentalism to such tendencies in Islamic thought as stress the transcendence of God as opposed to his immanence, unity as opposed to diversity and authenticity as opposed to openness. In my opinion a further characteristic ought to be added: the emphasis on the essential equality of all believers.[127]

The religious implications of the Bahá'í outlook on *taqlíd*, however, go far beyond the sphere of explicit denunciations of it, and can be noted in several aspects of Bahá'í doctrine and organization. In its broader sense the strong Bahá'í position contrary to 'imitation' (*taqlíd*) is said to be a consequence of the Bahá'í belief in the maturing of humanity as a whole. Mankind's coming of age is related by Bahá'u'lláh and Shoghi Effendi to a number of signs denoting the dignity of human beings and as members of the transcending collective unit with which they stand identified: the human race.[128] Interestingly, in the *Seven Valleys* Bahá'u'lláh defines the overcoming of *taqlíd* as one of three basic conditions to be fulfilled by the wayfarer who sets out on his spiritual journey: 1) he must cleanse his heart;

2) must 'turn away from imitation, *which is following the traces of their forefathers* (*taqlíd kih az athar-i-ábá' va ajdád ast*); and 3) shut the door of friendship and enmity upon all the people of the earth'[129] (emphasis added).

In a narrower sense, however, the denunciation of *taqlíd* is a consequence of the principle of 'free and independent investigation of truth', which places all human beings on an equal footing in matters of conscience and faith. This principle amounts to an explicit superseding of the Islamic doctrine of *taqlíd,* be it in the form of allegiance to the four Islamic schools of law,[130] or in the form of a patterning of one's behaviour after the models provided by the living religious authorities (*mujtahids*). Bahá'u'lláh makes this point explicit by stating:

> The founder of the principles of Islamic jurisprudence (*uṣúl*) was Abú-Ḥanífih, who was a prominent leader of the Sunnis. Such principles had existed in former times as well, as hath already been mentioned. In this day, however, the approval or rejection of all things depended wholly upon the Word of God [i.e. the Manifestation of God].[131]

The possibility of 'reconstituting', as it were, a *maktab* of Bahá'í jurisprudence, in the Islamic sense, is therefore clearly neutralized, though Bahá'u'lláh makes it clear that jurisprudential differences among the existing schools were of no real significance 'for they do not contradict that which is essential' and should rather be viewed, as many other things of the past, through the eye of divine mercy.[132] This in itself is a confirmation of the Báb's repudiation of the entire edifice of *taqlíd* and *zunún* which justified the consolidation of Shí'i jurisprudence.[133] Bahá'u'lláh also denounces the kind of borrowing (or rather plagiarism) that would take place among the learned clerics: 'This limited knowledge they even stealthily borrow one from the other, and vainly pride themselves therein!'[134]

More specifically, 'Abdu'l-Bahá's critique of 'imitations' entails a complete departure from established Shí'i doctrine concerning the role of the Supreme Exemplar (*marja'at-i-taqlíd*), which at His time was already solidified. This in turn presupposes a different approach to the place of personal interpretation in the shaping of the Bahá'í community (*qíyás, ijtihád*) as well as to the limits to cultural and religious innovation (*bid'a*).[135] As 'Abdu'l-Bahá repeatedly stated, Bahá'ís were 'lovers of illumination and not of lamps and candles'.[136]

A major elaboration on the social implications of the Bahá'í position on *taqlíd* is shown at work in 'Abdu'l-Bahá's treatise *The Secret of Divine Civilization* (*Risaliy-i-Maddaníyyih)*, where 'Abdu'l-Bahá advocates the very possibility of innovating and borrowing foreign ideas (denounced by the Shí'í clergy as 'imitations', that is, in fact 'heretic innovations') while criticizing the blind imitation of the clergy itself. The paradox here is that 'Abdu'l-Bahá could have been seen as embracing the adoption (emulation, or 'imitation') of foreign practices while repudiating a supposedly 'self-initiated', autarchic process of nativization. 'Abdu'l-Bahá's critical approach is further reinforced by the stress laid on the importance of forming a public opinion and of consultation as a truth-finding and decision-making tool. Imitation, by contrast with personal inquiry, does not work:

> We must not be content with simply following a certain course because we find our fathers pursued that course. It is the duty of everyone to investigate reality, and investigation of reality by another will not do for us.[137]

Imitations or superstitions can also be taken as unwarranted accretions to the fundamental tenets of religion, which are perpetuated solely on the putative merits of traditional authority (tradition being, as seen above, just one of the four or five forms of knowing).[138] For at a deeper level, imitation is basically the outcome of a defection of one's conscience whereby the person enters into a false relationship with oneself, adopting a position of convenience in connection with his own opinions and desires, in a vain effort to maximize personal advantage at the cost of consistency and truthfulness (truthfulness, *ṣidáqat*, regarded as the foundation of all other virtues). In keeping with this view of human nature, the Bahá'í writings identify 'vain imaginings' and 'prejudices' as the main barriers intervening in man's approach to his own exalted condition. These writings convey a vision in which violence is the result of injustice, and this is related to the predominance of untruth and, in consequence, of tyranny:

> In these days truthfulness (*rastí*) and sincerity (*ṣadiq*) are sorely afflicted in the clutches of falsehood (*kazb*), and justice (*'adl*) is tormented by the scourge of injustice (*ẓulm*). The smoke of corruption (*khan-i-fasád*) hath enveloped the whole world in such wise that naught can be seen in any direction save regiments of soldiers and nothing is heard from any land but the clashing of swords. We beseech God, the True One, to strengthen the wielders of His power in that which will rehabilitate the world and bring tranquillity to the nations.[139]

23
Violence and the Individual: The Power of Vain Imaginings and Idle Fancies

Doubtless from a Bahá'í perspective war, crime, and conflicts have a rooting in man's [lower] nature. These happen not just by chance nor are they a mere outcome of a sick or insane society; they are also the consequence of a declining human condition, both individually and collectively.

From a Bahá'í viewpoint, whenever mankind is out of touch with its Creator, and grows unable to creatively draw on the teachings of a former Dispensation of God, divisions and strife find their way into its ranks. The decline of religion itself compounds this state and aggravates circumstances by leading into fanaticism and superstitions. But irrespective of the state of degradation that may affect a given culture or civilization, men and women are still held responsible for their own individual beings. Their belief or unbelief, their service and usefulness depend to a great extent on their willingness to make use of their own endowments. This is not to deny that social conditions may hinder or prevent the expression of these potentialities; yet, the dignity inherent in mankind is never annulled by the imposition of external, tyrannical conditions, nor fully erased by man's own sinking into sinful behaviour, a point most forcefully conveyed in 'Abdu'l-Bahá's recounting of His own state while in prison.[140] That man can be at peace is, therefore, a consequence of his own inherent dignity and perfectibility:

> Each man has been placed in a post of honour, which he must not desert. A humble workman who commits an injustice is as much to blame as a notorious tyrant. Thus all human beings have a choice between justice and injustice.[141]

And this is so because all human beings are in a position to choose between honour or abasement, heaven or earth, cruelty or mercy: 'Every good habit, every noble quality', avers 'Abdu'l-Bahá, 'belongs to man's spiritual nature, whereas all his imperfections and sinful actions are born of his material nature. If a man's Divine nature dominates his human nature, we have a saint.'[142]

Bahá'ís are in consequence called upon to reverse the terms normally associated with states of necessity and to combine seemingly opposing extremes:

> The realization of these two opposite attitudes [severance from and attachment to the things of this world] in a single individual is very rare. In the Bahá'í Cause it is taught that we must devote the utmost attention to the pursuit of our worldly affairs but at the same time be severed from all else save God. How can the mind and heart be entirely free, and detached from every pursuit, yet occupied with the solution of material problems? This is a most subtle, psychological question. To be in the water and not to get wet; to go through the fire and not to be burned – these are opposite, irreconcilable conditions. Still, in the spiritual world these two antipodes must meet and the two qualities of severance and attachment must be harmoniously combined.[143]

In the face of dire deprivation they are encouraged to show forth longanimity and forbearance;[144] if confronted with persecution and tribulations they are called upon to be contented;[145] if debarred from freedom, they are reminded that freedom 'is not a matter of place. It is a condition'.[146] Peace of mind can therefore be established in one's own self through faith and understanding:

> One of the bounties of religion and faith is the attainment of peace of the heart and soul and the joy of spirit and conscience. This station can only be gained through faith and understanding. Peace of mind is the soul's delight, as it is a means of acquiring that extraordinary state in which man finds happiness in times of affliction and tranquillity in trouble. In spite of poverty he acquires a sense of affluence and in a state of riches and power he offers help and protection to the weak because the well assured soul is like a tree which has strong roots and is not shaken by any event.[147]

Conversely, violence is originated in man's departure from his own higher nature: 'So long as one's nature yieldeth unto evil passions, crime and transgression will prevail.'[148] To redress that situation constitutes a titanic task calling for a rallying of all active forces available to society and every single individual. Although man-made laws may prove to have a deterrent effect, it is ultimately the fear of God that infuses into him an inner and outer sense of self-restraint:

> In formulating the principles and laws a part hath been devoted to penalties which form an effective instrument for the security and protection of men. However, dread of the penalties maketh people desist only outwardly from committing vile and contemptible deeds, while that which guardeth and restraineth man both outwardly and inwardly hath been and still is the fear of God.[149]

Retaliatory or punitive laws will not have a sufficient deterrent effect by themselves, nor will they prove effective in wiping out crime. The multiplication of legal codes and prisons will be of little avail unless a new spirit is infused into the system, one which combines education, prevention and new morals with the adoption of measures of a corrective rather than punitive nature. What is true of the treatment of criminals can be equally said about the handling of industrial disputes[150] or even the arms race in general. In all these cases, rather than relying on material and technical ingenuity, mankind should turn towards avoiding such excesses and balancing them out with a new approach to community and peace-building. This must be underpinned by some basic attitudes, including the fear of God, which Bahá'u'lláh represents as 'the essence of wisdom',[151] 'the chief cause of the protection of mankind, and the supreme instrument for its preservation'.[152] To the extent to which fear of God helps mankind to become aware of its true station, it can be regarded as the 'prime factor in the education' of men:

> It is incumbent upon thee to summon the people, under all conditions, to whatever will cause them to show forth spiritual characteristics and goodly deeds, *so that all may become aware of that which is the cause of human upliftment*, and may, with the utmost endeavour, direct themselves towards the most sublime Station and the Pinnacle of Glory. The fear of God hath ever been the prime factor in the education of His creatures.[153] (emphasis added)

Moreover, fear prevents human beings from indulging in unbecoming behaviour and children from expressing unworthy sentiments.[154] Yet, while fear as a force has a protective effect on society and its members, it cannot be considered entirely adequate as a human response unless it entails a degree of awareness and upliftment. In this connection the Bahá'í writings underline the importance of heightening one's vision as a form of rising above the narrow limits of daily experience, with its concomitant deceptions in the form of vain imaginings and idle fancies. The ordinary experience of the mirage or the optical illusion that fouls us into error becomes the standard metaphor to understand the more fundamental errors induced by vain imaginings.

To be able to 'see' with the eyes of the spirit means to take notice of things in their essentiality rather than in their accidental, often fortuitous, appearance. This operation requires a reversal of the ways humans tend to consider perception. For practical purposes, external objects, to be sure, can be apprehended for what they are; but this experience does not cancel the intuitive experience that they are much more than that on account of being inexhaustible realities and 'signs' pointing always towards a higher or deeper metaphysical source. For this appreciation to surface to the human conscience, a deliberate effort must be made not to mistake forms and shapes, names and attributes, for their substantive realities:

> Surely no man of intelligence and insight would ever pay attention unto limitations or names, but rather unto that with which Muḥammad was invested, which was none other than the Cause of God.[155]

In a way, a major Bahá'í critique is devoted to the human fixation on 'names' and 'titles', rather than on their meaning and true import. Names and attributes can easily take on a fake currency deriving its sense of worth from the names themselves rather than from their realities, a simple synecdoche, yes, but one that changes everything.

Statements such as the one just quoted seem to imply that if a uniting vision is to be achieved there should be an accompanying effort to engage one's faculties in the same direction. The whole being must act in unison. The psychological principle is clear: 'Approach not the things which your minds condemn.'[156] There must be some form of spiritual frugality to comply with the call to Bahá'ís to 'forsake the things current amongst them';[157] a frugality which has to do with things as much as it does with desires and thoughts: 'He should be content with little, and be freed from all inordinate desire.'[158] Thinking and the imaginative processes must too be moderated and tamed.[159] Even pious desires should be reconsidered, for:

> The true worshipper, while praying, should endeavour not so much to ask God to fulfil his wishes and desires, but rather to adjust these and make them conform to the Divine Will. Only through such an attitude can one derive that feeling of inner peace and contentment which the power of prayer alone can confer.[160]

Yet imagination and worldly desires work more in the opposite way. Instead of renunciation and detachment they provide constant ammunition to keep the mind and the will 'busy':

> Vague fancies have encompassed the dwellers of the earth and debarred them from turning towards the Horizon of Certitude, and its brightness, and its manifestations and its lights. Vain imaginings have withheld them from Him Who is the Self-Subsisting. They speak as prompted by their own caprices, and understand not.[161]

But vain imaginings are not just related to a disturbance of the imagination: they are inducers of power and wealth. This idea is conveyed most emphatically by Bahá'u'lláh:

> Their hearts [of the Muslim divines] seem not to be inclined to knowledge and the door thereof, neither think they of its manifestations, *inasmuch as in idle fancy they have found the door that leadeth unto earthly riches, whereas in the manifestation of the Revealer of knowledge they find naught but the call to self-sacrifice*. They therefore naturally hold fast unto the former, and flee from the latter.[162] (emphasis added)

The human mind needs to be continually focused on the right objects and deeds. The notion of God's remembrance (*dhikr*) is clearly meant to provide not so much a topic of meditation as a handle for the right inspiration linking present states of mind and actions with their only legitimizing source. A duly moderated imaginative faculty may prove very useful in the conceiving of worthy projects. Yet, imagination can easily become a trap whereby the human mind engages in a derivative kind of experience, quite removed from the God-given centre of its being. If the faculty of knowledge condescends to work on the basis of imaginative proposals not subject to critical scrutiny, the mind itself becomes corrupted. The following oral statement attributed to 'Abdu'l-Bahá elaborates upon this point:

> The Word of God is revealed according to the degree of Spiritual Sight, no matter who the messenger may be. Again, people do not receive the Manifestation of God because they are veiled by their imaginations. Imagination is one of our greatest powers and a most difficult to rule. Imagination is the father of superstition . . . We are led astray by imagination, even in violation of will and reason. It is our test power. We are tested by our ability to control and subdue it. A man imagines he is wealthy. Some day real wealth comes to him, but it is never what he imagined it would be. *Imagination is our greatest misleader. We hold to it until it becomes fixed in memory. Then we hold to it the stronger, believing it to be a fact.* It is a great power of the soul but without value unless rightly controlled and guided.[163] (emphasis added)

Accordingly, there is an important difference between an imagination that simply projects illusions and a creative imagination that gives shape to objects worthy of consideration. The iconoclastic power wielded by God's Messengers defines a characteristic aspect of their 'message' particularly linked to the unrealistic world of imagination: 'Blessed is that strong one who will shatter the gods of vain imaginings through the potency of the Name of his Lord . . .'[164] Idolatry, in the Bahá'í writings, has not the restricted sense of mere adoration of images, nor is any more concerned with Trinitarian or anthropomorphic temptations. By identifying 'idols' and 'gods' with vain imaginings, Baha'u'llah points to the spiritual or ideological dynamics behind the power struggle between God and ungodliness. It is to these 'representations' to which human beings surrender their faculties in a servile, delusional and self-interested fashion. The forbidden fruit always comes with promises of an enhanced reality beyond the ken of ordinary existence. 'Abdu'l-Bahá further confirms this by conceding that even idols (*aṣnám*) have a material existence compared to the purely fictional one of vain fantasies, which in the context of His discussion he identifies with the theological and mystical representations of the *ahl-i-tawḥíd*.[165] 'Multiple identities' can be regarded as accretions of passions in contradiction with the oneness of God:

> Let all be set free from the multiple identities (*ka<u>th</u>rat-i-nafs va havá*) that were born of passion and desire, and in the oneness of their love for God find a new way of life.[166]

That all this makes up idolatry is evinced by the following statement where idolatry is further dissected into its spiritual and psychological barebones:

> Were these to ask the Light of Truth concerning those images which their idle fancy hath carved, and were they to find His answer inconsistent with their own conceptions and their own understanding of the Book, they would assuredly denounce Him Who is the Mine and Wellhead of all Knowledge as the very negation of understanding.[167]

These products of imagination are 'extensions" 'of the world of dreams into vigil time.[168] Nonetheless they are extremely powerful, as confirmed by the qur'ánic dictum 'For [such as these] have taken to worshipping deities other than God, hoping that they would be [a source of] strength to them'.[169] Understandably so, since those deities are fixations of human passions.[170]

> Inasmuch as they have not apprehended the meaning of Knowledge, and have called by that name those images fashioned by their own fancy and which have sprung from the embodiments of ignorance, they therefore have inflicted upon the Source of Knowledge that which thou hast heard and witnessed.[171]

Violence in society: Prejudices and imitation

The 'path' of imitation is one which although adopted willingly by the individual is nevertheless made excusable by the law of great numbers. Human beings engage in this imitation in order to cash in on their withdrawal from truth and coherence (their dignity). As seen above, only rarely do expectations become rewarded as initially imagined; eventually, man 'sacrifices', gives away or barters his integrity to a figment or false representation of reality (the idols of his vain imaginings),[172] thus forfeiting his own rights implied in the divine trust:

> Take heed, O friends, that ye forfeit not so inestimable a benefit, or disregard its transcendent station. *Consider the multitude of lives that have been, and are still being, sacrificed in a world deluded by a mere phantom which the vain imaginations of its peoples have conceived.* Render thanks unto God, inasmuch as ye have attained unto your heart's Desire, and been united to Him Who is the Promise of all nations. Guard ye, with the aid of the one true God – exalted be His glory – the integrity of the station which ye have attained, and cleave to that which shall promote His Cause. He, verily, enjoineth on you what is right and conducive to the exaltation of man's station.[173] (emphasis added)

In a similar vein 'Abdu'l-Bahá affirms:

> They have deluded themselves with a fable, and to indulge their appetites

> they have done away with their own selves. They gave up everlasting glory in exchange for human pride, and they sacrificed greatness in both worlds to the demands of the insistent self.[174]

Bahá'u'lláh equals self-concern, or simply concern with these worldly things, with a form of self-inflicted punishment:

> Had the world been of any worth in His sight, He surely would never have allowed His enemies to possess it, even to the extent of a grain of mustard seed. He hath, however, caused you to be entangled with its affairs, in return for what your hands have wrought in His Cause. This, indeed, is a chastisement which ye, of your own will, have inflicted upon yourselves, could ye but perceive it.[175]

At this individual level, violence admits of being described as a violation perpetrated by the individual against his own deeper nature:

> all prejudices between man and man are falsehoods and violations of the will of God. God desires unity and love; He commands harmony and fellowship. Enmity is human disobedience; God Himself is love.[176]

There cannot be social violence or institutionalized violence without prior and concomitant assent given by the individual. This does not mean that social violence is a mere by-product, only on a larger scale, of individual violence. Just as the individual person engages in self-delusion, society has also the ability to produce its own false conceptions and entrap itself into collective forms of deception that require full commitment on the part of individuals. In the works of Bahá'u'lláh and 'Abdu'l-Bahá almost any scenario of violence and confrontation is in fact described as the consequence of large-scale generalized and collective expressions of fanaticism/prejudice (*ta'aṣṣub*) and imitation (*taqlíd,* dogmatic belief, blind following). Thus, referring to the conditions prevailing in the world, 'Abdu'l-Bahá explains that the ravages of modern warfare exceed those of previous times.[177] The cause seems clear to him:

> And the breeding-ground of all these tragedies is prejudice (*ta'aṣṣub*): prejudice of race and nation, of religion, of political opinion (*jinsí, vaṭaní, díní, síyásí*); and the root cause of prejudice is blind imitation of the past – imitation in religion, in racial attitudes, in national bias, in politics. So long as this aping of the past (*taqlíd*) persisteth, just so long will the foundations of the social order be blown to the four winds, just so long will humanity be continually exposed to direst peril.[178]

Likewise the decline of the people of Persia has its source in this imitating. Hence 'Abdu'l-Bahá's exhortation:

> Release yourselves from this blind following (*taqlíd*) of the bigots (*nufús-i-mutiváhimih*, literally 'self-conceited'), this senseless imitation which is the principal reason why men fall away into paths of ignorance and degradation.[179]

This is not to say that there is no room for some form of moderate national pride and intense religious sentiment. Yet, as seen previously, all 'collective centres' need to be reshaped and given new meaning by subjecting themselves to the discipline of God's new Dispensation. Religions can be regarded as the most powerful collective centres available (as opposed to imitations), and are conducive to peace:

> The divine religions are collective centres in which diverse standpoints may meet, agree and unify. They accomplish oneness of native lands, races and policies. For instance, Christ united various nations, brought peace to warring peoples and established the oneness of humankind.[180]

But even religion may also degenerate into a spiral of self-righteousness. When this happens, religion becomes a most deleterious source of destructiveness.

> . . . I wish to explain to you the principal reason of the unrest among nations. The chief cause is the misrepresentation of religion by the religious leaders and teachers. They teach their followers to believe that their own form of religion is the only one pleasing to God, and that followers of any other persuasion are condemned by the All-Loving Father and deprived of His Mercy and Grace. Hence arise among the peoples, disapproval, contempt, disputes and hatred. If these religious prejudices could be swept away, the nations would soon enjoy peace and concord.[181]

In order to counter such a risk, it is vital to ensure that religion is purged from those ills which bring with them divisiveness. In the long term and at a societal and historical level, those purges take place from time to time, be it by way of a divine interposition, or else through the spiritual renewal brought about by a new revelation.

24
Conclusion

The Bahá'í writings implicitly define Reality (and Truth) as an interconnected, living,[182] and moving order of things which, extending from the most insignificant being (starting at the mineral and atomic level) to the most exalted realities, follows patterns and contains a myriad of degrees and stations. The world of nature, in which man stands as the apex, is a dynamic reality subject to a continuous flux of changes, yet harmoniously contained and sustained through the omnipresent grace of God. From a human point of view, the preservation, progression and advancement of this general order are possible only if those things are known and related to in their truest essence, that is, if they are seen through God's eyes. Conversely, reality becomes disturbed when man meddles with that order in ignorance or disregard of its nature and subtle connection with other realities.

In view of what precedes, peace can be regarded at the individual level as a state of being characterized by a harmonious, healthy integration of man's inner powers, first within himself, and then with his fellow human beings and other creatures. The human heart, as the unifying symbol of the most important faculties in the spirit of man ('knowledge, volition and action')[183] is connected with the world of affections and desires. In other words, the integration of those faculties must be 'willed' for them to come to fruition. Thus unity or disunity within one's own self is itself dependent on free choice. For humans are creatures halfway between the animal and the angelic. At birth, a person is not determined by any of the two natures, as he or she has the potential for developing qualities belonging to both realms. 'Salvation' lies in integrating the animal and human natures into a higher spiritual dimension, which, if properly developed, will secure for man a 'sure handle' in the after-life.[184] Furthermore, the spiritual dimension in man is not subject to the same laws of causation and effect, progress and regress applicable to everyday phenomena: 'The soul', states 'Abdu'l-Bahá, 'does not evolve from degree to degree as a law.'[185] Thus a spiritual being is free from the need to retaliate when belittled, remains unruffled by the shifting of events, withstands trials,[186] undergoes poverty or riches with equanimity.[187] In this process of long endurance, tests will help the person to become detached from the trappings of this world.[188] This purging of oneself is necessary not because human beings are meant to be unconcerned about or contemptuous of the world, but because of their simultaneous awareness of the divine reality. The overcoming of divisions and violence requires this special presence of mind. Thus, spiritualization is typically defined as an awakening of the conscious soul to the reality of the Godhead.[189] It is this awareness of the real world of the divine impulses that, by comparison, causes ordinary consciousness to look like a dream-like state. God-consciousness is often depicted as implying forgetfulness of all other things ('Forget all save Me and commune with My spirit'),[190] and as a permanence of the remembrance of God in the light of which things are seen immersed in the sea of mercy and forgiveness. This consciousness allows human beings to be non-reactive when faced with adversities and hostility. In other words, human beings can be liberated from the endless cycle of action and reaction, strike and counter-strike, because there is no need for them to be intellectually and emotionally trapped into the seemingly insoluble dilemmas these situations portray. An integrated undivided self will not fight against itself, nor will it engage in reactive forms of aggression against others. This can only be achieved through a regulation or subduing of man's animal nature to his rational and spiritual faculties, that is by creating a state of 'readiness' or 'receptivity', which implies both an acceptance of limits and an openness to a higher form of awareness, which is the concomitant of such recognition. Man is invited to see his true self in God's image, and to pattern his whole existence as one belonging to a deeper and more exalted station than the one he finds as his starting point in life. The realization of this inherited nobility, excellence and perfectibility is dependent on whether he retains this spiritual orientation or fixation throughout her life. This operation has definitely a cosmic ring:

> Likewise, were the perfections of the spirit not to appear in this world, it would become dark and wholly animalistic. It is through the appearance of the spirit in the material body that this world is illumined. *Just as the spirit of man is the cause of the life of his body, so is the whole world even as a body and man as its spirit.* If man did not exist, if the perfections of the spirit were not manifested and the light of the mind were not shining in this world, it would be like a body without a spirit.[191] (emphasis added)

The Bahá'í writings point markedly to a series of counter-themes of man's dignity and perfectibility: vain imaginings, idle fancies, imitations and prejudices. These are defined as 'images' or 'idols', in other words pseudo-representations of truth which while satisfying 'formally' man's need for truth in actual fact cave in to motives totally spurious, thus opening the way to violence and the corruption of life at the intellectual and moral level. A spiritual frugality and some iconoclastic vision is therefore needed to offset the illusory nature of the engaging, manifold and insistent representations which the self is wont to display. One of the fundamental functions filled by God's Messengers is the removal of these ideological barriers that stand between human beings and their Creator:

> The divine Manifestations have been iconoclastic in Their teachings, uprooting error, destroying false religious beliefs and summoning mankind anew to the fundamental oneness of God.[192]

Moreover, man is not the 'fallen creature' which he is held up to be in the moralistic Christian interpretation of the story of Adam and Eve, nor the imitating creature who relinquishes his own efforts and gives away his freedom to conform to the elaborate formalities of *taqlíd.* An important aspect of the Bahá'í denunciation of *taqlíd* lies precisely in the fact that this institution disempowers the individual and reinforces extraordinarily the authority wielded by a caste of self-appointed religious leaders.

Prejudices, which are the breeding ground of most forms of violence, are made up to a large extent of imitations and traditional received knowledge that is passed on to the next generations in an uncritical way. Such imitations can become extraordinarily dangerous when massive uncritical assent becomes also a way of strengthening the plausibility of their proposed truths. While prejudices tend to focus attention on certain exclusivist notes, thus justifying violence and aggression, by contrast, 'collective centres' such as patriotism, religion, science or even economic interests may have a unifying effect whenever they are used as rallying points, rather than as barriers set up against each other.

> Whatsoever instilleth assurance (*ráḥat*) into the hearts of men, whatsoever exalteth their station (*buzurgí*) or promoteth their contentment (*raḍí*), is acceptable in the sight of God. How lofty is the station (*maqám*) which man, if he but choose to fulfil his destiny, can attain![193]

PART V

A FRAMEWORK FOR PEACE
THE BAHÁ'Í ETHOS

> True peace and tranquillity will only be realized when every soul will have become the well wisher of mankind.[1]

Historically, the Bahá'í religion has partly broken away from prevailing codes of morality by setting meanings and terms of reference which give new currency to what otherwise the Bahá'í scriptures regard as exalted 'eternal verities' and perennial divine attributes (*ṣifát*). References in the Bahá'í writings to the raising of a 'new race of men'[2] – presented as 'the supreme and distinguishing function of His Revelation'– suggest a conscious effort at attaining personal excellence and moral integrity to a degree. Ringing as it does with echoes of Paul's 'new man', and with reverberations of the 'new heaven and new earth' of the Book of Revelation,[3] this view of a glorified humanity carries important implications for the development of Bahá'í morals and for any conceptualization of peace, as the following chapters will endeavour to expound. Thus the emphasis placed on the uniqueness and excellence of Bahá'u'lláh's Dispensation can be taken as a summons calling upon the people of Bahá to rise above ordinary experience in order to realize the meaning invested in the inner reality of all things. Terms like *badí'* ('new', 'unparalleled', 'wonderful'), or *a'ẓam* ('most excellent'), often found in the Bahá'í writings, are employed to characterize the depth and scope intended for Bahá'u'lláh's Revelation. Moreover, the new aeon is said to be unparalleled in that it supplies the yardstick against which not only present realities must be measured, but all previous Dispensations as well.[4]

In this context Bahá'í moral life is not conceived as a regularization through atonement of past and present sins or, in more eschatological terms, as a climatic triumph of the good over the bad; nor is it understood as scrupulous adjustment to the codified requirements of the Law, with its corollary of a patterning (*taqlíd*) of one's conduct after the example and rulings of a jurisprudential elite. It is conceived, rather, as a gradual decantation, refinement and increasing reflection of divine virtues. The inner impulses driving this process ('the love of transcendence')[5] come from the same build-up towards perfection that characterizes the movement of creation through its various realms, as well as the expansion of human 'collective centres' towards wider and stronger forms of incorporation (culminating in the kingdom of God), or the personal refinement leading to a second birth. It is a transformative process whereby prejudices, idle fancies and vain imaginings – which can be taken as culturally-determined accretions (*idola*, idols, false representations) of 'sin'– are definitely overcome and the inherent human nobility is brought to the fore.

Yet the Bahá'í writings do not offer a solidification of these virtues[6] in the form of a set of prescribed, ritualized or intellectualized behaviours. The rigidity of quantifying or qualifying behaviours is constantly avoided by relating the quality of a human action to its acceptability by God (*riḍáy-i-Ḥaqq*, good-pleasure), or to the only living model in the person of 'Abdu'l-Bahá (the perfect exemplar, *mat͟hal-i-á'lá*). In the words of Bahá'u'lláh, the acceptability of man's actions 'in this Day' depends on their being 'matchless'.[7] Only the 'purest deeds' will win God's good-pleasure.[8]

While Part IV has dealt with some basic features of a Bahá'í anthropology, the present Part V will move a step forward in an attempt to examine some of the key moral dimensions that reciprocally link individuals to their communities through accepted standards of personal and social behaviour. The account will commence by providing a brief outline of Bahá'í morality. Following my previous presentation,I will adopt as a given the consideration that human beings are defined in the Bahá'í writings as noble creatures potentially able to realize God's will (or His 'image', i.e. the embodiment of all divine virtues), and thus acquire the spiritual organs of 'a new eye, a new ear, a new heart, and a new mind'.[9] As 'Abdu'l-Bahá repeatedly pointed out, it is for the cultivation of this second spiritual nature that the Manifestations of God gave up their all:

> This spiritual nature (*ṭabí'at-i-rawḥáníyih*), which has come to exist through the grace of the Divine Reality (*fayḍ-i-ḥaqíqat-i-raḥmáníyih*), is the sum of all perfections (*jámi' jamí'y-i-kamálát ast*) and proceeds from the breath of the Holy Spirit. It is the divine perfections; it is light, spirituality (*rawḥaníyat*), guidance (*hidáyat*), exaltation (*'úlúvvíyat*), high-mindedness (*bolandíy-i-himmat*), justice (*'idalat*), love (*mawḥibbat*), generosity, kindness (*mihrabání*) to all, and charitable deeds (*k͟hayrát*):It is life upon life. This spiritual nature is an effulgence of the splendours of the Sun of Truth.[10]

But the conquering of this second spiritual nature is defined in terms of a dilemma apparently irresolvable: how can an ethics that reclaims autonomy for human beings (as in 'Abdu'l-Bahá's advocacy of an 'unfettered investigation of truth'), yet ground this autonomy on the realization of the divine 'trust' (*amánat*), in complete submission to God's will? This will mark the beginning of my exploration.

In characterizing the Bahá'í ethos I will stress the importance attached to dialogue and kindness in any communication exchanges as an alternative to violent or aggressive persuasion. Similarly, the service-orientation of this morality, as opposed to theoretical lip-service to humanity, will be underlined. This will be followed by a discussion of two key 'Bahá'í principles', namely, those of religious and organic unities, both of which are of fundamental import to a Bahá'í understanding of peace and to any conception of the Bahá'í ethos. The connection between the two will be clarified, and in the process some light will be added as to how the Bahá'í writings approach the reconciliation of religious differences, a question that from a Bahá'í standpoint occupies a paradigmatic place in the world problematic. The attention will then be turned to Bahá'í consultation, an institution in itself that, in a collegiate culture devoid of clergy, takes on a far more significant role than is usually credited. Consultation becomes in a way the Bahá'í procedural panacea for the peaceful settlement of differences. Nonetheless, its true worth is perhaps better defined by its function as the breeding ground for the cultivation of a new type of collegiate leadership (no campaigning, no conception of 'sides') based on a core of virtues such as moderation, service, truth-searching (for instance in discriminating needs and priorities from interests and secondary matters), fair-mindedness and reconciliation of interests.

In using this rather indirect approach to a delimitation of the Bahá'í ethos I have been guided by the notion that in the study of any religious system due weight must be given to the background provided by its own historical record, its stated doctrinal and moral tenets, its world perspective, and the general relationships it fosters from within and from without. In this broader view, ethics becomes an integral, albeit more specialized, province in the realm of what, for want of a better word, we may term 'ethos', a concept which Keck has pointedly described in these terms:

> That ethos is not ethics should be clear enough, for ethics is the systematic reflection on the nature of the good or the right, whereas ethos refers to the life-style of a group or a society. An ethic can be the rationale for an ethos or a critique of it. While an ethos can result from the working out of principles or convictions, it is never explainable on this basis alone, for, among other reasons, an ethos always includes assumptions, values, and habits which are not produced by conscious reasoning but which may actually be the controlling factors in the formulation of the principles and convictions themselves. In religion, as elsewhere, practices and habits more often receive interpretations than interpretations generate practices. One thinks readily of festivals such as Passover or Christmas, or of rites such as circumcision or baptism.[11]

Given the scope of this part of the book, a conscious choice has been made to leave out of its purview a number of issues that relate to this broader perspective. With the exception of the themes of organic unity and unity in diversity (both conceptual metaphors), often illustrated by analogues of harmonious plurality, no attempt will be made to explore how the Bahá'í ethos has been moulded by a number of what elsewhere I have termed 'ethical representations', that is, 'a set of stories, symbols or images destined to represent a number of values or a borderline ethical situation'.[12] As pointed out in the introduction, the Lovejoyan idea (and 'organic unity', and 'consultation' can be counted as such) is descriptive in principle, but prescriptive at heart. Of interest, but equally beyond the range of this work, would be to determine how these ethical representations are actually transmitted, learned and reinterpreted in different cultural contexts and by successive Bahá'í generations.

25
Bahá'í Morality

Moral life can be defined primarily as the prevailing over one's self and secondarily as the determination of one's conduct in light of what is regarded as good. The first aspect deals with the relationship that the individual keeps with his or her own self. The second concerns the determination or regulation of actions or omissions *ad extra*. Concerning in particular the first part 'Abdu'l-Bahá is reported to have said:

> Moral life consists in the government of one's self. Immortality is government of a human soul by the Divine Will.[13]

From this point of view, self-ruling, or autonomy, is seen as the legitimate goal of a truly moral life. Since the Enlightenment this has been, for the most part, the accepted view among contemporary moralists and educationalists. Yet 'Abdu'l-Bahá's parallelism underlines a second dimension of moral life, that of immortality, which in a sense appears as contradicting the autonomy principle: the surrender of one's autonomy to God's Will. The implicit question rests on the apparent incompatibility between the realization of an autonomous moral life and the willing subjugation of one's will to an 'external' moral source. A distinctive Bahá'í approach to morality cannot be dissociated from both aspects.

The first part in 'Abdu'l-Bahá's dictum seems to refer to a preparatory task, which is essentially human, a reordering of one's house, or pulling together of oneself (see Part IV). Both Bahá'u'lláh's *Kitáb-i-Íqán* and the *Seven Valleys* begin with a description of the state of mind and preliminary work which the individual must accomplish in order to reconcile with himself or herself prior to achieving communion with God. It is clearly a 'purifying' phase characterized by the cleansing of the soul from worldly attachments, especially those that are the product of human love and knowledge; it is also a transitional phase in which distance between the subject and the goal is gradually removed.[14]

The second half in 'Abdu'l-Bahá's sentence links this effort to subservience to God's will, and is presented no longer as a task that human beings can accomplish by themselves, but rather as a consequence of their own activity. This is God's domain and is governed by laws and conditions beyond the ken of human understanding. In the first half of 'Abdu'l-Bahá's sentence ('moral life consists in the government of one's self') the subject is the 'I' with which any person stands identified; in the second half ('immortality is government of a human soul by the Divine Will') the moral agent becomes a recipient dissolving itself into God's Providence.[15] While the disciplining of one's self seems to imply effort, merit, the acquiring of capacity, conversely the surrendering of oneself – a true inversion of the normal perspective – carries with it notes of self-evanescence, cessation of volition and desire ('death', extinction, *faná*). In a Bahá'í sense, therefore, the subject of a moral life is the individual; but in a truly spiritual life the subject must in fact become the object, and as such renounce any claims over personal autonomy, in which case the transfer of the spiritual senses is made possible: 'With the ear of God he heareth; with the eye of God he beholdeth the mysteries of divine creation.'[16]

In everyday life personal merit or demerit have a relative justification. A person is not censored for inherited or innate traits – explains 'Abdu'l-Bahá – but because of acquired characteristics.[17] Virtuous works retain intrinsic value to the extent that they help man to model himself by his own action. 'However, unto them that are rid of all attachments a deed is, verily, its own reward.'[18] Here distinctions based on categories such as merit or distinction disappear and are regarded as naught insofar as they appear in their undivided inherent unity. In this dimension silence seems the only way of acknowledging that discourse must lead to a cessation of differences (already conciliated within oneself); this condition is often signified by the silence and self-oblivion induced by the state of awe and wonder.[19] Bahá'u'lláh explicitly appears to be reluctant to dwell on the relationships between the various states and conditions prevailing in the human self:

> Much hath been written in the books of old concerning the various stages in the development of the soul, such as concupiscence, irascibility, inspiration, benevolence, contentment, Divine good-pleasure, and the like; the Pen of the Most High, however, is disinclined to dwell upon them. Every soul that walketh humbly with its God, in this Day, and cleaveth unto Him, shall find itself invested with the honour and glory of all goodly names and stations.[20]

A similar prevention seems to explain why no effort is made in the Bahá'í writings to categorize, and much less legislate, what constitutes 'good works', a fact obviously related to the emphasis placed by Bahá'u'lláh on God's *own* good-pleasure when assessing the moral value of good works. Understood as a mechanical way of 'trapping' the object of one's aspiration, good works cannot be relied upon, for the Ultimate Objective cannot be objectified:

> Make not your deeds as snares wherewith to entrap the object of your aspiration, and deprive not yourselves of this Ultimate Objective for which have ever yearned all such as have drawn nigh unto God. Say: The very life of all deeds is My good pleasure, and all things depend upon Mine acceptance.[21]

This emphasis on the spiritual element that must animate good works is also at the heart of 'Abdu'l-Bahá's explanation on the merits and condition of those who, while disbelieving in God, perform the very same deeds that are supposed to characterize believers:

> . . . good deeds alone, without the recognition of God, cannot lead to eternal redemption, to everlasting success and salvation, and to admittance into the Kingdom of God.[22]
>
> Briefly, good deeds become perfect and complete only after the knowledge of God has been acquired, the love of God has been manifested, and spiritual attractions and goodly motives have been attained. Otherwise, though good deeds be praiseworthy, if they do not spring from the knowledge of God, from the love of God, and from a sincere intention, they will be imperfect.[23]

In view of the above it can be seen that 'Abdu'l-Bahá's use of the term 'immortality' has little to do with the survival of the 'I' (immortality in a materialistic sense), and much more with the transcendence of 'salvation' (*niját*). In referring to immortality 'Abdu'l-Bahá, therefore, is not concerned with a *post-mortem* life, but with an immortality predating death, a point he often illustrated with elaborations on the Christian second birth and the baptism of 'water and fire'.[24]

How can man reach that condition? How can this plane, which 'Abdu'l-Bahá links to man's second birth, be defined? The same question could also apply to the social or collective counterpart of this question: how can God's Kingdom, its peace and justice, be enthroned upon earth? The reason seems to lie in the internal dynamism that is present in creation, the same dynamism that presides over the movement of God's creatures from one plane of existence to the next, or the articulation of ever more complex forms of integration among civilized societies now moving towards their climax: the unification of mankind. In reality – explains 'Abdu'l-Bahá – one of the basic driving forces in human beings compels them to aim for the sublime:

> Praise be to God! Man ever aspires to greater heights (*tavajuhish bih 'uluvv ast*) and loftier goals. He ever seeks to attain a world (*'álam*) surpassing that which he inhabits, and to ascend to a degree (*darrijih*) above that which he occupies. This love of transcendence is one of the hallmarks of man (*ḥubb-i-'ulúvvíyat az khaṣa'iṣ-i-insán ast*).[25]

While human aspirations to secure continuity after death are by no means disregarded in Bahá'í doctrine, quite on the contrary, here the emphasis is on access to another plane of life within present existence, one that would accordingly find exalted continuity in the next life. Thus, the bond between life after death and life on a mortal plane is not a sequential or chronological one; indeed the connection between the Kingdom of Abhá (which in a sense is also the world of the deceased) and that of the living is subjected to constant renewal. This spiritual communication, mysterious though it might be, never ceases and accounts for the spiritual energies that have set humanity in motion towards its exalted goal. Spirituality, or the 'morals of the Kingdom',[26] is what gives substance to this higher sphere. The essence of religion can then be considered as revolving on 'that mystic feeling which unites Man with God':[27]

> The Bahá'í Faith, like all other Divine Religions, is thus fundamentally mystic in character. Its chief goal is the development of the individual and society, through the acquisition of spiritual virtues and powers.[28]

'Love of transcendence' is the driving force behind this movement, a vital energy whose atrophy or absence leads to the inertia of everyday experience, or worse, to the countermovement or vertigo of 'self' and 'passion'.[29] The overcoming of these contrasts or contrary trends requires active involvement on the part of the individual through discrimination. Bahá'u'lláh emphatically asserts that human beings have been called upon to exert their intelligence in order to discern between good and evil, what is and is not. To know oneself, to debase or to exalt one's nature, to seek glory or to inflict humiliation upon oneself, all are moral choices that human beings cannot avoid making:

> . . . the first effulgence which hath dawned from the horizon of the Mother Book is that man should know his own self (*ma'arifat-i-insán ast bi nafs-i-khud*) and recognize that which leadeth unto loftiness or lowliness (*'uluvv va dunuvv*), glory or abasement (*zillat va 'izat*), wealth or poverty (*tharvat va faqr*).[30]

Bahá'u'lláh's exhortation to be just and fair belongs clearly in the same category and retains the same degree of primacy, for 'justice' (fair-mindedness, *inṣáf*), presented as the 'most beloved of all things', is clearly defined as the heart's discerning capacity whereby one's moral or spiritual behaviour is not only determined but also disciplined:

> By its aid thou shalt see with thine own eyes and not through the eyes of others, and shalt know of thine own knowledge and not through the knowledge of thy neighbour. Ponder this in thy heart; how it behooveth thee to be. Verily justice is My gift to thee and the sign of My loving-kindness. Set it then before thine eyes.[31]

This kind of discernment which is justice (also translated as 'equity' or 'fairmindedness') cannot be deferred nor delegated. Each person is a discriminating agent and hence responsible for his or her own acts *in fairness*. For no one can exercise virtues in the place of others, except in an exemplary manner, without by the same token subtracting from them what is inalienable. In this sense moral life is primarily directed towards oneself: First each person must engage himself in his own training, thinking of how to perfect himself, for what is needed foremost is the education of one's own soul;[32] it does not consist in the moralizing of others, an activity which Shoghi Effendi describes plainly as a 'waste of time':

> Each of us is responsible for one life only, and that is our own. Each of us is immeasurably far from being 'perfect as our heavenly Father is perfect' and the task of perfecting our own life and character is one that requires all our attention, our will- power and energy. If we allow our attention and energy to be taken up in efforts to keep others right and remedy their faults, we are wasting precious time.[33]

Elsewhere, justice – emphatically reasserted as the essence of Bahá'u'lláh's Revelation – is associated with the freeing from imitation, as well as with discernment and a searching eye:

> The essence of all that We have revealed for thee is Justice (*inṣáf*), is for man to free himself from idle fancy (*waḥm*) and imitation (*taqlíd*), discern with the eye of oneness (*tawḥíd*) His glorious handiwork, and look into all things with a searching eye.[34]

In this connection the image of the heart as a well-established citadel or a fortress underscores the notion that the self must conquer an impregnable condition free from the mutability and capricious oscillations attached to ordinary experience:

> For every one of you his paramount duty is to choose for himself that on which no other may infringe and none usurp from him. Such a thing – and to this the Almighty is My witness – is the love of God, could ye but perceive it.
>
> Build ye for yourselves such houses as the rain and floods can never destroy, which shall protect you from the changes and chances of this life.[35]

Naturally, this does not mean that virtues lack a collective dimension, or, to put it differently, that they cannot be appropriated in a social context:

> . . . the merciful God, our Creator, has deposited within human realities certain latent and potential virtues. Through education and culture these virtues deposited by the loving God will become apparent in the human reality, even as the unfolding of the tree from within the germinating seed.[36]

A divine civilization, emerging from the collective centre of religion, is understood as a matrix where human beings obtain refinement and cultivate spiritual virtues. But this does not imply that spirituality is induced solely 'from without' the individual. The establishment of a new world order – stresses Shoghi Effendi – depends largely on the regeneration which the believers are capable of effecting in their own lives, as well as on a correlative purification of social maladies: 'Its chief goal [of the Bahá'í Faith] is the development of the individual and society, through the acquisition of spiritual virtues and powers.'[37] The first task is vital in that it requires that Bahá'ís focus their attention on themselves, their needs and deficiencies, as a means to clear the way for the establishing of a rightful and healthy society, which would be a peaceful one. That this is the most important single task that Bahá'ís should undertake is illustrated by Shoghi Effendi's reference to Bahá'u'lláh's words:

> The most vital duty, in this day, is to purify your characters, to correct your manners, and improve your conduct . . . inasmuch as the purpose of the Manifestation of God . . . is to educate the souls of men, and refine the character of every living man.[38]

Among the moral prerequisites that Bahá'ís should strive to fulfil the following stand out:

> a high sense of moral rectitude in their social and administrative activities, absolute chastity in their individual lives, and complete freedom from prejudice in their dealings with peoples of a different race, class, creed or colour.[39]

Expatiating further on this point, Shoghi Effendi links rectitude of conduct to a set of virtues implicated by it, such as 'justice, equity, truthfulness, honesty, fair-mindedness, reliability, and trustworthiness',[40] all of which possess an individual and trans-personal dimension. Through these 'dynamic virtues'[41] the believers become, by way of example, the 'lump that must leaven the peoples of the world'.[42]

26
Spiritual Behaviour: Action as Service to Humanity

Spirituality, the conscious cultivation of one's divine endowment (*amánat*), is the main defining activity of human beings. This cultivation or education, which can be represented variously as the act of toiling the land, polishing a jewel, or bringing out pearls from the riches of the ocean to the surface, constitutes the heart of religious doctrine:

> Every other word of Bahá'u'lláh's and 'Abdu'l-Bahá's writings is a preachment [sic] on moral and ethical conduct; all else is the form, the chalice, into which the pure spirit must be poured; without the spirit and the action which must demonstrate it, it is a lifeless form.[43]

In the Bahá'í writings the emphasis on leading a virtuous life is distinguished from mere piety[44] and ritual law, and carefully detached from any priestly associations,[45] especially all those that would belie double standards. In effect, some of Bahá'u'lláh's harshest words appear to be significantly reserved for behaviours often misidentified as marks of superior knowledge and morals. Sciences that 'begin in words and end in words' or 'metaphysical hair-splitting',[46] mystic anomy, idle contention,[47] reliance on miracles[48], ascetic practices and mortifications,[49] public displays of religiosity, mendicancy,[50] the shunning of certain professions or trades, 'excessive reading'[51] and 'excess of speech',[52] all are rejected. The value of words, traditionally the preserve of the interpretative elite, is not sacralized, but suspended or relativized unless translated into action. 'Guidance (*hidáyat*)', states Bahá'u'lláh, 'hath ever been given by words, and now it is given by deeds', for 'words are the property of all alike, whereas such deeds as these belong only to Our loved ones'.[53] In fact, previous religions have been equally responsive to this leitmotif:

> The Books, the Scriptures and Holy Writings of previous ages have all proclaimed the joyful tidings that the purpose underlying this most mighty Revelation is none other than the rehabilitation of the world and its nations; *that*

> *perchance the power of utterance may prevail over the power of arms, and the world's affairs be administered through the potency of love.*[54] (emphasis added)

The superiority of words – i.e. dialogue and peaceful speech – is emphasized by Bahá'u'lláh in contrast with the violent religious practice of suppressing others or bringing them into submission. The power of the word to effect changes of heart (for 'Every word is endowed with a spirit'[55]) is restated, but on condition that it be timely and appropriately expressed, otherwise its influence may be compared to the effects of fire or poison:

> Human utterance is an essence which aspireth to exert its influence and needeth moderation. As to its influence, this is conditional upon refinement which in turn is dependent upon hearts which are detached and pure. As to its moderation, this hath to be combined with tact and wisdom as prescribed in the Holy Scriptures and Tablets.[56]

Following in the tradition initiated by the Báb in His celebrated exhortation addressed to the peoples of the West calling them to leave their cities (in the *Qayyúmu'l-Asmá*),[57] and the farewell speech addressed by the Báb to the Letters of the Living, modelled on those of Jesus to His disciples,[58] Bahá'u'lláh summons His followers to spread God's fragrances and the good tidings with utmost consideration:

> Show forbearance and benevolence and love to one another. Should any one among you be incapable of grasping a certain truth, or be striving to comprehend it, show forth, when conversing with him, a spirit of extreme kindliness and good-will. Help him to see and recognize the truth, without esteeming yourself to be, in the least, superior to him, or to be possessed of greater endowments.[59]

Bahá'u'lláh stresses that he has 'annulled the rule of the sword, as an aid to Our Cause, and substituted for it the power born of the utterance of men'.[60] His message must be spread exclusively through the instrumentality of words: 'Aid ye your Lord with the sword of wisdom and of utterance'[61] and by way of an exemplary conduct. The peaceful nature of this propagation is itself a mark of the sacred nature of the divine message; no degree of coercion nor violence is deemed to be acceptable: 'Arise for the triumph of My Cause, and, through the power of thine utterance, subdue the hearts of men.'[62] Engaging in discourse in turn requires the observance of some basic rules, the first among them being that the teacher must first teach himself: 'Unless he teacheth his own self, the words of his mouth will not influence the heart of the seeker.'[63] Concomitant with this is the duty of cladding oneself with a 'saintly character', an obligation which, in the absence of a clerical class and given that all Bahá'ís are exhorted to teach His Cause,[64] implies an added effort at excelling oneself and disregarding one's own interests:

> O people of God! Do not busy yourselves in your own concerns; let your thoughts be fixed upon that which will rehabilitate the fortunes of mankind and sanctify the hearts and souls of men. This can best be achieved through pure and holy deeds, through a virtuous life and a goodly behaviour. Valiant acts will ensure the triumph of this Cause, and a saintly character will reinforce its power.[65]

When engaging in dialogue with other people, Bahá'ís must become intent listeners who in responding to questions or arguments should avoid assuming either a condescending or a belligerent attitude:

> A kindly approach and loving behaviour toward the people are the first requirements for the teaching of the Cause. The teacher must carefully listen to whatever a person has to say – even though his talk may consist only of vain imaginings and blind repetitions of the opinions of others. One should not resist or engage in argument. The teacher must avoid disputes which will end in stubborn refusal or hostility, because the other person will feel overpowered and defeated. Therefore, he will be more inclined to reject the Cause. One should rather say: 'Maybe you are right, but kindly consider the question from this other point of view.' Consideration, respect and love encourage people to listen and do not force them to respond with hostility. They are convinced because they see that your purpose is not to defeat them, but to convey truth, to manifest courtesy, and to show forth heavenly attributes. This will encourage the people to be fair. Their spiritual natures will respond, and, by the bounty of God, they will find themselves recreated.[66]

Furthermore, the quality of one's discourse must be honey or 'mild as milk, that the children of men may be nurtured and edified thereby and may attain the ultimate goal of human existence which is the station of true understanding and nobility (*maqám-i-idrák va buzurgí*)'.[67] This etiquette extends to the consideration that must be accorded to the sayings and writings of other fellow-human beings. These should not be viewed, Bahá'u'lláh counsels, 'with too critical an eye', rather they should be approached 'in a spirit of open-mindedness and loving sympathy'.[68]

Likewise, similar consideration must be extended to all those who, although working on materialist premises, still render worthy services to mankind, as noted by 'Abdu'l-Bahá in His letter to Auguste Forel,[69] or in His explanation to Laura Clifford Barney[70] with regard to philanthropists who work for the welfare of mankind with no religious motivation.

Yet, compared to the eloquence of good deeds, words recede in importance and hence are placed in a subordinate position within the overall ethical framework: 'Let deeds (*'amál*), not words (*aqvál*), be your adorning,' proclaims Bahá'u'lláh.[71] Instances of this idea are common stock in the Bahá'í writings. Often good deeds, or their underlying virtues, are metaphorically compared to handsome robes or mantles:

> The purpose of the one true God in manifesting Himself is to summon all mankind to truthfulness (*ṣidq*) and sincerity (*ṣifá*), to piety (*díyánat*) and trustworthiness (*amánat*), to resignation (*taslím*) and submissiveness (*riḍá*) to the Will of God, to forbearance (*rifq*) and kindliness (*mudárá*), to uprightness (*taqá*) and wisdom (*ḥikmat*). His object is to array every man with the mantle of a saintly character (*akhláq-i-marḍíyyih*), and to adorn him with the ornament of holy and goodly deeds (*a'mál-i-muqaddasih*).[72]

Conversely, lack of deeds – including at an elementary level idleness or resistance to occupying oneself in gainful employment – is portrayed sometimes in the strongest language reminiscent of the Gospels:

> Thus it is incumbent on every one to engage in crafts and professions, for therein lies the secret of wealth, O men of understanding! For results depend upon means, and the grace of God shall be all-sufficient unto you. Trees that yield no fruit have been and will ever be for the fire.[73]

Texts such as the one quoted above have important implications for the development of a work ethic stressing responsibility towards oneself and one's dependants and, when linked to a broader ideal of service, to the welfare of the entire community. Thus the acquisition of virtues as the way of spiritualizing life in all its dimensions becomes a pervasive Bahá'í theme: 'The betterment of the world can be accomplished through pure and goodly deeds, through commendable and seemly conduct.'[74] Elaborations of how these moral qualities or 'dynamic virtues' may interrelate were given by Shoghi Effendi in connection with the qualifications of the believer and, especially, members of Bahá'í institutions.[75] Similar qualifications can also be found in different contexts with regard, for instance, to the attributes of the learned,[76] as well as the wayfarer and seeker,[77] teachers of the Faith,[78] and statesmen,[79] or in connection with family relationships,[80] social intercourse and business transactions.[81] In all such instances the appropriate code of behaviour is sketched only in its broad lines. The absence of legalistic derivations, inferences or further scholastic elaborations in the overall Bahá'í moral system seems to be a deliberate feature of its open-ended nature rather than a mark of a-systemacity. Entire areas of private law, manners and civility in general are left to the discretion of the believer or regulated to a minimum. Issues concerning personal appearance and apparel, disposal of personal property, consumption of food and beverages, family relationships, forms of public and private worship, business transactions and like matters are treated succinctly, usually appealing to moderation or in some cases hinting at the most agreeable or noblest course of action. Even a work such as Bahá'u'lláh's *Hidden Words*, which in some respects can be construed as a collection of ethical exhortations and maxims couched in the evocative language of sapiential literature, is most prominently set in the context of a mystical relationship with the Beloved, rather than as a moral compendium.

Moral behaviour is thus redefined in accordance with the enhanced states of consciousness and aesthetic perceptions that prevail in a love connection. The attitude towards the law is depicted in similar terms, for instance by likening the law to inebriating wine or by praising obedience as love subjugation:

> Observe My commandments, for the love of My beauty. Happy is the lover that hath inhaled the divine fragrance of his Best-Beloved from these words, laden with the perfume of a grace which no tongue can describe.[82]

Under these terms, moral behaviour takes on the nature of the object of love itself, and is thereby less determined by the objective conditions that obtain in a given situation. A blend of planes, physical and spiritual, constitutes the deliberate aim pursued in modelling the functioning of the Bahá'í community and the strengthening or shaping of personal bonds. The Nineteen Day Feast, for instance, is described by 'Abdu'l-Bahá in this vein as involving the mirroring of the spiritual world so that the 'flesh take on the qualities of soul; and just as the spiritual delights are here in profusion, so too the material delights'.[83] Seen from this perspective, the act of moving beyond the plane of limitations becomes a liberating, bird-flying experience. The following explanation of 'Abdu'l-Bahá with regard to riches is particularly representative in this regard:

> Luxuries cut off the freedom of communication. One who is imprisoned by desires is always unhappy; the children of the Kingdom have unchained themselves from their desires. Break all fetters and seek for spiritual joy and enlightenment; then, though you walk on this earth, *you will perceive yourselves to be within the divine horizon*. To man alone is this possible. When we look about us we see every other creature captive to his environment.[84] (emphasis added)

The aptitude for freeing one's perception from the conditioning of one's immediate circumstances (whether our own limiting circumstances – the prison of ego – or others') is suggested in the above passage by the metaphor of the horizon. The same spatial and visual metaphor can be applied to multiple areas of personal and interpersonal experience. The overcoming of prejudices would be impracticable without this projective capacity. In the area of interpersonal relationships, for instance, 'changes of heart' can be induced by adopting a higher and more self-removed perspective. Transcending the 'particularity' of a certain point of view becomes then key to resolving seemingly insoluble tensions:

> There are imperfections in every human being, and you will always become unhappy if you look toward the people themselves. But if you look toward God, you will love them and be kind to them, for the world of God is the world of perfection and complete mercy. Therefore, do not look at the shortcomings of anybody; see with the sight of forgiveness. The imperfect eye beholds

> imperfections. The eye that covers faults looks toward the Creator of souls. He created them, trains and provides for them, endows them with capacity and life, sight and hearing; therefore, they are the signs of His grandeur. You must love and be kind to everybody, care for the poor, protect the weak, heal the sick, teach and educate the ignorant.[85]

In the absence of an interpretive or legislative class, the responsibility to discern the meaning of the Word of God and its accompanying duties is placed on the conscience of each individual. Truth – spiritual, ethical, practical – is realized then in the personal encounter of the believer with the Word of God and its living embodiments. At a community level, truth appears as a perfectible outcome of spiritual consultation, with its formal and informal learning opportunities. At both levels the emphasis is on combining rightly motivated knowledge with action, rather than on knowledge alone.[86]

Individual and collective moralities

The blend of a highly autonomous human being and a highly developed civilization is thought to be possible only through the transformation of the individual and the correlative infusion of spiritual values into culture. If the world is to become a mirror of the unity of God, then the individuals themselves must become perfect embodiments of the 'new creation'. In the words of 'Abdu'l-Bahá:

> We are striving with heart and soul, resting neither day nor night, seeking not a moment's ease, to make this world of man the mirror of the unity of God (*á'íniy-i-vaḥdat-i-ilahí*). Then how much more must the beloved of the Lord reflect that unity? And this cherished hope, this yearning wish of ours will be visibly fulfilled only on the day when the true friends of God arise to carry out the Teachings of the Abhá Beauty . . .[87]

The dynamics of this twofold process have already been examined to some extent. It remains to be shown what elements of Bahá'í doctrine support a non-individualistic understanding of behaviour. In other words, why and in what sense does the Bahá'í ethos imply essentially an ethics of action or, perhaps more accurately described, an ethics focused on a personalist approach to community building. Although admittedly the energetic denunciation of *taqlíd* could have supported the development of an individualistic ethics resulting in a largely liberal, atomistic and non-conformist sectarian faith, the parallel emphasis on service to humanity and on concerted unified efforts contained since its inception the elements of a strong communitarian movement. The harmonizing of these tendencies into a new synthesis was largely due to Shoghi Effendi's work. The process, however, as we know from the historical record of well-established communities, was far from being a straightforward one.

In particular, the appeal to a non-individualistic concept of salvation and ethics was made explicit by Bahá'u'lláh in one of His letters bidding Christians to recognise Him. In His own words:

> Verily, He [Jesus] said: 'Come ye after Me, and I will make you become fishers of men.' In this day, however, We say: 'Come ye after Me, that We may make you to become quickeners of mankind.'[88]

This well-known passage has a foundational value for Bahá'í theology and ethics. Shoghi Effendi, for instance, refers to it in connection with the decline of Christian civilization.[89] The new Bahá'í theophany, in contrast, is said to give salvation new meaning and a broader scope. The reference to 'men' and 'mankind' in Bahá'u'lláh's passage places the individual, or the single collective, in contrast with mankind taken as a whole, that is without any exclusion. This universalistic appeal is further reinforced by the fact that Bahá'u'lláh warns Christians not to tarry at the gate inasmuch as 'they who were not in the Kingdom have now entered it'.[90] This allusion shows that the Kingdom has widened to incorporate peoples of other faiths. It also indicates that now Christians can become relegated as a result of their own exclusivist and individualistic understanding of salvation.

The collective interests of humanity now take on the nature of a moral imperative that ought to guide the actions and policies adopted by rulers. If implemented, this perspective, which must be supported by a universal hospitality, may ultimately lead to the establishment of the reign of justice:

> The tabernacle of unity hath been raised (*sirápardiy-i-yigánigí buland shud*); regard ye not one another as strangers (*bi chashm-i-bígánigán*). Ye are the fruits of one tree, and the leaves of one branch. We cherish the hope that the light of justice (*núr-i-inṣáf*) may shine upon the world and sanctify it from tyranny. If the rulers and kings of the earth, the symbols of the power of God, exalted be His glory, arise and resolve to dedicate themselves to whatever will promote the highest interests of the whole of humanity, the reign of justice (*'adl*) will assuredly be established amongst the children of men, and the effulgence of its light will envelop the whole earth.[91]

Unity and justice appear in this text tightly interrelated. To overcome estrangement, one of the causes of disunity, Bahá'u'lláh proposes an all-inclusive definition of man as part of one single identity (one tree, one branch). This new vision, however, must be reflected in the way justice is administered by those in authority. Following the traditional pattern, justice is made the opposite of tyranny; but its range of meaning is much broader as now the highest interests of the whole of mankind are to be considered before those of its constituent parts (the nation states). The importance attached to this perspective can be gathered by the fact that Bahá'u'lláh quoted this or similar statements in other works. The following passage, for instance, goes a step further by defining a human being in terms of 'service':

> That one indeed is a man, who, today, dedicateth himself to the service of the entire human race. The Great Being saith: Blessed and happy is he that ariseth to promote the best interests of the peoples and kindreds of the earth. In another passage He hath proclaimed: It is not for him to pride himself who loveth his own country (*vaṭan*), but rather for him who loveth the whole world (*'álam*). The earth is but one country (*fi'l ḥaqíqah 'álam yik vaṭan maḥsúb ast*), and mankind its citizens.[92]

The inversion of the terms 'country' and 'earth/world' is indisputable. All men and women must see themselves in the light of their common humanity, which today entails a global conscience and an ethics of service. The election of the term *vaṭan,* a word chosen in Arabic to cover the same semantic field as the French *patrie* shows a clear intention to enlarge the concept by countering its potentially threatening nationalistic overtones.[93] Consistent with this stance are Bahá'u'lláh's injunctions to enforce a system of collective security (see Part I) and His exhortations addressed to all the various sections of religion as well as to the nations of the world. Thus, the individual man is inseparable from an undivided mankind. No greater good can be conceived than becoming the cause of peace:

> Is any larger bounty conceivable than this, that an individual, looking within himself, should find that by the confirming grace of God he has become the cause of peace and well-being, of happiness and advantage to his fellow men? No, by the one true God, there is no greater bliss, no more complete delight.[94]

Knowledge is also redefined in terms of its contribution to the welfare of mankind, as when Bahá'u'lláh declares that 'the choicest fruit of the tree of knowledge is that which serveth the welfare of humanity and safeguardeth its interests'.[95]

Understandably, the upholding of this universalistic view implied a moral decision to widen the radius of one's loyalty and to rein in the drive towards a jingoistic or solipsistic identity. At a time when the western powers had not even completed their imperial designs, and notions of racial and class superiority were rife, universalistic ideas seemed to be able to succeed only under an imperialistic or socialist guise. But a truly universal outlook on life, as 'Abdu'l-Bahá states, calls for a capacity to put the interests of the public first:

> Sincerity is the foundation-stone of faith. That is, a religious individual must disregard his personal desires and seek in whatever way he can wholeheartedly to serve the public interest (*khayríat-i-jumhúr*).[96]

In Ramleh (Egypt) 'Abdu'l-Bahá expressed this view even more forcefully, noting how the benefits of one's good works need to be made available to all without exception and not restricted to Bahá'ís alone or to a specific people or nation. A strong public or socially-minded morality seems clearly to be the hallmark of a Bahá'í code of conduct: what is generally public, that which transcends the scope of the private (good as it might be), is then a public good and divinely sanctioned, a point that itself reads very much like a paraphrase from Imam Ali's dictum 'Everything that is individual is human, everything that is social is divine'.[97]

27
Divine Philosophy and Religious Unity

A further aspect of the Bahá'í ethos, in addition to those matters already examined, consists in its open admission of the truth found in previous religions. From the outset the cosmopolitanism of the Bahá'í perspective described so far received a further impetus by the statement that 'all religions' came from one and the same divine source. It was this bold assertion that lent the Bahá'í Faith its characteristic appeal.

The Bahá'í 'principles' of the oneness of God and that of the oneness of religion often presented by 'Abdu'l-Bahá (see Part II) were intimately linked, but did not necessarily lead to an affirming theology of religions. For this to eventuate an understanding of religious pluralism (the why and how of different religions and religious communities) was required as well as a disposition to explore the questions that such a standpoint would raise at a practical and theoretical level. The Bahá'í writings supplied some basic schemata that made sense of this diversity and, above all, helped to counter the negative associations attached to religious divergences. Hence, the resulting approach to the matter of religious unity was many-sided.

At one level religious unity was intimately tied to a broader conception of reality. 'Abdu'l-Bahá's emphasis on the notion that reality is one found a close parallel in His conviction that an untrammelled quest after truth would result in a new partnership between science and religion:

> Religion must agree with science, so that science shall sustain religion and religion explain science. The two must be brought together, indissolubly, in reality. Down to the present day it has been customary for man to accept blindly what was called religion, even though it were not in accord with human reason.[98]

While the idea here conveyed suggests a strong interpenetration between science and religion, 'Abdu'l-Bahá seems to suggest in actual fact a deeper common thread or a convergence on what he calls 'divine philosophy'. This shared area of knowledge would hinge around the pivotal concept of the 'oneness of humanity' and would impregnate, together with its contents – the various Bahá'í principles and modalities of unity – all the 'distinguishing character, sentiment, moral nature or guiding beliefs' of the new aeon.[99] As stated by 'Abdu'l-Bahá in the address he delivered at Columbia University:

> The most important principle of divine philosophy is the oneness of the world of humanity, the unity of mankind, the bond conjoining East and West, the tie of love which blends human hearts.[100]

'Abdu'l-Bahá made it clear that divine philosophy aims at the 'the training of the human realities so that they may become clear and pure as mirrors and reflect the light and love of the Sun of Reality'.[101] Elsewhere, 'Abdu'l-Bahá expanded the same concept by stating that the goal of divine philosophy is the 'sublimation of human nature, spiritual advancement, heavenly guidance for the development of the human race, attainment to the breaths of the Holy Spirit and knowledge of the verities of God'.[102] Divine philosophy was contrasted with, but was not opposed to, natural philosophy:

> Natural philosophy seeks knowledge of physical verities and explains material phenomena, whereas divine philosophy deals with ideal verities and phenomena of the spirit.[103]

Socrates, Plato and Aristotle 'discoursed upon the world of nature as well as the supernatural world', and in so doing 'rendered praiseworthy service to humanity'.

> Man should continue both these lines of research and investigation so that all the human virtues, outer and inner, may become possible. The attainment of these virtues, both material and ideal, is conditioned upon intelligent investigation of reality.[104]

However, given the neglect in which 'divine philosophy' finds itself among the various nations of the world, declared 'Abdu'l-Bahá, there is a great need for it to run apace with 'natural philosophy', an activity which entails the discarding of imitations and dogmas and their replacement by an unstinting investigation of reality in all its forms. Accordingly, dogmatic or formulaic notions of God and religion must give way to a wider understanding of His being, an operation which 'Abdu'l-Bahá described in quasi-poetic terms:

> Ordinarily when the word Divinity is mentioned, it is associated in the minds of the hearers with certain formulas and doctrines, whereas it essentially means the wisdom and knowledge of God, the effulgence of the Sun of Truth, the revelation of reality and divine philosophy.[105]

Similarly, 'true evolution' consists in the glorification of the world of humanity.

It cannot be construed in purely material terms, however necessary and valuable material progress might be in and by itself:

> . . . by simple development along material lines man is not perfected. At most, the physical aspect of man, his natural or material conditions, may become stabilized and improved, but he will remain deprived of the spiritual or divine bestowal. He is then like a body without a spirit, a lamp without the light, an eye without the power of vision, an ear that hears no sound, a mind incapable of perceiving, an intellect minus the power of reason.[106]

All efforts must be focused then on coupling material and physical advancements with a concentration of efforts 'to advance humanity toward the nobility of its true and intended station',[107] for 'just as man is in need of outward education, he is likewise in need of ideal refinement'.[108] Religion and religious law are revealed with the one primary purpose of bringing 'about happiness in the after life and civilization and the refinement of character in this'.[109] How this refinement of character should operate and what ethical principles or tenets underpin this vital function in the Bahá'í writings are important questions, the answers to which will help us to complete our view of peace in the Bahá'í religion.

As hitherto noted, the general Bahá'í ethos appears to be characterized by a considerable stress on achieving 'moderation in all things',[110] hence the emphasis on bringing unity to a divided world and developing a civilization where the fruits of the material and the spiritual are blended together rather than defined in mutual opposition: East or West, unity and diversity, soul and spirit, material and divine civilizations have a rightful place in the order of creation. Religion itself, particularly the power of the Holy Spirit, is defined essentially as a moderating force allowing for the harmonious operation of realities that by themselves would either drift away or cancel each other out. Knowledge, technical prowess and freedom will not work to the full advantage of humanity unless tempered or complemented by the spirit of faith:

> Therefore, it is evident that no means but an ideal means, a spiritual power, divine bestowals and the breaths of the Holy Spirit will heal this world sickness of war, dissension and discord. Nothing else is possible; nothing can be conceived of. But through spiritual means and the divine power it is possible and practicable.
>
> . . . The divine religions are collective centres in which diverse standpoints may meet, agree and unify. They accomplish oneness of nativities, races and policies.[111]

Yet, the cause of peace is important in the sense that its mandate transcends formal religion, and hence, as explained by 'Abdu'l-Bahá, 'any movement which brings peace . . . is truly a divine movement':

> The divine religions were founded for the purpose of unifying humanity and establishing universal peace. Any movement which brings about peace and agreement in human society is truly a divine movement; any reform which causes people to come together under the shelter of the same tabernacle is surely animated by heavenly motives.[112]

In Bahá'í terms this capacity of mediation, moderation, balancing and bridging of differences, defined as inherent in the power of religion, not only confers a mandate on religion but also defines it, providing a test of its own authenticity. Thus, when 'Abdu'l-Bahá stated that religion 'must be the cause of unity', the assertion of this ethical imperative seems to suggest that all religions are meant to unify mankind, not only in recognition that their original impulse is geared toward unity, but also in the sense that historical religions must ultimately converge by overcoming some of the more obvious and destructive differences generated over time among themselves.

> The foundations of the divine religions are one. If we investigate these foundations, we discover much ground for agreement, but if we consider the imitations of forms and ancestral beliefs, we find points of disagreement and division; for these imitations differ, while the sources and foundations are one and the same. That is to say, the fundamentals are conducive to unity, but imitations are the cause of disunion and dismemberment. *Whosoever is lacking in love for humanity or manifests hatred and bigotry toward any part of it violates the foundation and source of his own belief and is holding to forms and imitations.*[113] (emphasis added)

> The fundamental truth of the Manifestations is peace. This underlies all religion, all justice. The divine purpose is that men should live in unity, concord and agreement and should love one another.[114]

At its deepest this effort requires a capacity to relativize one's religion by perceiving other religions as authentic repositories of truth, originated in a common spiritual source or, alternatively, as genuinely responsive to the deep-seated spiritual needs of the individual. Bahá'í statements illustrating this point of view are abundant:

> Religions are many, but the reality of religion is one. The days are many, but the sun is one. The fountains are many, but the fountainhead is one. The branches are many, but the tree is one . . . The subject is one, but predicates are many.[115]

The above similes suggest naturally that religions are changing 'expressions' of a more enduring and unifying reality, and that choosing whether to accentuate the unifying theme or, on the contrary, magnify the differences between them is as much a hermeneutical option as a consequence of an ethical choice:

> Let us strive with all our powers to unite the East and West so that the nations of the world may be advanced and that all may live according to the one foundation of the religions of God. The essentials of the divine religion are one reality, indivisible and not multiple. It is one. And when through investigation we find it to be single, we have a basis for the oneness of the world of humanity.[116]

'Abdu'l-Bahá defines the 'core' or foundational reality shared by most religions as being 'essentially' the same: knowledge of God through recognition and embodiment of His attributes, coupled with love, compassion and service towards His creatures. Other elements of existing religions assume a peripheral position in the 'divine Economy', and can be modified in accordance with circumstances, for in reality 'religion is the outer expression of the divine reality' and hence 'it must be living, vitalized, moving and progressive'.[117]

At a less deep, yet very important level, the effort calls for a capacity to generate a culture of tolerance and peaceful coexistence between different and often quite divergent belief systems:

> Christ was the Prophet of the Christians, Moses of the Jews – why should not the followers of each prophet recognize and honour the other prophets also? If men could only learn the lesson of mutual tolerance, understanding, and brotherly love, the unity of the world would soon be an established fact.[118]

This approach to the unity of religions, which constitutes a rhetorical Bahá'í topos[119] was particularly emphasized by 'Abdu'l-Bahá in His travels throughout the West. By speaking from the vantage point of view of 'religion' (i.e. religion in general), revealed religions were pictured as instances of one and the same overarching reality – the phenomenon of religion. From this perspective differences between religions were then attributable to differences of time, place, tradition, temperament, mentality, capacity, and even expediency:

> There can be no doubt whatever that the peoples of the world, of whatever race or religion, derive their inspiration from one heavenly Source, and are the subjects of one God. The difference between the ordinances under which they abide should be attributed to the varying requirements and exigencies of the age in which they were revealed. All of them, except a few which are the outcome of human perversity, were ordained of God, and are a reflection of His Will and Purpose.[120]

Logic and other rational standards of enquiry could be brought to bear on some of the theological moot points, thereby introducing a degree of reasonableness into matters that have often been cluttered by theological accretions. Casting away 'dogmas and ritualism' (*taqálíd*) would give pre-eminence to the realities of the Books, thus paving the way for the 'unification of religion' (*ittiḥád-i-adián*).

New hermeneutic principles could then be applied to the explanation of profound theological issues with more satisfying results. For this to happen, a re-evaluation of symbolic language may be required, for core differences among existing faith communities often originated in terminological questions and in reified interpretations of metaphors or symbols. 'Abdu'l-Bahá illustrated this process in His dialogue with the protestant theologian Pasteur Monnier over the relationship of Christ, Bahá'u'lláh and God by stating: 'We say that this Fatherhood and Son-ship are allegorical, and symbolical' (*tafsírí*). In fact, and independently of the proper names or titles ascribed to it, all believers – explained 'Abdu'l-Bahá – are agreed that an intermediary and beneficent reality acts as a link between God and His creatures:

> Now mark well that none of these religionists have ever seen the Founders, they have only heard His name. If they overlooked these names they would realize that they all believed in a perfect Reality which is an intermediary between the Almighty and His creatures. Their dissension is over a word, otherwise they all share in common the belief of a Mediatorship between the Creator and the creature.[121]

In this sense it is worth noting that in the Kitáb-i-Íqán, Bahá'u'lláh had de-emphasized, if not refuted, the well-known standard Muslim argument that the text of the divine Torah or the Gospel had been tampered with or corrupted. There was no need to resort to this kind of reason to explain why and how historical religions, rather than their canonical texts, would differ among themselves without resorting to a putative deviation from the Abrahamic belief. The texts themselves were indeed a testimony to their own truth. 'By corruption of the text is meant that in which all Muslim divines are engaged today, that is the interpretation of God's holy Book in accordance with their idle imaginings and vain desire.'[122]

Those differences could indeed be present at the genesis of the new religion as part of its response to general conditions, needs and requirements; or could result from the organic process of maturation and decay that inexorably accompanies the gestation of historical religion. In this perspective religious ordinances and doctrines, after fulfilling a positive role, become 'exhausted, and cease to exert their influence'.[123] The following quotation of Siyyid Kaẓim by Nicolas, as given by Shoghi Effendi, is all the more expressive in this context as it further illustrates a preferred Bahá'í locus (namely humanity's passage from adolescence to maturity) linking it to the fulfilment of the eschatological promises in the new revelation:

> You have understood, I think, that the religious law and the precepts of morality are the food of the Spirit. It is then necessary that these religious laws be diverse; it is necessary that sometimes the older regulations be annulled; it is necessary that these precepts contain some things which are doubtful and some things which are certain; some things general and some things specific;

> some things absolute and some things finite; some of appearances and some of inner realities, so that the child may reach adolescence and may be perfect in his power and his capacity. 'It is, at that time, that the Qa'im will appear and after his manifestation the length of his days will come to an end and he will be martyred, and when he is martyred, the world will have reached its eighteenth year.'[124]

Taken in its broader terms the above approach exhibits both the interconnection as well as the limits between Bahá'í theology ('the oneness of religion') and Bahá'í ethics ('religion must be the cause of unity'). The Bahá'í understanding of religious pluralism acknowledges the truth of historical religions, values their diversity, establishes tolerance as a basic requirement for their interrelationship, pays homage to their founders, cultural and human attainments, and posits a convergence between religions as a result of a double dynamics of investigation of commonalities amongst religious systems – a point especially stressed by 'Abdu'l-Bahá – and the ultimate acceptance of Bahá'u'lláh as 'the Manifestation for this Day'. Unity among religions may thus take on an elastic meaning stretching from a realization of a *pax religiosa* based on toleration, or even acceptance of variable degrees of truth in all other religions, up to a recognition of Bahá'u'lláh as the Promised One of all Ages. The image of an eschatological convergence of religious perspectives in the Bahá'í Revelation may in a logical turn give way to a back-reading of sacred history: 'This day [religious Dispensation] may be likened to a sea and all other [previous] days to gulfs and channels that have branched therefrom.'[125] This interpretation is even more explicitly stated further on by Bahá'u'lláh:

> In a sense this day and that which appeareth therein are to be regarded as the primary principles, while all other days and whatsoever appeareth in them are to be viewed as the secondary ordinances deduced therefrom, and which as such are subordinate and relative.[126]

At any rate, religious unity, or unity in religion (*vaḥdat-i-dín*) is so central that 'Abdu'l-Bahá places it at the centre of the Seven Candles of Unity. This is said to be the 'the corner-stone of the foundation itself (*aṣl-i-asás*), and which, by the power of God, will be revealed in all its splendour'.[127]

Since this theology implies a progressive movement towards recognition of the Bahá'í Faith as *the* religion of mankind, and the Bahá'í writings stress avoidance of confrontational missionary work, there is a clear Bahá'í preference to perhaps understate the universal nature of the Bahá'í claims to universality[128] in favour of a more pluralistic view of religion, with the Bahá'í Faith presented more as a form of religion that clears the way for the reconciliation of existing religious differences. This more nuanced view was repeatedly put forward by Shoghi Effendi:

> The Revelation, of which Bahá'u'lláh is the source and centre, abrogates none of the religions that have preceded it, nor does it attempt, in the slightest degree, to distort their features or to belittle their value. It disclaims any intention of dwarfing any of the Prophets of the past, or of whittling down the eternal verity of their teachings. It can, in no wise, conflict with the spirit that animates their claims, nor does it seek to undermine the basis of any man's allegiance to their cause. *Its declared, its primary purpose is to enable every adherent of these Faiths to obtain a fuller understanding of the religion with which he stands identified, and to acquire a clearer apprehension of its purpose.* It is neither eclectic in the presentation of its truths, nor arrogant in the affirmation of its claims. *Its teachings revolve around the fundamental principle that religious truth is not absolute but relative, that Divine Revelation is progressive, not final.*[129] (emphasis added)

In the process, the absoluteness of religion, particularly in its monotheistic variety, is relativized. Historical religions appear as links in an uninterrupted chain of revealed truth, or rather as phases in the ascending parable trailed by the 'light of divine Revelation'. The intensity of the light is thus 'vouchsafed unto men in direct proportion to their spiritual capacity'. Otherwise, a sudden manifestation of its energies at an early stage would only wreak havoc, 'for men's hearts would neither sustain the intensity of its revelation, nor be able to mirror forth the radiance of its light'.[130]

Contemplated from this perspective, claims by most existing religions to be regarded as unique and exclusive expressions of the infinite truth must of necessity be viewed in the context of their relative position in the horizon of God's will: 'We must be adorers of the sun of reality from whatsoever horizon it may appear, rather than adorers of the horizon,' says 'Abdu'l-Bahá.[131] The same meaning is conveyed in many other variations: 'The sun is always the sun. According to the position of the earth we receive its radiation differently.'[132] Hence the singularity of all religions must be taken as an outcome of divine creativity, not as a proof of their exclusive entitlements over truth. The following passage depicts 'Abdu'l-Bahá in a typical remonstrance of sectarianism from a Bahá'í perspective:

> It was while Abdul Baha was in Paris that a group composed of different sects awaited an audience to argue their various faiths. Suddenly this divine teacher of men swept into the room and pointing out of the window, exclaimed: 'The sun of truth rises in each season from a different point of the horizon – to-day it is here, yesterday it was there, and to-morrow it will appear from another direction. Why do you keep your eyes eternally fixed on the same point? Why do you call yourselves Christians, Buddhists, Mohammedans, Bahá'ís? You must learn to distinguish the sun of truth from whichever point of the horizon it is shining! People think religion is confined in an edifice, to be worshipped at an altar. *In reality it is an attitude toward divinity which is reflected through life.*'[133]

The concomitant belief that witnessing to one's truth may necessarily exclude or even confront other religious beliefs, and that this kind of witnessing is conducive to one's salvation, does not escape 'Abdu'l-Bahá's critical comments: 'To label ourselves will not be sufficient.'[134] In actual fact, names and attributes – in other words, the specific traits of any religion – may just like other representations, become major obstacles towards unity.

Various syntheses of the above positions were given by Shoghi Effendi at various stages of his ministry. Perhaps none as significant as the following statement conveyed to the UN commission:

> The fundamental principle enunciated by Bahá'u'lláh, the followers of His Faith firmly believe, is that Religious truth is not absolute but relative, that Divine Revelation is a continuous and progressive process, that all the great religions of the world are divine in origin, that their basic principles are in complete harmony, that their aims and purposes are one and the same, that their teachings are but facets of one truth, that their functions are complementary, that they differ only in the non-essential aspects of their doctrines and that their missions represent successive stages in the spiritual evolution of human society.[135]

True to this same spirit, Shoghi Effendi went on to explain that the Bahá'í Faith represents, therefore, a restatement of the truths 'in a manner that would conform to the needs, and be in consonance with the capacity, and be applicable to the problems, the ills and perplexities, of the age in which we live'. This adaptability of religion, in its various epiphanies, is what explains the appearance of the Bahá'í Faith as yet another phase in the 'eternal history and constant evolution of one religion, Divine and indivisible, of which it itself forms but an integral part'.[136] This view of an open-ended religion was in stark contrast with the characteristic view of the established monotheistic religions.

Simultaneous awareness as to both the historical caducity and timelessness of religion explains another important feature of religion that Shoghi Effendi was careful to underline. While former religions were able to supply some varying measure of specifics – in the way of laws, standards of behaviours and organizational patterns – at the same time for them to be effective they had to be supported by a powerful undercurrent of spirituality and ethical dynamics. If observed from this standpoint, the demise of established religions would have accrued from an increasing inability, as time goes by, to provide a balance between the static and the temporal. In the last analysis some of the major break-ups which occurred in the Christian and Muslim religions were as much a product of human intervention as an outcome of the constraints and limits which these religions encountered almost from the outset. A paramount example of this kind of mysterious, in-built contingency of historical religions was afforded by the very question of succession in both Christianity and Islam.[137] By contrast, this depiction allowed Shoghi Effendi to characterize Bahá'u'lláh's system as endowed with the requisite features of flexibility and solidity, of the temporal and the timeless.[138] 'Secondary matters' – explained Shoghi Effendi – would have to be decided at the appropriate decision-making level 'according to the exigencies of their respective circumstances'.[139] And what was true of National Spiritual Assemblies was all the more applicable to the Guardianship and the Universal House of Justice.[140] Of the latter, Shoghi Effendi commented on this passage from the Will and Testament of 'Abdu'l-Bahá:

> 'Thus for example, the House of Justice enacteth today a certain law and enforceth it, and a hundred years hence, circumstances having profoundly changed and the conditions having altered, another House of Justice will then have power, according to the exigencies of the time, to alter that law. This it can do because that law formeth no part of the divine explicit text. The House of Justice is both the initiator and the abrogator of its own laws.' Such is the immutability of His revealed Word. Such is the elasticity which characterizes the functions of His appointed ministers. The first preserves the identity of His Faith, and guards the integrity of His law. *The second enables it, even as a living organism, to expand and adapt itself to the needs and requirements of an ever-changing society.*[141] (emphasis added)

28
The Organic Analogy: Organic Unity and Unity in Diversity

The quotation at the end of the preceding chapter, and particularly its reference to the 'living organism', illustrates a major sub-theme with considerable repercussions on the Bahá'í ethos. If Lakoff's image of 'metaphors we live by'[142] is more than a suggestive turn of phrase, then the use of organic imagery in the Bahá'í writings deserves closer attention inasmuch as it plays a crucial role in generating positive responses to the challenges of accepting and harmonizing diversity.

As seen in the previous section, the Bahá'í conception of religion as a continuum of unfolding revealed material (progressive revelation) that follows a sacred rhythm marked by successive Dispensations is paralleled by the belief that humanity as a whole is moving from an adolescent phase to its coming of age. Humanity is likened to an embryo in which all divisive differences, including religious ones, are finally merged:

> The whole earth, He, moreover, has stated, '*is now in a state of pregnancy*. The day is approaching when it will have yielded its noblest fruits, when from it will have sprung forth the loftiest trees, the most enchanting blossoms, the most heavenly blessings.' 'All nations and kindreds', 'Abdu'l-Bahá likewise has written, '. . . will become a single nation. Religious and sectarian antagonism, the hostility of races and peoples, and differences among nations, will be eliminated. All men will adhere to one religion, will have one common faith, will be blended into one race, and become a single people. All will dwell in one common fatherland, which is the planet itself.'[143] (emphasis added)

As can be inferred from the two passages just quoted, organic imagery occupies an important place in the Bahá'í writings. Nature in all its multifarious levels, from the mineral to the human reality, is considered as a source of metaphors or similes that, when properly viewed, offer easier to grasp models of comparable yet more complex phenomena. The transposition of properties or features from one realm of experience to another is made possible because of the underlying correspondences between those different levels. The generative world of creation is represented as a text – the product of the Word of God – and hence saturated with meanings, signs or emblems that act as pointers. Bahá'u'lláh and 'Abdu'l-Bahá make reference to the heuristic properties that are inherent in things and are brought further to light by the revealing power of symbolic language and imagery. Exploiting the heuristic properties of the highly metaphorical and symbolic language is both a necessary task and a pleasure for the truly spiritual mind.[144] Expressions and descriptions of natural processes, whether in connection with the vegetable kingdom, the succession of the seasons, the physical beauty of natural phenomena, the ascendancy of the sun, or the allusions to the unity of the body and its constituent members, all become Bahá'í images, some of which, as in the case of the wine and the vineyard, evoke immediately the referential world of biblical, qur'ánic and mystical poetry.[145]

In contrast with the direct coinage of symbolic and organic imagery carried out by Bahá'u'lláh and 'Abdu'l-Bahá, the writings of Shoghi Effendi seem to have made a more indirect or conceptualized use of organic language. Although this did not prevent him from using some remarkable symbolic figurations, his tendency is more towards a further denouement of the abstract essential Bahá'í idea, a feature already examined with regards to his preference for patterns, particularly binary patterns, symmetries and synchronicities.[146] This tendency, which may reflect Shoghi Effendi's self-perception as an interpreter, can be seen at work in two of Shoghi Effendi's terminological innovations,[147] namely the concepts of 'organic unity' and 'unity in diversity', both of which can be taken as partially synonymous or, to some extent, coextensive.[148] The success of these terms lies in their capacity to conjure up the referential world of images embodying their meaning. In these and similar expressions the evocative world of organic metaphors is just suggested through the use, in connection with the expansion and development of the Bahá'í community, of the rather conceptual terms 'organic' and 'embryonic'.[149] In what follows I will illustrate some of the uses or meanings attributable to the extensive presence of organic language in the Bahá'í scriptures. Their relevance to a definition of the Bahá'í ethos and their pertinence to the theme of peace will be further explored after considering their closest associations.[150]

The term 'organic' denotes in Shoghi Effendi's writings a gradual adaptive growth and a healthy correspondence between the constituent members of a whole. The word itself, although well-fitted to describe concepts derived from the writings of Bahá'u'lláh and especially 'Abdu'l-Bahá,[151] constitutes an innovation whose entry into the Bahá'í repertoire largely reflected Shoghi Effendi's preference for the term. It was a natural choice, as the organic mode of thought was prevalent among such authors as Thomas Carlyle – who was assiduously read by Shoghi Effendi – or Constantin Brunner (recognized as an organicist thinker whose ideas find interesting parallels in the Bahá'í writings), Ralph Waldo Emerson, or Horace Bushnell,[152] to name but a few.[153] A more contemporary usage of the term 'organic' which Shoghi Effendi must have encountered directly or indirectly is the one illustrated by Spengler in his *The Decline of the West*, where the term is employed to describe some 'general biographic archetypes' (*allgemeine biographische Urformen zugrunde*), such as birth, youth, ageing and death, that would apply to the life courses of social organisms.[154] It should be noted, however, that the use of organic imagery in the Bahá'í writings, particularly with its illustrations of the 'unity in diversity' principle, takes on a meaning at odds with the category of 'organicism' analysed by Opler,[155] the sources of which can be traced back to common origins branching off into opposite directions.[156] Thus, while the Bahá'í 'unity in diversity' principle stresses the essential compatibility of diverse expressions of unity – a feature underlined by the pluralistic notion of a diversity of unities – the racialist notions of organicism described by Opler as inherent in Nazi and Fascist thinking are in fact murderous derivations of nature's killing instinct.[157]

The term 'embryonic' for its part refers more specifically to the rapidly changing period of growth which is characteristic of the first developmental stages in most living organisms. In this case, the reference denotes the unfoldment of the Bahá'í organism through its 'formative period' up to the Golden Age. Through these lenses, the Bahá'í community is envisioned as a body endowed with a soul whose mission is to translate the spiritual impulses into visible forms. In this perspective stability (as shown in the previous section), is provided by the law of God, given by the Manifestation of God, whereas movement, flexibility and adaptation is on the side of man. Not surprisingly, Shoghi Effendi relates the very principle of oneness to the institutional framework provided by the Bahá'í administrative system:

> It [the principle of oneness] does not constitute merely the enunciation of an ideal, but stands inseparably associated with an institution adequate to embody its truth, demonstrate its validity, and perpetuate its influence. It implies an *organic change in the structure of present-day society, a change such as the world has not yet experienced.*[158] (emphasis added)

The above passage also summarizes some of the features characteristic of Shoghi Effendi's approach to unity, as well as to change, and the role of the Bahá'í community in bringing it about. A distinction is drawn between idealism and spiritual realism by referring to the key notion of 'embodiment'. Whatever the initial stage at which the Bahá'í administrative system may find itself, its institutions are said to be framed in such a way that they are regarded as apt to not only translate seminal truths into reality, but also to resist the test of time and to induce an 'organic change in the structure of present-day society', a change simply radical.

In consequence, the expression 'organic unity' used by Shoghi Effendi suggests a sense of continuity of identity in the face of seemingly irrevocable changes. It evokes the capacity to relate changing realities, perceived in a state of flux (rather than as static snapshots), to a unifying principle which holds them together in a mesh of relations that enable them to endure further organic transformations. It is that plastic capacity that allows for the mutations that both simple and composite organisms must undergo while moving from minute formations to larger and more complex ones. As an analogy or metaphor of social and religious life, the principle of organic unity describes how societies can evolve into highly complex, diversified yet life-sustaining entities that hold together successfully. The organic cycle of birth, maturation and decay, so characteristic of the vegetable kingdom, the development of the human embryo in the womb, the progression of various growth stages from childhood to old age become then standard Bahá'í analogies applicable in various degrees to human and historical phenomena. Instances of these are the frequently used Bahá'í analogy likening the transformation undergone by religions to the changes experienced by the seedling as it traverses the cycle of the seasons,[159] the powerful Bahá'í organic analogy describing humanity as passing from adolescence to adulthood, and the no less important metaphor of life after death as the culmination of an embryo-like existence on earth.

For its part, 'unity in diversity' can be considered a conceptual couplet often seen in various Latin formulations such as 'e pluribus unum' or similar, and adopted by a number of government and non-governmental organizations, conveying the belief or recognition that diversity (of opinions, races, classes, religions, interests) can take place productively without necessarily having to be resolved through exclusion, unification or uniformity. Shoghi Effendi defines 'unity in diversity' as 'the bedrock of the Bahá'í administrative order . . . so strongly and so repeatedly emphasized in the writings of the Cause'.[160] Typically, in Bahá'í terms, differences can be explained metaphorically as waves in a sea, or roses in a garden; besides adding with their variety and plurality to the larger reality of which they are part, they also contribute to the aesthetic recreation, beauty and resilience of the general fabric of existence.[161] This is so because the various parts or constituents in an organic whole are not juxtaposed or mutually tangential but truly interconnected in a maze of relationships and dynamic equilibria governed by what 'Abdu'l-Bahá calls the laws of mutuality and reciprocity. This is true not only of members of one and the same species, but in fact of all beings contained 'in the unified body of the world', as 'Abdu'l-Bahá puts it:

> Were one to observe with an eye that discovereth the realities of all things, it would become clear that the greatest relationship that bindeth the world of being together lieth in the range of created things themselves, *and that co-operation, mutual aid and reciprocity are essential characteristics in the unified body of the world of being*, inasmuch as all created things are closely related together and each is influenced by the other or deriveth benefit therefrom, either directly or indirectly.[162] (emphasis added)

The degree of reciprocity may however differ depending on the degree of evolution in the 'arc of ascent'.

> The supreme need of humanity is cooperation and reciprocity. The stronger the ties of fellowship and solidarity amongst men, the greater will be the power

> of constructiveness and accomplishment in all the planes of human activity. Without cooperation and reciprocal attitude the individual member of human society remains self-centered, uninspired by altruistic purposes, limited and solitary in development like the animal and plant organisms of the lower kingdoms. The lower creatures are not in need of cooperation and reciprocity. A tree can live solitary and alone, but this is impossible for man without retrogression.[163]

The strength of this organic relationship is also pre-eminently applicable to the bonds of love uniting Bahá'ís in a mystic embrace:

> We also have the example of the Master before us. The individual Bahá'ís were organic parts of His spiritual being. What befell the least one of the friends brought deep affliction and sorrow to Him also.[164]

In addition to reciprocity and mutuality, the properties of flexibility and adaptability referred to above by Shoghi Effendi are characteristically organic features. They allow for the appearance in the course of time of new needs, limbs, extremities, elements or substances that, while differentiated from the original mould, belong to it as its inherent property, just as the branches of a tree are 'contained' in the seed.[165] Such plasticity is associated with the capacity to bring about changes or give rise to new institutions in response to the general requirements of the time. It may, conversely, explain the lack of functionality or temporary underdevelopment in some element of the divine economy. Moreover, crises are often construed as opportunities for the 'cleansing' of the body of the believers. Far from being an insurmountable obstacle in the evolution of humanity, spiritual crises afford greater opportunities to rethink and remodel social and personal values, address the problems and search for new answers. This adaptability is an essential feature of a living organism and can be adopted as a model of the Bahá'í organism with all the more reason. In keeping with this perception, the progressive application of the laws of the Aqdas, the configuration of the administrative system through the addition of intermediate administrative layers (National Assemblies, Auxiliary Board Members, Counsellors, Regional Councils), and the transformation of the knowledge and training arrangements along more formal lines (Bahá'í schools, training institutes) have often been rationalized as part of the exigencies of such an organic process.

Understood as an ethical ideal, the organic analogy furnishes a general model for the acceptance of diversity, the recognition of the time-boundness of cultural realities, and perhaps, more importantly, for the embracing of change and the need to bring diversity to bear in all processes, as illustrated in 'Abdu'l-Bahá's exegesis of the woman in labour in the Book of Revelation,[166] where the matricial metaphor carries significant implications. Furthermore, ethical exhortations to unity based on organic images can range from simple analogies illustrating the concept of unity in diversity to more complex elaborations. An instance of the former is Bahá'u'lláh's advice: 'Be ye as the fingers of one hand, the members of one body.'[167] A far more elaborate derivation of the latter can be shown in the following passage by Shoghi Effendi:

> In the body of a man, which is the true divine example or parallel, the spirit, when in ideal control of all the lesser parts of the organism, finds the utmost harmony throughout the whole body – each part is in perfect reciprocity with the other parts. The commands and impulses of the spirit are obeyed by the body and the body in turn in its actions and functions identifies and determines the expression the spiritual impulses shall take. *This is divine unity – and this law, being universal and found in every created object in the universe, has full application to the universal Bahá'í organism made up of believers everywhere,* which has been established by the Manifestation of God.[168] (emphasis added)

The human body here described is not a mere extension of matter but an agency that plays an active role consisting in identifying and determining 'the expression the spiritual impulses shall take'.[169] Insofar as a 'true divine example, or parallel', the healthy human body implies harmony and reciprocity between the constituent parts of the whole. In this sense harmony manifests itself as the state of equilibrium ensuing from an ideal working correspondence between the different bodily parts and functions. Harmony, however, appears not so much as a changeless state, but rather as a fluid balance compatible with movement and even periods of crisis. A second trait in the 'universal law' identified by Shoghi Effendi is the mutual dependency between the different components of the whole. As in any relationship, no part can be defined without taking into consideration the rest and the nature of the relationship itself. Here the analogy of the body tends to stress the inseparable linking between the spiritual and the material, the Manifestation of God and the *Bahá'í organism.* Other references by Shoghi Effendi take the analogy one step further by describing the relationship between Bahá'í administrators and the 'body' of the believers. In such instances, Shoghi Effendi underscores notions of mutuality and service as paramount. Those called to serve as administrators are urged to avoid turning the 'administrative machinery of the Cause' into an end itself.[170]

References such as the above supply what we may call a 'figurative world' where the tension between the individual and society is no longer perceived as a dominant theme or, at any rate, is reformulated in terms that help to renegotiate it. In this great scheme the universal Bahá'í organism appears as a whole made up of institutions and believers who interact in organized communities whose relationships branch out into new living formations. A Bahá'í society, in consequence, appears not so much as an aggregate of individuals confronted by society, but rather as a community in which the institutions constantly interact among themselves (as well with their members and the wider society), providing some direction to the initiative and efforts of the individuals, who seen from this perspective, are the main agents of the civilizing process. Diversity is consciously sought after and experienced both aesthetically and ethically as enrichment. Progress is conceived not so much as a linear progression but rather in terms of wavy incorporations and enlargements, often dotted with crises, in which the effective integration of diversity constitutes a hallmark of authenticity. In the end organicity becomes a mental representation of the way peace and unity move from strength to strength. Syntheses of these notions have been articulated variously in the most recent past by the Universal House of Justice, as in the following text, which furnishes a clear connection between the themes of organic unity, unity in diversity, recognition of the oneness of religion, and the role of consultation, to which I will turn my attention before closing:

> [the Bahá'í community] is a single social organism, representative of the diversity of the human family, conducting its affairs through a system of commonly accepted consultative principles, and cherishing equally all the great outpourings of divine guidance in human history.[171]

29
Bahá'í Consultation

While the metaphor of organic unity and the ethics of unity, service to humanity, moderation and personal growth provide the bedrock of a Bahá'í morality, this would be incomplete without reference to the broader implications of Bahá'í consultation. The absence of a living successor of Shoghi Effendi, or of a priestly parallel structure that could play a role in the authoritative interpretation of the *magisterium*, has if anything brought the matter into sharper relief. While collegiality has perforce assumed an even more visible role in the day-to-day running of the Bahá'í community, this feature has been present in Bahá'í life since its early beginnings, the Conference of Badasht being the first early instance that comes to mind. In effect, the main features of Bahá'í consultation and its expected role in a social setting were laid out by Bahá'u'lláh and 'Abdu'l-Bahá in a variety of contexts susceptible of wide-ranging applications before Shoghi Effendi would incorporate them into the fabric of the Bahá'í administrative system and its social organism, first in the form of codified by-laws for Assemblies (local or national), and second as general guidelines for the conduct of national conventions.[172] In addition, a series of interrelated Bahá'í principles have highlighted the underlying notion that humanity is coming of age and that its very organicity requires, effectively, a new way of approaching communication and interaction between individuals, institutions and nations:

1) Oneness of mankind	The gift of God to this enlightened age is the knowledge of the oneness of mankind and of the fundamental oneness of religion. War shall cease between nations, and by the will of God the Most Great Peace shall come; the world will be seen as a new world, and all men will live as brothers. ('Abdu'l-Bahá, *'Abdu'l-Bahá in London*, pp. 19–20)
2) Federalism	The United States may be held up as the example of future government – that is to say, each province will be independent in itself, but there will be federal union protecting the interests of the various independent states. ('Abdu'l-Bahá, *The Promulgation of Universal Peace*, p. 167)

3) Decentralization	To cast aside centralization which promotes despotism is the exigency of the time. This will be productive of international peace. ('Abdu'l-Bahá, *The Promulgation of Universal Peace*, p. 167)
4) Information/publicity/ communication	The publication of high thoughts is the dynamic power in the arteries of life; it is the very soul of the world. Thoughts are a boundless sea, and the effects and varying conditions of existence are as the separate forms and individual limits of the waves; not until the sea boils up will the waves rise and scatter their pearls of knowledge on the shore of life. ('Abdu'l-Bahá, *The Secret of Divine Civilization,*, pp. 109–110) A mechanism of world inter-communication will be devised, embracing the whole planet, freed from national hindrances and restrictions, and functioning with marvellous swiftness and perfect regularity. (Shoghi Effendi, *The World Order of Bahá'u'lláh*, p. 203)
5) Independent search after truth	God has given man the eye of investigation by which he may see and recognize truth . . . This is his endowment and equipment for the investigation of reality. Man is not intended to see through the eyes of another, hear through another's ears nor comprehend with another's brain. Each human creature has individual endowment, power and responsibility in the creative plan of God. ('Abdu'l-Bahá, *The Promulgation of Universal Peace*, p. 293)
6) Consultation (*mas<u>h</u>virat*)	In this Cause consultation is of vital importance, but spiritual conference and not the mere voicing of personal views is intended. ('Abdu'l-Bahá, *The Promulgation of Universal Peace*, p. 72)

The last two principles appear intimately interrelated. In Bahá'í practice independent search after truth – or intellectual freedom from imitation – not only is not seen as cancelling collective methods of enquiry, but in fact it implies them to the extent to which epistemological equality and devolution lead in that direction. As shown in previous chapters, the success of this process depends on the provision of a context that achieves some degree of 'unity of conscience' and is backed up by an informed public opinion. Without the consequent enlargement of the public sphere, regarded by 'Abdu'l-Bahá as a necessary instrumentality for the inchoation of unity in its manifold forms, neither 'unity in world undertakings' nor 'universal peace' would be feasible.

But in addition to the bolstering of an enlightened public sphere, truth-finding and the processes of communication that make for a deliberative society require a broader view of knowledge. They also demand, ultimately, a method of enquiry that balances the spiritual and the scientific by integrating the various approaches to learning identified by 'Abdu'l-Bahá (sensorial, rational, traditional, intuitive, spiritual). This tenor is further stressed by Shoghi Effendi's bold assertion that the

Revelation of Bahá'u'lláh is 'scientific in its method'.[173] As though to compensate for the strong emphasis on individual conscience, and for the corresponding absence of an interpretive elite, Bahá'í consultation takes on a pivotal role as a framework for the socialization of personal and collective opinions, perspectives, projects, interests and needs. Consultation becomes the preferred channel for the regularization of meanings through an open process of enquiry and consensus building. Its main regulatory condition is that consultation must be held in unity and lead to unity of purpose and action.

Sociologically, Bahá'í consultation can be regarded as an institution in its own right. This understanding is explicitly pointed out by 'Abdu'l-Bahá when he refers to it as 'one of the fundamental elements of the foundation of the Law of God'.[174] Likewise, Shoghi Effendi describes it as a 'principle' and 'one of the basic laws' of the Bahá'í Administrative Order.[175] More recently and in more current idiom Bahá'í consultation has also been defined as a 'method of non-adversarial decision-making'.[176]

The universalization of consultation is a matter of course in the Bahá'í writings. In the Tablet to Queen Victoria Bahá'u'lláh calls for the efforts of the elected representatives to be redirected towards the common good of humanity:

> O ye the elected representatives of the people in every land! Take ye counsel together, and let your concern be only for that which profiteth mankind and bettereth the condition thereof, if ye be of them that scan heedfully. Regard the world as the human body . . .[177]

In *The Secret of Divine Civilization*, the case for the institution of parliamentary life (*maḥáfil-i-mas͟hvirat*)[178] is supported on the exigencies of the time as well as on the qur'ánic injunctions to consult. In more general terms, 'Abdu'l-Bahá, for instance, affirms that consultation should be held to discuss matters, 'whether major or minor', pertaining to 'trade or commerce', 'when a believer is uncertain about his affairs, or when he seeketh to pursue a project or trade', as well as among family relations and friends.[179] Far from being confined to just some administrative levels in the Bahá'í hierarchy, consultation must be relied upon by the entire Bahá'í community for its operation and proper functioning, from the Nineteen Day Feast (itself an institution) to the Universal House of Justice. Shoghi Effendi emphasizes the importance of consultation by stating:

> The *principle of consultation*, which constitutes one of the *basic laws of the Administration*, should be applied to all Bahá'í activities which affect the collective interests of the Faith, for it is through co-operation and continual exchange of thoughts and views that the Cause can best safeguard and foster its interests.[180]

Consultation, therefore, is to be understood as the preferred method of truth/reality-finding. Set in a spiritual and ethical context of service to humanity, it works through a process of collective inquiry that relies on rational argumentation and persuasion to achieve the negotiation of practical meaning. The reason alleged by Shoghi Effendi for the pre-eminent position accorded to consultation is in itself revealing of the new pattern of inquiry which is to be implemented universally in Bahá'í communities:

> Individual initiative, personal ability and resourcefulness, though indispensable, are, unless supported and enriched by the collective experiences and wisdom of the group, utterly incapable of achieving such a tremendous task.[181]

One fundamental role of the branch of the 'learned in Bahá', which specifically aims at extending the benefits of consultation, is to infuse the governing bodies of the Bahá'í community with an additional layer of experience that must bear on community issues. And although the Hands of the Cause first, and subsequently the Counsellors and Auxiliary Board members, function mainly in a personal advisory capacity, their activities are also to a large extent informed by regular processes of consultation.

Granted, then, that Bahá'í consultation implies more than a parliamentary regime, it is worth noting what the implications of this institution might be. Several answers suggest themselves. First, Bahá'í consultation seems to favour the formation of a new pattern of leadership. Bahá'u'lláh explicitly declares: 'From two ranks amongst men power hath been seized: kings and ecclesiastics.'[182] This remark alone, which can be taken as both descriptive and prescriptive, would not suffice to warrant the inference that royalty and the institution of the religiously learned must hence disappear. In fact, Bahá'u'lláh foresees a role for both monarchs and the learned, but their functions, as further reflected in 'Abdu'l-Bahá's *The Secret of Divine Civilization*, are no longer defined in terms of power-wielding. Second, Bahá'í consultation shifts the focus of attention from defining who has the authority to decide for others or how power is shared among the various branches of power, to ensuring that effective consultation and participation takes place all across the board, a position that assumes an inherent right among all people and parties concerned to become active participants and discussants.

Framed in these terms consultation is not a perfunctory adjunct to the adoption of executive decisions but a necessary means – and a moral duty – for the validation of the decisions thus arrived: 'In all things it is necessary to consult. This matter should be forcibly stressed by thee, so that consultation may be observed by all.'[183] This point may also have important implications in a proper understanding of the consultative status of the learned in Bahá (i.e. Counsellors and their Auxiliary Board members). Benefits accruing from consultation are said to exceed personal advantage, for consultation is 'the cause of awareness and of awakening and a source of good and well-being'.[184] Consultation enhances personal and social consciousness, and promotes the welfare of the community:

> Say: No man can attain his true station except through his justice. No power can exist except through unity. No welfare and no well-being can be attained except through consultation.[185]

Bahá'u'lláh places consultation so highly, in point of fact, that is linked to one of His major concerns, namely mankind's maturity as a species as well as individually: 'The maturity of the gift of understanding is made manifest through consultation.'[186] It should be noted in this regard that two hallmarks signifying the development of mankind as defined by Bahá'u'lláh appear to be significantly the result of consultative processes. The convening of the Peace Conference among the great world powers, and the selection of an auxiliary international language, two of Bahá'u'lláh's peace proposals *par excellence*, must be decided upon through vast and unprecedented rounds of consultation on a world scale.[187] And again, the main duties incumbent upon the members of the House of Justice mentioned in the Kitáb-i-Aqdas are headed by the injunction 'to take counsel together and to have regard for the interests of the servants of God, for His sake'.[188] But while the significance of consultation as a major Bahá'í theme can be clearly inferred from the above assertions, it is only in considering its distinguishing features that a proper understanding of its place in the Bahá'í economy can be reached.

The starting point in Bahá'í consultation is not so much individual ideas as personal contributions to the common good, however filtered these might be by personal views. Learning to unlearn, in other words, learning to give up a representation of truth is part of the process of spiritual transformation. Significantly the first valley (valley of search, *vadíy-i-ṭalib*) in the spiritual quest described by Bahá'u'lláh contains words of advice that can be equally related to any search or fact-finding operation. The wayfarer is invited to exert patience (*ṣabr*), to 'shut the door of friendship and enmity upon all the people of the earth', and to 'sacrifice all things. That is, whatever he hath seen, and heard, and understood – all he must set at naught . . .' This injunction is not a recipe for isolation or solipsism but, on the contrary, a mandate for comingling with all other peoples.[189] 'Attachment to lamps and candles' has long been repudiated by Bahá'ís as one of the main causes of 'imitation' (*taqlíd*) and prejudice (*ta'aṣṣub*) in religious history. These basic understandings guide the process and interactions taking place in Bahá'í consultation. Since deliberations ought to be framed in the context of needs rather than interests, as clearly implied by Bahá'u'lláh's exhortations,[190] emphasis on 'spiritual conferencing' seems to be geared to remind participants that consultation requires a special vigilance to overcome particularistic stances. Various deliberate consultation strategies appear to be geared towards this overall goal:

1) Reliance on spiritual means. Prayer and reading of relevant scriptural texts are recommended, especially when contentious issues warrant regular re-focusing.[191]
2) Understanding of certain virtues and values as crucial precursors and

elements of any true dialogue: 'The prime requisites for them that take counsel together are purity of motive, radiance of spirit, detachment from all else save God, attraction to His Divine Fragrances, humility and lowliness among His loved ones, patience and long-suffering in difficulties and servitude to His Threshold.'[192] Other elements include:

a. Truthfulness[193]
b. Trustworthiness[194]
c. Patience[195]
d. Courtesy[196]
e. Search after truth[197]
f. Strongest condemnation of backbiting,[198] cursing,[199] and mendacity
g. Attentive, respectful listening
h. Speaking from a position of humility[200]
i. Engaging in seemly talk[201]
j. No excess of words[202]

3) Avoidance of contention.[203] In some settings this may entail deferring to the other party for the sake of unity, or simply withdrawal; but by and large this seems to mean the adoption of a non-confrontational style in the discussion of issues, premised on:
   a. A positive affirmation of the right of participants to free speech,[204] and more specifically the right to differ, and to appeal decisions.[205]
   b. The countering of stereotyping by questioning hearsay information, vague assumptions, received knowledge, etc.[206]
   c. Elimination of electioneering,[207] power-brokering tactics and 'representative' thinking.[208]
4) Stress on the importance of paying respect to procedures.[209]
5) Aiming for unanimity.[210] A consequence of this practice is that issues tend to be explored more in depth, differing or silent voices are invited to make their views known, and margins for accommodation are broadened so as to deliver inclusive decisions through consensus building. In consequence, the quest for unanimity fosters greater participation and may break the cycle of majority/minority decisions, together with the risks of consolidating 'sides'.
6) Respect for minorities.
7) Acceptance and endorsement of decisions taken by majority vote at various levels.[211] This acceptance requires a combination of loyalty and self-discipline, as well as refraining from using means that may undermine the implementation of decisions, including the unwise questioning of the authority to do so.

One of the specific aims of consultation is to provide a safe environment for the expression of personal views. Freedom of expression, as stressed by Shoghi Effendi, is a vital requirement of the Bahá'í Administrative Order:

> Let us also remember that at the very root of the Cause lies the principle of the undoubted right of the individual to self-expression, his freedom to declare his conscience and set forth his views.[212]

However, this freedom must operate in a safe environment, that is, one that provides the amplest opportunities for the exchange of views, for a majority of people, with a minimum of friction. In a broad sense, safe conditions depend on a number of factors such as access to education, equality between men and women, overcoming of psychological fears, etc.[213] Life in a mature Bahá'í community is intended to reinforce these formative processes. In addition, safety is also achieved through some basic safeguards. Vote-soliciting,[214] for instance, and grouping along ideological lines are strictly forbidden in the Bahá'í Administrative Order;[215] contributions to the funds are strictly confidential[216] and earmarking of these[217] subject to approval by the relevant institution. Accordingly, issues must be debated on the basis of individual conscience and factual merits:

> The members thereof must take counsel together in such wise that no occasion for ill-feeling may arise. This can be attained when every member expresseth with absolute freedom his own opinion and setteth forth his argument. Should any one oppose, he must on no account feel hurt for not until matters are fully discussed can the right way be revealed. The shining spark of truth cometh forth only after the clash of differing opinions.[218]

Insisting on one's own opinion is to be avoided at all cost,[219] and under no circumstances is the belittling of another's opinion acceptable. Criticisms of decisions already arrived at are not permissible as this kind of behaviour leads to 'estrangement', 'coolness' and 'alienation'. Instead, wholehearted support for such decisions is encouraged in the belief that any shortcomings may stand a better chance to be redressed in the normal course of events than through active dissidence or opinionatedness:

> What the Master desired to protect the friends against was continual bickering and opinionatedness. A believer can ask the Assembly why they made a certain decision and politely request them to reconsider. But then he must leave it at that, and not go on disrupting local affairs through insisting on his own views. This applies to an Assembly member as well. We all have a right to our opinions, we are bound to think differently; but a Bahá'í must accept the majority decision of his Assembly, realizing that acceptance and harmony – even if a mistake has been made – are the really important things, and when we serve the Cause properly, in the Bahá'í way, God will right any wrongs done in the end.[220]

Such constraints cause Bahá'í consultation to be a demanding exercise in balancing one's own impulses and motives (in view of the feelings and varying capabilities of other participants) with the need to express frankly any views relevant to the matters discussed. Indirect ways of expressing oneself must be avoided.[221] And the discussion of hypothetical questions, for their own sake, with only a remote bearing on the issues at hand, must also be bypassed (a clear safeguard against casuistry or excess of legislation). Moreover, there should be no room for an atmosphere of secrecy and exclusiveness, all incompatible with Bahá'í procedure.[222]

The importance of proper, solidly-based argumentation is also a key point underlined by Bahá'u'lláh and 'Abdu'l-Bahá when stressing the education of Bahá'í children, and in general when it comes to 'proving' religious matters by rational means.[223] A great deal of the Bahá'í de-emphasis of religious clashes is achieved through a representation of a triumph of virtues (such as tolerance, patience, etc.) and the power of the word over its opposites – intolerance, the sword, hair-splitting, casuistry.

At variance with top-down and forensic decision-making models, the starting point in Bahá'í consultation is the assumption that decision-making is not best served by either the instalment of a firm line of command or the confrontation of opposing camps. Current agonic views of argumentation sanction as ultimately 'positive' elements such as denunciation, aggressiveness and even self-pandering, which in the context of ordinary relationships (among neighbours, at the work place) would be regarded as seriously disruptive. The agonic model also tends to reward conflict by conferring upon contending sides a capacity for interlocution which third parties, including victims, are often denied, itself a major breeding ground of resentment and future problems. Unrestricted applications of this model in the socio-economic world through the mystifying of competition, aggressiveness, risk-taking, adventure, and survival of the fittest, also contradict basic Bahá'í assumptions about human nature to the extent that they cancel out the power of cooperation and reciprocity to overcome differences.

In contrast, Bahá'í consultation focuses on the gradual building of shared understandings – 'unity of conscience' – through collaborative efforts. This perspective, while taking diversity as a natural fact of life ('the shining spark of truth cometh forth only after the clash of differing opinions')[224] seems to aim at effecting a reconciliation of points of view for the sake of both truth and harmony.

Bahá'u'lláh underlines the deliberative and process-dependent nature of social decisions – and the knowledge that sanctions them – by pointing to the transmuting effect that consultation has in changing the status of issues from doubtful or problematic to certain: 'Consultation bestoweth greater awareness and transmuteth conjecture into certitude.'[225] As pointed out, its range of application is not confined to specific matters, but rather is applicable to all departments of life. Its placement under the orbit of wisdom, together with compassion, seems to suggest a benign overall-protective role for consultation, a factor especially relevant bearing in mind that Bahá'u'lláh warns that His laws and justice should nevertheless not be nullified through excessive compassion:

> The heaven of divine wisdom is illumined with the two luminaries of consultation and compassion (*mashvirat va shafagat*). Take ye counsel together in all matters, inasmuch as consultation is the lamp of guidance which leadeth the way, and is the bestower of understanding (*agahí*).[226]

In the main, Bahá'í consultation can be defined as a tool to reach a shared and practical understanding of matters affecting the common good. Hypotheses, theories and simple suggestions can be put forward freely; but great care must be exercised to avoid placing undue pressure on the members of the elected bodies to conform to established or general opinion. Shoghi Effendi stresses that the elected members of a Bahá'í council do not have a mandate from their electors other than the generic one to act and decide on principle. They are not elected on the basis of platforms but rather of personal attributes. In consequence, the members of a Bahá'í council are not responsible for their decisions before a constituency whose views or interests they would embody.[227] The elected members are free to think and vote according to conscience, regardless of whether this entails a change of mind or even a radical shift from previous positions. The confidentiality of discussions, again a basic requirement, helps to maintain the fluidness of opinions. Face-saving and playing-to-the-gallery are then minimized.

Bahá'í consultation establishes its agenda in accordance with community needs and requirements. Although the building of Bahá'í communities can be seen as a gradual rapprochement to the wider society, this process is not meant to be a reaction to the world problematique. Here the words of 'Abdu'l-Bahá can be taken as an insightful guide as to the antidote to being deluded by a problem-oriented vision of things:

> The afflictions which come to humanity sometimes tend to centre the consciousness upon the limitations, and this is a veritable prison. Release comes by making of the will a Door through which the confirmations of the Spirit come.[228]

A similar attitude is implicit, as seen in Part II, in 'Abdu'l-Bahá's depiction of peace as an integrative process whereby peace itself is defined not so much as a single item or occurrence (the absence of war), but rather as an outcome of action emerging decisively from different social and political areas in human affairs.

Consequently, the community-building process consciously undertaken by Bahá'ís strives to identify needs and to uncover harmful uncritical assumptions.[229] To achieve this, Bahá'í practice seeks above all to empower its community base to articulate its views on matters of common concern. A generalization of consultative processes along these lines, especially one that reaches its grass-roots levels, can be regarded as a major goal of Bahá'í community life and the main mechanism to ensure the healthy functioning of the community. It is this understanding which explains why consultation has been defined by the Bahá'í International

Community as 'the operating expression of justice in human affairs'.[230] This definition parallels that of justice as an act of discernment according to which the person regulates his or her personal life.[231] The definition is based on a text by Bahá'u'lláh where justice, unity and consultation are linked:

> No man can attain his true station except through his justice. No power can exist except through unity. No welfare and no well-being can be attained except through consultation.[232]

Consultation, therefore, is seen here as a collective exercise of discernment whose rulings affect the functioning of the community. If conducted appropriately it also tends to be self-correcting. Community-building requires permanent empirical evidence in order to perfect its own machinery, whether conceptual, moral or material. Once a decision is arrived at, Bahá'ís are called to give it their full-hearted support, regardless of whether one personally agrees with it. Such an endorsement is necessary simply to allow the decision to follow its natural course. If the decision is undermined by objectors, the goodness, or otherwise, of the decision can be severely affected. Internal opposition can then easily turn into a self-fulfilling prophecy and predispose negatively future decisions. Conversely, if a decision which is carried out with the support of its main proponents as well as contradictors fails, the community not only has an opportunity to assess where things went wrong, but it also feels greatly reassured by the display of solidarity shown in the process. This method, however idealized, contrasts with the treatment of error in complex top-down organizations where often accountability processes stigmatize error and thus vitiate feedback by distorting error-reporting or ostracizing whistle-blowers. Since Bahá'í consultation fosters a mature assumption of error as collective risk and as part of the gathering of knowledge, failures tend to be fed back into consultation through a process of evaluation, redefining of goals and behavioural changes, if and when required.

Implications of Bahá'í consultation

Strong parallels between the Bahá'í understanding of consultation and dialogic ethics have been noted. The emphasis on dialogue as providing in itself a moral legitimization to human projects is common to both perspectives. However, this does not mean that Bahá'í ethics just takes just correct procedures as the main criteria to assess the value of norms and decisions. Unity rather than consensus, or correct decisions in the formal sense of discourse ethics, is the overriding concern present in Bahá'í consultation. Unanimity is pursued as a goal because the arrival at unanimity, although not an end in itself, guarantees that all voices (including those in the minority) are heard and their views legitimately understood or considered in the overall process of dialogue.

Bahá'í consultation aims at becoming a universal process. First of all, it establishes that discussions must be framed in such a way as to encompass as many interlocutors as possible. In one of the latest statements by the Bahá'í International Community this idea has been stressed:

> The institutions of society will succeed in eliciting and directing the potentialities latent in the consciousness of the world's peoples to the extent that the exercise of authority is governed by principles that are in harmony with the evolving interests of a rapidly maturing human race. Such principles include the obligation of those in authority [1] to *win the confidence, respect and genuine support* of those whose actions they seek to govern; [2] to *consult openly and to the fullest extent possible with all those whose interests are affected by the decisions being arrived at*; [3] to assess in an objective manner both the *real needs and the aspirations* of the communities they serve.[233] (emphasis and numbering added)

The generalization of consultative processes at all levels of the social scale is one of the salient features of the Bahá'í administrative system. In particular, the institution of a consultative part at the Nineteen Day Feast draws the institutional process of dialogue to the grass-roots level of the Bahá'í community.[234] Yet, from a Bahá'í point of view, the Habermasian demands that all the people concerned in a situation of dialogue be given the opportunity to voice their concerns and to question any statement, require important qualifications. To uphold these demands as overriding principles may simply disrupt any real consultative process in the name of correctness. Not everyone affected by a decision or a public matter can enter into a situation of effective dialogue, nor is prepared to do so, nor is there a possibility to provide social spaces ample enough to welcome all the likely participants.[235] Discourse philosophers tend not to be too worried about these questions because they are prepared to concede that in a deliberative democracy allowances can be made for the functioning of institutions, with their various levels of representation and hierarchy and their constitutional safeguards and provisions for the respect of human rights. But if this is so, and qualifications of such great import are introduced via a detour, there seems to be not much point in undermining discourse ethics by conceding that the extrapolation of small-scale situations of communicative dialogue into large-scale settings is fraught with major problems. In the second place, in Bahá'í consultation universalization must also be introduced into discussions, through a conscious effort to take into consideration the needs, interests, wishes and concerns of humanity as a whole. This is a Bahá'í moral standard and holds true for governments as well as individuals. In other words, it is not enough to have a system that ensures access to decision-making, it is also necessary that decision-making itself be patterned after such consciousness.[236] The monological and the dialogical dimensions of conventional and post-conventional ethics must be therefore re-combined.[237]

30
Towards the Most Great Peace

The characterization of the Bahá'í ethos attempted in the previous chapters has shown the correspondence between a highly personalistic conception of individual agency, and a cosmopolitan, community-oriented outlook mediated by a strong ethical view of the importance of proper communication and the institution of a universal consultative process. The tension between these two poles is rationalized and negotiated in several ways.

First of all, deprecations of *taqlíd* and exhortations to exert intellectual and spiritual freedom are intended to act as emancipatory and unencumbering mechanisms. They devolve the ultimate responsibility to decide on religious matters upon the individual's conscience ('independent' search after truth). This activity, however, is not restricted to conscience matters, as it becomes a universalizable 'model' applicable to all other departments of human life in which human beings find their own identities, needs and interests at stake. This is further reinforced by a lack of a priestly structure and the fostering of a culture of democratic collegiality.

Second, the stress on personal salvation is given a distinct focus. While the spiritual survival of the 'I', in other words the preparation for the next life, continues to be the determinant component of one's purpose in life, this preparation is described in terms of what the spiritual soul does effectively in this world for the benefit of others. Spiritualization and civilization are then defined in terms mutually inclusive. Service and sacrifice assume here a key role as guarantors of mankind's salvation. The resulting morality is one fundamentally preoccupied with the good of mankind as a whole, but also critically aware of the need to anchor service in the robust acquisition of both personal and public virtues. The pursuit of good works and practical attainments not only determines the shape of preferences in the cultivation of knowledge and morality, it also extends to the way the mature person understands the salvific potentialities of purposeful action. Since ultimately the salvific value of good works depends on God's acceptance and hence can be regarded as imponderable, moral life ultimately resolves itself in a relationship of trust in God, His grace, His promises and His rightful channels.

Third, the very movement towards a world-embracing morality that overcomes individualistic motives and favours a universalistic approach is inclusive of a teleology of history and a theology of religions in which humanity advances from various stages of development towards new levels of maturity and inclusiveness. This inclusiveness explicitly contains a critique of prejudices, fanaticism and vain imaginations, portrayed as the major intellectual and moral counter-themes underlying most conflicts among human beings. The scope of Bahá'í morality remains largely an open one, hinging around a number of core values such as unity, justice, service, sacrifice, moderation, truthfulness, courtesy, refinement, all buttressed by a set of guiding tenets, goals or principles that provide a constructive direction to the virtues concerned. In this context, peace appears linked positively to the cultivation of definite and appropriate behaviours.

An illustration of how unity is understood in a pluralistic fashion is shown in the very notions of the oneness of religion and of organic unity, both of fundamental importance for a Bahá'í approach to peace. The first concept is usually explained in terms of either an historical progression of revealed religions (progressive revelation),[238] or, more usually, as a coincidence in fundamentals (laws of love, justice, fairmindedness, truthfulness)[239] yet compatible with a divergence in non-essentials (rituals, social laws and cultural adaptations). 'Abdu'l-Bahá's standard explanations would emphasize the importance of achieving such an understanding among existing religions to bridge their differences and thereby secure a strong basis for the attainment of peace, or rather a true *pax religiosa*. The coincidence with Küng's dictum 'no peace among the nations without peace among the religions' should deserve more than a note in passing.[240]

For its part, the theme of 'organic unity' (assisted by other quasi-organic concepts such as the 'eternal Covenant of God', 'creative Word')[241] furnishes a common thread to understand how continuity can operate despite discontinuities, lapses and crises, or how solidity can coexist with flexibility, or similarities with differences, while maintaining a wholesome balance. The strength of this conception relies considerably on the generative capacity of organic metaphors to supply an emblematic world allowing Bahá'ís to 'figure out' the accommodation of differences in a number of ways.[242] These 'expressions', to adopt Opler's terminology, can be taken as prefigurations of major attitudinal shifts in the conception of power and human relations as a whole. As seen above, Bahá'í explanations of such an organic process in sacred history provide a global understanding not only of the transformations taking place in the 'womb' of humanity, but of the new combinatory of elements (religious law) required to assist in what is regarded as a birth-like experience of cosmic proportions. As such, this maieutic process, brought about by the succession of revealed dispensations, is bound to lead to the efflorescence of a divine civilization where the ideal of one common humankind is realized in and made possible by an abiding peace.

In this connection the notions of 'organic unity' and 'unity in diversity', both inseparable from the concept of organic growth, illustrate a highly dynamic conception of human life as something that happens at the intersection of the personal and the civilizational, more as a balanced approaching of higher integrative patterns of interaction than as the mimetic copying of a blueprint. This was paradigmatically highlighted in a letter written on behalf of Shoghi Effendi:

> We cannot segregate the human heart from the environment outside us and say that once one of these is reformed everything will be improved. *Man is organic with the world. His inner life moulds the environment and is itself also deeply affected by it.* The one acts upon the other and every abiding change in the life of man is the result of these mutual reactions.[243] (emphasis added)

Fourth, the institution of Bahá'í consultation serves as a case in point of how Bahá'u'lláh's emphasis on the prevalence of the word (the 'power of utterance'), as against persuasion by coercion, turns into a paradigm of governance evolved out of a deliberative community which values collective wisdom in a context of hermeneutical equality and refinement. More significantly, it also suggests how a diversity of points of view and interests can be resolved with a minimum of conflict. At any rate, the priority accorded to unity in the Bahá'í writings and the emphasis on the power of utterance (dialogue), embodied by virtuous individuals, recalibrate the demands imposed on any situation of dialogue. This goal is pursued in a setting that, through universal participation, aims consciously at integrating as many actors as possible in the decision-making process. This entails not only an effort at proper devolution (maximum decentralization compatible with unity), but also a more resolute willingness to strengthen the sphere of publicity and the resolve of public opinion to count effectively in the decisions that concern them. 'Abdu'l-Bahá's repeated calls for a widening of religious dialogue entailed a new opening for religious studies, and, perhaps more significantly, created fresh conditions for a re-definition of the institution of the learned (*'ulamá*), now recast into a new humbled lay class ministering to the needs of humanity.

Although here the ethics of communicative action does not emerge from an analysis of the speech acts and its exigencies, as in Habermas's theory, some of the anthropological and philosophical presuppositions underlying both the Habermasian and the Bahá'í communities are exchangeable (epistemic equality, universalization principle, broadening of the public sphere, belief in the perfectibility of man and society through education/communication). Bahá'í consultation appears to be the form truth-seeking adopts in a medium guided by an ethics of unity which sees the oneness of humanity as both its moral bedrock and ultimate goal. The basic tenet of independent search after truth – which, it should not be forgotten, is linked to an understanding of justice as fairmindedness in discerning truth/reality – results in the emerging of Bahá'í consultation as an institution in its own right. Less clear, however, is to what extent Bahá'í consultation may affect in the long term an understanding of argumentation, knowledge building and a socially assumed form of orality and textuality. As in the case of dialogue ethics, Bahá'í consultation tends to remove the abrasiveness of the agonistic, adversarial and logomachic practices present in democratic deliberative societies, including the latent and only apparently paradoxical drive towards an imposition of democratic values by force.[244] In this regard 'Abdu'l-Bahá's reflections suggest that a truly spiritual ethos may not only assist in the creation of a more levelled terrain for the interplay of diverse and contrary positions, but also endow it with a more potent and stable foundation for peace and conflict resolution than that obtained through a minimalist secular morality.

31
Summary and Conclusions

Bahá'u'lláh's explicit abrogation of *jihád* and His summons to a concomitant partial relinquishment of sovereignty by the state rulers for the sake of peace – as implied in His letters to the kings – brought to the fore the question of Bahá'u'lláh's religious authority to issue forth a new canon transcending Islam and, indeed, all the religions 'of the past'. This was not, however, a hollowing out of the *Sharí'a* through *gnosis ('irfán)*, and then made more or less admissible through dissimulation (*taqíyya*), but a complete, open overturning of it via a new revelation (*wahí*).[1]

By obliterating *jihád* Bahá'u'lláh disclaimed any associations with seditious elements engaged in *fitna* (rebellion or subversion), and more importantly He cut through the maze of *Sharí'a* binding formulations and customary practice by turning them upon themselves. With this first move, Bahá'u'lláh created a point of no return for His own followers, leaving no room for confusion as to the place of violence, coercion, dissimulation or imitation in the new Bahá'í system (a point which 'Abdu'l-Bahá further elevated to a central theme in His work *The Secret of Divine Civilization*). In addition, Bahá'u'lláh's rejection of *jihád* laid out the basis for the centrality of peace in the Bahá'í teachings. It did so not so much by crushing one of the basic tenets of the Muslim system, but fundamentally by divesting it of its supportive legal, social and political ramifications, the more obvious of which were the concept of ritual impurity and the strict separation between the religious communities of the Book, both of which were rejected. Much of the preliminary work, which was contained in the *Kitáb-i-Íqán* (Bahá'u'lláh's reinterpretation of apocalyptic and eschatological imagery), emphasized the spiritual nature of the eschatological and moral struggles that must precede or accompany the soul's occupancy of the 'peaceful city of the divine presence'.[2]

At an elementary level the annulment of *jihád* entailed a new understanding not only of how communities within the new *ummah* would relate to each other, but also, and perhaps more significantly, of how states – regardless of their religious makeup – would have to conduct their own affairs and manage their conflicts in a non-violent way. In this new normative approach the time-honoured division between the Muslim community (*dár-al Islám*, the world of Islam) and the realms of those not yet converted, subjected or vanquished (*dár-al ḥarb*, the world of war) became definitely relegated to the past. Thus, the abrogation of *jihád* effectively put an end to the rather fictional Islamic understanding of conflicts in terms of an alleged normative tension between believers and unbelievers. Such a division had historically operated, as the cases of *jihád* in Bahá'u'lláh's own lifetime demonstrated all too clearly, as a fig leaf to fuel or justify conflicts with infidel nations or with internal enemies assimilated to them.

Moreover, the abrogation of *jihád* wiped out a second form of violent tensions in the form of military preparedness for the coming of the Promised Qá'im or Mahdí. While the abrogation was a most conspicuous and symbolically significant act of spiritual authority, it was not an isolated phase, as made evident by Bahá'u'lláh's subsequent pronouncements reproving all forms of intolerance, fanaticism, hypocrisy and dissimulation. The condemnation of these was positively affirmed by Bahá'u'lláh in His role as lawgiver and Messiah both through His general counsels and admonitions addressed to potentates of His time, and through His own repository of laws (the Kitáb-i-Aqdas) destined for His own followers.

In effect, Bahá'u'lláh's major legislative actions entailed a reversal of millennialist expectations (especially those of a triumph of faith by the sword), which Bahá'u'lláh reframed in a largely symbolical context of eschatological fulfilment in which God's sovereignty (*sulṭanatí*) materializes through the power of the Word. Yet, instead of placing God's sovereignty exclusively in the metaphysical realm, or in the thereafter, this sovereignty is said to be destined for more rounded religious and civilizational expressions, for such is the inner impetus of (re)revelation. The visionary thrust behind these declarations is made apparent in Bahá'u'lláh's statements that the world 'in this Day' is rapidly moving closer towards maturity. Signs of its impending approach are characteristically couched in the language of prophetic and mystic fulfilment; behaviours (unity, consultation) in keeping with it are noted, and calls for a sublimation of motives in a form of global loyalty to humanity, unequivocally made. In this context, the principle of 'collective security' (not His words) enunciated by Bahá'u'lláh appears as a requisite corollary of humanity's coming of age or, expressed in socio-political terms, as a reflection of God's increasing sovereignty.

In some important respects Bahá'u'lláh's principle of collective security works as the secular counterpart of the abolition of *jihád* and all its derivative forms of religiously motivated violence. Just as religious violence was removed by Bahá'u'lláh as a valid ground for waging war or justifying violent conflicts, similarly interstate war was no longer viewed as a morally acceptable state of affairs, but rather as a source of evil which needed to be redressed through collective security arrangements. Seen from this perspective, the anarchic condition of inter-state war (however justifiable 'just wars' might appear) was as deserving of condemnation as holy wars, civil strife, insurgencies and seditious acts.

Bahá'u'lláh's texts succinctly outlined three fundamental but minimum requirements: disarmament; a mechanism for the resolution of outstanding disputes, including the use of force; and a limited suite of supportive measures. As suggested in Bahá'u'lláh's conversation with Edward Granville Browne, the

Cambridge orientalist, the eventual attainment of peace was set in a context of messianic fulfilment. Peace was an integral part of the eternal Covenant of God and was reflective of the unfolding nature of God's Kingdom. The almost baffling distinction between the Lesser and Most Great Peace, perhaps modelled on a reversal of the Islamic pair Lesser/Greater *Jihád*, corresponded to the lower and higher end of a scale that would gradually take humanity to its final consummation. The whole process was indirectly portrayed in terms of a progressive maturation of mankind set in motion through the potencies released by God's new Revelation. At this level peace *(ṣulḥ)* was the process rather than the result (*salám*) of pacifying the evil forces at work in the world. The new terms and conditions envisaged by Bahá'u'lláh for the renewal of humanity were thus similar, only on a global plane, to those that obtained between the times of *jáhilíyya* in pre-Islamic tribalistic Arabia and those introduced by Muhammad into the Islamic *ummah.*

'Abdu'l-Bahá's elaborations on peace provided from the outset a wider context to His Father's injunctions. Two major texts, *The Secret of Divine Civilization* (1875) and the Tablet to The Hague (1919) defined the main framework of the Bahá'í approach to peace. Between the two intervened 'Abdu'l-Bahá's travels to the West and the horrors of a world war which he announced as an almost inevitable outcome of European warmongering. In addition to Bahá'u'lláh's proposals, some further elements were introduced into the equation. Peace was not merely an issue of special interest, indeed it had to become the defining theme of the twentieth century, for nothing else was as pressing as building a society free from the scourge of war, with its distortions of human, social, moral and economic relationships. This enterprise, furthermore, was not an isolated feature, but had to be placed on a par and in logical continuance with the struggle for the abolition of slavery achieved during the nineteenth century (a feature specially singled out by Bahá'u'lláh as an evil specifically abrogated by God's new Law).

Adding to Bahá'u'lláh's vision of collective security, 'Abdu'l-Bahá underscored in His *The Secret of Divine Civilization* the consultative nature of the arrangements agreed upon by the superpowers. Solid guarantees would need to be incorporated into its legal instruments, including a full ratification process of endorsement by parliamentary and public opinion. The representatives of humanity, appointed to the world parliament in proportion to their countries' populations, would deliberate on a broad range of matters bearing upon peace and security. Frontiers would be fixed and a world auxiliary language chosen. As a result, a world tribunal would be established to adjudicate on international disputes. Given these guarantees, any act of aggression would be repelled unitedly by the world's political body with due resort to force if necessary.

Whatever the importance of taking steps in this direction, 'Abdu'l-Bahá was careful to point out some forty-five years later in His Tablet to The Hague that these bare elements (amounting perhaps to the basics of the Lesser Peace, *ṣulḥ-i-asghar*) would not afford a firm grounding for universal peace (*ṣulḥ-i-'umúmí*). The end to war and violence had to also be related to a number of principles that demanded no less attention than arms reductions, arbitration or security measures among nations. For this to take root, a much wider concept had to be envisioned. Other issues had to be added to the world agenda of reforms; matters such as gender equality, universal education, the adoption of a universal auxiliary language, cooperation between science and religion, and the elimination of prejudices needed to be contemplated as part of a comprehensive global platform. In the end, the much greater scope afforded by these additional dimensions of peace may have justified 'Abdu'l-Bahá in His statement to Andrew Carnegie to the effect that 'in the future his [Bahá'u'lláh's] teachings will act as a deterrent and preventive from the occurrence of the most great danger, i. e. universal war'.[3]

In His articulation of the Bahá'í teachings (or 'principles') as the main content of a 'positive peace', 'Abdu'l-Bahá provided a convenient device to systematize some Bahá'í essentials, albeit without implying that the list was exhaustive. In the absence, however, of an overtly logical rationale that would expand and interrelate these principles, and given the loss of the immediate context and the illocutionary effect surrounding His speeches (that contemporary listeners often reported in terms of awe and spellboundness), the 'list' of Bahá'í principles often assumed unofficial status as a creedal formulation of sorts. Yet, if our analysis of the critical passage in *The Secret of Divine Civilization* and the Tablet to The Hague serves as an indication, an underlying pattern or hierarchy of principles seems undeniable. To start with, truth/reality was presented as a network of embedded realities and necessary relationships, a dynamic flow of manifestations and ramifications which defied conventional wisdom. An interrelated world meant that wars and conflicts were now sending powerful shockwaves whose effects could be felt everywhere. Modern warfare and violence, and their attending ideologies, were simply far more than anything witnessed before. The sufferings of the toiling *fellahin* of Egypt would not end with the conscription and ordeals experienced in armed service, grave as these were given the deadly power of modern warfare, but they would be compounded with the miseries of crop failure and severe economic depression following in its aftermath. In order to apprehend this reality in its multifarious complexity, 'unity of conscience' was required. This kind of integrative perception was extremely important because the implied opposite view was prone to overstate the fragmentary condition of reality (or rather of its perception), and then elevate one single aspect to a gnoseologically dominant yet unwarranted position. While the way in which unity of conscience was implicitly defined reconnected with almost identical definitions of religion and science given by 'Abdu'l-Bahá,[4] as a concept it seemed to transcend or combine the senses of both ideas. Unity of conscience was not to be equated with similar notions such as 'public consensus', 'public opinion' or 'unity in belief', equivalents of which had currency in the thought and doctrine conveyed by 'Abdu'l-Bahá. Unity of conscience was perhaps the objective way of referring to the eminent capacity to transcend all particularistic points of view and to integrate all principles and issues bearing on reality in a creative way, for 'all created things have their degree or stage of maturity',[5] or as Bahá'u'lláh expressed it:

> Every age hath its own problem, and every soul its particular aspiration. The remedy the world needeth in its present-day afflictions can never be the same as that which a subsequent age may require. Be anxiously concerned with the needs of the age ye live in, and centre your deliberations on its exigencies and requirements.[6]

Human problems and their corresponding needs had to be interpreted and articulated in this integrative and more dialectical way. This method of arguing the world was exemplified, for instance, in the new phase of peace building that would correspond to the new realities now forcefully emerging:

> According to an intrinsic law all phenomena of being attain to a summit and degree of consummation, after which a new order and condition is established. As the instruments and science of war have reached the degree of thoroughness and proficiency, it is hoped that the transformation of the human world is at hand and that in the coming centuries all the energies and inventions of man will be utilized in promoting the interests of peace and brotherhood. Therefore, may this esteemed and worthy society for the establishment of international peace be confirmed in its sincere intentions and empowered by God. Then will it hasten the time when the banner of universal agreement will be raised and international welfare will be proclaimed and consummated so that the darkness which now encompasses the world shall pass away.[7]

By the same token, it was imperative to discard or rather replace false notions with others truer to reality. False notions (whether in the form of prejudices, pseudo-scientific truths, or ideologies) had the potential to divert the creative energies of humanity into worthless if not criminal designs. A good example of a polarizing idea with the capacity to engender conditions for its own fulfilment was the prevailing notion about war as a natural accoutrement of civilization. This was felt as a 'fact of life', in the naturalistic sense conveyed by Darwinistic ideas such as 'struggle for existence' which 'Abdu'l-Bahá condemned as the 'fountain head of all calamities' and 'supreme affliction', but which interlocutors of 'Abdu'l-Bahá such as Maxim Hudson would embrace with gusto:

> Self-preservation is the first law of Nature, and this law applies to nations exactly as it applies to individuals. Our American Republic cannot survive unless it obeys the law of survival, which all individuals must obey, which all nations must obey, and which all other nations are obeying. No individual, and no nation, has ever disobeyed that law for long and lived; and it is too big a task for the United States of America.[8]

Likewise the socio-political significance accorded to differences among human beings attributable to an 'inherited' and 'innate' character, or alternatively to a particular type of group identity (race, class, religion, ethnicity, gender), was never denied by 'Abdu'l-Bahá, but their effects on society were said to be such that either they could be put to good use or otherwise harmonized through education and the motivational forces of love and religion. Differences were good to the extent that they added variety, freshness, nimbleness, resilience and beauty; but if used to fuel a false and exclusivist sense of identity or dominance they were detrimental. Accordingly, prejudices originating in the belief of an inherent superiority of a category of men over other human beings on account of such differences were condemned by 'Abdu'l-Bahá as utterly groundless. Complacent theories built on the belief in the supremacy of a given race, class, gender, nation or religion were denounced as inimical to humanity's progress, which historically, as explained repeatedly by 'Abdu'l-Bahá, had been the result of an ever-widening dynamics of expansion stemming from what he termed 'collective centres of unity'. Stress on the goodness of all things, appreciation for truth irrespective of where it was found, and a radical admission that if religion is a cause of conflict then it is better to do without it, further enhanced this general sense of toleration.

As presented by 'Abdu'l-Bahá, the teachings of His Father and the different varieties of unity examined in Part II constituted a simple yet comprehensive framework of tenets which operated at various levels informing essential aspects of the Bahá'í ethos. In particular, the pervasive Bahá'í principle of the oneness of humanity, together with its close ally – the oneness of God and of religion – were the first such principles to be proclaimed by 'Abdu'l-Bahá from the vantage point of 'unity of conscience'. These three, in turn, implied or embraced other principles which at least for expository purposes may be regrouped or related as more specialized subsets. For instance, unity of conscience implied in this sense independent investigation of truth, harmony between science and religion, and universal education; and the principle of the oneness of mankind entailed equality between men and women and the overcoming of the prejudices of race, religion, class and ideology. The acceptance of these doctrines or 'principles' acted as heuristic and moral pointers to a series of desired logical outcomes (the establishing of a world tribunal, the election of a universal language, the setting up of other 'world undertakings', the acceptance of a divine source of all religions) whose shape and form would need to be adjusted to the needs and requirements of the time.

In this approach, peace itself (in its more limited sense, usually associated with the establishment of collective security and a world tribunal) was no longer the dominant feature, but in fact one among many decisive factors contributing to the establishment of a new civilization. The attainment of such general conditions were then regarded as indicative of the attainment of a universal peace (*ṣulḥ 'umumí*, *ṣulḥ-i-akbar*) far greater than anything previously experienced, certainly more so than the still precarious peace resulting from the legalistic and purely political approach informing collective security. Since the conception of reality and knowledge contained in these expressions was implicitly a dynamic one, none of these 'Bahá'í' principles could strictly speaking be determined in a precise fashion. Our understanding of how these realities would interact and inform each other, including the extent to which they can be widened or implemented, must move at a pace with the needs of humanity and with the learning involved in the new dynamics. As reiterated by Bahá'u'lláh and 'Abdu'l-Bahá, and even more explicitly, by Shoghi Effendi, formulaic knowledge and dogmatic approaches have no place in the satisfaction of humanity's needs. This was if anything reinforced by clear hints as to the significant limitations attributable to contemporary ideological approaches, as implied by 'Abdu'l-Bahá at the end of the Tablet to The Hague with reference to the major political ideologies, and as noted by Shoghi Effendi in unambiguous terms in his 'World Order' letters, where the evils of racism, nationalism and communism (in other words the supremacy of the interests of a particular race, nation or class) were decried as antithetical to unity.

This worldview was also consistent with the emphasis placed by 'Abdu'l-Bahá on the notion of an 'unlearning of war', the need to experiment with peace after six thousand years of violence, and on the cultivation of the 'blessed arts of peace'. These and similar ideas, including the emphasis on a non-retaliatory system for the treatment of criminals and a moderate approach to the settlement of industrial disputes, were suggestive of an almost counter-intuitive process of detoxification from war and its supportive thinking based on the dialectics of confrontation and power brokering. New and fresher insights into the reality of the person, his or her mutability, educability and progression towards more integrated forms of personal and collective attainment were considered essential. This was a global educational enterprise involving all human beings, or to be more precise the 'armies of peace', the new scholars who would serve the body politic of the world, from mothers to university professors:

> The thoughts of universal peace must be instilled in the minds of all the scholars, in order that they may become the armies of peace, the real servants of the body politic the world. God is the Father of all. Mankind are His children. This globe is one home. Nations are the members of one family. The mothers in their homes, the teachers in the schools, the professors in the colleges, the presidents in the universities, must teach these ideals to the young from the cradle to maturity.[9]

Consistent with this approach and what we know were the main trends within the American peace movement, 'Abdu'l-Bahá was also quick to point out the special position that the United States of America was bound to occupy on the world scene and likewise the role that women would be forced to perform as natural allies, if not main drivers, of the peace cause. America was indeed in a unique position to champion a world peace modelled on an extension of the federal principle to international relationships. By comparison with its European counterparts, the United States was free from imperialistic designs and thereby better placed to lead the process.

A number of these themes were synthetically summarized by 'Abdu'l-Bahá in a letter where the role of America and Iran were mentioned, and respect for all forms of life, let alone human life, were taken as a given:

> O ye loved ones of God! In this, the Bahá'í dispensation, God's Cause is spirit unalloyed. His Cause belongeth not to the material world. It cometh neither for strife nor war, nor for acts of mischief or of shame; it is neither for quarrelling with other Faiths, nor for conflicts with the nations. Its only army is the love of God, its only joy the clear wine of His knowledge, its only battle the expounding of the Truth; its one crusade (*jihád*) is against the insistent self, the evil promptings of the human heart. Its victory is to submit and yield, and to be selfless is its everlasting glory. In brief, it is spirit upon spirit . . .[10]

There fell upon Shoghi Effendi in his role as Guardian of the Bahá'í Faith (1921–1957) the dual task of 'recasting' the Bahá'í teachings into the idiom of the West as well as gathering what was until then a heteroclite grouping of dispersed communities under the aegis of a fully functional set of 'world-shaking, world-embracing, world-directing administrative institutions'.[11] The first aspect of this task assumed a literal expression in the monumental amount of fresh authoritative translations undertaken by Shoghi Effendi. These were complemented by a considerable amount of new translations integrated into his book-size letters dealing with the administrative machinery (*Bahá'í Administration*), the worldwide expansion of the Bahá'í community (*The Advent of Divine Justice*), its constitutional foundations (*The Dispensation of Bahá'u'lláh*), and a world historical perspective set in terms of the past (*The Promised Day Is Come*, *God Passes By*) and the future ('The Unfoldment of World Civilization' in *The World Order of Bahá'u'lláh*). This enterprise was closely mirrored by the construction programme undertaken at the heart of the Bahá'í holy places, that is, at the intersection of sacred space and sacred time. None of Shoghi Effendi's engagements took place in favourable circumstances but in the midst of two major global upheavals: two world conflagrations, and the convulsions accompanying the formation of the State of Israel.

These efforts resulted in a considerable clarification of the place that Bahá'ís would occupy in the general scheme of things. Gradually, the new believers were led to see themselves in a perspective that made positive sense of their own early Bahá'í history and hence their position in the context of the great world religions. The indispensable 'fundamental verities' of the Faith were identified and explained, in particular with regard to the seminal value of such texts as the *Will and Testament of 'Abdu'l-Bahá*, the *Tablets of the Divine Plan* or Bahá'u'lláh's Tablet of Carmel. Similarly, the essential mechanics of the Bahá'í community were laid out, and the expansive dynamism of the community, fuelled by a vision of sheer will power and urgency, was focused on a series of teaching plans. In this teleological and eschatologically-driven vision of history, the Lesser Peace and the Most Great Peace were essential pointers of the divine economy, which Shoghi

Effendi clarified by association with a series of parallel, synchronous processes. The tension between the 'erelong' of prophetic time and the disappointing 'here and now', in eager anticipation of fulfilment, was creatively managed by pointing to the unparalleled transcendence of the Bahá'í mission, as further corroborated by an immensely glorious past. The 'spiritual conquest' of the world was thus associated with the erection, however modestly, of the building blocks of the Bahá'í administrative system, which, moving from local to national levels, would eventually lead to the election of the Universal House of Justice and, in the fullness of time, to the blossoming of a wholesome divine civilization. Shoghi Effendi's periodification of Bahá'í history, with its three major ages (apostolic, administrative or formative, golden), and its synchronization of events with the outside world, helped to infuse into the new believers a sense of sacred history, a rhythm of the divine which was on the march towards its apogee when the Minor and Greater Plans of God would converge. These concepts acted as powerful propellers that, buttressed by the notion of God's Covenant, reconnected both fulfilled and unfulfilled eschatology with the notion of progressive revelation. Glimpses foreshadowing the beauty and grandeur of that glorious time were identified not only with the sacrificial feats of the apostolic times, but also with the spotless arrangements embellishing the Bahá'í holy places. These were foretastes that would help Bahá'ís realize the potentialities latent in their Faith and gain assurance in the promises of Bahá'u'lláh of a world replete with His peace and justice.

The relationship of the incipient Bahá'í communities with the world was clarified by identifying the Bahá'í system with the nucleus, pattern, and last refuge of an embattled humanity. This idea, variously expressed in conjunction with the key concepts of eschatological fulfilment (Daniel's prophecies in the Old Testament), and the pairs of crisis and victory, major and minor plans, combined to imprint upon the nascent communities a sense of sacral responsibility towards the world. The people of Bahá, whom Bahá'u'lláh had already furnished with a new canonical expression of the eternal Covenant of God, and whom 'Abdu'l-Bahá had established as a model of successful integration of differences (typically the various religious backgrounds of the new adherents), were now to ready themselves to embody the redeeming qualities of Bahá'u'lláh's 'wondrous system' on a global scale.

The role of the North American continent in leading the world community towards the fulfilment of Bahá'u'lláh's vision of collective security was if anything reinforced by a number of Shoghi Effendi's statements pointing out the meagre, yet highly significant, steps already achieved in that direction.[12] His lamentation about the fate of President Wilson's vision after his country's defection from the League of Nations, the conviction that the world was already 'contracted into a neighbourhood', and that the principle of national sovereignty was a 'fetish' made his appeal for a decisive involvement of America in world affairs all the more pregnant. Yet, only to the extent that America was able to divest itself of its narrow insularity, not to mention the perennial issue of race segregation, would it become worthy of the mission with which she was entrusted. In some important respects this was manifest destiny in reverse, as made clear by Shoghi Effendi's explicit words casting the parallel mission of the American Bahá'í community (and its counterpart, the Iranian Bahá'í community) in terms of a thorough purge of the manifest evils corroding the vitals of their society.

A similar pattern was emerging from the experience of the Iranian Bahá'í community. The fact that its engagement with the surrounding culture was 'interrupted' by the violent outbursts of the first Iranian Constitutional Revolution and later by further secularizing measures by Reza Shah, was no obstacle for the Bahá'í community of that country to continue engaging with society by spearheading the first modern schools and instituting democratic and gender equality in their own internal processes under the ministries of both 'Abdu'l-Bahá and Shoghi Effendi. In combination with its North American counterpart, the Iranian Bahá'í experience, even if limited by societal and political constraints, helped to lay down the foundations of the model that Shoghi Effendi put in place on a global scale in his series of ground-breaking plans which, starting in 1937, when the first plan of the North American community was launched, culminated in the Ten Year Crusade (1953–1963), efforts which were symbolized by the erection of the first continental Houses of Worship.

The greater engagement of Baha'is with society also required further clarification concerning the degree to which Bahá'ís were to participate in politics, retain relationships with their religions of origin, serve in the military forces, carry arms, or be allowed to defend themselves against aggression. An emphasis on law-abidance meant that Bahá'ís would not entertain any sympathies with revolutionary thinking, or any flirtations with violence. By the same token, it also meant that absolute pacifism in the form of a complete surrendering to the dictates of one's conscience was regarded as unacceptable. An intermediate stance was to be adopted whereby Bahá'ís would seek non-combatant status avoiding the carrying of arms other than those required for other legitimate purposes such as hunting or sport. The Bahá'í commitment to non-resistance and to the avoidance of the taking of life was thus mediated or limited in an Oplerian sense by a clear acknowledgement of the prerogatives of the state to regulate law enforcement and socially-sanctioned violence, cases of complete anarchy or tyranny aside.

The above peace ideals, as conveyed in Part IV, were buttressed by a spiritual anthropology in which the person also evolves by degrees, just as humankind has been moving from one stage to another in the ladder of historical evolution. The individual, in other words, is not conceived in the Bahá'í writings as a 'complete' entity of its own who is thrown into the world to lead a life in isolation from, or competing with, other human beings. Rather, he or she is best defined as a creature of God, the result as it were of a continual process of recreation set in motion through a myriad of interactions. The individual appears suspended as though by a mesh of relationships that puts the person constantly at the crossroads of a series of ascending grades of existence that must be traversed in order to achieve corresponding degrees of personal fulfilment, mostly through the acquiring of qualities in service to the 'cause of humanity'.[13] This ascension or spiritual journey is in fact the individual's prime reason of existence; but in contrast with the purely mystical ascension of the few, the spiritual journey described in the Bahá'í writings takes on a parallel social and civilizational dimension due to the impetus brought about by the succession of divine revelations. The interplay of both the vertical and horizontal dimension is nowhere better symbolized than in the conception of the institution of the Mashriqu'l-Adhkár,[14] but it is not confined to it, as the institution of the Nineteen Day Feast makes abundantly clear by blending again the spiritual with practical deliberative democracy and festive elements. The 'this-worldliness' orientation of the Bahá'í Revelation is reinforced by situating the realization of the individual not so much in the world beyond but, as Bausani would put it, in its present reverberations.[15] The importance attached to the present here-bound reality is in fact a function of the greatness imputed to the current aeon, a perspective which in essence is metaphysical and eschatological rather than secular (despite the obvious secularist themes running through much of the Bahá'í outlook):

> The world's equilibrium hath been upset through the vibrating influence of this most great, this new World Order. Mankind's ordered life hath been revolutionized through the agency of this unique, this wondrous System – the like of which mortal eyes have never witnessed.[16]

The influence of the new World Order of Bahá'u'lláh is rendered visible in a 'new creation', a 'new springtime', and a new 'race of men'[17] endowed with energies that will allow them to overcome the obstacles that for millennia have dragged human societies into the whirlpool of violence. Yet, instead of conceiving the dignity of man in terms of inherent rights, the Bahá'í perspective concentrates on man's potential for realizing the divine trust, or God's image, whether individually (by embodying God's good names), or collectively by mirroring forth God's kingdom (that is, developing a divine civilization). It is the realization of God's image in man that explains why human beings, who are said to occupy such a position of honour within the scheme of creation, cannot be treated in ways that may detract from their (largely potential) station. Similarly, it is the approaching of God's kingdom which confers upon human societies (cultures and civilizations) their sacral dimension, often reinforced by the recognition of timeless intergenerational and spatial bonds. Most importantly, this capacity for the attainment of a fuller expression of humanity, whether at the individual or collective level, is not seen as static, but rather as a dynamic phenomenon which is commensurate with the greatness of the Day of God and expresses itself through a renewed commitment to please God by serving the whole of humanity.

In this complex view of human beings, as reiterated by 'Abdu'l-Bahá, the main barriers standing in the way of humankind and the prime causes of bloodshed are the various kinds of prejudices prevailing everywhere. These are not mere superstitions or anachronisms that need to be superseded through reasoning (often the Enlightenment view), but indeed 'forces' or 'counter-themes' in an Oplerian sense (the expressions of self-interest) that require being neutralized by stronger counterforces. In a profound sense, prejudices are collective representations fashioned or carved out of reality to the point where they become idolized in themselves. Typically, prejudices (of race, nation, gender, colour, religion, class and station) work as false identities that stand vicariously for a much larger, all-encompassing universalistic whole. What they lack in truth they compensate for by exacerbating the passional (*awḥam*) and imaginary elements, which are the concomitants of fanaticism (*ta'aṣṣub*). Prejudices act then as 'veils' that colour or blind perceptions by aligning them with man's baser interests in what amounts to a betrayal of the genuine intellectual life of the spirit.[18] Thus the violence encountered by the Prophets of God and their chosen ones, far from being accidental, summarizes prototypically all conceivable forms of violence perpetrated by human beings; likewise the endurance and courage displayed by the Prophets in the face of adversity are taken as vindications of another and more real level of freedom in response to violence and the bare necessities of life. Accordingly, the Bahá'í writings place a heavy burden and a high prize on the achievement of a truly discerning, non-imitating behaviour on the part of each single human being (capacity building, empowerment), and a no less onerous mission on society's role in fostering those same qualities through community-building.

This view of the inherent nobility of man and his perfectibility (which appears reinforced by a parallel perception that all the realms of creation move by degrees towards enlarged forms of integration), is served by a purposeful morality in which mutual interdependence, reciprocity and collaboration are stressed. The Bahá'í ethos, so far as it has been determined in this study, stresses the contiguity and even intimacy of the vertical and the horizontal, the eternal and the ephemeral, the individual and the collective, the autonomous and the heteronomous, life after death and present life. Rather than denying the tension between these poles, Bahá'í morality stresses the value of placing them together and moderating them out in an exercise of moral strength which 'Abdu'l-Bahá characteristically links to the moderating or regulatory influence of the Holy Spirit. Preserving innocence in full consciousness of the world's challenges and tests gives the measure of the mature and noble person. The act of embodying virtues in this rather tensional way becomes an energizing 'exertion' whose models can be found in the example set by the Bahá'í heroes of the apostolic times, and then replicated in the following generations by the ever-growing waves of sacrificial Bahá'í pioneers. This morality stresses the value of constant indefatigable endeavours towards the accomplishment of unity and peace at all levels, especially by laying emphasis on the need to govern one's conduct by the ethical imperative of service to the whole of humanity. The defining characteristic of an individual is then measured in terms of his or her positive contribution towards the advancement of society; and vice versa, the wealth of any society resides in its capacity to assist its members to achieve this higher purpose through its institutional and community frameworks. Lower forms of loyalty such as attachment to one's race, country, class, and even religion are constantly checked against this touchstone.

Given the premium placed on the peaceful settlement of differences that may result from conflicting loyalties, the Bahá'í ethos seems to rely for their resolution on a 'unitarian' view of reality or truth. Truth is posited as an approaching rather than as a dogmatic fixation of second or third level partial truths. The 'divine philosophy' emerging from this belief in the internal coherence and cohesiveness of all realities – whether scientific or spiritual – is given impetus by a concomitant belief in their 'organicity'. The concept of the 'organic', and especially that of 'organic unity', as displayed by Shoghi Effendi, implies an acceptance of differences in the first place (differences of needs, growth, size, conditions and other externals); second, a commitment to allow the passage of time to bring to fruition the various potentialities inherent in this diversity; and third, a reintegration or harmonizing of those differences in terms of their contribution to the whole. Social and moral realities are subjected to continuous reappraisals that are meant to refine our understanding and enjoyment of life. Peace is thus the result of a harmonizing of the individual impulses towards transcendence and those of society towards more refined forms of integration. Civilization in this context takes on the form of a veritable flourishing.

The substance of the organic metaphor appears replicated in another vital element of the Bahá'í ethos, namely the conception of the transcendent oneness of religions. Often represented as a majestic display over time of a series of tree-like revelations that have taken humanity by degrees of social evolution (clan, tribe, city-state, nation-state) and spiritual perfection (from the salvation of the few to the redemption of all mankind), this pattern would explain the underlying unity of existing religions. Religious renewal, as manifested by the appearance of newer and more fulsome revelations, would in reality be an expression of the eternal Covenant of God and His pledge to perfect His light.[19] Obvious differences in theological and spiritual conceptions can thus be reconciled through a series of rhetorical strategies that minimize their import, for instance by pointing out the dual nature of religions (temporal and eternal, mutable and immutable, dynamic and static, accidental or essential), as well as to their eschatological convergence, or to the translatability of their symbolic, moral and mystic worldviews.[20] Major steps towards neutralizing religious prejudices as a potential *casus belli* require a conscious cultivation of this kind of perspective. Eventually, an almost natural acceptance of these views will not only assist in divesting war and violence of their religious and moralizing guise or appeal, but will gradually prepare the way for a recognition of Bahá'u'llah's Faith as the spiritual expression where these views are best blended into a moral and intellectually coherent resolution.

The reconciliation of religious differences implicit in this roundabout approach is similar to the settlement of international disputes through collective security arrangements. Both 'solutions' entail an equalization of authority (no clergy system, unfettered search after truth, consultation, a cessation of absolute national sovereignty), as well as an implicit theory of cognition (justice as commitment to truth and fair-mindedness), and a conception of the supremacy of unity and peace as guiding values. Bringing all these elements together is the institutionalization of dialogue in the form of 'Bahá'í consultation' at all levels of the Administrative Order, from the Nineteen Day Feast to the Universal House of Justice. Problem areas, new challenges and emerging needs can thus be addressed by instituting processes of discussion in a system aimed at universal participation. Differences, as repeatedly conveyed in the Bahá'í writings, can be of two kinds, that is, destructive (de-unifying, solved by violent means) and constructive (unifying). An appreciation of differences can only be achieved if our way of knowing as human beings is previously re-set or predisposed accept them. The metaphor of organic unity, with its vast richness of analogues, provides that sort of understanding. This precursor theory (of knowledge, growth, religious change throughout history) has a corresponding correlate in the notion of Bahá'í consultation, which is the testing ground of how differences can be articulated into practical shared understandings. It would not be too much of an exaggeration to say that the ideas of 'organic unity', 'unity in diversity' and 'consultation' are in reality compound ideas themselves. Following Bredsdorff, it could be argued that they fulfil the implicit Lovejoyan mandate for concepts or conceptualizations to qualify as true ideas, that is, they must be descriptive on the surface and normative at heart.[21]

An evolving peace pattern

The overall concept of peace emerging from our examination of the Bahá'í sources can be better described as a cluster of understandings whose implications have tended to become magnified in the interplay between the successive authoritative interpretations (i.e. those of 'Abdu'l-Bahá and Shoghi Effendi) and the unfolding of a Bahá'í community increasingly able to engage with the world at large. Rather than an 'evolution' in the sense of a transformation into something else, the process has operated as a succession of layers of more or less transparent unit ideas which add or open new significations into the core theme of peace.

Three main streams of peace thinking can be discerned at the heart of Bahá'í peace proposals. The first two have to do with the basic mechanics of political and social peace, and it is those two that have tended to claim the attention of both Bahá'í authors and the general public. The third stream, however, links peace to its deeper metaphysical, eschatological and anthropological foundations. By and large, Bahá'í proposals in the first two areas were couched in the language of other contemporary western peace proposals, and as such met with the usual alternations of dismissiveness, if not ridiculing (too Utopian), and not infrequently, with a wholehearted yet imprecise understanding of their applicability to real life situations. Notwithstanding, compared to other elaborate peace projects, the main distinguishing factor of the Bahá'í approach seems to rest on its deliberately broad and principled framing of the problem. As shown in Part I, the collective security arrangements proposed by Baha'u'llah were preceded by the articulation of a number of unit ideas, first and foremost the explicit abolition of *jihád* or just war thinking equivalents. In doing so a plain field for the interaction amongst state actors as equals was created. This was further reinforced by a second unit idea, or rather, theme (given its pervasiveness): the demilitarization of eschatology and the consequent spiritualization of the militant ethics of 'self' discipline. Second, the concept of collective security propounded by Bahá'u'lláh and 'Abdu'l-Bahá was not tied, for instance, to a parallel defence of republicanism (as Kant or Paine would have it), nor confined to European countries (Saint Pierre, Rousseau, Kant), nor focused on juridical conflict management, for instance through international arbitration or replacement altogether by the comparatively much more benign impulses of free trade (Saint Simon, Cobden). While attaching utmost importance to the universality of agreements that would set peace on a new footing, the soundness of the system was not made to rest on the voluntary submission of countries to the provisions of the International Covenant (as in the League of Nations), nor did it count on the tribunal of public opinion to make the covenanted decisions enforceable (William Ladd) as a result of the shaming of offending nations. Moreover, it did not regard unilateral disarmament or a hegemonic peace as solutions to the endemic underlying problems. To be sure, the system envisaged was to lead in the end, as Shoghi Effendi had visualized, to a federated world organism, a world super-state (not to be confused with a cyclopean hydra-like mega-state); but the achievement of this goal was to be preceded by arms reductions, the securing of frontiers and other collective security arrangements, including a strong world tribunal for the settlement of international disputes. The latter, however, was not meant to be a weak world tribunal. Representative of the governments and its peoples, it would possess binding jurisdiction on matters serious enough to lead to violent escalation. Taken as a whole, the Bahá'í proposals in this regard were devoid of most of the particulars that turned similar peace projects into unworkable propositions *ab orto*. No hard and fast rules were given that would radically ill-dispose their adoption by a number of leading statesmen and rulers. The pursuit of peace in the form of arms reductions and universal arbitration could be initiated by a hard core of rulers, for instance; and the mechanics to operationalize the agreements could then be worked out in accordance with the needs and circumstances. The attention paid to arms reductions and the fixing of frontiers – again important Bahá'í unit ideas – through negotiated settlement was, however, sufficiently suggestive of where the priorities would lie and how vast the 'all-embracing assemblage of men' had to be for peace to materialize in the form of the Lesser Peace. Other peace-relatable issues could then be added to the discussions or be dealt with by world experts, the choice of a universal auxiliary language being a case in point.

The above general distinctions do not cancel the overall coincidence between the Bahá'í approach and the so-called 'idealist' position in international relationships, which deserves some further comment at this point. In effect, a baseline of liberal internationalism is easily recognizable in Bahá'í statements (up to the present) implying a positive appreciation of what the sheer force of travel, trade, commerce and communications may do of themselves as enablers for the pacification of the world.[22] In common with liberal idealist and neo-idealist positions,[23] the Bahá'í view indicates that these forces need to be harnessed through a 'system' of international governance in which collective security provisions are put in place, and the 'global' interests of humanity, as distinct from other legitimate interests, are represented through institutions duly empowered to act on its behalf. This new level of governance can be best imagined in the context of two tensional world trends that need to be positively promoted: one that moves in the direction of a 'human scale' where grass-roots communities and existing identities are secured (rights of minorities, decentralization, devolution of authority), and the other that extends the logic of the rule of law and democratic principles to the regulation of international and human relations. This position, usually termed 'neo-idealist', can be argued and derived from the analyses of Bahá'í writings in the present study. Yet, a point of crucial difference setting Bahá'í positions apart from the above liberal positions, including neo-institutionalism, is the much stronger emphasis on humanity as an actor itself and as an ethical premise. Typical articulations of this concept imply a recognition of the indivisibility of humanity, a moral/legal imperative – a *raison d'humanité*, to follow Yehezkel Dror – that must permeate any deliberations, and a move to embrace world citizenship as the new frontier where states and individuals must meet by recognizing the higher interests and needs of humanity.

In common with social constructivist theories, the Bahá'í approach to peace posits a far more malleable state of affairs in the global scene than usually taken for granted in realist, liberal and Marxian theories. Seeing reality as a mesh of dynamic interrelationships of mutuality and dependency is crucial in how reality as a whole is perceived, including the human actions and interventions that reshape them. This has an empowering effect, in that the theory of peace itself is seen less as a calculation (for instance, of power imbalances) serenely made in the midst of an essentially predatory world fit only for the fittest actors. The Tablet to The Hague, as well as the Tablet to Dr Auguste Forel, made these points abundantly clear. Importantly the Tablet to The Hague provides an outline of a world agenda that calls into question basic ingrained premises of international and political thought, many of which resurface at their ugliest when the call of war and violence is made. 'Abdu'l-Bahá's oft-repeated descriptions of the impending carnage of war, as confirmed later by the 'war to end all wars', were not acts of doomsaying, nor even an antidote to rife delirious war-mongering propaganda,[24] but, at one level, truthful depictions of a reality that materialistic realism and idealism, as well as revolutionary approaches to social change and international order, tended to push to the sidelines of their ideological and theoretical lenses.[25]

Shoghi Effendi's move for the Bahá'í community to achieve observer status at the United Nations at a very early date has in time consolidated the Bahá'í International Community as a transnational actor, and is a further instance of Bahá'í engagement with worldwide consultative and deliberative processes.[26]

More profoundly, perhaps, Bahá'í positions see an in-built connection between the self-clarification implied in these postulations and a teleological view of human evolution or, rather, perfectibility. It is this added dimension that may explain the prominence attached to knowledge and education – moral education in particular – as levellers and enhancers of human-beingness. This aspect reconnects the Bahá'í project with some of the moral optimism and push for self-improvement that was so characteristic of the Socratic and Enlightenment traditions, with their belief in the maieutic properties of knowledge and culture.[27]

A second stream of Bahá'í peace thinking relates the mechanics of collective security (arms reductions, delimitation of frontiers and collective use of force against recalcitrant nations) to a larger core of Bahá'í tenets whose implementation is said to be instrumental to the securing of peace on solid foundations. This second tier of Bahá'í thought shows much more clearly the underpinnings of the peace process (i.e. *ṣulḥ*, pacification, as opposed to *salám*, the definite state and enjoyment of peace). The key text illustrating this is part of 'Abdu'l-Baha's introductory paragraphs in the Tablet to The Hague:

> But the wise souls who are aware of the essential relationships emanating from the realities of things (*muṭṭali' hastand bar ravábiṭ-i-ḍurúríyyih kih monba'ith az ḥaqáyiq-i-ashiást*) consider that one single matter (*masa'iliy-i-váḥidih*) cannot, by itself, influence the human reality as it ought and should, for until the minds of men (*'uqúl-i-bashari*) become united, no important matter can be accomplished. At present universal peace (*ṣulḥ-i-'umúmí*) is a matter of great importance, but unity of conscience (*vaḥdat-i-vujdán*) is essential, so that the foundation of this matter may become secure, its establishment firm and its edifice strong.[28]

Our discussion of these principles in Parts II and V has shown that these tenets implied not only a wider positive concept of peace, in that peace is no longer the opposite of war (or its absence), but also a theory of human reality (unity of mankind), which carries special weight as a moral imperative. Thus the pursuit of the unification of mankind at all levels is underscored by the acceptance of the imputed underlying unity of religions, and the surmised capacity of the human mind not only to discern reality free from prejudices, whether through the eyes of science or religion, but to act on it by extending the radius of spiritual and material education to all human beings.

In particular, 'Abdu'l-Bahá's reference to unity of conscience indicates perhaps more clearly the ethical and gnoseological dimension that the search for appropriate principles ought to assume, especially in connection with the kind of world undertakings that will lend peace the kind of firm grounding it necessitates. Both

The Secret of Divine Civilization and the Tablet to The Hague show in this regard a strong commonality, as both are prefaced by explicit references to an underlying theory of knowledge and reality. The Tablet to The Hague adopts as a starting point the notion that war is the antithesis of life, and that life reigns supreme as a value or good that needs preserving and fostering through a nurturing process involving wide-ranging knowledge, a concordant morality (the 'morals of the kingdom', no coercion, freedom from material dependency), and its confident projection into the world arena in the form of world enterprises. This vision, reinforced considerably by the stress laid on the importance of creating an informed public opinion, in turn activated through the pursuit of global enterprises, marks a sharp contrast with historical trends to try piecemeal approaches to peace-building.

In an almost Socratic and Enlightenment fashion, the Bahá'í vision conceives of problems as the result of excesses committed in ignorance of the complex interrelationships that bind all phenomena between each other. The critical comments reserved by 'Abdu'l-Bahá for the religiously-driven jingoism of the Iranian clergy serves as an index:

> A few, who are unaware of the reality below the surface of events, who cannot feel the pulse of the world under their fingers, who do not know what a massive dose of truth must be administered to heal this chronic old disease of falsehood, believe that the Faith can only be spread by the sword, and bolster their opinion with the Tradition, 'I am a Prophet by the sword.'[29]

What applies to 'prejudices', as counterthemes, can also be said of the way of framing unity in almost kaleidoscopic terms. The various 'unities' identified by Baha'u'llah in the Lawḥ-i-Ittiḥád, by 'Abdu'l-Bahá in the 'Seven Candles of Unity', and by Shoghi Effendi's own terminological innovations ('unity in diversity' and 'organic unity') outline a basic landscape of partial unities. Each of these emphasize some important aspect under which a protean unity needs to be considered for its fulsome effects to be irradiated to the rest of humankind. This way of looking at life's phenomena *sub specie unitatis* seems to counter the reductionistic approach that derives all phenomena, and hence all explanations, from one single and exclusivist form of unity, however exalted this might be. Baha'u'llah's less than emphatic allusions to the doctrine of *tawḥíd* can be seen in this light.

A third stream of Bahá'í thought relates peace to its eschatological, anthropological, and ethical underpinnings. The eschatological element places peace in the perspective of prophetic fulfilment. Peace is here seen as the supreme realization of God's kingdom on earth; this dimension is referred to and finds echo in numerous passages in the writings of Baha'u'llah. The promise of a world filled with the Lord's peace, knowledge and justice is thus identified with the fruits accruing from the new Law of God. As for the anthropological and ethical underpinnings, the discussions in Parts IV and V suggest that peace at this level is seen as feasible because man is perceived to be, above all, a noble creature, perfectible and potentially capable of overcoming violence in its individual or collective varieties. As a creature, the human being finds itself in a realm of its own, surrounded by and intimately linked to other planes of reality which appear to be in a state of orderly flux, moving as it were to a climax, and under the constant care of a Creator Who provides and tends to all His creatures, visible or invisible, large or small.

This vision appears in marked contrast with the reassertions of war and violence not just as obvious historical constants but even as a source of good and progress, the exponents of which 'Abdu'l-Bahá was to encounter all throughout His travels.[30] The denunciation of the notion of struggle of existence, and the parallel negation of the concept of 'inexistence', with its dangerous nihilistic or, paradoxically, 'existentialist' ramifications, stemmed from this deeper conception of the human being as a creature of God endowed with an eternal soul rather than as a sensory and almost purposeless being thrown into a senseless world. Our examination of *taqlíd* has shown that in refuting these arguments 'Abdu'l-Bahá was targeting for His critical remarks not just erroneous concepts, susceptible of empirical or logical rebuttal, but also, and more importantly, the power and knowledge relationships that engender such notions. The main thrust behind a work such as *The Secret of Divine Civilization* focused its criticisms firstly on the Muslim clergy, but the problem analysed there was in fact much wider in scope. This point was made all the more clear by 'Abdu'l-Bahá's refusal to endorse the shallow materialism of the West, with its thirst for war and its false morality. The difficulty with 'imitation', as seen by 'Abdu'l-Bahá, ran much deeper. Imitations or prejudices, together with fancies and vain imaginings, passions and fanaticism belong in an intermediate realm of veils that obfuscate and lure the human mind towards the attainment of a false sense of self-reliance and sufficiency truly at odds with reality.

Taken together the three streams suggest a flow moving seamlessly from an elementary modality of peace, which forms a bare core of collective security arrangements (the Lesser Peace, *ṣulḥ-i-asg͟har*), towards a broader concept of positive peace (the Great Peace, *ṣulḥ-i-akbar*). The latter type of peace is the result of combining efforts in different areas of the world agenda including the universalization of education, the overcoming of prejudices based on race, class, gender and culture differences, the adoption of an auxiliary world language, the embracement of an attitude of unfettered search after truth, and the harmonization of science and religion as sources of knowledge. This broader conception of peace is inclusive of collective security but, by contrast with the Lesser Peace, its scope is visualized in 'universal' *('umumí)* positive terms, no longer tied to the suppression and control mechanisms inherent in and indeed required by a system of collective security. The dimension of this broader peace is properly speaking civilizational, if one is to take seriously the logic of *The Secret of Divine Civilization*, and global as it encompasses or rather transcends the primordial division between East and West.

While these two imbricate 'peaces' are by no means minor achievements, they leave partially intact the deeper level of motivational forces and understandings which inform the substance of a third level of attainment, as implied by the term Most Great Peace (*ṣulḥ-i-a'ẓam*). At this level peace taps directly into a dynamic conception of knowledge, anthropology and morality characterized by a pervasive non-authoritarian, transformative, service-oriented and deliberative ethos.

This third conception identifies itself openly with the teachings of Bahá'u'lláh, exploits the insights thereof and works them through a process of modelling in permanent interaction with the world at large. Since this third and broader conception of peace is more clearly related to processes, both internal and external, collective and individual, taking place within the Bahá'í community, 'peace' has here direct denotations of eschatological fulfilment, directly relatable to the presence or rapid approaching of God's Kingdom. This translates into a redefined morality with fresh demands in terms of how the diversity of needs, interests and opinions are negotiated within a constantly expanding community framework where collective action stems from a flux of shared understandings. The stress placed by the central figures of the Bahá'í religion, including Shoghi Effendi, on establishing a working model for humanity, one which must be 'transferable', respectful of rational enquiry, conscious of its own 'organic' nature, bent on dialogue and committed to non-violent processes of needs-based social and moral transformation, seems to be at the heart of the important change of paradigm witnessed during the last 25 years within the worldwide Bahá'í community. Structural aspects of the new paradigm quickly setting in are:

1) The worldwide introduction of the 'Training Institute process'. Designed to provide new and old believers with an understanding of Bahá'í fundamentals, the currently available courses centre around a series of books facilitated by coordinators within a participatory dynamic that applies insights from adult education principles, community development theory, and learning through the systematization of experiences.[31]

2) The parallel reframing of institutional and community practices, including significant structural changes in the machinery of the Bahá'í administrative system.[32]

3) The shift in emphasis from a 'proclamation' approach to the expansion of the Bahá'í Faith, largely reliant on the self-evidence of the Baha'i teachings, to one that accords Bahá'u'lláh a central stage within a clearly articulated narrative. This is illustrated at all levels of the spectrum, including statements released by the Bahá'í International Community.

4) The systematization of Bahá'í learning in terms of experimentation through trial and error, documenting of processes and, perhaps more notably, evaluative reflection. Although most of these efforts have been directed towards reaching a sustainable pattern of growth, they also increasingly inform all

> other processes in the Bahá'í community. The net result is an increasing capacity to relate Bahá'í principles to actual Bahá'í-generated experiences. Thus, rather than being referred to in the abstract or offered as reiterations of authoritative statements by the central figures, Bahá'í principles can be seen now in real-life contexts, promoted as thick descriptions or tentative proposals rather than prescriptions. Some areas of growth in this sense can be identified, such as educational initiatives, women's advancement, social and economic development projects, conceptual initiatives, human rights advocacy, and interfaith dialogue.

This phenomenon may have important consequences for a furtherance of a Bahá'í understanding of peace and can manifest itself mainly in two ways: first, a more nuanced distinction between what is (the factual, the real, what can be observed), what should be (the intended, the tensional world of principles, values and projects) and what may lie in between in the form of intermediate stages; second, an ability to deduce from significant Bahá'í experiences lessons that may in turn give shape to or inform any understanding of those distinctions. This is especially important if the gap between an internal and external Bahá'í discourse is to be bridged in more creative ways. Representative illustrations of this capacity, albeit still in a largely conceptual domain, are the statements of the Bahá'í International Community such as *The Prosperity of Humankind, Turning Point for All Nations*, or *A Governance Befitting: Humanity and the Path Toward of a Just Global Order*, and, more recently, the document summarizing learnings from fifty roundtable discussions facilitated by the Australian Bahá'í Community in order to discern 'how we can work towards a more cohesive society'.[33] The experience gathered over the past four decades in defending the rights of the Iranian Bahá'ís in particular has also gone a long way in establishing the Bahá'í Faith in the public arena; but in addition, it has illustrated how a community of law-abiding citizens may still engage in the defence of their interests and legitimate rights in the face of religious persecution, by using institutional channels while strictly avoiding disruptive, let alone violent, methods.

Final remarks

The idea of peace in the Bahá'í religion was from the outset established by Baha'u'llah as a two-pronged continuum marked by two connected unit ideas: first, the abrogation of *jihád* and 'just war' thinking, with its concomitants of impurity and segregation, and second, the institution of collective security with its corollary of arms disarmaments, securing of frontiers, etc. Both main sub-ideas were set in the dynamics of a basic progressive movement from the Lesser Peace to the Most Great Peace. 'Abdu'l-Bahá further enlarged the concept by making explicit new dimensions to the core concepts supplied by His Father. Peace was presented not so much a matter of state or even interstate security, nor as a mere counter-image of war and violence, but in fact as the outcome of the implementation of a set of new principles and assumptions logically derived from the essential notion of the unity of mankind and a supple yet firmer connection between reality and knowledge. War belonged definitely in the old aeon, while peace was to provide the basis of a new form of politics:

> I wish this blessing to appear and become manifest in the faces and characteristics of the believers, so that they, too, may become a new people, and having found new life and been baptized with fire and spirit, may make the world a new world, to the end that the old earth may disappear and the new earth appear; old ideas depart and new thoughts come; old garments be cast aside and new garments put on; ancient politics whose foundation is war be discarded and modern politics founded on peace raise the standard of victory.[34]

It was Shoghi Effendi's role to firmly implant the concepts of peace and unity in the historical interplay of a Faith and a humanity that were both drawn together by the powerful forces present in the new Dispensation. Since the growth of the Bahá'í community was described by Shoghi Effendi in terms of organic development, and then the relationship between the nascent Bahá'í community and the wider community was often expressed in terms of the model/refuge metaphors, there can be little doubt that the concrete expression of the relationship is better left open. This would be in keeping with Baha'u'llah's injunction to be 'anxiously concerned with the needs of the age', as well as with the gradualist approach to the implementation, through methodical trial and error, of the principles of the Bahá'í Faith in a setting increasingly porous, responsive and receptive to society's demands.

As more and more aspects of collective security regimes become mainstream, and new bolder initiatives at the international level operationalize other aspects of the world agenda customarily associated by Bahá'ís with their own social and humanitarian programme,[35] the concept of peace in the Bahá'í religion may increasingly gravitate towards a furtherance of its modelling role. If this is so, then how the Bahá'í community manages its own growth in keeping with its essential principles and how it infuses its own processes with a stronger spirit of tolerance, universal participation and empowerment of institutions, individuals and communities, will become further litmus cases of its capacity to re-conceptualize its understanding of peace. The importance attached to knowledge, wisdom and learning, both in the Bahá'í writings and in the current practice of the Bahá'í community worldwide, seems to suggest that Bahá'í peace proposals may in future emphasize more descriptively those aspects that are of direct benefit to humanity, particularly in the area of educational practices and general organizational principles. Just as importantly, the quality of discourse and transformative communication among all levels of the Bahá'í Administrative Order may inform to what extent social action and personal realization can be fuelled by a culture governed by the laws of solidarity and reciprocity, rather than by the agonistic presuppositions still prevalent in most accounts of the nature of politics. Contemporary concerns with the role of civilization, the politics of identity and, not least, the requirements for a global governance, are very much also at the heart of the preoccupations with which Bahá'ís have been contending for generations, often in the face of insidious persecutions.

It does not seem unwarranted, therefore, to assume that a more vocal and socially involved Bahá'í community may be progressively able to shape itself and its relationships in light of the now considerable historical baggage it has mustered, its redefinition of history and, consequently, its own projection towards a peaceful future.

BIBLIOGRAPHY

'Abdu'l-Bahá. *'Abdu'l-Bahá in Canada.* Toronto: National Spiritual Assembly of the Bahá'ís of Canada, 1962.

— *'Abdu'l-Bahá in London: Addresses and Notes of Conversations* (1912, 1921). London: Bahá'í Publishing Trust, 1982.

— *Abdul Baha on Divine Philosophy.* Ed. I. F. Chamberlain. Boston, MA: The Tudor Press, 1918.

— *Foundations of World Unity: Compiled from Addresses and Tablets of 'Abdu'l-Bahá.* Wilmette, Ill.: Bahá'í Publishing Trust, 1972.

— *Khiṭábát-i-Ḥaḍrat-i-'Abdu'l-Bahá* [Addresses by 'Abdu'l-Bahá]. Hofheim-Langenhain: Bahá'í Verlag, 1984.

— *Muntakhabátí az Makátíb-i-Ḥaḍrat-i-'Abdu'l-Bahá.* Vol. 4, Hofheim-Langenhain: Bahá'í Verlag, 2000; vol. 5. Hofheim-Langenhain: Bahá'í Verlag, 2003.

— *Paris Talks: Addresses Given by 'Abdu'l-Bahá in Paris in 1911–1912.* London: Bahá'í Publishing Trust, 12th ed. 1995.

— *The Promulgation of Universal Peace: Talks Delivered by 'Abdu'l-Bahá during His Visit to the United States and Canada in 1912.* Comp. Howard MacNutt. Wilmette, Ill.: Bahá'í Publishing Trust, 1982.

— *The Secret of Divine Civilization.* Wilmette, Ill.: Bahá'í Publishing Trust, 1983; Persian edition under the title *Risáliy-i-Madanníyyih.* 'Aṣr-i-Jadíd: Darmstadt, Germany, 2006. French edition: *Le Secret de la Civilisation Divine.* Bruxelles: Maison d'Éditions Bahá'íes, 1973.

— *Selections from the Writings of 'Abdu'l-Bahá,* Haifa: Bahá'í World Centre, 1978.

— *Some Answered Questions* (1908). Comp. and trans. Laura Clifford Barney. Haifa: Bahá'í World Centre, rev. ed. 2014. Persian edition under the title *An-Núr fí Mufaviḍát-i-'Abdu'l-Bahá, Guftugúy-i-bar Sar-i-Náhár*, National Spiritual Assembly of the Bahá'ís of India: New Delhi, 1983.

— *Risáliy-Síyásíyyih.* Darmstadt, Germany: 'Aṣr-i-Jadíd, 2006.

— *Tablets of Abdul-Baha Abbas.* 3 vols. Chicago: Bahá'í Publishing Society, 1909–1916. Wilmette, Ill: National Spiritual Assembly of the Bahá'ís of the United States, 1980.

— *Tablets of the Divine Plan: Revealed by 'Abdu'l-Bahá to the North American Bahá'ís.*

Wilmette, Ill.: Bahá'í Publishing Trust, 1993. Persian edition under the title *Farámín-i-Tablighíy-i-Ḥaḍrat-i-'Abdu'l-Bahá*. Persian/American Affairs Committee of the National Spiritual Assembly of the Bahá'ís of the United States, 1985.

— 'Tablet to Dr. Auguste Henri Forel', in *The Bahá'í World, 1968–1973*, vol. XV, pp. 37–43. Complete Persian text available in Dávúdí, 'Alí Murád, *Malakút-i Vujúd: Nigáhí bar Lawḥ-i Ḥaḍrat-i 'Abdu'l-Bahá Khiṭáb bih Duktúr Agust Furil*. Darmstadt, Germany: 'Aṣr-i Jadíd, 1998, pp. 33–40.

— *A Traveler's Narrative Written to Illustrate the Episode of the Báb* (1891). Trans. E. G. Browne. Wilmette, IL: Bahá'í Publishing Trust, rev. ed. 1980.

— *Will and Testament of 'Abdu'l-Bahá*. Wilmette, Ill: National Spiritual Assembly of the Bahá'ís of the United States, 1944.

Abizadeh, Arash. 'Politics beyond War: Ulrich Gollmer's Contribution to Bahá'í Political Thought', in *World Order*, 2004.

Abrahamian, Ervand. *A History of Modern Iran*. Cambridge: Cambridge University Press, 2008.

Abrams, M. H. *The Mirror and the Lamp: Romantic Theory and the Critical Tradition*. Oxford: Oxford University Press, 1971.

Addams, Jane. *Newer Ideals of Peace*. Syracuse, NY: Mason-Henry Press, 1907.

Afroukhteh, Youness. *Memories of Nine Years in 'Akká*. Oxford: George Ronald, 2005.

Afshari, Reza. 'Religious Minorities in Iran', review in *Human Rights Quarterly*, vol. 23 (2001), no. 4, pp. 1121–1133.

Algar, Hamid. 'Dár Al-Harb', in *Encyclopædia Iranica*, 1993. http://www.iranica.com/articles/dar-al-harb-the-realm-of-war-lands-not-under-islamic-rule-a-juridical-term-for-certain-non-muslim-territory-though-of.

Alkan, Necatí. *Dissent and Heterodoxy in the Late Ottoman Empire: Reformers, Babis and Baha'is*. Istanbul: The Isis Press, 2008.

— 'The Eternal Enemy of Islam': Abdullah Cevdet and the Baha'i Religion', in *Bulletin of the School of Oriental and African Studies*, vol. 68 (2005), no. 01, pp. 1–20.

Amanat, Abbas. *Pivot of the Universe: Nasir al-Din Shah Qajar and the Iranian Monarchy 1831–1896*. Berkeley: University of California, 1997.

— *Resurrection and Renewal: The Making of the Bábí Movement in Iran, 1844–1850*. Ithaca: Cornell University Press, 1989.

—; Vejdani, Farzin (eds). *Iran Facing Others*. New York: Palgrave Macmillan US, 2012.

Anonymous. 'In Memoriam: Pasquale Fiore', in *The American Journal of International Law*, vol. 9, no. 2 (April 1915), pp. 496–7.

Appel, Otto. 'El proyecto filosófico para la paz perpetua de Kant como cuasi-pronóstico de la filosofía de la historia a partir del deber moral', in Kant: *La Paz Perpetua, doscientos años después*. Valencia: Nau Libres, 1997.

Arbab, Farzam. *La senda del aprendizaje en Latinoamérica: Opción moral*. Colombia: Editorial Nur, 1991.

Aron, Raymond. *L'Opium des intellectuels*. Paris: Calmann-Lévy, 2002.

— *War and Industrial Society*. New York: Basic Books, 1964.

Attinà, Fulvio. *El sistema político global, Introducción a las relaciones internacionales*. Barcelona: Paidós, 2001.

Australian Bahá'í Community. 'Creating an Inclusive Narrative'. Office of External Affairs, 2020. https://news.bahai.org/story/1470/.

Avery, Peter. *Modern Iran*. London: Ernest Benn, 1965.

Ayalon, Ami. *Language and Change in the Arab Middle East: The Evolution of Modern Political Discourse*. New York: Oxford University Press, 1987.

Ayman, Iraj. 'Maqáṣid-i-Dín va Ma'múriyyat-i-Á'yn-i-Bahá'í', in *Safíniy-i-'Irfán*, vol. 2, pp. 11–30. Darmstadt, Germany: Aṣr-i-Jadíd, 1999.

Ayoub, Mahmoud. *Redemptive Suffering, in Islam: A Study of the Devotional Aspects of 'Ashura' in Twelver Shi'ism*. The Hague: Mouton Publishers, 1978.

Báb, The. *Selections from the Writings of the Báb*. Haifa: Bahá'í World Centre, 1976.

Bahador, Babak; Ghanea, Nazila (eds). *Processes of the Lesser Peace*. Oxford: George Ronald, 2002.

Bahá'í International Community. 'A Governance Befitting Humanity: Humanity and the Path to Global Order', A Statement of the Bahá'í International Community on the Occasion of the 75th Anniversary of the United Nations. New York, 2020.

— *The Bahá'ís: A Profile of the Bahá'í Faith and Its Worldwide Community.* London: Bahá'í Publishing Trust, 1992.

— *Ḥaẓrat-i-Bahá'u'lláh*. London: Bahá'í Publishing Trust, 1992.

— *The Prosperity of Humankind.* New York, 1994.

— *Turning Point for All Nations*. New York, 1995.

— *Who is Writing the Future? Reflections on the Twentieth Century* (1999). Wilmette, Ill: Bahá'í Publishing Trust, 2000.

Bahá'í News. Periodical, published by the National Spiritual Assembly of the Bahá'ís of the United States.

Bahá'u'lláh. *Ad'iyyah-i Ḥaḍrat-i Maḥbúb*. Hofheim-Langenhain: Bahá'í Verlag, 1980. Original edition: Cairo: Faraju'llah al-Kurdi, 76 B.E./1920.

— *The Call of the Divine Beloved: Selected Mystical Works of Bahá'u'lláh.* Haifa: Bahá'í World Centre, 2018.

— *Epistle to the Son of the Wolf.* Trans. Shoghi Effendi. Wilmette, Ill., rev. ed. 1988.

— *Gems of Divine Mysteries*. Haifa: Bahá'í World Centre, 2002.

— *Gleanings from the Writings of Bahá'u'lláh*. Trans. Shoghi Effendi. Wilmette, Ill.: Bahá'í Publishing Trust, 1983.

— *The Hidden Words of Bahá'u'lláh*. Trans. Shoghi Effendi. Wilmette, Ill.: Bahá'í Publishing Trust, 1939, 1970.

— *The Kitáb-i-Aqdas: The Most Holy Book*. Haifa: Bahá'í World Centre, 1992.

— *Kitáb-i-Íqán: The Book of Certitude*. Trans. Shoghi Effendi. Wilmette, Ill.: Bahá'í Publishing Trust, 1983.

— *Prayers and Meditations by Bahá'u'lláh*. Trans. Shoghi Effendi. Wilmette, Ill.: Bahá'í Publishing Trust, 1987.

— 'Surih-i-Sabr, or Lawh-i-Ayyub', n.d. http://Bahá'ístudies.net/kf/sabr.html.

— *Tablets of Bahá'u'lláh Revealed after the Kitáb-i-Aqdas*. Haifa: Bahá'í World Centre, 1978.

— *The Summons of the Lord of Hosts: Tablets of Bahá'u'lláh*. Haifa: Bahá'í World Centre, 2002.

— *The Tabernacle of Unity, Bahá'u'lláh's Responses to Mánikchí Ṣáḥib and Other Writings*. Haifa: Bahá'í World Centre, 2006.

Balyuzi, Hasan M. *'Abdu'l-Bahá: The Centre of the Covenant of Bahá'u'lláh*. Oxford: George Ronald, 1972.

— *Bahá'u'lláh, the King of Glory*. Oxford: George Ronald, 1980.

— *Edward Granville Browne and the Bahá'í Faith*. Oxford: George Ronald, 1975.

— *Eminent Bahá'ís in the Time of Bahá'u'lláh*. Oxford: George Ronald, 1985.

Banani, Amin. '*Modernity and Millenium,* by Juan Cole: Some Reflections', in *Bahá'í Studies Review*, vol. 9 (1999), pp. 159–62. http://bahai-library.com/banani_reflections_modernity_millennium.

Bausani, Alessandro. 'Can Monotheism Be Taught?: (Further Considerations on the Typology of Monotheism)', in *Numen*, vol. 10 (1963), no. 3, pp. 167–201.

— *El Islam en su cultura*. México: Fondo de Cultura Económica, 1988.

— *Religion in Iran: From Zoroaster to Bahá'u'lláh*. New York: Bibliotheca Persica Press, 2000.

— *Saggi sulla Fede Bahá'í*. Rome: Casa Editrice Bahá'í, 1991.

Bayat, Mangol. *Iran's First Revolution: Shi'ism and the Constitutional Revolution of 1905-1909*. New York: Oxford University Press, n.d.

— *Mysticism and Dissent: Socioreligious Thought in Qajar Iran*. Syracuse: Syracuse University Press, 1982.

— 'The Concepts of Religion and Government in the Thought of Mírzá Áqá Khán Kirmání, a Nineteenth-Century Persian Revolutionary', in *Journal of Middle East Studies*, vol. 5 (1974), pp. 381–400.

Baylis, John; Smith, Steve. *The Globalization of World Politics*. Oxford: Oxford University Press, 2nd ed.

Benda, Juliene. *The Treason of the Intellectuals*. New York: W. W. Norton, 1969.

Berger, Peter Ludwig. *From Sect to Church: A Sociological Interpretation of the Baha'i Movement.* New York: New School for Social Research, 1954.

— 'Motif messianique et processus social dans le Bahaisme', in *Archives de Sociologie des Religions*, vol. 2 (1957), no. 4, pp. 93–107.

— 'Sectarianism and Religious Sociation', in *American Journal of Sociology*, vol. 64 (1958), no. 1, pp. 41–4.

Blainey, Geoffrey. *The Causes of War*. Melbourne: Macmillan, 1988.

Blomfield, Sara. *The Chosen Highway*. Oxford: George Ronald, RP 2007.

Boas, George. 'Types of Internationalism in Early Nineteenth-Century France', in *International Journal of Ethics*, vol. 38 (1928), no. 2, pp. 141–52.

Booth, K. 'Security in Anarchy: Utopian Realism in Theory and Practice', in *International Affairs* (Royal Institute of International Affairs 1944-) vol. 67 (1991), no. 3, pp. 527–45.

Boroujerdi, Mehrzad. *Iranian Intellectuals and the West: The Tormented Triumph of Nativism*. New York: Syracuse University Press, 1996.

Bramson, Leon; Goethal, George. *War: Studies from Psychology, Sociology, Anthropology*. New York: Basic Books, 1964.

Bredsdorff, T. 'Lovejovianism – or the Ideological Mechanism: An Enquiry into the Principles of the History of Ideas According to Arthur O. Lovejoy', in *Orbis Litterarum*, vol. 30 (1975), no. 1, pp. 1–27.

— 'Lovejoy's Idea of "Idea"', in *New Literary History*, vol. 8 (1977), no. 2, pp. 195–211.

Brown, Keven. *Evolution and Baha'i Belief: 'Abdu'l-Bahá's Response to Nineteenth-Century Darwinism*. Los Angeles: Kalimát Press, 2001.

Brown, Michael. *Theories of War and Peace: An International Security Reader*. Cambridge, Mass: MIT Press, 1998.

Browne, Edward G. *Materials for the Study of the Bábí Religion*. Cambridge, UK: Cambridge University Press, 1918.

— *Selections from the Writings of E. G. Browne on the Bábí and Bahá'í Religions*. Edited by Moojan Momen. Oxford: George Ronald, 1987.

Buck, Christopher. *Paradise and Paradigm: Key Symbols in Persian Christianity and the Bahá'í Faith*. New York: State University of New York Press, 1999.

— *Symbol and Secret: Qur'án Commentary in Bahá'u'lláh's Kitáb-i-Iqán*. Los Angeles: Kalimát Press, 1995.

— 'The Eschatology of Globalization, the Multiple Messiahship of Bahá'u'lláh Revisited', in Moshe Sharon (ed), *Studies in Modern Religions, Religious Movements and the Bábí–Bahá'í Faiths*, pp. 143–77. Leiden: Brill, 2004.

—; Ioannesyan, Youli A. 'Baha'u'llah's Bishārāt (Glad-Tidings): A Proclamation to Scholars and Statesmen', in *Baha'í Studies Review*, vol. 16 (2010), no. 1, pp. 3–28.

Bull, Hedley. *The Anarchical Society: A Study of Order in World Politics*. New York: Columbia University Press, 1977.

Bullock, Alan et al. *The Fontana Dictionary of Modern Thought*. London: Fontana, 1988.

Burgel, Johan Christoph. 'The Bahá'í Attitude towards Peace and its Christian and Islamic Background', in Heshmat Moayyad (ed), *The Bahà'i Faith and Islam: Proceedings of a Symposium, McGill University, March 23–25, 1984*, pp. 29–46. Ottawa: Association for Bahá'í Studies, 1990.

Bushnell, Hart; Lovejoy, Arthur (eds). *Handbook of the War, for Readers, Speakers and Teachers*. New York: National Security League, 1918.

Bushrui, Soheil. *The Style of the Kitáb-i-Aqdas: Aspects of the Sublime*. Bethesda: University Press of Maryland, 1994.

Cahen, Claude. *El Islam: Desde los orígenes hasta el comienzo del Imperio Otomano*. Madrid: Siglo XXI, 1972.

Caillois, Roger. *La cuesta de la guerra*. Mexico: Fondo de Cultura Económica, 1975.

Calduch, Rafael. *Dinámica de la sociedad internacional*. Madrid: Editorial Centro de Estudios Ramón Areces, 1993.

Cannadine, David. *The Undivided Past: Humanity beyond Our Differences*. New York: Knopf, 2013.

Carr, Halett Edward. *The Twenty Years Crisis 1919–1939: An Introduction to the Study of International Relations* (1939). New York: Harper Perennial, 2001.

Chatfield, Charles. 'World War I and the Liberal Pacifist in the United States', in *The American Historical Review*, vol. 75 (1970), no. 7, pp. 1920–37.

Cherry, Conrad. 'The Structure of Organic Thinking: Horace Bushnell's Approach to Language, Nature, and Nation', in *Journal of the Academy of Religion*, vol. 40 (1972), no. 1, pp. 3–20.

Cobb, Stanwood. *Tomorrow and Tomorrow* (1956). Wilmette, Ill.: Bahá'í Publishing Trust, 1960.

Cole, Juan R. 'Commentary: On Amin Banani, Some Reflections on Juan Cole's *Modernity and the Millennium'*. http://www-personal.umich.edu/~jrcole/bahai/2001/colerepl.htm.

— 'The Concept of Manifestation in the Baha'i Writings', in *Bahá'í Studies*, vol. 9 (1982), pp. 1–38.

— 'Imami Jurisprudence and the Role of the 'Ulama: Mortiza Ansari on Emulating the Supreme Exemplar', in Nikki R. Keddie (ed), *Religion and Politics in Iran, Shi'ism from Quietism to Revolution*. New Haven: Yale University Press, 1984.

— 'Iranian Millenarianism and Democratic Thought in the 19th Century', in *International Journal of Middle East Studies*, vol. 24 (1992), no. 1, pp. 1–26.

— *Modernity and the Millennium: The Genesis of the Bahá'í Faith in the Nineteenth-Century Middle East*. New York: Columbia University Press, 1998.

Comenius, John Amos. *Panorthosia or Universal Reform*. Trans. A. M. O. Dobbie. Sheffield Academic Press, 1993.

The Compilation of Compilations. Mona Vale: Bahá'í Publishing Trust of Australia, 1991.

Compilation of the Holy Utterances of Baha'o'llah and Abdul Baha Concerning the Most Great Peace, War and Duty of the Bahais toward their Government (Chicago, 1918). HardPress Publishing, 2013.

Cook, David. *Understanding Jihad*. Berkeley: University of California Press, 2001.

Corbin, Henri. *En Islam iranien*, 4 vols. Paris: Gallimard, 1972.

— *History of Islamic Philosophy.* Trans. Liadain Sherrard, with Phillip Sherrard. London: Kegan Paul, 1993.

— *Spiritual Body and Celestial Earth: From Mazdean Iran to Shiite Iran.* Princeton, NJ: Princeton University Press, 1977.

Cortina, Adela. 'Ética discursiva', in *Historia de la ética.* Barcelona: Editorial Crítica, 1989.

Coulson, Noel. *Historia del derecho islámico.* Barcelona: Ediciones Bellaterra, 1998.

Danesh, John; Fazel, Seena. *Search for Values: Ethics in Bahá'í Thought.* Los Angeles: Kalimát Press, 2004.

Danesh, Roshan. 'Internationalism and Divine Law: A Baha'i Perspective', in *Journal of Law and Religion*, vol. 19 (2003), no. 2, pp. 209–42.

Darling, Linda T. 'Do Justice, Do Justice, For That Is Paradise: Middle Eastern Advice for Indian Muslim Rulers', in *Comparative Studies of South Asia and the Middle East*, vol. 22 (2002), no. 1, pp. 3–19.

Davidi, Avi; Sanasarian, E. 'Domestic Tribulations and International Repercussions: The State and the Transformation of Non-Muslims in Iran', in *Journal of International* Affairs, vol. 60, no. 2 (1 June 2007), pp. 55–68.

Dávúdí, 'Alí Murád. *Malakút-i Vujúd: Nigáhí bar Lawḥ-i Ḥaḍrat-i 'Abdu'l-Bahá Khiṭáb bih Duktúr Agust Furil.* Darmstadt, Germany: 'Aṣr-i Jadíd, 1998.

Díaz, Carlos. *Manual de historia de las religiones.* Madrid: Desclée de Brouver, 1997.

Dunne, Tim. 'Liberalism', in John Baylis and Steve Smith (eds), *The Globalization of World Politics: An Introduction to International Relations.* Oxford: Oxford University Press, 2001.

Eco, Umberto. *The Search for the Perfect Language.* Oxford: Wiley-Blackwell, 1997.

Egea. Amin. *The Apostle of Peace: A Survey of References to 'Abdu'l-Bahá in the Western Press 1871–1923.* 2 vols. Oxford: George Ronald, 2017, 2018.

— 'Reading Reality in Times of Crisis', online article 8 May 2021. https://bahaiworld.bahai.org/library/reading-reality-in-times-of-crisis/.

Eliade, Mircea. *The Myth of the Eternal Return: Or, Cosmos and History.* New Jersey: Princeton University Press, 2018.

— *Tratado de historia de las religiones.* Mexico: Biblioteca Era, 1975.

Elias, Norbert. *The Germans.* Edited by Michael Schröter. New York: Columbia University Press, 1998.

Eshráqí, Armín. (In Persian: The Báb's Movement: Peasant Uprising or a Free Thought Movement?). http://www.bbc.co.uk/persian/blogs/2013/11/131127_l44_nazeran_babism_shtml

Encyclopedia Iranica Online. Editor-in-chief Danel Elton. Ehsan Yarshater Center for Iranian Studies, Columbia University. Leiden: Brill. https://referenceworks.brillonline.com/browse/encyclopaedia-iranica-online.

Esslemont, J. E. *Bahá'u'lláh and the New Era.* Wilmette, Ill.: Bahá'í Publishing Trust, 5th rev. ed. 1990.

Faizi, Gloria. *The Bahá'í Faith: An Introduction.* New Delhi: Bahá'í Publishing Trust, 1990.

Faydí, Muḥammad-'Alí. *Hayát-i-Ḥaḍrat-i-'Abdu'l-Bahá, va Havádith-i-Dawriy-i-Mitháq.* Tehran: Mu'assisiy-i-Millíy-i-Maṭbu'át-i-Amrí, 128 BE.

Fazel, Seena. 'Baha'i Approaches to Christianity and Islam: Further Thoughts on Developing an Inter-Religious Dialogue', in *Bahá'í Studies Review*, vol. 14, pp. 39–51.

— 'The Bahá'í Faith and Academic Journals', in *Bahá'í Studies Review*, vol. 3 (1993), no. 2.

Ferguson, Niall. *The War of the World.* New York: Penguin, 2007.

Ferrín, González. *La angustia de Abraham: Los orígenes culturales del Islam.* Madrid: Almuzara, 2013.

Fischer, Michael. 'Social Change and the Mirrors of Tradition: The Bahá'ís of Yazd', in Heshmat Moayyad (ed), *The Bahá'í Faith and Islam: Proceedings of a Symposium, McGill University, March 23–25, 1984*, pp. 25–53. Ottawa: Association for Bahá'í Studies, 1990.

Flori, Jean. *Guerre Sainte, Jihad, Croisade, violence et religion dans le christianisme e l'Islam.* Paris: Éditions du Seuil, 2002. Spanish edition: *La guerra santa: La formación de la idea de cruzada en el Occidente cristiano.* Madrid: Trotta, 2003.

Frithjof, Schuon. *Comprendre l'Islam.* Paris: Seuil, 1976.

Gail, Marzieh. *Arches of the Years.* Oxford: George Ronald, 1991.

Galtung, Johan. *Peace by Peaceful Means: Peace and Conflict, Development and Civilization.* London: Sage, 1996.

Gaudefroy-Demonbynes, Maurice. *Mahomet.* Paris: Albin Michel, 1969.

Gheissari, Ali. *Iranian Intellectuals in the 20th Century.* Austin: University of Texas Press, 1998.

Giachery, Ugo. *Shoghi Effendi: Recollections.* Oxford: George Ronald, 1973.

Giddens, Anthony. *The Consequences of Modernity.* Cambridge: Polity Press, 1991.

Gil Santesteban, Miguel. *Diálogo de religiones, Camino de paz*, Barcelona: Arca, 2001.

— *Hacia un discurso bahá'í.* Terrassa: Editorial Bahá'í de España, 1996.

Gouldner, Alvin. *The Future of Intellectuals and the Rise of the New Class.* London: MacMillan, 1979.

Gregor, James. *Mussolini's Intellectuals: Fascist Social and Political Thought.* Princeton: Princeton University Press, 2005.

Grundy, Julia M. *Ten Days in the Light of 'Akká.* Wilmette, Ill.: Bahá'í Publishing Trust, RP 1979.

Guardian, The. 'Aristide Briand's Plan for a United States of Europe: Archive 1929', 5 September 2019. http://www.theguardian.com/theguardian/from-the-archive-blog/2019/sep/05/aristide-briands-plan-for-united-states-of-europe-september-9.

Guenon, René. *The Multiple States of Being.* Burdett, NY: Larson, 1984.

— *Symbolism of the Cross.* London: Luzac, 1975.

Gulpáygání. Mírzá Abu'l-Faḍl. *Letters and Essays, 1886–1913*. Trans. Juan Ricardo Cole. Los Angeles: Kalimát Press, 1985.

— *Miracles and Metaphors*. Trans. Juan Ricardo Cole. Los Angeles: Kalimát Press, 1981.

Gutiérrez de Terán, Ignacio Gómez-Benita. *Estado y confesión en Oriente Medio, el caso de Siria y Líbano: Religión, taifa y representatividad*. Madrid: Ediciones de la Universidad Autónoma, 2003.

Hansell, William H. 'The Spiritual Unity of Robert Hayden's Angle of Ascent', in *Black American Literature Forum*, vol. 13, no. 1 (Spring 1979), pp. 24–31.

Hassall, Graham. 'Bahá'í History in the Formative Age: The World Crusade, 1953–1963', in *Journal of Bahá'í Studies*, vol. 6 (1995), pp. 1–22.

— 'Rights to Human and Social Development: A Survey of the Activities of the Bahá'í International Community', in T. Tahririha-Danesh (ed): *Bahá'í-Inspired Perspectives on Human Rights*, pp. 102–22. Hong Kong: Juxta Publishing, 2001.

Hatcher, John S. *The Ocean of His Words: A Reader's Guide to the Art of Bahá'u'lláh*. Wilmette, Ill.: Baha'i Publishing Trust, 1997.

Hatcher, William S.; Martin, Douglas J. *The Bahá'í Faith: The Emerging Global Religion*. Sydney: Harper & Row, 1986.

Hay, Stephen. 'Rabindranath Tagore in America', in *American Quarterly*, vol. 14, no. 3 (23 January 1962), pp. 439–463.

Ḥaydar-'Alí, Ḥájí Mírzá. *Stories from the Delight of Hearts*. Los Angeles: Kalimát Press, 1980.

Hayes, Terrill; Hill, Richard; Scheffer, AnneMarie; Atkinson, Anne; Fisher, Betty (eds). *Peace, More than an End to War: Selections from the Writings of Bahá'u'lláh, the Báb, 'Abdu'l-Bahá, Shoghi Effendi and the Universal House of Justice*. Wilmette, Ill.: Baha'i Publishing Trust, 1986.

Hermann, Denis. *Le shaykhisme à la période qajare: Histoire sociale et doctrinale d'une Ecole chiite*. Miroir de l'Orient Musulman Series, vol. 3. Turnhout: Brepols, 2017.

Hinnells, John R. *The New Penguin Handbook of Living Religions*. London: Penguin, 2nd ed. 2003.

Hobsbawm, Eric J. *The Age of Capital, 1848–1875*. London: Abacus, 1995.

Hofstadter, Richard. *The Age of Reform, from Bryan to T.D.R.* New York: Knopf, 1969.

— *Anti-Intellectualism in American Life*. New York: Vintage Books, 1963.

— *Social Darwinism in American Thought*. Boston: Beacon Press, 1983.

Hogenson, Kathryn Jewett. 'The Cause of Universal Peace', in *The Bahá'í World* online, 23 February 2021. https://bahaiworld.bahai.org/library/the-cause-of-universal-peace/.

Højsgaard, M. T.; Warburg, M. *Religion and Cyberspace*. London: Routledge, 2005.

Holley, Horace. *Religion for Mankind* (1951). Oxford: George Ronald, 1976.

Holliday, Oscar Jara. *La sistematización de Experiencias práctica y teoría para otros mundos posibles*. Bogotá, Colombia: Fundación Centro Internacional de Educación y Desarrollo Humano (CINDE), 2018.

Hollinger, Richard. 'Bahá'ís and American Peace Movements', in Antony Lee (ed), *Circle of Peace: Reflections on the Bahá'í Teachings*. Los Angeles: Kalimát Press, 1985.

Holsti, Kalevi J. *Peace and War: Armed Conflicts and International Order, 1648–1989*. Cambridge: Cambridge University Press, 1998.

Hoonaard, Will C. van den. 'Inside the Origins of the Baha'i Community of Canada, 1898–1948: A Personal Narrative'. http://Bahá'í-library.com/index.php5?file=mcmullen_hoonaard_origins_Bahá'í.

— *The Origins of the Bahá'í Community of Canada, 1898–1948*. Waterloo, Ontario: Wilfrid Laurier University Press, 1996.

Hourani, George F. 'The Basis of Authority of Consensus in Sunnite Islam', in *Studia Islamica*, vol. 21 (1964), pp. 13–60.

Hovannisian, Richard G.; Sabagh, Georges (eds). *The Persian Presence in the Islamic World*. Cambridge: Cambridge University Press, 1998.

Howard, Michael. *La invención de la paz: Reflexiones sobre la guerra y el orden internacional*. Barcelona: Salvat, 2001.

— *War in European History*. Oxford: Oxford University Press, 1976.

— *War in History*. Oxford: Oxford University Press, 1977.

Huddleston, John. *Achieving Peace by the Year 2000: A Twelve Point Proposal*. London: OneWorld, 1988.

— *The Earth is But One Country*. London: Bahá'í Publishing Trust, 1976.

— *The Search for a Just Society*. Oxford: George Ronald, 1989.

Hudson, Maxim. *Defenseless America*. New York: Hearst's International Library, 1916.

Huffines, Jeffrey. 'Bahá'í Proposals for the Reformation of World Order', in Babak Bahador and Nazila Ghanea (eds), *Processes of the Lesser Peace*, p. 43. Oxford: George Ronald, 2002.

Ḥuqúqu'lláh: The Right of God. Comp. Research Department of the Universal House of Justice. London: Bahá'í Publishing Trust, 1986.

Hvithamar, Annika. *Holy Nations and Global Identities: Civil Religion, Nationalism, and Globalisation*. International Studies in Religion and Society Series, vol. 10. Leiden: Brill, 2009.

—; Warmind, M.; Warburg, M. *Baha'i and Globalisation*. Aarhus: Aarhus University Press, 2006.

Inis, Claude. *Swords into Plowshares:The Problems and Progress of International Organization*. New York: Random House, 1971.

'In Memoriam: Pasquale Fiore', in *The American Journal of International Law*, vol. 9, no. 2 (April 1915, pp. 496–7.

Iqbal, Z.; Lewis, M. K. 'Governance and Corruption: Can Islamic Societies and the West Learn from Each Other?', in *American Journal of Islamic Social Sciences*, vol. 19 (2002), no. 2, pp. 1–33.

Ishráq-Khávarí (comp.). *Ma'idiy-i-Ásmání*. A compilation of Bahá'í Writings. 9 vols. Tehran: Bahá'í Publishing Trust, BE 129 (1974).

Issawi, Charles Philip (ed). *The Economic History of Iran, 1800–1914*. Chicago: University of Chicago Press, 1971.

Ives, Howard C., and Senator Borah of Idaho. *Discussion*, 1932.

Izutsu, Toshihiko. *The Concept of Belief in Islamic Theology, A Semantic Analysis of Imám and Islám*. Kuala Lumpur: Islamic Book Trust, 2006.

— *Ethico-Religious Concepts in the Qur'án*. Montreal: McGill-Queen's University Press, 2002.

— *God and Man in the Qur'an: Semantic of the Qur'anic Weltanschauung*. Kuala Lumpur: Islamic Book Trust, 2008.

— *Sufismo y Taoísmo: Ibn 'Arabí*. Madrid: Ediciones Siruela, 1997.

Jahanbegloo, Ramin (ed). *Iran: Between Tradition and Modernity*. New York: Lexington Books, 2004.

Jaldún, Ibn. *Introducción a la historia universal: Al-Muqaddimah*. Mexico: Fondo de Cultura Económica, 1977.

Jouvenel, Bertrand de. *Les débuts de l'état moderne: Une histoire des idées politiques au XIXe siècle*. Paris: Fayard, 1976; Spanish edition: *Los orígenes del Estado moderno: Historia de las ideas políticas en el siglo XIX*. Madrid: Magisterio Español, 1977.

Jünger, Ernst. *La Paz, seguido de El nudo gordiano, El Estado mundial y Alocución de Verdún*. Barcelona: Tusquets, 1996.

— *Storm of Steel*. Oxford: Penguin, 2004.

Kant, Immanuel. *Perpetual Peace: A Philosophical Essay* (1795). London: S. Sonnenschein, 1903. http://archive.org/details/perpetualpeaceph00kantiala.

Karimi, Dariush. 'Muhammad Amíní, Saíd Payvandí, and Iraj Ishráqi: Amir Kabir and his legacy (Amir Kabir kih bud va chih kard?)' Interview, Pargar, BBC, 21 October 2018. https://youtu.be/f3hgT5mxmK4.)

Karlberg, Michael. *Beyond the Culture of Contest*. Oxford: George Ronald, 2004.

Katz, Jonathan G. 'Shaykh Aḥmad's Dream: A 19th-Century Eschatological Vision', in *Studia Islamica*, no. 79 (1994), pp. 157–80.

Keck, L. E. 'On the Ethos of Early Christians', in *Journal of the American Academy of Religion*, vol. 42 (1974), no. 3, pp. 435–52.

Keddie, Nikki R. *Modern Iran, Roots and Results of Revolution*. New Haven and London: Yale University Press, 2003.

— 'Religion and Irreligion in Early Iranian Nationalism', in *Comparative Studies in Society and History*, vol. 4, no. 3 (April 1962), pp. 265–95.

— (ed). *Religion and Politics in Iran: Shi'ism from Quietism to Revolution*. New Haven: Yale University Press, 1984.

— *Religion and Rebellion in Iran: The Iranian Tobacco Protest of 1891-1982*. London: Frank Cass, Routledge, 1966.

Keegan, John. *A History of Warfare*. New York, NY: Vintage Books, 1994.

Keene, James J. 'Baha'i World Faith: Redefinition of Religion', in *Journal for the Scientific Study of Religion*, vol. 6, no. 2 (Autumn 1967), pp. 221–35.

Kelly, Sean. 'Morrison's Outrage over Chinese Tweet a Tried and True Tactic', in *The Age*, 6 December 2020.

Kennedy, Paul. *The Parliament of Man: The United Nations and the Quest for World Government*. London: Allen Lane, 2006.

Keynes, John Maynard. *The Economic Consequences of the Peace*. New York: Harcourt, Brace and Howe, 1920.

Khadem, Riaz. *Prelude to the Guardianship*. Oxford: George Ronald, 2014.

— *Shoghi Effendi in Oxford*. Oxford: George Ronald, 1999.

Khurshid, Anjam. *The Seven Candles of Unity: The Story of 'Abdu'l-Bahá in Edinburgh*. London: Bahá'í Publishing Trust, 1991.

King, Richard. 'Introducing Intellectual History', in *Culture, Theory & Critique*, vol. 47, no. 1 (1 April 2006), pp. 1–6.

Kissinger, Henry. *Diplomacy*. New York: Simon & Schuster, 1994.

Kohlberg, David Cook. *Understanding Jihad*. Berkeley: University of California Press, 2001.

Knox, Geoffrey. *Religion and Public Policy at the UN*. Washington DC: Religion Counts, 2002. https://www.geoffreyknox.com/pdf/Religion_Counts.pdf.

Küng, Hans. *The Catholic Church: A Short History*. New York: Modern Library, RP 2003.

— *Islam, Past, Present and Future*. Oxford: OneWorld, 2007.

— *Proyecto de una ética mundial*. Madrid: Trotta, 1991.

—; Kuschel, Karl-Josef (eds). *Global Ethic: The Declaration of the Parliament of the World's Religions*. New York: Continuum, 1993.

—; van Ess, Joseph; von Stietencron, Heinrich; Bechert, Heinz. *Christianity and World Religions: Paths to Dialogue with Islam, Hinduism, and Buddhism*. New York: Orbis Books, 1999.

Kupchan, Charles A.; Kupchan, Clifford A. *The Promise of Collective Security*. Cambridge, Mass: MIT Press, 1988.

LaCapra, D. 'Tropisms of Intellectual History', in *Rethinking History*, vol. 8, no. 4 (1 December 2004), pp. 499–529.

Lacroix-Hopson, Eliane, *'Abdu'l-Bahá in New York, The City of the Covenant*. New York: NewVista Design, 1999.

Lakoff, George; Johnson, Mark. *Metaphors We Live By*. Chicago: University of Chicago Press, 1980.

Lambden, Stephen. 'The Voice of God and the Supreme Pen: Some Aspects of the Letters to Kings and Rulers of Muhammad, the Bab (d. 1850) and Baha'-Allah (d. 1892)'. n.d. http://www.hurqalya.pwp.blueyonder.co.uk/.

Lambton, A. K. 'A Nineteenth Century View of Jihad', in *Studia Islamica*, no. 32 (1970), pp. 181–92.

— *State and Government in Medieval Islam*. Oxford: Oxford University Press, 1981.

Lample, Paul. *Revelation and Social Reality: Learning to Translate What Is Written into Reality*. West Palm Beach, FL: Palabra Publications, 2009.

Lee, Antony (ed). *Circle of Peace: Reflections on the Bahá'í Teachings*. Los Angeles: Kalimát Press, 1985.

— *Circle of Unity: Bahá'í Approaches to Current Social Issues*. Los Angeles: Kalimát Press, 1984.

Lee, Kathy. *Prelude to the Lesser Peace*. New Delhi: Baha'i Publishing Trust, 1989.

Leibniz, Gottfried. *Leibniz: Political Writings*. Cambridge: Cambridge University Press, 2006.

Lepard, Brian. *Rethinking Humanitarian Intervention: A Fresh Legal Approach Based on Fundamental Ethical Principles in International Law and World Religions*. University Park: Pennsylvania State Press, 2002.

Lerche, Charles O. *Emergence: Dimensions of a New World Order*. London: Bahá'í Publishing Trust, 1991.

— *Healing the Body Politic: Bahá'í Perspectives on Peace and Conflict Resolution*. Oxford: George Ronald, 2004.

— *Towards the Most Great Justice: Elements of Justice in the New World Order*. London: Baha'i Publishing Trust, 1996.

Lewis, Bernard. *The Crisis of Islam, Holy War and Unholy Terror*. London: Phoenix, 2003.

— *The Political Language of Islam*. Chicago: The University of Chicago Press, 1991.

Lichtheim, George. *Imperialism*. London: Allen Lane, 1971

Lights of Guidance: A Bahá'í Reference File. Comp. Helen Hornby. New Delhi: Bahá'í Publishing Trust, 3rd rev. ed. 1994.

Lovejoy, Arthur O. *Great Chain of Being*. Harvard: Harvard University Press, 1936.

— 'The Historiography of Ideas', in *Proceedings of the American Philosophical Society*, vol. 78, no. 4 (31 March 1938), pp. 529–43.

— 'Reflections on the History of Ideas', in *Journal of the History of Ideas*, vol. 1 (1940), no. 1, pp. 3–23.

— *Reflections on Human Nature*. Johns Hopkins University Press, 1968.

Ma'ani Ewing, Soveida. *Collective Security within Reach*. Oxford: George Ronald, 2007.

MacEoin, Denis Martin. 'Bábí Concept of Holy War', in *Religion*, vol. 12 (1983), no. 2, pp. 93–129.

— 'Divisions and Authority Claims in Babism (1850–1866)', in *Studia Iranica*, vol. 18 (1989), no. 1, pp. 93–129.

— 'From Babism to Baha'ism: Problems of Militancy, Quietism, and Conflation in the Construction of a Religion', in *Religion*, vol. 13 (1983), no. 3, pp. 219–55.

— 'Hierarchy Authority and Eschatology in Early Babi Thought', in *Iran: Studies in Bábí and Bahá'í History*, pp. 95–141. Los Angeles: Kalimát Press, 1986.

— *The Messiah of Shiraz: Studies in Early and Middle Babism*. Iran Studies, vol. 3. Leiden: Brill Academic Publishers, 2008.

— 'Peter Smith: *The Babi and Baha'i Religions: from Messianic Shi'ism to a World Religion*, xiv, 243 pp. Cambridge, etc.: Cambridge University Press, 1987'. Book review in *Bulletin of the School of Oriental and African Studies*, vol. 51 (2009), no. 03, pp. 557–8.

— *The Sources for Early Babi Doctrine and History: A Survey*. Leiden: Brill Academic Publishers, 1991.

Malaparte, Curzio. *Técnica de un golpe de Estado*. Barcelona: Plaza y Janés, 1960.

Malouf, Diana. *The Hidden Words of Bahá'u'lláh: Translation Norms Employed by Shoghi Effendi*. New York: State University of New York at Binghamton, 1988.

Mandelbaum, Maurice. 'Arthur O. Lovejoy and the Theory of Historiography', in *Journal of the History of Ideas*, vol. 9, no. 4 (October 1948), pp. 412–23.

— 'The History of Ideas, Intellectual History, and the History of Philosophy', in *History and Theory*, no. 5 (1965), pp. 33–66.

Mannheim, Karl. *Ideology and Utopia: An Introduction to the Sociology of Knowledge*. San Diego: Harcourt Brace Jovanovich, 1985.

Maragall, José Antonio. *Estudios de la historia del pensamiento español, s. XVIII*. Madrid: Mondadori, 1991.

Marchand, C. Roland. *The American Peace Movement, and Social Reform 1898–1918*. Princeton, New Jersey: Princeton University Press, 1972.

Martin, Douglas. 'The Missionary as Historian', in *Bahá'í Studies*, vol. 4 (1978), pp. 1–29.

Martínez Guzmán, Vicent. *la paz perpetua, doscientos años después*. Valencia: Nau Libres, 1997.

Masroori, Cyrus. 'European Thought in Nineteenth-Century Iran: David Hume and Others', in *Journal of the History of Ideas*, vol. 61, no. 4 (October 2000), pp. 657–74.

Mattelart, Armand. *La comunicación-mundo: Historia de las ideas y de las estrategias*. Madrid: Fundesco, 1993.

Mazgaj, Paul. 'The Young Sorelians and Decadence', in *Journal of Contemporary History*, vol. 17, no. 1 (January 1982), pp. 179–99.

McCants, W.; Milani, K. 'The History and Provenance of an Early Manuscript of the Nuqtat al-Kaf Dated 1268 (1851–52), in *Iranian Studies*, vol. 37 (2004), no. 3, pp. 431–49.

McGlinn, Sen. 'Baha'u'llah's "Tablet of the Banu Qurayza"'. n.d. http://senmcglinn.wordpress.com/2010/03/06/lawh_banuqurayza/#more-4179.

— *Church and State: A Post-modern Political Theology*. Los Angeles: Kalimát Press, 2005.

— 'A Difficult Case: Beyer's Categories and the Bahá'í Faith', in *Social Compass*, vol. 50, no. 2 (June 2003).

McLean, Jack. *Dimensions of Spirituality*. Oxford: George Ronald, 1994.

— *Revisioning the Sacred: New Perspectives on a Bahá'í Theology*. Los Angeles: Kalimát Press, 1997.

— 'Shoghi Effendi's *The Dispensation of Bahá'u'lláh*: A Theology of the Word', in *Lights of 'Irfán*, vol. 9 (2008), pp. 239–80.

McNamara, Brendan. *The Reception of 'Abdu'l-Bahá in Britain: East Comes West.* Leiden and Boston: Brill, 2020.

The Ministry of the Custodians, 1957–1963: An Account of the Stewardship of the Hands of the Cause. Haifa: Bahá'í World Centre, 1992.

Moayyad, Heshmat (ed). *The Bahá'í Faith and Islam: Proceedings of a Symposium, McGill University March 23–25, 1984.* Ottawa: Association for Bahá'í Studies, 1990.

Moghadam, Assaf. 'Mayhem, Myths, and Martyrdom: The Shi'a Conception of Jihad', in *Terrorism and Political Violence*, vol. 19 (2007), no. 1.

Momen, Moojan. "Abdu'l-Bahá's Tablet on the Functioning of the Universal House of Justice: A Provisional Translation and Commentary', in Iraj Ayman (ed), *Lights of 'Irfán*, vol. 8 (2007), pp. 257–97.

— 'The Babi and Baha'i Community of Iran: A Case of "Suspended Genocide"?', in *Journal of Genocide Research*, vol. 7 (2005), no. 2, pp. 221–41.

— (ed). *The Bábí and Bahá'í Religions, 1844-1944: Some Contemporary Western Accounts.* Oxford: George Ronald, 1981.

— (ed). *The Bahá'í Faith and the World's Religions: Papers presented at the Irfan Colloquia.* Oxford: George Ronald, 2003.

— 'The Baha'is and the Constitutional Revolution: The Case of Sari, Mazandaran, 1906–1913', in *Iranian Studies*, vol. 41 (2008), no. 3, pp. 343–63.

— *An Introduction to Shi'i Islam.* Oxford: George Ronald, 1985.

— 'Insider and Outsider Scholarship in Bahá'í Studies', in *Lights of 'Irfán*, vol. 9 (2008), pp. 281–6.

— "Marginality and Apostasy in the Baha'i Community', in *Religion*, vol. 37 (2007), no. 3, pp. 187–209.

— 'Messianic Concealment and Theophanic Disclosure', in *Online Journal of Bahá'í Studies*, vol. 1 (2007), pp. 71–88.

— 'Millennialism and Violence: The Attempted Assassination of Nasir al-Din Shah of Iran by the Babis in 1852', in *Nova Religio*, vol. 12 (2008), no. 1, pp. 57–8.

— 'Millennialist Dreams and Apocalyptic Nightmares', in Moshe Sharon (ed), *Studies in Modern Religions, Religious Movements and the Bábí–Bahá'í Faiths*, pp. 97–126. Leiden: Brill Academic Publishers, 2004.

— *Scripture and Revelation.* Oxford: George Ronald, 1997.

— 'The Social Basis of the Babi Upheavals in Iran (1848–53): A Preliminary Analysis', in *International Journal of Middle East Studies*, vol. 15 (1983), no. 2, pp. 157–83.

Mooten, Nalinie. 'The Bahá'í Contribution to Cosmopolitan International Relations Theory', in *Online Journal of Bahá'í Studies*, vol. 1 (2007), pp. 4–70.

Morgenthau, Hans J. *Politics among Nations: The Struggle for Power and Peace.* New York: McGraw Hill, 2005.

Morrison, Gayle. *To Move the World: Louis Gregory and the Advancement of Racial Unity in America.* Wilmette, Ill.: Bahá'í Publishing Trust, 1982.

Mosse, George L. 'Caesarism, Circuses, and Monuments', in *Journal of Contemporary History*, vol. 6 (1971), no. 2, pp. 167–82.

— 'Introduction: The Genesis of Fascism', in *Journal of Contemporary History*, vol. 1 (1966), no. 1, pp. 14–26.

— 'The Political Culture of Italian Futurism: A General Perspective', in *Journal of Contemporary History*, vol. 25, no. 2 (June 1990), pp. 253–68.

Muḥammad Ḥussayní, Nuṣratu'lláh. 'Páṣukh-i-Yik Naqdnámih', in *Pazhuheshnameh*, vol. 5 (11 Khurdád 1378).

Muqaddam, Síyámak Dhabíḥí. 'Pírámún-i-Kitáb-i-Ḥaḍrat-i-Báb', in *Pazhuheshnameh*, vol. 4 (Khurdád 1377). http://www.pazhuheshnameh19.info/content/category/8/106/139/.

Murray, Gilbert; Tagore, Rabindranath Tagore. *East and West.* Oxford: International Institute of Intellectual Co-Operation, League of Nations, 1935. http://archive.org/details/dli.ministry.25700.

Nabíl-i- A'ẓam (Muḥammad-i-Zarandí). *The Dawn-Breakers: Nabíl's Narrative of the Early Days of the Bahá'í Revelation.* Trans. Shoghi Effendi. Wilmette, Ill.: Bahá'í Publishing Trust, 1932.

Nakhjavání, 'Alí. *Towards World Order.* Rome: Casa Editrice Bahá'í, 2005.

Nakhjavani, Bahiyyih. *Asking Questions: A Challenge to Fundamentalism.* Oxford: George Ronald, 1990.

National Spiritual Assembly of the Bahá'ís of the United States. 'A Bahá'í Declaration of Human Rights and Obligations: A Statement Presented to the First Session of the United Nations Commission on Human Rights.' n.d. http://info.Bahá'í.org/article-1-8-3-1.html.

— (comp.). *Developing Distinctive Baha'i Communities.* Wilmette, Ill.: Bahá'í Publishing Trust, 1998.

Nye, Joseph S. 'Soft Power', in *Foreign Policy*, no. 80 (1990), pp. 153–71.

Opler, Edward Morris. 'Component, Assemblage, and Theme in Cultural Integration and Differentiation', in *American Anthropologist*, vol. 61, no. 6, New Series (December 1959), pp. 955–64.

— 'The Context of Themes', in *American Anthropologist*, vol. 51, no. 2, New Series (June 1949), pp. 323–5.

— 'Cultural and Organic Conceptions in Contemporary World History', in *American Anthropologist*, vol. 46, no. 4 (December 1944), pp. 448–460.

— 'Themes as Dynamic Forces in Culture', in *The American Journal of Sociology*, vol. 51 (1945), no. 3, pp. 198–206.

Ortega y Gasset, José. *España Invertebrada: Bosquejo de algunos pensamientos históricos.* Madrid: Revista de Occidente, 1983.

— *The Revolt of the Masses.* London: Allen and Unwin, 1951.

Pareja, Félix M. *La religiosidad musulmana.* Madrid: BAC, 1975.

The Pattern of Bahá'í Life. Compilation of Bahá'í Writings. London: Bahá'í Publishing Trust, 1983.

Peters, Rudolph. 'Idjtihád and Taqlíd, in 18th and 19th Century Islam', in *Die Welt des Islams*, vol. 20 (1980), no. 3.

Phelps, Myron H. *The Master in 'Akká.* Los Angeles: Kalimát Press, 1985. Reprinted from *The Life and Teachings of Abbas Effendi*, New York and London: G. P. Putnam's Sons, 1912.

Pokorny, Brad. 'Bahá'ís and American Peace Movements', in Antony Lee (ed), *Circle of Unity: Bahá'í Approaches to Current Social Issues.* Los Angeles: Kalimát Press, 1984.

Quinton, René. *Maximes sur la guerre.* Paris: B. Grasset. Available at http://quinton.chat.ru/rqtable.html,

Rabbani, Ruḥíyyih. *The Priceless Pearl.* London: Bahá'í Publishing Trust, 1969.

Radhakrishnan, S. *The Philosophy of Rabindranath Tagore.* London: Macmillan, 1919.

Rafati, Vahid. 'The Development of Shaykhí Thought in Shí'í Islam'. Unpublished Ph.D. dissertation, University of California, Los Angeles, 1979.

— *Malakút-i-Vujúd: Nigáhí bar Lawḥ-i Ḥaḍrat-i 'Adbu'l-Bahá Khiṭáb bih Duktúr Ugúst Furil.* Darmstadt, Germany: 'Aṣr-i Jadíd, 1998.

Randall, John Herman. 'Arthur O. Lovejoy and the History of Ideas', in *Philosophy and Phenomenological Research*, vol. 23, no. 4 (June 1963), pp. 475–9.

Rassekh, Shapour. 'Haft Gúniy-i-vaḥdat: Nigáhí bih Lawḥ-i-Mubárak-i-Haft Sham', in *Pazhuheshnameh*, no. 5 (11 Khurdád, 1378).

Religion Counts. *Religion and Public Policy at the UN.* Chicago: Religion Counts, 2002.

Research Department of the Universal House of Justice. *Conservation of the Earth's Resources.* New York, 1989.

Remey, Charles Mason. *The Peace of the World.* Chicago: Bahai Publishing Society, 1919.

Renouvin, Pierre. *Historia de las Relaciones Internacionales.* Madrid: Akal, 1982. A translation of *Histoire des relations internationales.* Paris: Hachette, 4 vols. 1954.

Ringer, Monica M. *Education, Religion and the Discourse of Cultural Reform in Qajar Iran.* Costa Mesa, Ca, 2001.

— 'Negotiating Modernity, Ulama and the Discourse of Modernity in Nineteenth-Century Iran', in Ramin Jahanbegloo (ed), *Iran: Between Tradition and Modernity*, pp. 39–50. New York: Lexington Books, 2004.

Rodinson, Maxime. *Mahoma, el nacimiento del mundo islámico.* Madrid: Biblioteca Era, 1974.

Ropp, Theodore. *War in the Modern World.* New York: Collier Books, 1992.

Ross, C. N. B. 'Lord Curzon and E. G. Browne Confront the "Persian Question",', in *Historical Journal*, vol. 52, no. 2 (30 June 2009), pp. 385–411.

de Rougemont, Denis. *Pensar con las manos: Sobre las ruinas de una cultura burguesa.* Madrid: EMESA, 1977. A translation of *Penser avec les mains* (1936).

Rousseau, Jean-Jacques. *A Lasting Peace through the Federation of Europe and The State of War*. London: Constable and Co, 1917. https://oll.libertyfund.org/title/rousseau-a-lasting-peace-through-the-federation-of-europe-and-the-state-of-war.

— *The Social Contract and Discourses by Jean-Jacques Rousseau*. Edited by G. D. H. Cole. London & Toronto: J. M. Dent and Sons, 1923.

Ruhe, David S. *Robe of Light: The Persian Years of the Supreme Prophet Bahá'u'lláh*. Oxford: George Ronald, 1994.

Ruiz de los Paños, Alberto Brosi. 'La prohibición del uso de la fuerza', in *Derecho Internacional Humanitario*. Valencia: Tirant lo Blanch, 2002.

Rutherford, Ken. 'The Hague and Ottawa Conventions: A Model for Future Weapon Ban Regimes', in *The Nonproliferation Review*, vol. 6, no. 3 (Spring–Summer 1999), pp. 36–50.

Sabet, Ariane. 'Bahá'u'lláh's Concept of Collective Security in Historical and Theoretical Perspective', in Babak Bahador and Nazila Ghanea (eds), *Processes of the Lesser Peace*. Oxford: George Ronald, 2002.

Sachedina, Abdulaziz Abdulhussein. *The Just Ruler (al-sultánal-'ádil): The Comprehensive Authority of the Jurist in Imamite Jurisprudence*. New York: Oxford University Press, 1998.

Sadri, M. ; Sadri, A. et al. *Reason, Freedom, & Democracy in Islam: Essential Writings of 'Abdolkarim Soroush*. New York: Oxford University Press, U2000.

Saiedi, Nader. *'Aql, Dín va Jam'ih dar Andíshiy-e Bahá'í* [Intellect, Religion and Society in Bahá'í Thought].

— 'Az Demukrásíy-i-Farhangí bih Demukrásíy-i-Síyásí', in *Payám-i-Bahá'í*, September 2020.

— *Gate of the Heart: Understanding the Writings of the Báb*. Ontario: Wilfrid Laurier University Press, 2008.

— *Logos and Civilization*. Bethesda: University Press of Maryland, 2000.

— *Maẓharíyyát, Shálúdiy-i-Ilahíyyát-i-Bahá'í (Theophany, Foundations of Bahá'í Theology)*. Bahá'i Studies Series, vol. 8. Institute for Bahá'í Studies in Persian, 1995.

— 'Replacing the Sword with the Word', in *The Bahá'í World* online, 22 May 2019. https://bahaiworld.bahai.org/library/replacing-the-sword-with-the-word/.

— *Risáliy-i-Madanníyyih va Mas'aliy-i-Tajaddud Dar Khávar-i-Míyánih (The Secret of Divine Civilization and the Problem of Modernization in the Middle East)*. Ontario: Institute for Bahá'í Studies in Persian, 1993. English expanded version titled *An Introduction to 'Abdu'l-Bahá's The Secret of Divine Civilization*, Converging Realities 1, St Gall, Switzerland: Landegg Academy, 2000.

Sánchez Nogales, Luis. *La nostalgia del Eterno*. Madrid: CCS, 1997.

de Santos, Aurelio Otero. *Los Evangelios Apócrifos: Edición crítica y bilingüe*. Madrid: BAC, 1979.

Savi, Julio. *The Eternal Quest for God: An Introduction to the Divine Philosophy of 'Abdu'l-Bahá*. Oxford: George Ronald, 1989.

Schaefer, Udo. *Bahá'í Ethics in Light of Scripture: An Introduction*. Vol. 1: *Doctrinal*

Fundamentals; vol. 2: *Virtues and Divine Commandments*. Oxford: George Ronald, 2007, 2009.

— *Beyond the Clash of Religions: The Emergence of a New Paradigm*. Prague: Zero Palm Press, 1992.

— 'Challenges to Bahá'í Studies', in *First European Conference on Bahá'í Activities in Universities*, vol. 2. Brno: Bahá'í Studies Review, 1992.

— 'Crime and Punishment: Bahá'í Perspectives for a Future Criminal Law', in *Law and International Order: Proceedings of the First European Bahá'í Conference on Law and International Order*, De Poort, Netherlands, 8–11 June 1995.

— *The Light Shineth in Darkness: Five Studies in Revelation after Christ*. Oxford: George Ronald, 1977.

—; Gollmer, Ulrich; Towfigh, Nicola. *Making the Crooked Straight: A Contribution to Bahá'í Apologetics*. Oxford: George Ronald, 2002. A translation and update of *Desinformation als Methode: Die Bahá'ísmus Monographie des F. Ficiccia*. Hildesheim: Georg Olms Verlag, 1995.

Scharbrodt, Oliver. *Islam and the Baha'i Faith: A Comparative Study of Muhammad Abduh and Abdul-Baha Abbas*.. New York: Routledge, 2008.

— 'The Salafiyya and Sufism: Muhammad 'Abduh and his Risalat al-Waridat (Treatise on Mystical Inspirations)', in *Bulletin of the School of Oriental and African Studies*, vol. 70 (2007), no. 01, pp. 89–115.

— 'Theological Responses to Modernity in the Nineteenth-century Middle East: The Examples of Bahá'u'lláh and Muhammad Abduh', in *Lights of 'Irfán*, vol. 3 (2002), pp. 139–54.

Schuon, Frithjof. *Comprendre l'Islam*. Paris: Seuil, 1976.

— *The Transcendent Unity of Religions*. Quest Books, 1984.

Sifídvash, 'Ináyatkhudá. *Pishgaman-i-Parsí Nizhad*. Dundas, Ontario: Association for Bahá'í Studies, 1999.

Sharon, Moshe. *Studies in Modern Religions, Religious Movements and the Bábí–Bahá'í Faiths*. Leiden: Brill, 2004.

Shoghi Effendi. *The Advent of Divine Justice* (1939). Wilmette, Ill.: Bahá'í Publishing Trust, 1990.

— *Bahá'í Administration: Selected Messages, 1922–1932*. Wilmette, Ill.: Bahá'í Publishing Trust, 1974.

— *Citadel of Faith: Messages to America, 1947–1957*. Wilmette, Ill.: Bahá'í Publishing Trust, 1965.

— *Dawn of a New Day: Messages to India 1923–1957*. New Delhi: Baha'i Publishing Trust, 1970.

— *Directives from the Guardian*. Comp. Gertrude Garrida. New Delhi: Bahá'í Publishing Trust, 1973.

— *God Passes By* (1944). Wilmette, Ill.: Bahá'í Publishing Trust, 1974.

— *Letters from the Guardian to Australia and New Zealand, 1923–1957*. Mona Vale, Sydney: National Spiritual Assembly of the Bahá'ís of Australia, 1970.

— *Messages to America, 1932–1946*. Wilmette, Ill: Bahá'I Publishing Committee, 1947.

— *Messages to the Bahá'í World, 1950–1957*. Wilmette, Ill.: Bahá'í Publishing Trust, 1971.

— *Messages to Canada*. Thornhill, Ontario: National Spiritual Assembly of the Bahá'ís of Canada, 1965, rev. ed. 1999.

— *Messages of Shoghi Effendi to the Indian Subcontinent, 1923–1957*. Comp. Iran Furutan Muhajír. New Delhi: Bahá'í Publishing Trust, rev. ed. 1995.

— *Principles of Bahá'í Administration: A Compilation*. London: Bahá'í Publishing Trust, 1973.

— *The Promised Day Is Come* (1941). Wilmette, Ill.: Bahá'í Publishing Trust, 1996.

— *Summary Statement, addressed to a Special UN Committee on Palestine*, 1947.

— *This Decisive Hour: Messages from Shoghi Effendi to the North American Bahá'ís, 1932–1946*. Wilmette, Ill.: Bahá'í Publishing Trust, 2003.

— *The Unfolding Destiny of the British Baha'i Community: The Messages from the Guardian of the Baha'i Faith to the Baha'is of the British Isles*. London: Bahá'í Publishing Trust, 1981.

— *The World Order of Bahá'u'lláh: Selected Letters* (1938). Wilmette, Ill.: Bahá'í Publishing Trust, 1991.

Sicre, José Luis. *Introducción al Antiguo Testamento*. Estella: Verbo Divino, 2000.

Simma, Bruno. *The Charter of the United Nations: A Commentary*. Oxford: Oxford University Press, 2002.

Siraj, Abu Bakr. 'The Spiritual Function of Civilization', in *The Sword of Gnosis*. London: Arkana, 1974.

Smart, Ninian. *The World's Religions*. Cambridge: Cambridge University Press, 2nd ed. 1998.

Smiley, Albert K. 'The Rise of the Peace Movement', in *The Yale Law Journal*, vol. 20 (1911), no. 5.

Smith, Christian. 'Future Directions in the Sociology of Religion', in *Social Forces*, vol. 86, no. 4 (30 June 2008), pp. 1561–89.

Smith, Peter. *The Babi and Baha'i Religions: From Messianic Shi'ism to a World Religion*. Cambridge: Cambridge University Press, 1987.

— (ed). *In Iran: Studies in Bábí and Bahá'í History*. Los Angeles: Kalimát Press, 1986.

— 'Millenarianism in the Babi and Bahá'í Religion', in Roy Wallis (ed), *Millennialism and Charisma*, pp. 231–83. Belfast: Queen's University, 1982.

—; Momen, Moojan. 'The Babi Movement: A Resource Mobilization Perspective', in Peter Smith (ed), *In Iran: Studies in Bábí and Bahá 'í History*. Los Angeles: Kalimát Press, 1986.

Souleyman, Elizabeth V. *The Vision of World Peace in Seventeenth and Eighteenth-Century France* (1941). Literary Licensing (LLC), 2012.

Sorel, George. *Reflexiones sobre la violencia*. Madrid: Alianza, 1976.

Sours, Michael. *Without Syllable or Sound: The World Sacred Scriptures in the Bahá'í Faith*. Los Angeles: Kalimát Press, 2000.

Spengler, Oswald. *The Decline of the West*. London: Allen & Unwin, 1918.

Star of the West: The Bahai Magazine. Periodical, 25 vols. 1910–1935. Vols. 1–14 RP Oxford: George Ronald, 1978. Complete CD-ROM version: Talisman Educational Software/Special Ideas, 2001.

Starr Jordan, David. *Days of a Man*. New York: World Book Company, 1922.

— *Waste and War*. New York: Doubleday, Page & Co, 1913.

Stockman, Robert. *'Abdu'l-Bahá in America*. Wilmette, Ill.: Bahá'í Publishing Trust, 2013.

— *The Bahá'í Faith in America*. Vol. 2: *Early Expansion 1900–1912*. Oxford: George Ronald, 1995.

Tag, Abd El-Rahman. 'Le Babisme et L'Islam: Recherche sur les origins du Babisme et ses rapports avec l'Islam.' Paris: Université de Paris, Librairie Generale de Droit et de Jurisprudence, 1942.

Tagore, Rabindranath. *Creative Unity*. London: Macmillan, 1922.

— *Nationalism*. San Francisco: The Book Club of California, 1917.

— *Oriente y Occidente, Epistolario*. Barcelona: Editorial Juventud, 1990.

Taherzadeh, Adib. *The Covenant of Bahá'u'lláh*. Oxford: George Ronald, 1992

— *The Revelation of Bahá'u'lláh*. 4 vols. Oxford: George Ronald, 1974–1987.

Tahririha-Danesh, Tahirih (ed).*Bahá'í-Inspired Perspectives on Human Rights*. Hong Kong: Juxta Publishing, 2001.

Thomas, Richard W. 'A Long and Thorny Path: Race Relations in the American Bahá'í Community', in Antony Lee (ed), *Circle of Unity, Bahá'í Approaches to Current Social Issues*, pp. 37–65. Los Angeles: Kalimát Press, 1984.

Thompson, R. D. 'The Wesleyan and the Struggle to Forgive', in *Wesleyan Theological Journal*, vol. 18 (1983), pp. 81–92.

Tillion, Germaine. *Le harem et les cousins*. Paris: Seuil, 1966.

Titus, Craig Steven. 'Resilience and Christian Virtues: What the Psychosocial Sciences Offer for the Renewal of Thomas Aquinas' Moral Theology of Fortitude and Its Related Virtues'. Faculty of Theology at the University of Fribourg, Switzerland, 2002.

Tryon, James L. 'The Rise of the Peace Movement', in *The Yale Law Journal*, vol. 20 (1911), no. 5, pp. 358–371.

Tyson, J. *World Peace and World Government: From Vision to Reality*. Oxford: George Ronald, 1986.

Universal House of Justice. *Century of Light*. Haifa: Bahá'í World Centre, 2001.

— *The Constitution of the Universal House of Justice*. Haifa: Bahá'í World Centre, 1972.

— *Letter to the World's Religious Leaders*. Haifa: Bahá'í World Centre, 2002. https://www.bahai.org/documents/the-universal-house-of-justice/letter-worlds-religious-leaders.

— *Messages from the Universal House of Justice, 1963–1986: The Third Epoch of the Formative Age*. Comp. Geoffry W. Marks. Wilmette Ill.: Bahá'í Publishing Trust, 1996.

— *One Common Faith*. Haifa: Bahá'í World Centre, 2005. https://www.bahai.org/library/other-literature/official-statements-commentaries/one-common-faith/.

— 'The Promise of World Peace' (1985), in *Messages from the Universal House of Justice, 1963–1986: The Third Epoch of the Formative Age*. Wilmette, Ill.: Bahá'í Publishing Trust, 1996.

— *Wellspring of Guidance: Messages, 1963–1968*. Wilmette, Ill.: Baha'i Publishing Trust, 1976.

Unrestrained as the Wind: A Life Dedicated to Bahá'u'lláh. Compilation by the US Bahá'í Youth Committee.Wilmette, Ill.: Bahá'í Publishing Trust, 1985.

Utas, Bo. *A Persian Sufi Poem: Vocabulary and Terminology*. London: Curzon Press, 1978.

Vahman, Fereydun. *Yik Ṣad va Shaṣt Sál Mubárizih bá Díyánnat-i-Bahá'í* (One Hundred of Sixty Years of Persecution against the Bahá'í Faith).Stockholm: Baran, 2010.

van den Hoonaard, Will C. 'Inside the Origins of the Bahá'í Community of Canada, 1898–1948: A Personal Narrative'. http://Bahá'í-library.com/index.php5?file=mcmullen_ hoonaard_ origins_Bahá'í.

— *The Origins of the Bahá'í Community of Canada, 1898–1948*. Waterloo, Ontario: Wilfrid Laurier University Press, 1996.

— 'The Social Organization of Mentorship in Bahá'í Studies', in *Journal of Bahá'í Studies*, vol. 8 (1998), no. 3, pp. 19–38.

— 'Unfreezing the Frame: The Promise of Inductive Research in Bahá'í Studies', in *Bahá'í Studies Review*, vol. 10 (2001), pp. 103–14.

van Evera, Stephen. *Causes of War, Power and the Roots of Conflict*. Ithaca: Cornell University Press, 1999.

Visiting Bahá'í Holy Places. Haifa: Bahá'í World Centre, 1992.

Von Grunebaun, Gustave E. *El Islam, desde la caída de Constantinopla hasta nuestros días*. Madrid: Siglo XXI, 1975.

Walbridge, John. *Sacred Acts, Sacred Space, Sacred Time*. Oxford: George Ronald, 1996.

Wallis, Roy (ed). *Millennialism and Charisma*. Belfast: Queen's University, 1982.

Waltz, Kenneth N. *Man, the State and War: A Theoretical Analysis*. New York: Columbia University Press, 2001.

Warburg, Margit. 'Baha'i: A Religious Approach to Globalization', in *Social Compass*, vol. 46 (1999), no. 1, pp. 47–56.

— *Citizens of the World: A History and Sociology of the Baha'is from a Globalisation Perspective*. Leiden: Brill, 2006.

— 'The Dual Global Field: A Model for Transnational Religions and Globalisation', in M. Warburg, A. Hvithamar, and M. Warmind (eds), *Baha'i and Globalisation*, pp. 152–72. Aarhus: Aarhus University Press, 2006.

—; Hvithamar, Annika; Warmind, Morten (eds). *Baha'i and Globalisation.* Aarhus: Aarhus University Press, 2006.

Watt, W. Montgomery. *Muhammad: Prophet and Statesman.* Oxford: Oxford University Press, 1961.

Webb, A. 'The Countermodern Moment: A World-Historical Perspective on the Thought of Rabindranath Tagore, Muhammad Iqbal, and Liang Shuming', in *Journal of World History*, vol. 19, no. 2 (1 June 2008), pp. 189–212.

Wehr, Hans; Cowan, J. M. *Arabic-English Dictionary.* 3rd ed. Spoken Language Services, 1976.

Weikart, Richard. 'The Origins of Social Darwinism in Germany, 1859–1895', in *Journal of the History of Ideas*, vol. 54, no. 3 (July 1993).

Weil, Henry A. *Closer than your Life-Vein: An Insight Into the Wonders of Spiritual Fulfillment.* Anchorage: National Spiritual Assembly of the Bahá'ís of Alaska, 1978.

Weinberg, Matthew. 'The Human Rights Discourse: A Bahá'í Perspective', in *The Bahá'í World*, 1996–1997, vol. 25, pp. 247–74. Haifa: Bahá'í World Centre, 1998.

Welch, Michael R.; Sikkink,. David; Loveland, Matthew T. 'The Radius of Trust: Religion, Social Embeddedness and Trust in Strangers', in *Social Forces*, vol. 86 (2007), no. 1, pp. 23–46.

Wiener, P. P. 'Some Problems and Methods in the History of Ideas', in *Journal of the History of Ideas*, vol. 22 (1961), no. 4, pp. 531–48.

— 'Towards Commemorating the Centenary of Arthur O. Lovejoy's Birthday (October 10, 1873)', in *Journal of the History of Ideas*, vol. 34 (1973), no. 4, pp. 591–8.

Willis, John Ralph. 'Jihad fi Sabil Allah: Its Doctrinal Basis in Islam and Some Aspects of Its Evolution in Nineteenth Century West Africa', in *Journal of African History*, vol. 8 (n.d.), no. 3, pp. 395–415.

Winters, Jonah. 'Communicative Interaction: Notes on Relating Habermasian Universalism to Bahá'í Consultation.' http://bahailibrary.com/index.php5?file=winters_communicative_interaction.html.

— 'Dying for God: Martyrdom in the Shii and Babi Religions.' University of Toronto, 1997. http://bahai-library.com/theses/dying/.

Wolfson, Harry Austryn. 'Albinus and Plotinus on Divine Attributes', in *The Harvard Theological Review* vol. 45, no. 2 (April 1952), pp. 115–30.

— 'The Double Faith Theory in Clement, Saadia, Averroes and St. Thomas, and Its Origin in Aristotle and the Stoics', in *The Jewish Quarterly Review*, vol. 33 (1942), no. 2, pp. 213–64.

Wright, Quincy. *A Study of War.* Abridged edition. Chicago: University of Chicago Press, 1983.

Yarshater, Ehsan. 'The Persian Presence in the Islamic World', in Richard G. Hovannisian and Georges Sabagh (eds), *The Persian Presence in The Islamic World.* Levi Della Vida Symposia. Cambridge: Cambridge University Press, 1998.

Yazdani, Mina. 'The Islamic Revolution's Internal Other: The Case of Ayatollah Khomeini and the Baha'is of Iran', in *Journal of Religious History*, vol. 36 (2012), no. 4, pp. 593–604.

— 'Towards a History of Iran's Baha'i Community During the Reign of Mohammad Reza Shah, 1941–1979', in *Iran Namag*, vol. 2 (2017), no. 1, p. 29.

Yoder, John Howard. *Chapters in the History of Religiously Rooted Nonviolence Work.* University of Notre Dame, 1994.

Zabihi-Moghadam, Siyamak. 'The Babi-State Conflict at Shaykh Tabars.', in *Iranian Studies*, vol. 35 (2002).

— 'Pírámún-i-Kitáb-i-Ḥaḍrat-i-Báb', in *Pazhuheshnameh,* vol. 4 (11 Khurdád 1377). http://www.pazhuheshnameh19.info/content/category/8/106/139/

Zamoyski, Adam. *Rites of Peace: The Fall of Napoleon and the Congress of Vienna.* London: Harper, 2007.

Zarqání, Maḥmúd. *Maḥmúd's Diary: The Diary of Mírzá Maḥmúd-i-Zarqání Chronicling 'Abdu'l-Bahá's Journey to America.* Oxford: George Ronald, 1998.

Zweig, Stefan. *World of Yesterday*. London: Cassell, 1943.

NOTES AND REFERENCES

Introduction

1 The word 'theme' is used here in the general sense applied to it by Opler, 'Themes as Dynamic Forces in Culture', in *The American Journal of Sociology*, vol. 51, no. 3 (1945). See discussion below.

2 Although 'unity' (rendered in the Bahá'í writings usually by a number of various Arabic/ Persian words such as *vaḥdat, ittiḥád* and *tawḥíd*) can be taken in some ways as synonymous with 'love', it lays the stress on the properties of solidarity and strength resulting from the bond of love and affection. 'The foundation of divine teachings is the unity (*vaḥdat*) of the world of humanity' ('Abdu'l-Bahá, *Khiṭábát-i-Ḥaḍrat-i-'Abdu'l-Bahá*, p. 18); 'Today is the day of the unity (*vaḥdat*) of mankind and the union (*ittiḥád*) of all its peoples' (ibid. p. 20). The Universal House of Justice, the highest Bahá'í governing body, defines, for instance, the oneness of mankind as being 'at once the operating principle and ultimate goal of His Revelation' (*Messages*, p. 602).

3 See Shoghi Effendi, *The Advent of Divine Justice*, pp. 28–9: 'Small wonder, therefore, that the Author of the Bahá'í Revelation should have chosen to associate the name and title of that House, which is to be the crowning glory of His administrative institutions, not with forgiveness but with justice, to have made justice the only basis and the permanent foundation of His Most Great Peace (. . .)', and *The Promised Day Is Come*, para. 8, pp. 7–8. See also 'Abdu'l-Bahá, *The Promulgation of Universal Peace*, p. 181: 'According to the divine Will and intention religion should be the cause of love and agreement, a bond to unify all mankind, for it is a message of peace and good-will to man from God.'

4 'Abdu'l-Bahá, *The Promulgation of Universal Peace*, p. 32.

5 ibid. p. 97.

6 As noted by Smart, the Bahá'í Faith is perhaps the latest historical worldwide religion born into the modern age and possibly the first one to have recognized the stirrings of religious globalization (*The World's Religions*). For a study of the relationship between globalization and the Bahá'í Faith see for instance McGlinn, 'A Difficult Case: Beyer's Categories and the Bahá'í Faith', in *Social Compass*, vol. 50, no. 2 (2003); also Warburg, 'Baha'i: A Religious Approach to Globalization', in *Social Compass*, vol. 46, no. 1 (1999): 47–56.

7 See, for instance, Díaz, *Manual de historia de las religiones.*

8 Fazel, 'The Bahá'í Faith and Academic Journals', in *Bahá'í Studies Review*, vol. 3, no. 2 (1993).

9 Smith, *The Bábí and Bahá'í Religions: From Messianic Shi'ism to a World Religion.*

10 Smith's work was hailed by MacEoin (book review in *Bulletin of the School of Oriental and African Studies*, vol. 51, no. 3 (2009), pp. 557–558) as a salutary contribution to the topic,

praising his intelligent use of secondary sources and the application of sociological categories to its subject matter; his only main reservation concerned Smith's 'non-committal' position with regards to a number of issues as well as his use of the expression 'world religion' in reference to the Bahá'í Faith.

11 Berger, 'Motif messianique et processus social dans le Bahaisme', in *Archives de Sociologie des Religions*, vol. 2, no. 4 (1957), pp. 93–107.

12 Smith, *The Bábí and Bahá'í Religions*, p. 71.

13 See Cole, *Modernity and the Millennium*, p. 138.

14 See Warburg, *Citizens of the World: A History and Sociology of the Baha'is from a Globalisation Perspective*; also Warburg, Hvithamar, and Warmind (eds), *Baha'i and Globalisation*.

15 See Cole's review of the modernity concept in the introduction to *Modernity and the Millennium*, pp. 1–15. Cole's views are quite attuned to the survey by Christian Smith of the latest trends in the sociology of religion; see his 'Future directions in the sociology of religion', in *Social Forces*, vol. 86, no. 4 (30 June 2008), pp. 1561–1589.

16 See Scharbrodt, *Islam and the Baha'i Faith*.

17 See Alkan, *Dissent and Heterodoxy in the Late Ottoman Empire, Reformers, Babis and Baha'is*. Alkan has made extensive use of primary sources extant in Turkish archives documenting some of the connections between Bahá'u'lláh, 'Abdu'l-Bahá and the Ottoman elites.

18 Cole, *Modernity and the Millennium*, pp. 123–4.

19 See Banani, 'Some Reflections on Juan Cole's *Modernity and the Millennium*'. *Bahá'í Studies Review*, vol. 9 (1999/2000): 159–162; and Cole's response at http://www- personal.umich.edu/~jrcole/bahai/2001/colerepl.htm.

20 See Cole, *Modernity and the Millenium*, pp. 5, 47, 110, and 128.

21 ibid. p. 195. The coinage 'utopian realism' is borrowed by Cole from Anthony Giddens' book *The Consequences of Modernity* (1991). Attempts to recombine utopian and realist positions have tended to be overconscious of H. E. Carr's critique of utopianism in his *The Twenty Years Crisis 1919–1939: An Introduction to the Study of International Relations*. For a discussion of the concept see Booth, 'Security in anarchy: Utopian realism in theory and practice', in *International Affairs*, vol. 67, no. 3 (1991), pp. 527–545. John Howard Yoder has also argued repeatedly about the realist (empirical) rootedness of a number of utopian projects (see his 'The Procession of Peace Plans', in Yoder, *Chapters in the History of Religiously Rooted Nonviolence Work* (1994).

22 Cole compares Bahá'u'lláh and 'Abdu'l-Bahá's ideas with the postulates of the Saint-Simonians to show both commonalities and important differences (*Modernity and the Millenium*, pp. 123–4). Similarly, one may notice important and perhaps more contemporaneous parallels with the various streams of liberal thought and their common causes: anti-dogmatism, anti-slavery, anti-imperialism, anti-colonialism, and anti-sacerdotalism. Indeed, the use of the adjective 'liberal' by Shoghi Effendi carries always the positive sense of generosity, magnanimity and tolerance.

23 George Boas has analysed the various streams of early French internationalism, including Maistre's and Lammenais' Christian varieties; see Boas, 'Types of Internationalism in Early Nineteenth-Century France', in *International Journal of Ethics*, vol. 38, no. 2 (1928), pp. 141–152.

24 Cole, *Modernity and the Millennium*, p. 138.

25 See Saiedi, *Logos and Civilization*, pp. 242–57.

26 See MacEoin, 'Bábí Concept of Holy War', in *Religion*, vol. 12, no. 2 (1983): 93–129.

27 See Opler, 'Themes as Dynamic Forces in Culture', p. 198.

28 It should be noted that the idea in Lovejoy is far from being circumscribed to a limited definitional range of meaning. In describing the business of the historian of ideas, Lovejoy

– it should be recalled – identified the following principal types, which he regarded as the 'elements, the primary and persistent or recurrent dynamic units, of the history of thought': 1) 'assumptions', 'more or less unconscious mental habits', 'types of imagery' (for instance 'simplicity/complexity'); 2) 'dialectical motives', 'one or another turn of reasoning, trick of logic, methodological assumption' (such as the 'nominalistic motive' or the 'organismic motive'); 3) 'metaphysical pathos' ('pathos of sheer obscurity', 'pathos of the esoteric', 'eternalistic pathos', 'monistic pathos', 'voluntaristic pathos'); 4) 'philosophical semantics'; and finally 5) the idea par excellence, consisting in 'a single specific proposition or "principle" expressly enunciated by the most influential of early European philosophers together with some further propositions which are, or have been supposed to be, its corollaries'. Lovejoy explains that this idea must be traced through all the fields in life where it manifests itself, if necessary transcending national boundaries or disciplinary barriers. It must additionally be possessed of a special generalness or massive projection, for it is this fact that lends the idea its colouring and ensures its diffusion and persistence (See Lovejoy, *Great Chain of Being*, pp. 7–17).

29 See Mandelbaum, 'The History of Ideas, Intellectual History, and the History of Philosophy', in *History and Theory*, no. 5 (1965), p. 38.

30 The overstating of these precedents and influences was a concern for Lovejoy, who worried about its deleterious implications, a point he saw illustrated in Mannheim's statement that 'even one's point of view may *always* be expected to be peculiar to one's [social] position'. See Lovejoy, 'Reflections on the History of Ideas', in *Journal of the History of Ideas*, vol. 1, no. 1 (1940): p. 17 (emphasis added).

31 This is of course akin to Lovejoy's insistent plea for a study that in transcending artificial boundaries is able to locate 'expressions' and currents of thought latent in areas where least expected: English eighteenth-century gardening and romanticism being but a case among many such instances.

32 Lovejoy insisted also in relating 'the particular facts with which their researches are concerned to the theory of human nature as a subject matter common to them all, and needing, for its adequate historical treatment, to be pursued through them all' (see *Reflections on Human Nature*, pp. 12–14).

33 Lovejoy, *Great Chain of Being*, p. 3: '[the idea is] not only a compound but an unstable compound . . . One of the results of the quest of the unit-ideas in such a compound is, I think, bound to be a livelier sense of the fact that most philosophic systems are original or distinctive rather in their patterns than in their components.'

34 See Opler, 'Themes as Dynamic Forces in Culture', p. 198.

35 The assessment of this question is in part clouded by the fact that, by association with the English terms 'prejudice' and 'fanaticism' (*ta'aṣṣub)*, the entire matter assumes additional dimensions amplified by the critique of 'tradition' usually found among enlightened authors, and the parallel conservative defence of both 'prejudice' and 'tradition'. The whole question is further magnified by the metaphysical and psychological concepts of *awḥam* (vain imaginings) and idle fancies, which refer back to an implicit spiritual anthropology (see Part IV).

36 The identification of themes and counterthemes when discussing key unit ideas such as peace could also prove illuminating when establishing differences and similarities between the Abrahamic religions. The fact that some of their building blocs are in fact almost interchangeable make it all the more necessary to look at the variety of combinations and re-combinations that these basic elements have originated in time. Their distinctiveness may, as suggested by González Ferrín, be the result of 'retroactive continuity', a rewriting of the past commensurate with present expectations (see *La angustia de Abraham: Los orígenes culturales del Islam*, Almuzara, 2013).

37 Not much has been made for instance of the fact that the first systematic accounts of Bahá'í principles about the Faith were produced in the context of 'Abdu'l-Bahá's first encounters in the West (when He was at greater liberty to speak out) and necessarily in the compacted way afforded by the format of public orations mediated by interpreters. Yet, no more than eight years elapsed from those momentous tours of the West to the issuance of the Tablet to The Hague, arguably the most comprehensive peace statement that Bahá'ís were to have at their disposal until 1985, the year when the statement *The Promise of World Peace* was released by the Universal House of Justice.

1 Bahá'u'lláh

1 Bahá'u'lláh, as reported by Edward Granville Browne, quoted in *The Compilation of Compilations*, p. 157. This quotation has been widely used by Bahá'ís and occupies an important place in Bahá'í literature.

2 Cole, *Modernity and the Millenium*, p. 76. This is not quite exact if the whole of Bahá'u'lláh's production is considered. Demonstrative tracts like the Kitáb-i-Íqán, or His Book of Laws (the Kitáb-i-Aqdas or *al-Kitáb al-Aqdas*) are written in remarkably lucid prose and it may not be too bold a claim to say that their respective aims were to render apocalyptic categories graspable and current, and to refashion divine law into a highly simplified and dynamic system.

3 Radhakrishnan, *The Philosophy of Rabindranath Tagore*, p. viii.

4 See in particular the recollections of Bahíyyih Khánum, Bahá'u'lláh's daughter, in Blomfield, *The Chosen Highway*.

5 See Shoghi Effendi, *God Passes By*, p. 138.

6 Bahá'u'lláh, Lawḥ-i-Ra'ís, para. 16, in *The Summons of the Lord of Hosts*, pp. 167–8.

7 The Banu Qurayzah was a Jewish tribe who allegedly betrayed the Muslim camp during the Battle of the Trench (or Moat) and was finally massacred after a protracted siege (See Cole, *Modernity and the Millenium*, p. 115, following Bahá'u'lláh as quoted by Ishráq-Khávarí (comp.), *Ma'idiy-i-Ásmání*, vol. 7, p. 136). The slaughter of the Qurayzah tribe has been a moot point in the biography of the Prophet and a stumbling block in the thorny relationships between Islam and Judaism from then onwards. The assessment of the event varies however from author to author; see Watt, *Muhammad, Prophet and Statesman*, pp. 171–5; Rodinson, *Mahoma, el nacimiento del mundo islámico*, pp. 195–7; and Gaudefroy-Demonbynes, *Mahomet*, pp. 142–6. For a new approach to the question see McGlinn, 'Baha'u'llah's "Tablet of the Banu Qurayza"'.

8 The religious significance of this episode in Bahá'u'lláh's life would certainly not be lost on future converts of Jewish background and has implications for religious dialogue as a whole, at least to the extent that the Banu Qurayzah massacre stands as a controversial point marking a gulf of division between the two 'Semitic' communities.

9 I follow Balyuzi's account in *Bahá'u'lláh, the King of Glory*. Of interest as well are data provided by Amanat, *Resurrection and Renewal: The Making of the Bábí Movement in Iran, 1844–1850,* particularly pp. 361–5.

10 See Blomfield, *The Chosen Highway*, p. 40.

11 See Balyuzi, *Bahá'u'lláh, the King of Glory,* pp. 13–18. Other details gleaned from various sources available in English can be found in Ruhe, *Robe of Light: The Persian Years of the Supreme Prophet Bahá'u'lláh*, pp. 43–7.

12 See Rafati, 'The Development of Shaykhí Thought in Shí'í Islam', pp. 3–7.

13 Amanat, *Pivot of the Universe: Nasir al-Din Shah Qajar and the Iranian Monarchy 1831–1896*, pp. 215–17. Bahá'u'lláh was at the time of His arrest a guest of the Prime Minister, the Sadr Azam, Mírzá Áqá Núrí. This fact alone put the minister under suspicion of collusion with Bahá'u'lláh. The Shah's mother exploited this connection not only to denounce Bahá'u'lláh,

but also to force Núrí to distance himself from the prisoner, a manoeuvre that allowed her to regain ascendancy over her young son. There are good reasons to believe that the particularly macabre ceremony of bloodshed, which involved the participation of all ranks and classes in the execution of the Bábís, was Núrí's way of proving himself innocent of any such collusion.

14 On the appearance of this Messianic figure, as well as on the various datings for his coming, and the number of claimants that appear to have proclaimed themselves after the execution of the Báb, see MacEoin, 'Hierarchy, Authority and Eschatology in Early Babi Thought' and 'Divisions and Authority Claims in Babism (1850–1866)'; also Saiedi, *Gate of the Heart*, passim.

15 The messianic secret theme is extensively explored by Buck in his *Symbol and Secret*, throughout his work, and by Saiedi in his *Logos and Civilization.*

16 Bahá'u'lláh, *Epistle to the Son of the Wolf*, p. 21.

17 Fear of revenge explains the formidable wave of repression unleashed to wipe out the remnants of Babism. In order to diffuse personal responsibility for the death of the Bábís, the State authorities, from the Shah's deputy down to the lower echelons in society, were forced to participate actively in the public executions. Gobineau, Lord Curzon and other authors have left us an impressive account of this elaborate execution (see the copious notes running from pages 599 to 621 in Nabíl, *The Dawn-Breakers*); see also Amanat, *Pivot of the Universe*, pp. 214–17.

18 To be sure, from the Bábí ranks there emerged so many claimants to the position of 'Him Whom God shall make manifest' (i.e. the next Manifestation of God) that the virtual disintegration of the Bábí community by the time Bahá'u'lláh resided in Baghdad was almost a foregone conclusion.

19 Regarding the appointment of Mírzá Yaḥyá, known by the title attributed to him by Browne, of Ṣubḥ-i-Azal (1831–1912), as a nominal figurehead, see Shoghi Effendi, *God Passes By*, pp. 28–9, as well as the elucidations on the subject by the Research Department of the Universal House of Justice in a memorandum dated 28 May 2004 (http://www.h-net.org/~bahai/docs/vol9/Research_Dept_2004_May_28.pdf). Of interest too are Ḥájí Mírzá Ḥaydar-'Alí's observations, op. cit, pp. 8–9. See also MacEoin, 'From Babism to Baha'ism', pp. 220–21, and *The Messiah of Shiraz*, pp. 370–407.

20 MacEoin has tended to portray the situation the other way around, in other words, it is Bahá'u'lláh who would have followed in the footsteps of his half-brother by moving to Iraq, and he again the one who returned from his two-year seclusion in Kurdistan at the behest of Ṣubḥ-i-Azal (*The Messiah of Shiraz*, pp. 384 and 396).

21 Quoted by Phelps, *The Master in 'Akká*, p. 24.

22 See Hatcher and Martin, *The Bahá'í Faith: The Emerging Global Religion*, pp. 35–6; and Schaefer, Towfigh and Gollmer: *Desinformation als Methode: Die Bahá'ísmus Monographie des F. Ficiccia*, pp. 492–503 (trans. *Making the Crooked Straight).* A similar and equally decisive cutting off from friends and foes occurred at a later period, in Edirne, when the Bábís were given the choice to accept the leadership of either Mírzá Yaḥyá or Bahá'u'lláh Himself.

23 *'Atabát* (lit. 'thresholds') are the Shí'i shrine cities in southern Iraq (i.e. Karbala, Najaf, Kaẓimayn, and Samarra).

24 See Balyuzi, *Bahá'u'lláh, the King of Glory*, pp. 145–6.

25 See Bahá'u'lláh, *Surih-i-Sabr, or Lawḥ-i-Ayyub,* provisional translation by Khazeh Fananapazir at http://Bahá'ístudies.net/kf/sabr.html.

26 See Momen, *An Introduction to Shi'i Islam*, p. 231.

27 See Willis, 'Jihad fi Sabil Allah – Its Doctrinal Basis in Islam and Some Aspects of Its Evolution in Nineteenth Century West Africa'.

28 See Nabíl, *The Dawn-Breakers*, p. 144.

29 For a review of *jihád* in the writings of the Báb see MacEoin, 'Bábí Concept of Holy War'.

30 Customarily, a declaration of *jihád* needs to be formalized through a *fatwa*, i.e. a decree issued by a properly recognized religious authority; such declaration must have been preceded by sufficient warnings summoning enemies to repentance.

31 See Note 108 in Bahá'u'lláh, *The Kitáb-i-Aqdas*, pp. 212–13.

32 See Saiedi, *Gate of the Heart*, pp. 357–71.

33 See Zabihi-Moghadam, 'The Babi-State Conflict at Shaykh Tabarsi'.

34 See Ayoub, *Redemptive Suffering, in Islam: A Study of the Devotional Aspects of 'Ashura' in Twelver Shi'ism*, p. 141.

35 See Nabíl, *The Dawn-Breakers*, p. 298: 'In the course of their journey to Mazindaran, a few of the followers of the Báb sought to abuse the liberty which the repudiation of the laws and sanctions of an outgrown Faith had conferred upon them. They viewed the unprecedented action of Ṭáhirih in discarding the veil as a signal to transgress the bounds of moderation and to gratify their selfish desires. The excesses in which a few indulged provoked the wrath of the Almighty and caused their immediate dispersion. In the village of Níyalá, they were grievously tested and suffered severe injuries at the hands of their enemies. This scattering extinguished the mischief which a few of the irresponsible among the adherents of the Faith had sought to kindle, and preserved untarnished its honour and dignity.'

36 This has become a moot point in reassessments of Iranian history by scholars of liberal and Shí'ih persuasions alike. On the one hand the upheavals of Zanján, Nayríz and Ṭabarsí are often interpreted, *tout court*, as religiously motivated 'rebellions' (*fitnih, surish*) against a legally constituted authority, hence deserving of condemnation. For lay and secularist historians part of the conundrum lies in the difficulty of reconciling a lionized image of Amir Kabir with the brutal quelling of the local 'revolts'. This reconciliation is made easier by overstating the political motivations of the Bábís and also by delegitimizing any of their claims for opposing resistance in what proved to be heavily charged contexts. An overlay of nationalistic modernizing pride also tends to project retrospectively an image of the Bábí upheavals as either anachronistic or 'pre-revolutionary'. On the other hand, the same qualms tend to disappear when the overall Constitutionalist Revolution (*inqiláb-i-mashuṭih*) and the Iranian Revolution itself are considered from the vantage point of their alleged intrinsic legitimacy. The taboo nature of the topic in contemporary Iran means that more often than not the question is bypassed or treated summarily in the conventional ways just mentioned. Outside Iran, however, re-evaluations of the phenomenon in public media are no longer an oddity, an instance of which is the reassessment of Amir Kabir achievements in the BBC's *Pargar* interview by Dariush Karimi in October 2018, 'Muhammad Amíní, Saíd Payvandí, and Iraj Ishráqi: Amir Kabir and his legacy'.

37 A summary of the questions put to Bahá'u'lláh by the Báb's uncle is included in Balyuzi, *Bahá'u'lláh, The King of Glory*, pp. 164–5.

38 Bahá'u'lláh, in *Tablets of Bahá'u'lláh*, p. 85.

39 ibid. p. 91.

40 ibid. p. 94. And again, on a more personal note, in one of the *Hidden Words* (Arabic no. 42) Bahá'u'lláh explains that triumph cannot be attained unless the believer humbles himself before God: 'O Son of Man! Humble thyself before Me that I may graciously visit thee. Arise for the triumph [*náṣrán*] of My cause, that while yet on earth thou mayest obtain the victory [*manṣúrín*].'

41 The idea that this world is but a reflection of another world – the Kingdom of Abhá – is important for an understanding of this question. Revelation is seen in Arabic and Muslim terms quite literally as a 'descent'. Bahá'u'lláh's first intimations of his mission at the Síyáh-Chál (the Black Pit) came, while he was asleep, as a sudden stream that would gush down from the

crown of his head onto his breast, resulting in a profusion of verses (See Bahá'u'lláh, *Kitáb-i-Íqán*, pp. 63–4).

42 Bahá'u'lláh, *Tablets of Bahá'u'lláh*, p. 21. Here the term 'Book' does not appear to signify so much a specific book, as the new Gospel (see Bahá'u'lláh, *Epistle to the Son of the Wolf*, p. 145), the 'Book' of his Revelation, inasmuch as the Mother Book can be taken as meaning the eternal Word of God. According to Bushrui: 'The term "Mother book" generally signifies the central book of a religious Dispensation, as for example, the Qur'án for Muslims, the Bayán for Bábís, and the Kitáb-i-Aqdas for Bahá'ís. According to Shoghi Effendi, it is also a "collective term indicating the body of the teachings revealed by Bahá'u'lláh". In a looser sense "Mother Book" is also the Divine Repository of Revelation' (*The Style of the Kitáb-i-Aqdas: Aspects of the Sublime*, pp. 57–8).

43 It is this act alone that seems to secure that the intended results are effected in due time. But since this is just a matter of course, the timeless view prevails and things are observed in their simultaneity from the vantage point of that primeval realm where the Word of God and its realization are one and the same.

44 Bahá'u'lláh, *Gleanings*, C, p. 203: 'It beseemeth all men, in this Day, to take firm hold on the Most Great Name, and to establish the unity of all mankind. There is no place to flee to, no refuge that anyone can seek, except Him.'

45 See Cole, 'Iranian Millenarianism and Democratic Thought in the 19th Century'.

46 See Bahá'u'lláh, *Hidden Words*, and also Taherzadeh, *The Revelation of Bahá'u'lláh*, vol. 2, p. 96.

47 See Part IV below.

48 During the period of his exile in Edirne (1863–68) and the early 'Akká period, Bahá'u'lláh addressed the kings, rulers and religious authorities of the world. The disclosure of his mission was emphatic and couched in eschatological terms.

49 See Amanat, *Pivot of the Universe*, pp. 232–7.

50 A *mujtahid* is a leading Islamic expert or jurisconsult entitled to exert *ijtihád* and hence to issue expert opinions on matters pertaining to the religious law; see Momen, *An Introduction to Shi'i Islam*, pp. 186–7.

51 Following Kohlberg (*Understanding Jihad*, pp. 90–92), who notes that the Persian calls to *jihád* lacked the intellectual grounding and incisiveness of similar pre- and post-dated documents.

52 'Abdu'l-Bahá would condemn even more explicitly the role that the *'ulamá* had played throughout history in meddling in political affairs, and especially in inflaming passions that would lead to wars of *jihád* with catastrophic results. In the *Secret of Divine Civilization* (1875) he describes the Crusades as wars of religion (*ḥarb-i-díní*) or *jihád* (p. 90; corresponding to p. 107 of the Cairo edition, and p. 62 of the 'Aṣr-i-Jadíd edition); and in a *Traveller's Narrative* (1886; see pp. 87–92 corresponding to pp. 94–8 of the German edition in Persian), as well as in his *Treatise on Governance (the Risáliy-Síyásíyyih)* (1892; see pp. 88–92 of the 'Aṣr-i-Jadíd edition in Persian) 'Abdu'l-Bahá provides further examples instantiating the kind of debacles propitiated at the instigation of the Muslim clerics both in Iranian and Ottoman territories.

53 See Shoghi Effendi, *God Passes By*, p. 143, and Balyuzi, *Bahá'u'lláh, the King of Glory*, p. 145.

54 See Buck, 'The Eschatology of Globalization, the Multiple Messiahship of Bahá'u'lláh Revisited'.

55 Bahá'u'lláh, *The Summons of the Lord of Hosts*, p. 109.

56 A *hadith* is a holy tradition reporting a saying uttered or an act performed by the Prophet Muhammad or his successors.

57 Bahá'u'lláh, *Epistle to the Son of the Wolf*, p. 90.

58 'Abdu'l-Bahá reaffirms this in *The Secret of Divine Civilization*, where he assigns the 'highest station . . . in creation' to 'the Prophets of God', followed by the Holy Ones, the kings, with their ministers, and then the learned and wise.

59 In the Shí'i twelver tradition the last of the twelve Imams is said to have moved into two phases of occultation, one known as the Lesser Occultation, where he would still communicate through a series of four deputies, known as the Gates or *Abwáb* (*Báb*), and the second known as the Great Occultation, which was to conclude with his victorious and military reappearance at the eschaton, when he is expected to defeat the unbelievers by the power of his sword.

60 See Balyuzi, *Bahá'u'lláh, the King of Glory,* pp. 306–7. This episode is exceptionally well documented. A photograph of Badí' was taken during the interrogation proceedings, a full account of which was provided by Muḥammad-Valí Khán who first heard it from the *farrash-báshí* responsible for torturing Badí'; see also Bahiyyih Nakhjavani, *Asking Questions: A Challenge to Fundamentalism*, pp. 120–21.

61 A petition would have entailed that not only was Bahá'u'lláh in a subordinate position, but also a recognition that the Shah had a discretionary capacity to accept or refuse His injunctions. On the significance of court etiquette and royal demeanour see the 'Murray incident' as recounted by Amanat, *Pivot of the Universe*.

62 See Lambden, 'The Voice of God and the Supreme Pen: Some Aspects of the "Letters to Kings and Rulers" of Muhammad, the Bab (d. 1850) and Baha'-Allah (d. 1892)'. For the text of Jesus' apocryphal letter to the Syrian King Abgar see de Santos, *Los Evangelios apócrifos, edición crítica y bilingüe*, pp. 662–9.

63 See *Selections from the Writings of the Báb*, p. 41: 'O concourse of kings and of the sons of kings! Lay aside, one and all, your dominion which belongeth unto God. Let not thy sovereignty deceive thee, O Shah, for "every soul shall taste of death", and this, in very truth, hath been written down as a decree of God.' For more details as to the content of the Báb's addresses to the kings and religious authorities, see Shoghi Effendi, *God Passes By*, pp. 23–4.

64 For a comprehensive introduction to the background of the Mirror of Princes literature see Darling, 'Do Justice, Do Justice, for That Is Paradise: Middle Eastern Advice for Indian Muslim Rulers'.

65 In his study of Biblical prophets, José Luis Sicre notes the following characteristics: a Prophet is an *inspired public man*, who *undergoes constant threat* and is endowed with a *charisma* that *shatters all human standards* (*Introducción al Antiguo Testamento*, pp. 187–190).

66 See note 19 above.

67 Bahá'u'lláh, *The Kitáb-i-Aqdas*, para. 75, p. 47.

68 The feeling of a shared or communal expression of faith is strong because faith through *taqlíd* (the emulating faith) is the natural condition in which the common people find themselves.

69 Bausani, 'Can Monotheism Be Taught?: (Further Considerations on the Typology of Monotheism)' pp. 174–5. Bausani goes on to explain why Islam has historically lacked missionaries, and the kind of contempt with which the proselytising efforts of Christian (and modern Muslim) missionaries have been seen.

70 'Abdu'l-Bahá, quoted in Esslemont, *Bahá'u'lláh and the New Era*, p. 170; Persian text available in *Bahá'u'lláh va 'Aṣr-i-Jadíd*, p. 191.

71 Bahá'u'lláh, *Kitáb-i-Aqdas*, para. 75, p. 47.

72 See Cole, *Modernity and the Millennium*, p. 33; for a more extensive treatment of the *Tanẓimát* see Gutiérrez de Terán, *Estado y confesión en Oriente Medio,* pp. 35–67, and *Encyclopedia Iranica* sv 'Tanẓimát', vol. 10.

73 Regarding the various acts of desacralization, the abolition of *jihád* one amongst them, performed by Bahá'u'lláh in His works, see Buck, *Paradise and Paradigm: Key Symbols in Persian Christianity and the Bahá'í Faith*, pp. 149–50.

74 Bahá'u'lláh, *Gleanings*, CXX, p. 255.
75 Shoghi Effendi, *God Passes By*, pp. 223–4.
76 This is particularly true of his Book of Laws; but it is equally applicable to other works such as the Lawḥ-i-Karmil or the Kitáb-i-Ahd (Bahá'u'lláh's Will and Testament), both of which are brief and highly symbolic in their allusions, yet vital for the virtual consolidation of the Bahá'í Faith. This condensation of meaning is a feature of Bahá'u'lláh's style in general.
77 Shoghi Effendi, *God Passes By*, p. 194.
78 The impact that this interview had on Browne is known to have been considerable, as further details of the experience make it abundantly clear. He had been somewhat ill-disposed towards Bahá'u'lláh, but the meetings reconciled him with his original interest and set him again on his single-handedly undertaking the task of studying the Bábí and Bahá'í religions; his efforts were later dampened by criticisms from fellow academics and his own advocacy of a Bahá'í endorsement of the pro-constitutionalist movement, which explains his subsequent interest in Azalí Babism. See Balyuzi, *Edward Granville Browne and the Bahá'í Faith*, pp. 55–60.
79 Quoted by Momen, *The Bábí and Bahá'í Religions*, p. 231.
80 This is one of the several symmetrical pairs of correlates that can be found in the Bahá'í writings. They usually mark a crucial difference in the understanding of a sequence, hierarchy or function.
81 See 'Abdu'l-Bahá, *Khiṭábát-i-Ḥaḍrat-i-'Abdu'l-Bahá*, pp. 20 and 457.
82 'Alí Nakhjavání, *Towards World Order*, p. 8.
83 The notion of a rejection of Bahá'u'lláh's message on the part of the great powers and of a consequent warning about the effects this would entail brings into relief the nature of Bahá'u'lláh's judgement. Shoghi Effendi's book *The Promised Day Is Come* can be regarded as a dramatized account of the retribution awaiting most of Bahá'u'lláh's powerful addressees. However, an even more penetrating insight into Shoghi Effendi's view on this issue is afforded by Rabbani, *The Priceless Pearl*, pp. 191–2.
84 Bahá'u'lláh, *Gleanings*, CXIX, pp. 253–4.
85 Bahá'u'lláh, *Tablets of Bahá'u'lláh*, p. 23.
86 ibid. pp. 89–90. Contrasts of this nature are not unfamiliar to a Muslim audience. Thus, for instance, in Sufi circles there is already an established contrast between the concept of holy war (understood as the spiritual struggle any person must engage in) and the minor holy war (the external and far less important struggle).
87 Burgel, 'The Bahá'í Attitude towards Peace and its Christian and Islamic Background', in Moayyad (ed), *The Bahá'í Faith and Islam*, p. 42.
88 See Cole, *Modernity and the Millennium*, pp. 113–14.
89 See *Encyclopedia Iranica*, new ed: 'Kull-i-Ṣulḥ' (by M. Athar Ali), vol. IX, p. 846.
90 Qur'án 4:128.
91 Lewis, *The Political Language of Islam*, pp. 78–80. The other word for peace is *salám*, which traditionally has been used in the non-political sense of religious security, i.e. denoting salvation. Its use to convey the notion of a state of peace, as opposed to war, is clearly modern (ibid. p. 79).
92 Hence the Arabic translation of famous European peace treaties such as those signed in Utrecht or Versailles using the word ṣulḥ. It should be noted that the triliteral root ṣ-l-ḥ, with the basic meaning of wholesomeness, rectitude and goodness, is present in at least two other key words from a political point of view, namely *iṣláḥ* (reform) and *maṣáliḥ* (vital interests, national interests).
93 See Cole, *Modernity and the Millennium*, pp. 120–21.
94 Crucé in his *Le Nouveau Cynée* (1623) and Comenius in his *Panorthosia* and *Angelus Pacis* had put forward proposals along similar lines (see Comenius, *Panorthosia or Universal*

Reform, chapters 19 to 26.) For a more detailed exposition of the French peace projects see Souleyman, *The Vision of World Peace in Seventeenth and Eighteenth-Century France.*

95 See for example Rousseau, *A Lasting Peace and the State of War*, pp. 36–91.

96 Rousseau believed that peace was a state of disguised war that was born out of specific social conditions; he also believed that war was an inter-State phenomenon (*The Social Contract,* pp. 5–13), and that a European confederation, such as the one proposed by Saint-Pierre, was not likely to be perceived as beneficial by the rulers and sovereigns since, in their minds, individual advantages would outdo collective ones, thus justifying them in taking the risk of mobilizing for war. Rousseau adduced Henri IV's project for a European union as an instance of how a coalition of sovereign powers would not succeed despite the obvious advantages which would accrue to each of the participating countries. Needless to say, he added, they would not resort to a supreme tribunal to settle their differences, any more than they would submit their dealings to the authority of one of their own tribunals.

97 See Kant, *Perpetual Peace: A Philosophical Essay*. Most of the peace programmes articulated by the above authors condensed ideas freely available in the way of enlightened commonplaces. Even in Catholic Spain, typically enlightened concepts such as peace, commerce, free trade, construction of channels and roads, or circulation of ideas had gained wide currency. As noted by Maragall, these notions were based on the discovery of an inherent dynamism in society, as revealed by the ubiquitous notions of progress, traffic, flows and exchanges. Most of the Enlightenment authors had nevertheless great difficulties in reconciling self-interest with public and private interests in a wholesome society (see Maragall, *Estudios de la historia del pensamiento español, s. XVIII*, pp. 254–5). This dichotomy remains still unsolved to this day. The Bahá'í response seems to have consisted in reclaiming the priority of moral impulses (as opposed to self-interest and prejudices), moderated by an informed religious conscience.

98 See de Jouvenel, *Los orígenes del Estado moderno: Historia de las ideas políticas en el siglo XIX*, pp. 279–80. The prevailing rhetoric at the time was one of optimism and in many ways a precursor of the ideology justifying the benefits of modern globalization.

99 See Mattelart, *La comunicación-mundo: Historia de las ideas y de las estrategias*, pp. 62–5.

100 In his book *The Search for the Perfect Language* Umberto Eco has documented the various streams of thought that went into the search for a 'perfect' language, whether a natural, re-created, logical or scientific one.

101 See Cole, *Modernity and the Millennium*, p. 130.

102 It should be noted that among the outcomes of the Treaty of Paris (1856) the following are commonly listed: the demilitarization of the Black Sea, the virtual independence of Moldavia and Valachia, the end of the protectorate extended over Christian followers by Russia and France, and the further independence of Serbia and other Romanian principalities from Ottoman rule.

103 See Hobsbawm, *The Age of Capital*, pp. 88–102.

104 Holsti, *Peace and War: Armed Conflicts and International Order, 1648–1989*, p. 137. Similarly, Henry Kissinger concludes in his book *Diplomacy*: 'The Concert of Europe was ultimately shattered on the anvil of the Eastern Question'. For his part, Adam Zamoyski in *Rites of Peace: The Fall of Napoleon and the Congress of Vienna*, questions the idealized image of the achievements imputable to the Vienna Congress, especially Kissinger's characterization of the nineteenth century as the century of peace (pp. 553–4).

105 See Calduch, *Dinámica de la sociedad internacional*, pp. 407–8.

106 At present discussions are centred on the regulation of the conditions that would make for a threat to peace, a breach of the peace or an act of aggression and the types of corresponding actions that these would trigger on the part of the UN Security Council. Unavoidably, the issue is bound up with the delimitation of powers between the Security Council and the International

Court of Justice, on the one hand, and the place of regional concerts of collective security, on the other. For a discussion on the pros and cons of collective security see Kupchan and Kupchan, 'The Promise of Collective Security'. On the prohibition of the use of force, see Ruiz de los Paños, 'La prohibición del uso de la fuerza', pp. 603–4.

107 Currently the distinction between 'collective security' and 'collective self-defence' has little value as most countries abide by the authority of United Nations (see Simma, *The Charter of the United Nations: A Commentary*, p. 42).

108 See Calduch, *Dinámica de la sociedad internacional*, pp. 411–13. According to Ch. Rousseau (cit. by Calduch, pp. 414–15), there are three basic elements in any effective system of collective security, to wit:

a) the regulation of the use of armed forces

i. prohibition of the recourse to force as a valid means for the conduct of international politics

ii. limitation of armed forces

iii. restrictions on the use of legal force

b) the adoption of procedures for the peaceful resolution of international conflicts

iv. creation of agencies and institutions to decide in cases of conflict

v. institution of norms for the peaceful settlement of international disputes

vi. adoption of effective sanctions in case of violation

c) the organization of collective action against the aggressor

vii. decision on whom and how to assess a threat or a violation

viii. adoption of a gradual system of coercion

ix. specifications on executive organs and conditions applying to the specific solutions adopted.

109 See Inis, *Swords into Plowshares: The Problems and Progress of International Organization*, pp. 245–85. For a comparative treatment of collective security in both Inis and the Bahá'í writings, see Sabet, 'Bahá'u'lláh's Concept of Collective Security in Historical and Theoretical Perspective'.

110 See the memorandum by the Research Department of the Universal House of Justice, dated 1 May 2001 (http://www.Bahá'í-library.com/resources/tablets-notes/lawh-maqsud/notes.html).

111 Bahá'u'lláh, Súriy-i-Haykal, para. 181, in *The Summons of the Lord of Hosts*, p. 93.

112 ibid. para. 182, p. 94.

113 The obvious connections and similarities between the two texts may dispense us from repeating Cole's observations regarding the immediate historic context for the Lawḥ-i-Maqṣúd, which coincided with the period when Egypt had just undergone an imposed restoration of the Khedive by British rule. In the Tablet of Bis͟hárát Bahá'u'lláh confirms that the sixth Glad-Tiding 'is the establishment of the Lesser Peace [*ṣulḥ-i-akbar*], details of which have formerly been revealed from Our Most Exalted Pen' (*Tablets of Bahá'u'lláh*, p. 23).

114 Bahá'u'lláh, Lawḥ-i-Maqṣúd, in *Tablets of Bahá'u'lláh*, pp. 165–6.

115 See Cole, *Modernity and the Millennium*, pp. 55–6, and 63.

116 Shoghi Effendi, *The Promised Day Is Come*, p. 45.

117 Bahá'u'lláh, *The Kitáb-i-Aqdas*, para. 88, p. 52.

118 Bahá'u'lláh, Súriy-i-Haykal, para. 181, in *The Summons of the Lord of Hosts*, p. 93.

119 Bahá'u'lláh, *Gleanings*, CXVIII, p. 249.

120 Bahá'u'lláh, *Gleanings*, CVI, p. 213.

121 Kant suggests that philosophers, and not just jurists, will have to be consulted in order to establish the new principles of war and peace.

122 Bahá'u'lláh, *Tablets of Bahá'u'lláh*, pp. 165–6. Other texts by Bahá'u'lláh regarding this question place the election of an international language in the hands of statesmen (ibid. p. 22),

or make it dependent upon a resolution to be made by 'the Trustees of the House of Justice' (ibid. p. 127; see also pp. 68 and 89). This is commonly taken to mean that whatever the chosen international language, it may ultimately fall upon the Universal House of Justice to endorse such a choice. UNESCO, which superseded the Intellectual Co-operation Committee which was part of the League of Nations, has dealt with the issue of the selection and adoption of an international auxiliary language, with no results other than some interesting reports.

123 See Appel, 'El proyecto filosófico para la paz perpetua de Kant como cuasi-pronóstico de la filosofía de la historia a partir del deber moral', in Kant, *La Paz Perpetua, doscientos años después*.

124 Balyuzi (*'Abdu'l-Bahá: The Centre of the Covenant*, pp. 440–41) refers to the following incident which occurred in late 1919: 'On October 4th, 'Abdu'l-Bahá, at the invitation of Major Williamson, the acting Military Governor of Haifa, went aboard a warship, H.M.S. Marlborough, which had taken part in the Battle of Jutland. He was shown round the ship, and when He was having tea with the Commander of the ship, Major Williamson, and Captain Lowick (deputy Military Governor of 'Akká), He said that this was the first time in His life that He had been on board a man-of-war, and He hoped and trusted that all the implements and means of warfare would be turned one day into means to promote peace and industrial prosperity, and that all the men-of-war would eventually become merchant ships, thereby stimulating trade and industry.'

125 Bahá'u'lláh, *Tablets of Bahá'u'lláh*, p. 23.

126 See Keegan, *A History of Warfare*, pp. 12–23. This is of course the 'realistic' premise par excellence underlying realist and neo-realist approaches to international relations.

127 Bahá'u'lláh, *Gleanings*, LXX, pp. 135–6, and *The Kitáb-i-Aqdas*, para. 157, p. 75 (and note 171), respectively.

128 Bahá'u'lláh, *Tablets of Bahá'u'lláh*, p. 167: "Blessed and happy is he that ariseth to promote the best interests of the peoples and kindreds of the earth. In another passage He hath proclaimed: It is not for him to pride himself who loveth his own country, but rather for him who loveth the whole world. The earth is but one country, and mankind its citizens.' 'Abdu'l-Bahá goes on to say in a similar context: 'wherever one inhabits that place is one's fatherland' (*Khiṭábát*, p. 715). Of course, a legal consequence of this thinking is that the citizenship of a person and hence their basic rights follows that person by virtue of their humanity, not on account of place of birth or nationality.

129 Bahá'u'lláh, Bishárát, in *Tablets of Bahá'u'lláh*, p. 28: 'Although a republican form of government profiteth all the peoples of the world, yet the majesty of kingship is one of the signs of God. We do not wish that the countries of the world should remain deprived thereof. If the sagacious combine the two forms into one, great will be their reward in the presence of God.'

130 Bahá'u'lláh, Súriy-i-Haykal, para. 173, in *The Summons of the Lord of Hosts*, p. 90.

131 Bahá'u'lláh, Lawḥ-i-Maqṣúd, in *Tablets of Bahá'u'lláh*, p. 167. There are probably very few texts that are better known and most widely quoted by Bahá'ís than this one. Significantly, this passage marks the conclusion of Bahá'u'lláh's address to the peoples of the world. E. G. Browne quotes almost identical words in the account of his personal encounter with Bahá'u'lláh (see Esslemont, *Bahá'u'lláh and the New Era*, pp. 37–8).

132 Bahá'u'lláh, Ishráqát, in *Tablets of Bahá'u'lláh*, p. 126.

133 'Abdu'l-Bahá quotes Bahá'u'lláh as follows: 'At one time We spoke in the language of the Law, at another time in the language of the Truth and the Way; and the ultimate object and remote aim was the showing forth of this high supreme station' (*A Traveller's Narrative*, p. 43).

134 Bahá'u'lláh, *Gleanings*, XXXIII, p. 77: 'No sooner had mankind attained the stage of maturity, than the Word revealed to men's eyes the latent energies with which it had been endowed –

energies which manifested themselves in the plenitude of their glory when the Ancient Beauty appeared, in the year sixty, in the person of 'Alí-Muḥammad, the Báb.'

135 ibid. CXX, p. 255.

136 Bahá'u'lláh, *Tablets of Bahá'u'lláh*, p. 89.

137 ibid. p. 168.

'Abdu'l-Bahá

1 'Abdu'l-Bahá, *Selections from the Writings of 'Abdu'l-Bahá*, no. 17, p. 36.

2 *Star of the West*, vol. 3, no. 7 (13 July 1912), p. 5.

3 See Bahá'u'lláh, *Tablets of Bahá'u'lláh*, pp. 219–23; and also Shoghi Effendi, *God Passes By*, pp. 237–43.

4 Although not regarded as a Manifestation of God, 'Abdu'l-Bahá is, as described by Shoghi Effendi, one of the three Central Figures of the Bahá'í Dispensation, thus bearing no possible comparison with any other creature. In this way, Shoghi Effendi made patently clear to the Bahá'í world at large the difference in station that was to characterize him as Guardian of the Bahá'í Faith compared to that of his Grandfather (see 'The Dispensation of Bahá'u'lláh', in Shoghi Effendi, *The World Order of Bahá'u'lláh*, pp. 130–40).

5 Fayḍí, *Hayát-i-Haḍrat-i-'Abdu'l-Bahá*.

6 Balyuzi, *'Abdu'l-Bahá: The Centre of the Covenant of Bahá'u'lláh*.

7 Of special value among the best-known reminiscences of 'Abdu'l-Bahá are the testimonials and memoirs of Youness Afroukhteh, *Memories of Nine Years in 'Akká*, and Maḥmúd Zarqání, *Maḥmúd's Diary: The Diary of Mírzá Maḥmúd-i-Zarqání Chronicling 'Abdu'l-Bahá's Journey to America*. See also, the series of memoirs by 'Abdu'l-Bahá's contemporaries and associates translated and made available online by Ahang Rabbani, at http://ahang.rabbani.googlepages.com/

8 Shoghi Effendi, *Bahá'í Administration*, p. 66: 'One thing and only one thing will unfailingly and alone secure the undoubted triumph of this sacred Cause, namely, the extent to which our own inner life and private character mirror forth in their manifold aspects the splendor of those eternal principles proclaimed by Bahá'u'lláh.'

9 In addition to the surveillance and restrictions imposed by the State authorities, 'Abdu'l-Bahá had to live at a time when personal security was still very much a private affair fraught with considerable dangers, only increased by the necessity of Bahá'ís to walk around unarmed (see Afroukhteh, *Memories of Nine Years in 'Akká*, pp. 123–5).

10 Opposition to 'Abdu'l-Bahá was particularly strong among some of his relatives and believers residing in 'Akká and Haifa. 'Abdu'l-Bahá's efforts at averting a spill-over effect on Iranian soil met with success, and the risk of a schism developing in the cradle of the Bahá'í Faith was thus completely averted.

11 The full picture of the reception of 'Abdu'l-Bahá in the West is only now starting to emerge in its proper historical context. See for instance, Stockman, *'Abdu'l-Bahá in America*; McNamara, *The Reception of 'Abdu'l-Bahá in Britain*; Egea, *The Apostle of Peace*.

12 This was reflected in the very title which 'Abdu'l-Bahá chose for the book containing the English version of his talks in North America: *The Promulgation of Universal Peace* (see p. xx, note).

13 Shoghi Effendi, *The Promised Day Is Come*, p. 116.

14 See Galtung, *Peace by Peaceful Means, Peace and Conflict, Development and Civilization*, pp. 2–8.

15 See Blomfield, *The Chosen Highway*, p. 194.

16 *The Secret of Divine Civilization* was written in Persian in 1875 and first published anonymously in Bombay in 1882. See *Le Secret de la Civilisation Divine* (Bruxelles: Maison D'Éditions Bahá'íes, 1973), p. 9.

17 'Abdu'l-Bahá, *Selections from the Writings of 'Abdu'l-Bahá*, no. 225, p. 284. The same idea is worded differently elsewhere: 'In material civilization good and evil advance together and maintain the same pace' ('Abdu'l-Bahá, *The Promulgation of Universal Peace*, p. 109); 'Natural civilization fosters both good and evil' (from *Ahmad's Diary*, 1913, quoted in *Compilation of the Holy Utterances of Baha'o'llah and Abdul Baha Concerning the Most Great Peace, War and Duty of the Bahais toward their Government*, Chicago, 1918, p. 188).
18 Bahá'u'lláh, *Gleanings*, CLXIV, p. 343.
19 Bahá'u'lláh, Kalimát-i-Firdawsíyyih, in *Tablets of Bahá'u'lláh*, p. 69.
20 'Abdu'l-Bahá, quoted in Blomfield, *The Chosen Highway*, pp. 183–4.
21 'Abdu'l-Bahá, *The Secret of Divine Civilization*, p. 46.
22 ibid. p. 63.
23 ibid. p. 64.
24 On the merits of The Hague Conventions see Rutherford, "The Hague and Ottawa Conventions: A Model for Future Weapon Ban Regimes'.
25 'Abdu'l-Bahá, *The Secret of Divine Civilization*, p. 64.
26 ibid. pp. 64–5.
27 ibid. p. 65.
28 ibid.
29 This would be a reversion to Ibn Khaldún's position, itself a progress.
30 'Abdu'l-Bahá, *The Secret of Divine Civilization*, p. 71.
31 See Ma'ani Ewing, *Collective Security within Reach*, pp. 10 and 54, who states that the principle of just war 'finds its corollary in Bahá'u'lláh's principle that force must be the servant of justice, that war fought for a righteous purpose can be a powerful basis of peace'. The first notion, i.e. force as the servant of justice, seems to be derived from Bahá'u'lláh, *The Kitáb-i-Aqdas*, para. 88, p. 52, as well as from the principle of collective security as defined by Bahá'u'lláh; the second seems more clearly deduced from 'Abdu'l-Bahá's above reference to cases when war might be justified. My position differs from Ma'ani's in that I consider that Bahá'u'lláh's 'abrogation' of *jihád* is also applicable, *mutatis mutandis*, to 'just war' theory (the two terms '*jihad*' and 'just' being functional equivalents in two different traditions that incorporate a full range of moral, religious and legalistic caveats). In reality, the 'abolition of war' requires a different standpoint from which the legitimacy of war and armed conflicts can be judged. True, the principle of collective security does not negate the use of force, but it implies the outlawing of war (any war) in principle between sovereign States living in an international condition of anarchy. 'Abdu'l-Bahá's recognition that force might be properly used in the cases He mentions (namely to 'to block the onset of the insurgent and the aggressor, or again . . . in a struggle to unify a divided state and people') may, if isolated from the important qualification that follows and the general context of His work, be taken as a backdoor way of receding into classical just war arguments, thereby voiding the concept of 'collective security' of its moral and practical content. One has only to see the use of 'just war' theory justifications supporting some twenty-first century egregious conflicts to realize the slippery nature of the argument when the overall political, legal and moral framework is overlooked.
32 This may be borne out specially by the charge given by Bahá'u'lláh in the Kitáb-i-Aqdas to the American republics to 'bind . . . the broken with the hands of justice, and crush the oppressor who flourisheth with the rod of the commandments of your Lord, the Ordainer, the All-Wise' (para. 88, p. 52).
33 See Lepard, *Rethinking Humanitarian Intervention: A Fresh Legal Approach Based on Fundamental Ethical Principles in International Law and World Religions*.
34 Esslemont, *Bahá'u'lláh and the New Era*, p. 172. Since Esslemont's work, originally published in 1923, was first read by Shoghi Effendi and subsequently in 1937 subjected to a major review

under his supervision, it can be said with some confidence that this particular understanding did enjoy a degree of endorsement by him.

35 'Abdu'l-Bahá, *'Abdu'l-Bahá in London*, p. 92.

36 See Wehr and Cowan, "umúmí', in *Arabic-English Dictionary*, p. 641.

37 'Abdu'l-Bahá, *Selections from the Writings of 'Abdu'l-Bahá*, no. 227, p. 297; *Muntakhabátí az Makátíb-i-Ḥaḍrat-i-'Abdu'l-Bahá* (Wilmette edition), p. 286.

38 'Abdu'l-Bahá, *Muntakhabátí az Makátíb-i-Ḥaḍrat-i-'Abdu'l-Bahá* (German edition), vol. 5, p. 226. See also p. 75 for a typical listing of the above terms in context.

39 See 'Abdu'l-Bahá, *The Promulgation of Universal Peace*, pp. 121 and 122–3; for the Persian transcript see *Khiṭábát*, p. 372.

40 'Abdu'l-Bahá, *'Abdu'l-Bahá in London*, pp. 69–70.

41 'Abdu'l-Bahá, *The Promulgation of Universal Peace*, p. 389. There seems to be an echo here of Tennyson's poem 'Locksley Hall': 'Till the war-drum throbb'd no longer, and the battle-flags were furl'd/ In the Parliament of man, the Federation of the world.' The same idea will be recaptured in the introductory sentences of *The Promise of World Peace*, the 1985 statement addressed by the Universal House of Justice to the peoples of the world.

42 *Tablets of Abdul Baha Abbas*, vol. 3, p. 595. See 'Abdu'l-Bahá, *'Abdu'l-Bahá in London*, p. 60: 'The Czar of Russia suggested The Hague Peace Conference and proposed a decrease in armament for all nations. In this Conference it was proved that Peace was beneficial to all countries, and that war destroyed trade, etc. The Czar's words were admirable though after the conference was over he himself was the first to declare war (against Japan).'

43 On the translation of these two words and the implied meaning see The Universal House of Justice, letter dated 9 May 1996.

44 'Abdu'l-Bahá, *Selections from the Writings of 'Abdu'l-Bahá*, no. 227, pp. 306–7.

45 'Abdu'l-Bahá, *The Promulgation of Universal Peace*, p. 389.

46 See also 'Abdu'l-Bahá, *Khiṭábát*, p. 453.

47 'Abdu'l-Bahá, *Selections from the Writings of 'Abdu'l-Bahá*, no. 202, p. 249 (Letter to Martha Root, dated Feb. (?) 1920).

48 See *'Abdu'l-Bahá in Canada*, pp. 31–9. University presidents welcomed 'Abdu'l-Bahá in a similar mood, as in the case of Howard University, a Washington college for black students (see Zarqání, *Maḥmúd's Diary*, p. 55).

49 ibid. p. 38.

50 ibid. p. 35.

51 The almost non-existent structure of the few western Bahá'í communities would obviously contribute to reinforce external perceptions of the Bahá'í message as one of 'pure' thought and 'lofty' ideals, devoid of rituals and clergy, yet practical in its orientation. In the minds of some early Bahá'ís their Faith was not so much a religion as a 'movement' breaking away from the established orthodoxies.It should be noted that many people who met 'Abdu'l-Bahá and the early Bahá'ís had the definite impression that the Bahá'í message was not 'a new religion' but a 'movement' and as such was often presented (see for instance the quotation attributed to 'Abdu'l-Bahá in *Star of the West*, vol. 5, no. 5 (5 June 1914), p. 67: 'The Bahá'í Movement is not an organization. You can never organize the Bahá'í Cause. THE BAHA'I MOVEMENT IS THE SPIRIT OF THIS AGE. IT IS THE ESSENCE OF ALL'). Bahá'ís might have been particularly keen on using the term 'movement' as it would divest their Cause from the current associations with notions of clergy and rituals (two instances can be found in two articles reporting 'Abdu'l-Bahá's activities in Montreal, in *'Abdu'l-Bahá in Canada*, p. 35). On the other hand, perceptions of the Bahá'í Faith as a movement were partly justified by the fact that dual membership was not a rare phenomenon among the early Bahá'ís. Some descriptions given by qualified exponents of the Faith blurred almost all distinctions: 'The adherents of the

Bahai teachings have no church organization or form of membership. They are composed of people drawn from all denominations, sects and religions' (Remey, *The Peace of the World*, p. 44). The term 'movement' was often used by Shoghi Effendi in his early writings, probably not only as a stylistic choice, but also as a way to deliberately defuse the more formal connotations of a word such as 'religion'. It was only in his letter 'The Unfoldment of World Civilization' that Shoghi Effendi thought it necessary to do away with this and expressions falling short of recognizing the Bahá'í Faith's pre-eminent position as the renewed religion which had always been and will always be (see Shoghi Effendi, *The World Order of Bahá'u'lláh*, p. 196: 'Ceasing to designate to itself a movement, a fellowship and the like – designations that did grave injustice to its ever-unfolding system').

52 'Abdu'l-Bahá, *Selections from the Writings of 'Abdu'l-Bahá*, no. 146, p. 174.

53 Bahá'u'lláh, Súriy-i-Haykal, para. 153, in Bahá'u'lláh, *The Summons of the Lord of Hosts*, p. 80.

54 'Abdu'l-Bahá, *Some Answered Questions*, ch. 11, para. 35, p. 65.

55 ibid. para. 37, p. 67.

56 'Abdu'l-Bahá, *Selections from the Writings of 'Abdu'l-Bahá*, no. 15, p. 32; also 'Abdu'l-Bahá, *The Promulgation of Universal Peace*, pp. 125–6.

57 See 'Abdu'l-Bahá, *The Promulgation of Universal Peace*, p. 16: 'A few days ago I arrived in New York, coming direct from Alexandria. On a former trip I travelled to Europe, visiting Paris and London. Paris is most beautiful in outward appearance. The evidences of material civilization there are very great, but the spiritual civilization is far behind. I found the people of that city submerged and drowning in a sea of materialism. Their conversations and discussions were limited to natural and physical phenomena, without mention of God.'

58 'Abdu'l-Bahá, *Selections from the Writings of 'Abdu'l-Bahá*, no. 224, p. 289.

59 See 'Abdu'l-Bahá, *Some Answered Questions*, ch. 12, p. 75.

60 See 'Abdu'l-Bahá, *The Promulgation of Universal Peace*, p. 414: 'And you must not think that this is ended [the persecution in Russia] . . . The time may come when in Europe itself they will arise against the Jews. But your declaration that Christ was the Word of God will end all such trouble. My advice is that in order to become honorable, protected and secure among the nations of the world, in order that the Christians may love and safeguard the Israelitish people, you should be willing to announce your belief in Christ, the Word of God.' (See also 'Abdu'l-Bahá, *Paris Talks*, no. 13).

61 One has only to read the story of 'Abdu'l-Bahá's delectation at watching an airplane in action to realize how unmixed this emotion was. Like so many other technical feats, the plane was symbolically another victory of man over nature through the power of his mind.

62 The Titanic tragedy, on which ship 'Abdu'l-Bahá was originally planned to be a passenger on its maiden voyage, could serve in 'Abdu'l-Bahá's words as a reminder of the false sense of security that derives from over-reliance on technical dexterity.

63 See 'Abdu'l-Bahá, *The Secret of Divine Civilization*, p. 66: 'Endeavour, ceaseless endeavour, is required. Nothing short of an indomitable determination can possibly achieve it.'

64 A point which needs to be stressed. Nineteenth and early twentieth pacifist movements were far from agreeing on the idea of a world federation and a world executive empowered to use legitimate force over nation states. As is well-known, the socialist dream of a revolutionary peace, attained through the international solidarity of the working classes in their common struggle against capitalist oligarchies, was shattered when World War I served them due notice of the strength of national barriers. Class struggle and revolutionary violence were the means to achieve the classless, peaceful State.

65 'Abdu'l-Bahá, *The Secret of Divine Civilization*, p. 66.

66 'Abdu'l-Bahá, *The Promulgation of Universal Peace*, p. 376.

67 ibid. p. 317: 'All the European nations are on edge, and a single flame will set on fire the whole of that continent.'
68 ibid. p. 376: 'The European continent is like an arsenal, a storehouse of explosives ready for ignition, and one spark will set the whole of Europe aflame, particularly at this time when the Balkan question is before the world.'
69 See *'Abdu'l-Bahá in Canada*, p. 35: 'There is nothing of the nature of prophecy about such a view . . . It is based on reasoning solely.'
70 See Balyuzi, *'Abdu'l-Bahá: The Centre of the Covenant*, p. 443; also Blomfield, *The Chosen Highway*, pp. 188–97.
71 See *Star of the West*, vol. 5, no. 11 (27 September 1914), p. 164.
72 ibid.
73 'Abdu'l-Bahá, *The Secret of Divine Civilization*, pp. 61–2.
74 'Abdu'l-Bahá, *The Promulgation of Universal Peace*, p. 124.
75 Zarqání, *Maḥmúd's Diary*, p. 27.
76 'Abdu'l-Bahá, *Khiṭábát*, pp. 713–14.
77 'I have just been told that there has been a terrible accident in this country. A train has fallen into the river and at least twenty people have been killed. This is going to be a matter for discussion in the French Parliament today, and the Director of the State Railway will be called upon to speak. He will be cross-examined as to the condition of the railroad and as to what caused the accident, and there will be a heated argument. I am filled with wonder and surprise to notice what interest and excitement has been aroused throughout the whole country on account of the death of twenty people, while they remain cold and indifferent to the fact that thousands of Italians, Turks, and Arabs are killed in Tripoli! The horror of this wholesale slaughter has not disturbed the Government at all! Yet these unfortunate people are human beings too' ('Abdu'l-Bahá, *Paris Talks*, no. 37, pp. 115–16).
78 'Abdu'l-Bahá, *The Promulgation of Universal Peace*, p. 103.
79 'Abdu'l-Bahá defines the 'fatherland' (*vaṭan*) as the place where one 'happens' to reside (*Khiṭábát*, p. 715).
80 'For instance, racial differences are a purely imaginary question, yet how much influence it exerts despite the fact that all are people . . . And the truth is that all the peoples belong to a single race' (ibid. p. 717).
81 'Abdu'l-Bahá, *The Promulgation of Universal Peace*, p. 102.
82 ibid. p. 42.
83 Words attributed to 'Abdu'l-Bahá, quoted in *Star of the West*, vol. 17 (1926), p. 238; for a similar quotation see vol. 7, no. 6 (24 June 1916), p. 41.
84 See 'Abdu'l-Bahá's description of the young Germans volunteering to sail for Germany on the day the announcement that war had broke out was made (*Khiṭábát*, p. 715, circa November 1915).
85 'Abdu'l-Bahá, *Selections from the Writings of 'Abdu'l-Bahá*, no. 68, p. 103.
86 'Abdu'l-Bahá, *Some Answered Questions*, ch. 78, para. 4, p. 316.
87 Words attributed to 'Abdu'l-Bahá, quoted in Zarqání, *Maḥmúd's Diary*, p. 36.
88 *'Abdu'l-Bahá in Canada*, p. 35.
89 ibid. p. 34; see also *Star of the West*, vol. 5, no. 8 (1 August 1914), p. 116: 'Now the question of disarmament must be put into practice by all the nations and not only by one or two.'
90 Afroukhteh, *Memories of Nine Years in 'Akká*, pp. 237–8.
91 'Abdu'l-Bahá, *The Promulgation of Universal Peace*, p. 455.
92 ibid. p. 125.
93 ibid. p. 388: 'In the Orient I was informed that there are many lovers of peace in America. Therefore, I left my native land to associate here with those who are the standard-bearers of

international conciliation and agreement.' Prior to his coming, 'Abdu'l-Bahá had stressed that his visit to America was conditional upon the love and unity achieved by the American Bahá'ís. It was solely through the power of the magnetic attraction thus generated that all the difficulties could be surmounted and the wishes of the American Bahá'ís be fulfilled (See *Selections from the Writings of 'Abdu'l-Bahá*, no. 68, p. 105).

94 For Tagore the American experience was an ordeal which drained all his energies. Tagore was quite aware of the challenges he was about to meet in America. His universalistic ideas closely resembled those expressed by 'Abdu'l-Bahá. In Tagore's view it was high time for surpassing nationalistic barriers. Only what was compatible with universalism had the capacity to endure. The time had come for peace and cooperation on a global scale. All the peoples would have to acquaint themselves with the cultural achievements that the others had to offer. See Murry and Tagore, *East and West*, and Tagore, *Nationalism.*

95 Hollinger, 'Bahá'ís and American Peace Movements', p. 4. The Lake Mohonk Conference on International Arbitration had been established by A. K. Smiley, a Quaker, in 1895, at Lake Mohonk, New York, a popular summer resort at the time. The purpose of the Conference evolved to include: '1) the promotion of arbitration among leaders of the American business community, particularly through trade associations; 2) national college essay and oratorical contests on the issue of arbitration; 3) supplying libraries and other educational institutions with information about arbitration and the Lake Mohonk Conferences; 4) creation of a type of Mohonk membership called "correspondents".' See http://www.swarthmore.edu/library/peace/DG051-099/DG054LakeMohonk.htm. Summaries of the Lake Mohonk Conferences on International Arbitration and the platforms therein adopted were regularly published in the *American Journal of International Law*. In 1911 James L. Tryon described the Lake Mohonk Conference in these words: 'Of the more recently founded agencies for the promotion of peace none has had more profound influence than the Lake Mohonk Arbitration Conference organized by Albert K Smiley' (Smiley, 'The Rise of the Peace Movement', in *The Yale Law Journal*, vol. 20, no. 5 (1911), pp. 358–371).

96 The reception at the Waldorf Astoria Hotel was attended by some two thousand people. For the notes of 'Abdu'l-Bahá's address at the reception extended to him by the New York Peace Society on 13 May 1912, see 'Abdu'l-Bahá, *The Promulgation of Universal Peace*, pp. 122–3.

97 'Abdu'l-Bahá's address at Lake Mohonk was delivered on 14 May 1912 (see Balyuzi, *'Abdu'l-Bahá*, p. 193, and Zarqání, *Maḥmúd's Diary*, pp. 100–03).

98 See Lacroix-Hopson, *'Abdu'l-Bahá in New York, The City of the Covenant*, p. 16.

99 *Star of the West,* vol. 6, no. 11 (27 September 1915), p. 82.

100 Fiore's name appears in the 'list of alien passengers' on board the *Cedric* bound for the United States (see record at http://www.ellisisland.org/). His address, delivered in April 1912 for the ASIL meeting, was titled 'Some Considerations on the Past, Present and Future of International Law' (see 'In Memoriam: Pasquale Fiore,' *The American Journal of International Law*, vol. 9, no. 2 (April 1915), p. 406).

101 Jane Addams was founder of the Hull House in Chicago and founder in 1920 of the Women's International League for Peace and Freedom. She was the author of *Newer Ideals of Peace* (1907). See Ruth Moffett's account of 'Abdu'l-Bahá's encounter with Jane Addams, in *Star of the West*, vol. 25, pp. 361–5.

102 Starr Jordan was the author of several books devoted to peace, among them *Waste and War*. In his memoirs (*Days of a Man*, vol. 2, p. 414), he recalls the visit of 'Abdu'l-Bahá, son of 'Baha'u'llah, the famous Persian devotee, founder and head of a widespread religious sect holding as its chief tenet the Brotherhood of Man, with all that this implies of personal friendliness and international peace. Through an interpreter the kindly apostle expressed with convincing force a message accepted, in name at least, by good men and women all through the ages.'

103 In *Star of the West*, vol. 3, no. 7 (13 July 1912), p. 5.
104 The conversation took place at the Ansonia Hotel on 15 April 1912, shortly after 'Abdu'l-Bahá's arrival in New York. Notes were taken by Howard MacNutt and the entire text was published in the *Star of the West*, vol. 3, no. 7 (13 July 1912), pp. 4–5, and 10.
105 'Abdu'l-Bahá, *The Promulgation of Universal Peace*, p. 388.
106 ibid. p. 83.
107 ibid. pp. 121–2; see also *Star of the West*, vol. 9, no. 17 (January 1919), p. 194: 'Abdu'l-Bahá looks to America which, being more disinterested than any European Power, will be able to help forward the realization of the world-wide unity and peace.' America's return to its isolationist policy, shortly after World War I, especially its withdrawal from the League of Nations, cancelled the possibility of its assuming the arbitral role that its prestige and war effort had conferred upon her.
108 See *Star of the West*, vol. 5, no. 11 (27 September 1914), p. 167.
109 See Hay, 'Rabindranath Tagore in America', p. 443. And in almost Hegelian spirit in 1916 Tagore was again to comment to journalists: 'Of course she [the United States of America] will make mistakes, but out of these series of mistakes she will come to some higher synthesis of truth and be able to hold up the banner of Civilization. She is the best exponent of Western ideals of humanity.' In 1940, once more, but now with a less diffident tone, he was commending the rest the world to President Roosevelt's intervention in the war engulfing Europe.
110 See Hofstadter, *The Age of Reform, from Byran to T.D.R,* pp. 270–80. The progressivist element was particularly visible in the 'need to phrase the problems of national policy in moral terms' (p. 274).
111 ibid. pp. 375–6. An interesting comment considering that California was not the leading state in peace activities. Bahá'ís do not fail to point out that San Francisco was the place where finally the United Nations Charter was approved.
112 See 'Abdu'l-Bahá, *Muntakhabátí az Makátíb-i-Ḥaḍrat-i-'Abdu'l-Bahá* (German edition), vol. 5, p. 75.
113 'Abdu'l-Bahá, *The Promulgation of Universal Peace*, p. 389.
114 'Abdu'l-Bahá, *Selections from the Writings of 'Abdu'l-Bahá*, no. 71, p. 109, and no. 232, p. 311. The fourteen Wilsonian principles stressed open diplomacy, freedom of navigation, elimination of trade barriers, disarmament to limits commensurable with internal policing needs, settlement of colonial disputes, rearrangement of European frontiers in recognition of the integrity of its constituent peoples, self-determination for the various non-Turkish nations under Ottoman rule, and, finally, the creation of a League or Union of Nations. It should be noted that 'Abdu'l-Bahá had double reason to convey his wishes in this way. In fact, there had been at least some indirect connection between 'Abdu'l-Bahá and Wilson via Secretary of State William Jennings Bryan, whose wife was personally visited by 'Abdu'l-Bahá during his stop at Lincoln, thereby returning Bryan's own failed attempt to visit 'Abdu'l-Bahá in Haifa (See Balyuzi, *'Abdu'l-Bahá*, pp. 279–80).
115 During his sojourn in England, upon seeing a woman riding on a horse completely at ease, her hair flying down, 'Abdu'l-Bahá is reported to have exclaimed: 'This is the age of woman. She should receive the same education as her brother and enjoy the same privilege; for all are equal before God' (*'Abdu'l-Bahá in London*, p. 81).
116 Balyuzi, *'Abdu'l-Bahá*, p. 347.
117 'Abdu'l-Bahá, *The Promulgation of Universal Peace*, p. 252.
118 See Amanat, *Resurrection and Renewal*, p. 305.
119 'Abdu'l-Bahá explains with regard to Ṭáhirih's removal of the veil: 'All women in Persia are enveloped in veils in public. So completely covered are they that even the hand is not visible. This rigid veiling is unspeakable . . . So excessive and compulsory is the requirement

for veiling in the East that people in the West have no idea of the excitement and indignation produced by the appearance of an unveiled woman ('Abdu'l-Bahá, *The Promulgation of Universal Peace*, p. 251). On the significance of the veil from an anthropological perspective see Tillion, *Le harem et les cousins*.

120 'Abdu'l-Bahá, *Paris Talks*, pp. 195–6.

121 ibid. p. 196. (in italics in the original).

122 See 'Abdu'l-Bahá, *The Promulgation of Universal Peace*, p. 283. Elsewhere 'Abdu'l-Bahá explains that whilst eastern men excelled eastern women in spreading the Bahá'í message, western women had a clear advantage over their male counterparts (ibid. p. 170).

123 'He [Bahá'u'lláh] made woman respected by commanding that all women be educated, that there be no difference in the education of the two sexes and that man and woman share the same rights' (ibid. p. 166)

124 'But while this principle of equality is true, it is likewise true that woman must prove her capacity and aptitude, must show forth the evidences of equality. She must become proficient in the arts and sciences and prove by her accomplishments that her abilities and powers have merely been latent. Demonstrations of force, such as are now taking place in England, are neither becoming nor effective in the cause of womanhood and equality. Woman must especially devote her energies and abilities toward the industrial and agricultural sciences, seeking to assist mankind in that which is most needful. By this means she will demonstrate capability and ensure recognition of equality in the social and economic equation' (ibid. p. 283).

125 These significant words are attributed to 'Abdu'l-Bahá by Miss E. H. C. Pagan, a woman who heard them in 1913 at the Whyte home, in Edinburgh, from 'Abdu'l-Bahá. Two years later the role of women in filling posts left vacant by conscripts gave them new meaning (see Khurshid, *The Seven Candles of Unity*, p. 153).

126 'Abdu'l-Bahá, *The Promulgation of Universal Peace*, p. 174.

127 'Abdu'l-Bahá would illustrate this statement with references to famous prominent women such as Catherine the Great, Isabella of Spain, Mary Magdalene and Zenobia (ibid. pp. 175 and 282).

128 ibid. p. 283.

129 ibid., see also 'Abdu'l-Bahá, *Paris Talks*, no. 50, pp. 169–70: '[T]he female sex is treated as though inferior, and is not allowed equal rights and privileges. This condition is due not to nature, but to education . . . It is not to be denied that in various directions woman at present is more backward than man, also that this temporary inferiority is due to the lack of educational opportunity.'

130 'Abdu'l-Bahá, quoted in Esslemont, *Bahá'u'lláh and the New Era*, p. 156.

131 'Abdu'l-Bahá, *Paris Talks*, p. 170.

132 'Abdu'l-Bahá, *The Promulgation of Universal Peace*, p. 284.

133 ibid. p. 375. The same analogy was applied by 'Abdu'l-Bahá to illustrate parity between religion and science.

134 ibid. p. 108.

135 ibid. p. 375: 'Woman by nature is opposed to war; she is an advocate of peace . . . for woman is naturally the most devoted and staunch advocate of international peace.'

136 ibid. p. 175.

137 ibid. p. 135; see also p. 167: 'When they [women] shall have a vote, they will oppose any cause of warfare.'

138 The 'Tablet to The Hague' is in fact the first Tablet known by that title addressed by 'Abdu'l-Bahá to the Committee; the second Tablet was dated 1 July 1920. Most of the text of the first Tablet is reproduced in *Selections from the Writings of 'Abdu'l-Bahá*, no. 227, pp. 296–307. The full text

of both Tablets is available from https://www.bahai.org/library/authoritative-texts/abdul-baha/tablets-hague-abdul-baha/. It should be noted that the first Tablet includes in appended form, as suggested by 'Abdu'l-Bahá, the text of a briefer letter written during the war years.

The Central Organization for a Durable Peace was established in April 1915 by 'thirty leading peace activists'. In 1916 and 1918, together with the Nederlandsche Anti-Oorlog-Raad, it was nominated for the Nobel Prize; both organizations were complementary and established a division of labour whereby the former would focus on influencing public opinion while the latter was to carry out the scientific work (see the list of nominees for the Nobel Prize in http://nobelprize.org/peace/nomination/database.html). The Organization included peace activists from various nations. It aimed to establish the principles of a new post-war diplomacy, and focused its studies in finding ways of establishing a system of workable sanctions for non-compliant States (http://www.swarthmore.edu/library/peace/CDGB/centralorganisation.htm). According to Balyuzi, the Tablet 'was addressed to the Central Organization For a Durable Peace at The Hague. This organization was not an official body. The president of its Executive Committee was Dr H. C. Dresselhuys of Holland. Great Britain was represented by G. Lowes Dickinson and Austria by Professor Dr H. Lammasch, well-known progressive thinkers in their respective countries' (*'Abdu'l-Bahá*, p. 438). Goldsworthy Lowes Dickinson (1862–1932) was a renowned Cambridge classicist, author of numerous works, among them *The International Anarchy 1904–1914*, (London: Allen & Unwin, 1937), *The Causes of International War* (London: Swarthmore Press, 1928) and a very influential essay on the League of Nations, *The Future of the Covenant* (London: League of Nations Union, 1920). H. Lammasch, the last prime minister of the Austro-Hungarian monarchy, was a politician and jurist well known for his pacifist positions; he served three times as chief justice of The Hague Tribunal.

139 'Abdu'l-Bahá, quoted in *Star of the West*, vol. 10, no. 7 (13 July 1919), p. 137.

140 The Versailles Pact had been hailed as a success and very few voices dared to express contrary views. Keynes was an exception.

141 'Abdu'l-Bahá, *Selections from the Writings of 'Abdu'l-Bahá*, no. 227, pp. 296–7.

142 References to the rule of brute force and the struggle for existence, both characteristics of nature, as being utterly contrary to the rule of love are frequent in 'Abdu'l-Bahá's writings and utterances. Thus, speaking about the Bahá'ís, 'Abdu'l-Bahá describes them as follows: 'They are awake and vigilant, they shun the obscurity of the world of nature, their highest wish centereth on the eradication from among men of the struggle for existence, the shining forth of the spirituality and the love of the realm on high, the exercise of utmost kindness among peoples, the realization of an intimate and close connection between religions and the practice of the ideal of self-sacrifice. Then will the world of humanity be transformed into the Kingdom of God' (ibid. no. 223, pp. 281–2).

143 'Abdu'l-Bahá, *The Promulgation of Universal Peace*, p. 400.

144 The notion of 'struggle for existence' was developed by Darwin in Chapter 3 of *The Origin of Species by Means of Natural Selection, or the Preservation of Favoured Races in the Struggle for Life*. 'Social Darwinism' is not Darwinism, but the term used to critically refer to the ideological and sociological positions taken by advocates of applying analogues of selective processes to the patterning of human societies. Social Darwinism was adopted in divergent ways by a number of theorists of *laissez faire* and in general by advocates of capitalism, racialism and eugenics; it also found its way as a justification for the prevalence of hegemonic nations (see Carr, *The Twenty Years Crisis 1919–1939*, pp. 46–50). The extent and uses of social Darwinism have been the object of much controversy since Richard Hofstadter published his ground-breaking *Social Darwinism in American Thought* (1983); for a more updated discussion see also Weikart, 'The Origins of Social Darwinism in Germany, 1859–1895'.

145 'Abdu'l-Bahá, *'Abdu'l-Bahá in London*, p. 20.

146 'Abdu'l-Bahá, *The Promulgation of Universal Peace*, p. 229.
147 'Abdu'l-Bahá, *Selections from the Writings of 'Abdu'l-Bahá*, no. 227, p. 297.
148 'Abdu'l-Bahá, *The Promulgation of Universal Peace*, p. 376.
149 'Abdu'l-Bahá, *Selections from the Writings of 'Abdu'l-Bahá*, no. 227, p. 297.
150 'While in America, I spoke before many Peace Societies, Churches and Conventions, and foretold the fearful consequences of armed peace in Europe' ('Abdu'l-Bahá, quoted in *Star of the West*, vol. 5, no. 11 (27 September 1914, p. 164).
151 'Abdu'l-Bahá, *Selections from the Writings of 'Abdu'l-Bahá*, no. 227, p. 304.
152 'Abdu'l-Bahá, quoted by Ahmad Sohrab in *Star of the West*, vol. 13, no. 6 (September 1922), p. 131.
153 'Abdu'l-Bahá, *Selections from the Writings of 'Abdu'l-Bahá*, no. 227, p. 298.
154 ibid. (emphasis added).
155 See Hayes et al. (eds), *Peace, More than an End to War*, p. 179.
156 'Abdu'l-Bahá, *Selections from the Writings of 'Abdu'l-Bahá*, no. 202, p. 249.
157 ibid. no. 227, p. 300.
158 ibid.
159 ibid. p. 301.
160 ibid.
161 ibid. p. 302.
162 ibid.
163 ibid. pp. 302–3.
164 ibid. p. 303.
165 ibid. pp. 303–4.
166 ibid. p. 304.
167 ibid. pp. 305–6.
168 Elsewhere 'Abdu'l-Bahá states that the mission of the Supreme Tribunal would be to prevent war (*Paris Talks*, no. 48, p. 161).
169 'Abdu'l-Bahá, *Selections from the Writings of 'Abdu'l-Bahá*, no. 227, p. 306.
170 ibid. no. 228, p. 307.
171 ibid.
172 Shoghi Effendi, *The World Order of Bahá'u'lláh*, pp. 29–30.
173 'Abdu'l-Bahá, quoted in Shoghi Effendi, *Citadel of Faith*, p. 37.
174 In this context the word 'principle' and 'Faith' occur for the first time in an article by Isabella Brittingham published in the *Bahá'í Bulletin* of December 1908 (see Stockman, *The Bahá'í Faith in America*, vol. 2: *Early Expansion 1900–1912*, pp. 367–8).
175 As Stockman has shown, between 1900 to 1912 leaflets and introductory materials by Bahá'í authors shifted attention from Christian and biblical prophecy to a greater focus on the humanitarian side of their Faith. This trend reflected an increasing movement of Bahá'í eastern missionaries and western pilgrims. First-hand accounts and fresh translations of Bahá'í writings unknown to the American believers acted as a catalyst for the North American Bahá'í community (see *The Bahá'í Faith in America*, vol. 2, pp. 232–43).
176 'Abdu'l-Bahá, *The Promulgation of Universal Peace*, p. 435; see also *Selections from the Writings of 'Abdu'l-Bahá*, no. 202, p. 249.
177 'Abdu'l-Bahá, *The Promulgation of Universal Peace*, p. 440. Horace Holley twice quotes this same list in his book *Religion for Mankind*, pp. 41–2, 71–2. In Paris 'Abdu'l-Bahá gave a similar outline consisting of eleven principles, among them 'non-interference of religion and politics', 'equalization of means of existence' and 'equality of men before the Law' ('Abdu'l-Bahá, *Paris Talks*, pp. 138–76).
178 Quoted in Stockman, *The Bahá'í Faith in America*, vol. 2, p. 380. Compared with the list by

'Abdu'l-Bahá, the only missing 'teaching' is 'the protection and guidance of the Holy Spirit'. Another minor change consists in the position of the principle of 'independent investigation of truth', placed second in the list.

179 'Abdu'l-Bahá, *Selections from the Writings of 'Abdu'l-Bahá*, p. 297 and ff.

180 Shoghi Effendi, *God Passes By*, pp. 281–2.

181 Van den Hoonaard recalls that Protestants, who made up three-quarters of the early middle-upper liberal class of the Bahá'í Canadian community, 'had a penchant for individual responsibility and the so-called twelve principles' ('Inside the Origins of the Bahá'í Community of Canada, 1898–1948: A Personal Narrative').

182 See Shoghi Effendi: *Principles of Bahá'í Administration.*

183 For instance, Horace Holley's *Religion for Mankind*, first published in 1956, and Stanwood Cobb, *Tomorrow and Tomorrow*, published in 1951.

184 Few references can be found to human rights as one of the teachings of Bahá'u'lláh. Yet 'Abdu'l-Bahá had clearly indicated that Bahá'u'lláh had taught that 'an equal standard of human rights' should be 'recognized and adopted' ('Abdu'l-Bahá, *The Promulgation of Universal Peace*, p. 182). The Persian transcript of the same is perhaps less conclusive since the reference is to a more general equality of rights: *'Jámí' bashar dar nazd-i-Khudá yik sánand, ḥuqúqishán ḥuqúq váḥidih; imtíází az baráy-i-nafsí níst. Kull dar taḥt-i-qánún ilahí hastand'* (*Khiṭábát*, p. 451). See also *The Promulgation of Universal Peace*, p. 318: 'There shall be an equality of rights and prerogatives for all mankind.'

185 As a general rule, introductions to the Bahá'í Faith relied heavily on scriptural quotations arranged in such a manner that they would render personal comments unnecessary (see Faizi, *The Bahá'í Faith: An Introduction*, or Holley, *Religion for Mankind*, pp. 157–66). In other cases, personal opinion was less in the way of a dialogue with the Bahá'í writings themselves, as with prevailing ideas. A Bahá'í author speaking from a Bahá'í perspective would then attempt to show how the concerns of modern man, his failures and high ideals, would relate to the new message.

186 As defined by the Merriam-Webster's Dictionary.

187 A good example of this can be seen in the summary of the discussion held between the prominent Bahá'í Howard Colby Ives and Senator Borah of Idaho, in *Star of the West*, vol. 22 (February 1932), pp. 328–30.

188 Shoghi Effendi's presentations of the Bahá'í Faith and the variety of the language he used to describe its many-faceted aspects bear witness to this.

189 Attempts at systematizing the essentials of the Bahá'í Faith through established 'deepening' courses were already well afoot during the 1970s in countries like the United States; but in the main the complete restructuring in terms of content, delivery and underlying educational philosophy was largely the work of the Ruhi Institute in Colombia.

190 Shoghi Effendi, *The World Order of Bahá'u'lláh*, p. 22; see also p. 19.

191 'Abdu'l-Bahá, *Selections from the Writings of 'Abdu'l-Bahá*, no. 202, p. 248.

192 Rassekh, 'Haft Gúniy-i-vaḥdat, Nigáhí bih Lawḥ-i-Mubárak-i-Haft Sham', in *Pazhuheshnameh*, no. 5 (Khurdád 11, 1378). Rassekh argues that the Bahá'í Faith promotes in essence three concepts of unity: oneness of God, unity of religion and oneness of mankind. His article is a commentary on the 'Seven Candles of Unity' (see below).

193 'Abdu'l-Bahá, *Selections from the Writings of 'Abdu'l-Bahá*, no. 227, p. 298. An even more forceful expression of the indissoluble bond connecting all realities and hence their truth is found in an address delivered by 'Abdu'l-Bahá (*Khiṭábát*, pp. 72–3).

194 'Abdu'l-Bahá, *Paris Talks*, no. 11, p. 34.

195 'Abdu'l-Bahá, *Selections from the Writings of 'Abdu'l-Bahá*, no. 15, p. 32.

196 'Abdu'l-Bahá, *The Secret of Divine Civilization*, p. 16. 'Abdu'l-Bahá looks favourably upon

the achievements of the Japanese in rallying public opinion in favour of reforms.

197 'Abdu'l-Bahá, *The Promulgation of Universal Peace*, p. 133. See also *Star of the West*, vol. 5, no. 8 (1 August 1914), p. 116: 'Consequently, the advocates of Peace must strive day and night, so that the individuals of every country may become peace-loving, public opinion may gain a strong and permanent footing, and day by day the army of International Peace be increased.'

198 'Abdu'l-Bahá, *The Promulgation of Universal Peace*, p. 454.

199 ibid.

200 Provisional translations of the Lawḥ-i-Ittiḥád are available at http://Bahá'í-library.com/provisionals/ittihad.cole.html (here followed) and http://Bahá'í-library.com/provisionals/ittihad.html. Original Persian text used: Bahá'u'lláh, Ad'íyyah-i-Ḥaḍrat-i-Maḥbúb (original edition: Faraju'lláh al-Kurdi, Egypt, 76 B.E./1920; reprint Germany 1980), pp. 388–406.

201 Also known as existential monism, and often translated as 'pantheism'. 'Abdu'l-Bahá clarifies in which sense, or senses, pantheistic statements can be taken as true, making it clear that no such a thing as an identification between the essence of God and the creatures is or has been ever possible (see 'Abdu'l-Bahá, *Some Answered Questions*, ch. 82).

202 'Abdu'l-Bahá, *The Promulgation of Universal Peace*, p. 156: 'The great and fundamental teachings of Bahá'u'lláh are the oneness of God and unity of mankind. This is the bond of union among Bahá'ís all over the world. They become united among themselves, then unite others. It is impossible to unite unless united. Christ said, "Ye are the salt of the earth; but if the salt has lost his savour, wherewith shall it be salted?" This proves there were dissensions and lack of unity among His followers. Hence His admonition to unity of action.'

203 Likewise, as already seen, the principle of 'oneness of religion' implies that *since* all revealed religions come from one divine source, they share 'at heart' the same truths and ethical principles, *despite* obvious differences, which for the most part are attributable to the changing needs of the time and the accumulated effect of man-made accretions.

204 Shoghi Effendi, *The Promised Day Is Come*, para. 276, p. 113. An important difference must be made between racism and racialism, which renders Shoghi Effendi's statement all the more significant. Racialism is a more generic belief in the important role that racial differences are imagined to play in historical, social, cultural and biological life. Racialism was, according to Niall Ferguson, far more determinant of the belligerent attitudes displayed by the various powers that fought each other during the two World Wars than other alleged factors (see Ferguson, *The War of the World*, pp. xlii–lix.

205 Shoghi Effendi, *The World Order of Bahá'u'lláh*, p. 202. Rabindranath Tagore had made strenuous and unsuccessful denunciations of this 'fetish', as he called it too, in his talks and writings.

206 Bahá'u'lláh (*Tablets of Bahá'u'lláh*, p. 71) sees this principle embodied in the qur'ánic verses (59:9) 'They prefer them before themselves, though poverty be their own lot.'

207 Bahá'u'lláh, *Gleanings*, XXIV, p. 59.

208 'Abdu'l-Bahá, *Selections from the Writings of 'Abdu'l-Bahá*, no. 79, p. 115, and no. 227, p. 302.

209 'Abdu'l-Bahá, *Some Answered Questions*, ch. 70, p. 289.

210 ibid. ch. 76, pp. 306–7.

211 ibid. p. 307.

212 ibid. ch. 84, p. 349; see also ch. 65.

213 'Abdu'l-Bahá, *The Secret of Divine Civilization*, p. 97; see also Bahá'u'lláh, *Epistle to the Son of the Wolf*, para. 50, p. 27: 'Indeed, there existeth in man a faculty which deterreth him from, and guardeth him against, whatever is unworthy and unseemly, and which is known as his sense of shame. This, however, is confined to but a few; all have not possessed, and do not possess, it.'

214 'Abdu'l-Bahá, *The Secret of Divine Civilization*, p. 98.
215 'Abdu'l-Bahá, *Some Answered Questions*, ch. 84, p. 304.
216 'Abdu'l-Bahá, *Abdul Baha on Divine Philosophy*, pp. 41–2.
217 'Abdu'l-Bahá, *Some Answered Questions*, ch. 77, p. 312.
218 ibid.
219 Bahá'u'lláh, Bishárát, in *Tablets of Bahá'u'lláh*, p. 27.
220 'Abdu'l-Bahá, *Some Answered Questions*, ch. 77, p. 313.
221 ibid.
222 To be sure, the nature of this executive power is not detailed, leaving room for speculation as to whether this could adopt various forms ranging from a bare-bones 'directorium' to the kind of world super-State which even Kant regarded as unlikely, if not undesirable. The United Nations has developed important rudiments of the former, but has still to contend with the institutionalization of a minimum system of 'world governance', let alone a world government.
223 The fleeting parallel marked with Japan could also serve as a case in point of comparative history, for both societies were faced with similar dilemmas: enormous pressures from western powers, absolutist regimes, dislocated societies, stiffening cultural traditions (Confucianism, Muslim clericalism) partly in conflict with other traditional roots.
224 See 'Abdu'l-Bahá, *The Promulgation of Universal Peace*, pp. 56–7.

3 Shoghi Effendi

1 Shoghi Effendi, Summary Statement, 1947, Special UN Committee on Palestine.
2 See Shoghi Effendi, *The World Order of Bahá'u'lláh*, pp. 58–60.
3 In keeping with this tradition, the Universal House of Justice supervised a lengthy review of the developments which have taken place in the Bahá'í community and the world at large for the one hundred years of the twentieth century, under the title *Century of Light*.
4 Shoghi Effendi was related to the Báb through his father, Mírzá Hádí Shírází, and to Bahá'u'lláh through his mother, Ḍíyá'íyyih Khánum, daughter of 'Abdu'l-Bahá. See Taherzadeh, *The Covenant of Bahá'u'lláh*, p. 280.
5 On Shoghi Effendi's early days and education see Rabbani, *The Priceless Pearl*, pp. 138; on Shoghi Effendi's training in languages see Malouf, *The Hidden Words of Bahá'u'lláh: Translation Norms Employed by Shoghi Effendi*, pp. 22–41.
6 Shoghi Effendi was among the party accompanying 'Abdu'l-Bahá on his journey to United States. However, on reaching Naples, he was returned to Palestine after being refused further passage by the Italian authorities on health reasons. The likely xenophobic implications of this measure were not lost on the young Shoghi Effendi. See Zarqání, *Maḥmúd's Diary*, pp. 22–3.
7 See Shoghi Effendi, *God Passes By*, p. 306. Jamal Pasha (Turkish Cemal Pasha), also known as Jamal the Butcher, was the military Governor of Syria from 1914 to 1917 and one of the members of the triumvirate that ruled over the tottering Ottoman Empire after a successful *coup d'état* staged in 1913. He was shot dead in 1922 when trying to reorganize the activities of his party. See also Alkan, *Dissent and Heterodoxy in the Late Ottoman Empire: Reformers, Babis and Baha'is*, pp. 173–6.
8 'Abdu'l-Bahá's career found in the opposition of his half-brother Muḥammad 'Alí a major impediment for the unfoldment of his activities at home and abroad. See Taherzadeh, *The Covenant of Bahá'u'lláh*, pp. 148–252.
9 For a detailed historical description of the course of studies undertaken by Shoghi Effendi while at Balliol College see Riaz Khadem's *Prelude to the Guardianship*, expanded from his *Shoghi Effendi at Oxford* (1999).
10 See Rabbani, *The Priceless Pearl*, p. 37.
11 ibid. pp. 43–8.

12 Shoghi Effendi's widow, Rúḥíyyih Rabbbani, has written: 'It is really during the 1930s that one sees a change manifest in Shoghi Effendi's writings ... Where before one could trace a certain diffidence, an echo of the affliction of soul he had passed through after the ascension of the Master and his assumption of his high office ... now the tone changes and a man speaks forth his assurance with great confidence and strength' (*The Priceless Pearl*, p. 214).
13 Shoghi Effendi, *God Passes By*, p. xii.
14 'Abdu'l-Bahá, quoted in *Star of the West*, vol. 5, no. 8 (1 August 1914), p. 122.
15 Siyyid Káẓim Ra<u>sh</u>tí, Head of the <u>Sh</u>ay<u>kh</u>í community from 1826 until 1843. Henri Corbin has devoted a lengthy study of <u>Sh</u>ay<u>kh</u>ism, in Corbin, *En Islam iranien*, vol. 4, pp. 205–300. For further references see Amanat, *Resurrection and Renewal*, pp. 48–69, and MacEoin, *The Messiah, of Shiraz*, pp. 59–137; also Rafati, 'The Development of Shaykhí Thought in Shí'í Islam'.
16 For a full discussion on the nature and continuity in the Báb's claims see Saiedi's discussion in *Gate of the Heart*, pp. 83–92; see also Amanat, *Resurrection and Renewal*, pp. 94–97 and passim; and MacEoin, *The Messiah of Shiraz*, pp. 168, 173–8.
17 Since no birth registers were in place at the time, the traditional date given in Bahá'í accounts for 'Abdu'l-Bahá's date of birth is assumed to be correct.
18 On the 'titles' and eschatological position of the Báb see Shoghi Effendi, *God Passes By*, pp. 57–9; also 'Abdu'l-Bahá, *Some Answered Questions*, ch. 8, pp. 30–31.
19 Shoghi Effendi, *God Passes By*, p. 3.
20 Shoghi Effendi, *The World Order of Bahá'u'lláh*, p. 56 (emphasis added).
21 Shoghi Effendi's letter *The Promised Day Is Come* constitutes an instance, if not the model, of the 'rewriting' of history which the advent of the Bahá'í revelation is bound to bring about.
22 See Shoghi Effendi, *God Passes By*, p. 245.
23 Isaiah 40:4; see also Bahá'u'lláh, *Gleanings*, CXXIII, p. 260.
24 See for instance Shoghi Effendi's periodization of the first four decades in American Bahá'í history, in 'America and the Most Great Peace', *The World Order of Bahá'u'lláh*, p. 80.
25 Characteristically, the work itself was intended as a fitting tribute to commemorate the one hundredth anniversary marking the inception of the Bahá'í Faith.
26 Shoghi Effendi devoted eight months to the task of translating *Nabíl's Narrative* and appending its accompanying 200 pages of copious notes. The book was originally published in 1931; yet the preliminary work for it was already in his mind as early as 1924, when instructions had been delivered to Iran for the collection of any items as would throw light on the history of the Faith (Shoghi Effendi, *Bahá'í Administration*, pp. 75–6). The original text remains unavailable. MacEoin has expressed doubts as to the degree to which Shoghi Effendi's version can be relied upon in view of comments by Rúḥíyyih <u>Kh</u>ánum, who compares the translation with that of Omar Khayyam's *Rubaiyyat* by Edward Fitzgerald (*The Sources for Early Babi Doctrine and History: A Survey*, pp. 166–7). On reading the work the Bahá'ís of the West '*caught a glimpse of the tradition behind them*, they saw that this was a Faith for which one carried one's life in one hand, they understood what Shoghi Effendi was talking about and what he expected from them when he called them the spiritual descendants of the Dawn-Breakers' (Rabbani, *The Priceless Pearl*, p. 218, emphasis added). The fact of regarding the Báb as one of the 'twin Manifestations for this Day' and a central figure of the Bahá'í Faith was a way of enhancing the Báb's figure in the eyes of the Bahá'ís, who at first used to think of the Báb merely as a forerunner of Bahá'u'lláh (see Shoghi Effendi, *The World Order of Bahá'u'lláh*, pp. 123–4). This was also made plain by the emphasis placed on formal recognition of the Báb as part of the minimum requirements for admission into the Bahá'í fold (compare Shoghi Effendi, *Principles of Bahá'í Administration*, p. 5, and *The Promised Day Is Come*, p. 114).
27 In 'The Dispensation of Bahá'u'lláh' (*The World Order of Bahá'u'lláh*, pp. 97–157), a letter

written in 1934 'coinciding' with the 90th anniversary of the Bahá'í Faith, Shoghi Effendi's purpose was described as follows: 'My chief concern at this challenging period of Bahá'í history is rather to call the attention . . . to certain fundamental verities the elucidation of which must tremendously assist them in the effective prosecution of their mighty enterprise' (pp. 98–9). Although on his own admission he was not intent on describing historical Bahá'í events and the forces the Faith had encountered, the fact that he laid out a clear-cut serialization was more than enough to provide a historical perspective which gave meaning to the erection of the 'administrative machinery', a task which was characteristic of the 'formative age', the transitional period beginning after 'Abdu'l-Bahá's decease. In *The Promised Day Is Come* and later in *God Passes By* Shoghi Effendi made two different attempts at both describing the forces unleashed by the Revelation of Bahá'u'lláh and at 'defining' the main events which could be discerned in Bahá'í and non-Bahá'í history.

28 See 'Abdu'l-Bahá, *Some Answered Questions*, p. 161: 'a universal **cycle** (*dawriy-i-kullí*) in the world of existence comprises a vast span of time (*muddatí madídih*), and countless ages (*qurún*) and epochs (*a'ṣar*)'.

29 See Bayat, *Mysticism and Dissent*, p. 52: '"Holy law and moral principles", he wrote, "are the nourishment of the spirit." It is, therefore, imperative that the laws be diverse; "sometimes earlier commands have to be cancelled", so that the child grows naturally in strength and ability.'

30 'No sooner had mankind attained the stage of maturity, than the Word revealed to men's eyes the latent energies with which it had been endowed – energies which manifested themselves in the plenitude of their glory when the Ancient Beauty appeared, in the year sixty, in the person of Ali-Muhammad, the Báb' (Bahá'u'lláh, *Gleanings* XXXIII, p. 77).

31 See 'Abdu'l-Bahá, *Some Answered Questions*, ch. 13, pp. 78–81.

32 'Abdu'l-Bahá, *The Promulgation of Universal Peace*, pp. 37–8.

33 See Rabbani, *The Priceless Pearl*, pp. 37–8, where Gibbon in particular, as well as Carlyle and the King James version of the Bible, is referred to as greatly admired for his style.

34 Shoghi Effendi, *The World Order of Bahá'u'lláh*, p. 74.

35 'The Goal of a New World Order', ibid. p. 33.

36 See Shoghi Effendi, *The Promised Day Is Come*, p. 19: 'Most of the pre-eminent embodiments of power and sovereignty in His day became, one by one, the object of Bahá'u'lláh's special attention, and were made to sustain, in varying degrees, the weight of the force communicated by His appeals and warnings.'

37 Shoghi Effendi, *God Passes By*, p. xvii.

38 Out of love and respect for Bahíyyih Khánum, 'Abdu'l-Bahá's sister, Shoghi Effendi dated the end of the heroic age 'more particularly' at the time of her death (*The World Order of Bahá'u'lláh*, p. 98). Bahíyyih Khánum had acted several times as deputy head of the Bahá'í Faith in the absence of Shoghi Effendi. Her role was crucial in securing that the Will and Testament of 'Abdu'l-Bahá and other Bahá'í properties would remain safe in the intervening period between 'Abdu'l-Bahá's death and Shoghi Effendi's arrival in Haifa.

39 Shoghi Effendi, letter to the National Spiritual Assembly of the Bahá'is of India dated 9 April 1949, in Shoghi Effendi, *Dawn of a New Day*, pp. 134–5.

40 Shoghi Effendi, *Bahá'í Administration*, p. 63.

41 See for example *The World Order of Bahá'u'lláh*, pp. 18–22, 56–7, 60–61.

42 'They must try to obtain, from sources that are authoritative and unbiased, a sound knowledge of the history and tenets of Islám – the source and background of their Faith – and approach reverently and with a mind purged from pre-conceived ideas the study of the Qur'án which, apart from the sacred scriptures of the Bábí and Bahá'í Revelations, constitutes the only Book which can be regarded as absolutely authenticated Repository of the Word of God' (Shoghi Effendi,

The Advent of Divine Justice, p. 41). Some knowledge of comparative religion and history was also very valuable (ibid. p. 43). Thus in a letter written on behalf of Shoghi Effendi the study of History, Economics and Sociology is recommended not only because of their intrinsic value as disciplines, but also because the Bahá'í teachings 'cast an entirely new light' upon them (quoted in the compilation by the Universal House of Justice *Unrestrained as the Wind*, p. 71.

43 'Therein lies the strength of the unity of the Faith, of the validity of a Revelation that claims not to destroy or belittle previous Revelations, but to connect, unify, and fulfil them' (Shoghi Effendi, *The World Order of Bahá'u'lláh*, p. 22). See Chapter 27 for a lengthier discussion of the concept of unity of religion in the Bahá'í writings.

44 See Shoghi Effendi, *Bahá'í Administration*, p. 92.

45 Shoghi Effendi, *The Advent of Divine Justice*, pp. 60–61 (emphasis added).

46 See for instance the opening words of Shoghi Effendi's message addressed to those attending the African Intercontinental Conference (February 1953, in Shoghi Effendi, *Messages to the Bahá'í World*, p. 135). Often important Bahá'í events, notably the series of Intercontinental Bahá'í Conferences, were marked by the display of some precious relics of Bahá'u'lláh, or by photos or designs showing the models of the buildings to be erected in the Holy Land. Significantly, one such building which was completed in Shoghi Effendi's lifetime was the Bahá'í International Archives (see Rabbani. *The Priceless Pearl,* pp. 264–5), the precursor of the future Bahá'í Archives which Shoghi Effendi urged national and local Bahá'í communities to establish. See also Shoghi Effendi, *Directives from the Guardian*, pp. 4–5.

47 See for instance the conjunction of events identified by Shoghi Effendi in the erection of the Báb's mausoleum and in the evolution of the American Bahá'í community (Shoghi Effendi, *Citadel of Faith*, p. 53).

48 ibid.p. 91. Shoghi Effendi refers to these two centres as 'the twin spiritual, administrative World Centres permanently fixed in the Holy Land constituting the midmost heart of the entire planet' (*Messages to the Bahá'í World*, pp. 8–9).

49 See Bahá'u'lláh, *The Kitáb-i-Aqdas*, para. 32, p. 30, and note 54, p. 191.

50 See *Visiting Bahá'í Holy Places*.

51 Shoghi Effendi, *Citadel of Faith*, p. 95. The remains were interred at the Shrine of the Báb on Mount Carmel. Since the Báb was known also for his title of 'Primal Point' (*Nuqṭiy-i-Ulá),* Shoghi Effendi establishes a 'physical description' of the world, divided in nine concentric circles, on the basis of this analogy, thus vindicating for the Báb the position which externally was denied him in his lifetime.

52 The actual line describing the arc was traced by hand by Shoghi Effendi on the slopes of Mount Carmel and was announced to the Bahá'í world community as a major event, doubtless a testimonial to the symbolical importance of this foundational act (see Rabbani, *The Priceless Pearl,* pp. 265–6).

53 Speaking of Shoghi Effendi's love for gardens, Professor Alain Locke wrote: 'They [gardens] were important because they all were meant to dramatize the emotion of the place and quicken the soul even through the senses' (quoted ibid. p. 85).

54 See Rabbani, *The Priceless Pearl,* p. 85. This description is said in connection with Shoghi Effendi's interest in gardens.

55 Shoghi Effendi makes extensive use of the binary system, for example, when referring to several instances of twin processes. His is a symmetrical arrangement which sees forces faced by counterforces, positive parts correlating with positive counterparts, processes synchronizing with other processes, and so on. There might be in this some strong affinity with Sufi thought. As Bo Utas has pointed out, 'many investigators have noticed the dichotomy or dualism inherent in Sufi terminology'. Dichotomies, pairs, pairs of opposites, paronyms, antithesis, synonyms,

antonyms appear quite abundantly in Sufi literature (See Utas, *A Persian Sufi Poem: Vocabulary and Terminology*, pp. 195–202.This mode of thinking had also parallels with the enlightenment penchant for dyads and triads, including the Hegelian dialectics of thesis and antithesis.

56 See Shoghi Effendi, *The Promised Day Is Come*, p. 119.

57 Shoghi Effendi, quoted in *The Compilation of Compilations*, vol. 2, no. 1619, p. 192.

58 Shoghi Effendi, *God Passes By*, pp. 223–4.

59 Shoghi Effendi, *The Advent of Divine Justice*, p. 74.

60 Shoghi Effendi was writing most of his main works during the mid-thirties and forties at a time when Carl Jung's theory of synchronicity had only started to be developed. Jung would also talk about 'acausal parallelism'.

61 See Shoghi Effendi, *Citadel of Faith*, p. 102.

62 For an instance of the language used by Shoghi Effendi in this connection, see *Citadel of Faith*, pp. 31–2: 'Indeed, if we would read aright the signs of the times, and appraise correctly the significance of contemporaneous events . . . we cannot fail to perceive the workings of two simultaneous processes . . .'

63 Shoghi Effendi, *The World Order of Bahá'u'lláh*, p. 170.

64 ibid. and ff.

65 This conception appears clearly illustrated in the description of the Báb's Manifestation as 'the opening scene of the initial act of this great drama (Shoghi Effendi, *God Passes By*, p. 4). The Ten Year Plan (1953–1963) was similarly described as 'the greatest spiritual drama the world has ever witnessed' (Shoghi Effendi, *Messages to Canada*, p. 44).

66 'Opportunities, though multiplying with every passing hour, will not recur, some for another century, others never again' (*Citadel of Faith*, p. 85).

67 The following is an instance of how the possibility of failure is used as a corrective: 'I refuse to believe that its members, invested with unique apostolic mission of 'Abdu'l-Bahá, will shrink from meeting the most challenging requirement of the present hour' (ibid. p. 45).

68 For a highly dramatized call by Shoghi Effendi directed to the Bahá'ís of the world in 1953 see ibid. p. 120: Bahá'ís must prepare themselves to disperse everywhere and get ready to have an 'inevitable encounter with the organized forces of superstition, of corruption and of unbelief'. Similar lists of ills can be found in Shoghi Effendi's summons to struggle against the: 'rising forces of materialism, nationalism, secularism, racialism, ecclesiasticism' (ibid. p. 149); 'evil forces which a relentless and all-pervasive materialism, the cancerous growth of militant racialism, political corruption, unbridled capitalism, wide-spread lawlessness and gross immorality' (ibid. p. 154). See also Shoghi Effendi, *Messages to the Bahá'í World*, p. 37.

69 Shoghi Effendi, *Citadel of Faith*, p. 93. It might be very tempting to trace back these images of dualistic confrontation to some sort of Zoroastrian origins; but there is scarcely any need for posing any indirect influences given the fact that apocalyptic imagery and its underlying Mazdean subthemes have been very present in Muslim messianic speculation. On the other hand, as Henri Corbin has shown, such themes can be found in many other areas of Muslim thought (see, for instance, *Spiritual Body and Celestial Earth, From Mazdean Iran to Shiite Iran*).

70 *Citadel of Faith*, pp. 56–7. Shoghi Effendi goes on to detail this inverted relationship (see also ibid. pp. 85–6).

71 See Sorel, *Reflexiones sobre la violencia*, originally published in 1908; and Jünger, *Storm of Steel*, originally published in 1920. Perhaps even more representative of the war mystique are the aphorisms of Quinton, *Maximes sur la guerre*, which constitute an unapologetic paean to all the alleged good that comes in the trail of war (see also Caillois, *La cuesta de la guerra*, pp. 212–17). Most of these works exalt 'instinct', the 'mass man', and above all 'action', all of them supremely incarnated in war, but also present in other myths of violence such as the general strike, the dictatorship of the proletariat, and the iron fist metaphor. The fascination

with 'action' as a value in itself explains, according to De Jouvenel, the admiration often felt by intellectuals and military men alike towards Napoleon or Stalin (see his *Los Orígenes del estado modern*: *Historia de las ideas polìticas en el siglo XIX*, pp. 22–30; French original title *Les débuts de l'Etat moderne: Une histoire des idées politiques au XIXe siècle.*

72 Shoghi Effendi, *The Promised Day Is Come*, para. 144, p. 57.

73 ibid. para. 146, pp. 58–9: 'Francis Joseph, Emperor of Austria, King of Hungary, a reactionary ruler, reestablished old abuses, ignored the rights of nationalities, and restored that bureaucratic centralization that proved in the end so injurious to his empire.'

74 ibid. para. 260, p. 105: 'What a sorry spectacle of impotence and disruption does this fratricidal war, which Christian nations are waging against Christian nations – Anglicans pitted against Lutherans, Catholics against Greek Orthodox, Catholics against Catholics, and Protestants against Protestants – in support of a so-called Christian civilization, offer to the eyes of those who are already perceiving the bankruptcy of the institutions that claim to speak in the name, and to be the custodians, of the Faith of Jesus Christ! The powerlessness and despair of the Holy See to halt this internecine strife, in which the children of the Prince of Peace – blessed and supported by the benedictions and harangues of the prelates of a hopelessly divided church – are engaged, proclaim the degree of subservience into which the once all-powerful institutions of the Christian Faith have sunk, and are a striking reminder of the parallel state of decadence into which the hierarchies of its sister religion have fallen.'

75 Shoghi Effendi, *Messages to the Bahá'í World*, 1950–1957, pp. 74–5.

76 Thus Shoghi Effendi explains in a cablegram that the inception of 'the intercontinental stage in administrative evolution' of the Bahá'í Faith 'acclaimed by posterity as *counterpart to consolidation Faith* at its World Centre through recent formation International Bahá'í Council in Holy Land' (ibid. p. 17; emphasis added).

77 See Shoghi Effendi, *The World Order of Bahá'u'lláh*, p. 162.

78 Shoghi Effendi clarifies: 'The founding of the Administrative Order of the Faith of Bahá'u'lláh – a system which is at once the harbinger, the nucleus and pattern of His World Order' (*God Passes By*, p. xv).

79 This seems to imply the election of a capital city which would act as the administrative seat of the Bahá'í Commonwealth of Nations.

80 Shoghi Effendi, *The World Order of Bahá'u'lláh,* p. 163: 'The emergence of a world community, the consciousness of world citizenship, the founding of a world civilization and culture – all of which must synchronize with the initial stages in the unfoldment of the Golden Age of the Bahá'í Era – should, by their very nature, be regarded, as far as this planetary life is concerned, as the furthermost limits in the organization of human society, though man, as an individual, will, nay must indeed as a result of such a consummation, continue indefinitely to progress and develop.'

81 Shoghi Effendi, *This Decisive Hour*, p. 36.

82 Shoghi Effendi, *Messages to the Bahá'í World*, p. 75.

83 Shoghi Effendi, *The World Order of Bahá'u'lláh*, p. 164.

84 See ibid. p. 163.

85 'Abdu'l-Bahá, *Tablets of Abdul Baha Abbas*, vol. III, p. 553.

86 Shoghi Effendi's visionary writings began in the 1930s. Shoghi Effendi's 'short term' is the very long term of politicians.

87 Shoghi Effendi, *Citadel of Faith*, p. 6.

88 See ibid. p. 32. According to Shoghi Effendi the end of the first epoch would coincide with the 'fulfilment of the prophecy mentioned by Daniel in the last chapter of His Book, related to the year 1335, and associated by 'Abdu'l-Bahá with the world triumph of the faith of His Father'. Shoghi Effendi identified that date with the conclusion of the Ten Year Crusade (ibid. p. 50) and

the celebration of the Most Great Jubilee, 'the hundredth anniversary of the formal assumption by Bahá'u'lláh of His Prophetic Office', i.e. 1963. As Shoghi Effendi passed away in 1957, it fell upon the institution of the Hands of the Cause to execute the rest of the Ten Year Crusade and make preparations for both the Most Great Jubilee and the election of the Universal House of Justice. The way for the election of this institution had been prepared by Shoghi Effendi when he created the Bahá'í International Council in 1951 (See Shoghi Effendi, *Messages to the Bahá'í World*, pp. 7–9, 22). The main reason for choosing 1963 for that election was made necessary by the course of events. In the absence of clear authoritative guidance from then onwards, it was imperative to appoint an institution which, following the provisions of 'Abdu'l-Bahá's Will and Testament and Shoghi Effendi's instructions, would be endowed with authority to take the reins of the Bahá'í community. See Shoghi Effendi, *The World Order of Bahá'u'lláh*, p. 148.

89 In 1992, coinciding with the centenary of Bahá'u'lláh's passing, the 'Scroll of Honour' mentioned by Shoghi Effendi (*Citadel of Faith*, p. 119) was deposited at the entrance door of Bahá'u'lláh's shrine at Bahjí. The Scroll contained the names of all those Bahá'í believers responsible for the opening of the territories mentioned.

90 Shoghi Effendi was punctilious in recording some events of particular import in this regard. A fatwa by the Supreme Religious Court of Egypt was hailed as a document demonstrative of the independent status of the Faith: 'This decision . . . may be regarded as an initial step taken by our very opponents in the path of the eventual universal acceptance of the Bahá'í Faith, as one of the independent recognized religious systems of the world' (Shoghi Effendi, *Bahá'í Administration*, p. 101). Subsequent cases of recognition were duly recorded in the *Bahá'í Year Book* (*Bahá'í World*). But perhaps the most outstanding instances of such recognition were those accorded to the Bahá'í International Community as a result of its interaction with the United Nations in connection with the creation of the State of Israel and the wave of persecutions of the Iranian Bahá'í community.

91 As Lichtheim recalls in his *Imperialism* (p. 92), nationalism and its populist expressions had been considered 'demagogic and subversive before becoming conservative and respectable' in the eyes of nineteenth century Russian and German governments. Shoghi Effendi's strong condemnation of nationalism (placed on a par with racism and communism) was couched in religious terms ('fetish', 'idol', 'gods') and hence regarded as a powerful destructive force devoid of reality. Soviet style internationalism had the added problem of disguising its increasing nationalistic turn with denunciations of always suspect bourgeois cosmopolitism. See *The Promised Day Is Come*, para. 291, pp. 117–18.

92 See 'The Unfoldment of World Civilization', in Shoghi Effendi, *The World Order of Bahá'u'lláh*, p. 180.

93 Letter on behalf of Shoghi Effendi to the National Spiritual Assembly of the United States, 14 March 1939, in *The Compilation of Compilations*, vol. 2, pp. 194–5.

94 'Abdu'l-Bahá, *Selections from the Writings of 'Abdu'l-Bahá*, no. 15, p. 32.

95 Cited in Lee, *Prelude to the Lesser Peace*, p. 83.

96 'Abdu'l-Bahá, *'Abdu'l-Bahá in London*, p. 106. For an equally clear statement to the same effect see 'Abdu'l-Bahá, *Muntakhabátí az Makátíb-i-Ḥaḍrat-i-'Abdu'l-Bahá*, vol. 4, pp. 227–8.

97 See Taherzadeh, *The Covenant of Bahá'u'lláh*, p. 413.

98 This can be documented in the case of the Bahá'í poet Robert Hayden; see Hansell, 'The Spiritual Unity of Robert Hayden's Angle of Ascent', in *Black American Forum*, vol. 13, no. 1 (1979), p. 24.

99 Bahá'u'lláh, *Gleanings from the Writings of Bahá'u'lláh*, LXI, pp. 118–19.

100 Bahá'u'lláh, *Hidden Words*, Persian no. 63.

101 Shoghi Effendi, *Citadel of Faith*, p. 58. By 'champion builders of Bahá'u'lláh's rising World

Order' Shoghi Effendi means the North American Bahá'í community, whose role throughout Bahá'í history has been vital, perhaps no more so than during the climactic Ten Year Crusade, between 1953 and 1963.

102 Letter written on behalf of Shoghi Effendi, 21 November 1949, in *Lights of Guidance*, no. 266.

103 Such an understanding would have placed the Bahá'í approach to peace on a similar footing with the Marxist stance, described by Raymond Aron as 'catastrophic optimism' ('War and Industrial Society', p. 361).

104 See Peter Smith, *The Babi and Baha'i Religions*, pp. 140–44. Smith illustrates the millenarian pattern of thought with examples from prominent Bahá'ís such as Martha Root, John Esslemont and Horace Holley.

105 *The Ministry of the Custodians, 1957–1963*, p. 115.

106 Shoghi Effendi, *The World Order of Bahá'u'lláh*, p. 46.

107 Shoghi Effendi, *The Promised Day Is Come*, para. 291, p. 117.

108 Shoghi Effendi, *The World Order of Bahá'u'lláh*, p. 202. Since Shoghi Effendi was writing at a time when the world map reflected enormous colonial boundaries, it seems obvious that he was not inferring that new nations were not or ought not to be born. Shoghi Effendi was referring critically to the processes that had been at work precisely between the leading nations of the world. It was this process of anarchy that Shoghi Effendi considered exhausted.

109 It should be recalled that the United Nations, just as its predecessor the League of Nations, is founded on the principle of equality among sovereign states and that this very definition imposes serious restrictions on the functioning of the UN system as a whole, particularly when the enforcing of its peace-keeping capabilities is put to the test.

110 'Abdu'l-Bahá, *Tablets of the Divine Plan*, p. 101.

111 ibid. p. 102.

112 Shoghi Effendi, *The Promised Day Is Come*, para. 294, p. 120.

113 Shoghi Effendi, *The Unfolding Destiny of the British Isles*, p. 456. In the absence of further explanations it remains rather conjectural to determine whether Shoghi Effendi was identifying perhaps the early ecumenism of the Islamic *ummah* as a crucible where tribal rivalries were transcended by a higher sense of loyalty (boosted by a common religious belief and a common language). How this would differ from the concept of 'Christendom', or rather *Corpus Christianum*, would be a matter for more serious comparative studies.

114 Shoghi Effendi did not hesitate to label unbridled nationalism as one of the three greatest scourges of contemporary humanity, the other two being racism and communism. See *The Promised Day Is Come*, para. 291, pp. 117–18.

115 Shoghi Effendi, *The World Order of Bahá'u'lláh*, p. 202.

116 This idea was expressed in 1994 by the Bahá'í International Community, *The Prosperity of Humankind*, in connection with the issue of power, p. 19.

117 Shoghi Effendi, *The World Order of Bahá'u'lláh*, p. 191.

118 Shoghi Effendi, *God Passes By*, p. 305.

119 See Renouvin, *Historia de las relaciones internacionales*, pp. 919–27; original in French: *Histoire des relations internationales*, 4 vols. (1954, rev. 1994).

120 Shoghi Effendi, *The World Order of Bahá'u'lláh*, p. 193.

121 Shoghi Effendi, *The Promised Day Is Come*, para. 144, p. 58.

122 The 'spirit of Locarno' would lead to a period of unprecedented optimism in war-ravaged Europe aptly described by Stefan Zweig in his melancholic 'Sunset' chapter in *The World of Yesterday*, pp. 248–70. The Stresman and Briand 1929 proposal for the formation of the United States of Europe would be met with failure one year later.

123 Shoghi Effendi, *Bahá'í Administration*, p. 146. The re-enactment referred to by Shoghi Effendi is a direct allusion to the process of nation building which transformed feudalistic European

nations into modern states. In this implicit analogy the world nations stand confronted before the super-state as the former feudal territories stood before the emerging monarchies.

124 Shoghi Effendi, *The World Order of Bahá'u'lláh*, p. 193. This move by the League was also hailed by Shoghi Effendi as 'an event without parallel in human history' (ibid. p. 191).

125 ibid. pp. 191–2.

126 ibid. pp. 193–4.

127 See Rabbani, *The Priceless Pearl*, p. 189: 'In the post-war years, as the victories the Bahá'ís were winning multiplied and the United Nations – the mightiest instrument for creating peace that men had ever devised – emerged, many of us no doubt hoped, and wishfully believed, that we had left the worst phase of humanity's long history of war behind us and that we could now discern the first light of that dawn we Bahá'ís are so firmly convinced lies ahead for the world.'

128 See Shoghi Effendi, *Messages to the Bahá'í World*, p. 27.

129 This took place in 1947. The successful application was accompanied soon by a Bahá'í Declaration of Human Obligations and Rights as well as a Bahá'í Statement on the Rights of Women. One year later the status was further strengthened with the establishment of the Bahá'í International Community (Rabbani, *The Priceless Pearl*, pp. 304–5).

130 Text of the declaration available from http://info.Bahá'í.org/article-1-8-3-1.html. A summary of the contribution of the Bahá'í International Community appears in Hassall, 'Rights to Human and Social Development: A Survey of the Activities of the Bahá'í International Community', in Tahirih Tahririha-Danesh (ed): *Bahá'í-Inspired Perspectives on Human Rights*, pp. 102–22. For a Bahá'í perspective on human rights see also Weinberg, 'The Human Rights Discourse: A Bahá'í Perspective,' http://info.Bahá'í.org/article-1-8-3-2.html.

131 See *The Bahá'í World*, vol. XIII (1954–1963), pp. 795–802, cit. by Huffines, 'Bahá'í Proposals for the Reformation of World Order', in Bahador and Ghanea, *Processes of the Lesser Peace*, p. 43.

132 Rommel's advances through Northern Africa on his way to Jerusalem were a source of concern for the Bahá'í sites. The Nazi regime suppressed the Bahá'í administrative system and confined to prison and executed some of the more prominent Bahá'ís under its rule. Moreover the Grand Mufti, whose pro-Nazi sympathies were no secret, was a declared opponent of the Bahá'í Faith (see Rabbani, *The Priceless Pearl*, pp. 183–4). Dangers continued looming on the horizon for some time. The outbreak of the first Arab–Israeli war was not exempted of its own quota of perils and crossfire (ibid. pp. 187–8).

133 The covering letter of the written submission is reproduced in Rabbáni, *The Priceless Pearl*, pp. 287–9. 'It must be remembered', writes Shoghi Effendi's widow, 'that the only oriental notable of any standing whatsoever who had not fled from Palestine before the War of Independence was Shoghi Effendi. This fact was not lost on the authorities of the new State . . .'

134 During the late 1920s representations were made before the Mandate Commission of the League of Nations to claim the property of Bahá'u'lláh's house in Baghdad (see Shoghi Effendi, *Bahá'í Administration*, pp. 180–81).

135 See Shoghi Effendi, *Messages to the Bahá'í World*, p. 43.

136 A cable sent by Shoghi Effendi in 1951 brings to relief such a correlation: 'Gigantic process now set in motion opening decade second Bahá'í Century synchronizing with, deriving notable impetus through birth of sovereign State, Holy Land, greatly accelerated through series of swiftly succeeding events originated in World Centre of Faith.' (*Messages to the Bahá'í World, 1950–1957*, p. 19) One of the main functions of the Bahá'í International Council, the forerunner of the Universal House of Justice, was that of assisting Shoghi Effendi in his dealings with the State of Israel (see Shoghi Effendi, ibid. p. 8; and *Citadel of Faith*, pp. 93. 147).

137 Shoghi Effendi, *God Passes By*, p. 224.

138 Shoghi Effendi, *Citadel of Faith*, p. 109.

139 'It was this community, the cradle and stronghold of the Administrative Order of the Faith of Bahá'u'lláh . . .' (ibid. pp. 34, 110–11; see also Shoghi Effendi, *The Advent of Divine Justice,* p. 7). For a historical summary of the steps involved in the evolution of the Bahá'í administrative system, see Smith, *The Bábí and Bahá'í Religions,* pp. 120–22. The organization of local and national communities and the way they were to interact were set forth respectively in the local and national by-laws of the Local Spiritual Assembly of the Bahá'ís of New York, and of the National Spiritual Assembly of the Bahá'ís of North America.

140 Shoghi Effendi, *Citadel of Faith*, p. 32.

141 Shoghi Effendi praised the American president as follows: 'To her President, the immortal Woodrow Wilson, must be ascribed the unique honour, among the statesmen of any nation, whether of the East or of the West, of having voiced sentiments so akin to the principles animating the Cause of Bahá'u'lláh, and of having more than any other leader, contributed to the creation of the League of Nations' (ibid. p. 36).

142 ibid. p. 33.

143 ibid.

144 ibid.

145 Shoghi Effendi brought home this idea to the American Bahá'í believers in *The Advent of Divine Justice.* There, an effort was made to discriminate between America's great potentialities and the crude reality of its condition. No 'inherent excellence or special merit' could explain their being singled out for that position of honour (pp. 15–16).

146 Shoghi Effendi, *Citadel of Faith*, p. 37.

147 ibid. p. 36.

148 See Shoghi Effendi, *The Advent of Divine Justice*, p. 74.

149 Shoghi Effendi, *Citadel of Faith*, p. 126.

150 Shoghi Effendi, *The Advent of Divine Justice*, pp. 76–7.

151 The American 'splendid isolation' was the main impediment preventing America from entering World War I. See for instance the positions advanced by Bushnell and Lovejoy, *Handbook of the War, for Readers, Speakers and Teachers*, pp. 3–4.

152 Shoghi Effendi, *The Advent of Divine Justice*, p. 74.

153 Kissinger, *Diplomacy*, pp. 18–19.

154 Shoghi Effendi, *Citadel of Faith*, p. 126.

155 ibid. The first national plan ever to be implemented by the North American Bahá'í community identified racism as the most 'challenging issue' (see Shoghi Effendi, *The Advent of Divine Justice*, pp. 28–34).

156 Shoghi Effendi, *Citadel of Faith*, p. 126.

157 For a description of Bahá'í activities concerning race relations see Thomas, 'A Long and Thorny Path: Race Relations in the American Bahá'í Community', in *Circle of Unity: Bahá'í Approaches to Current Social Issues*, pp. 37–65. The race amity meetings were praised by Shoghi Effendi (see Shoghi Effendi, *Bahá'í Adminsitration,* p. 129). See also Morrison, *To Move the World: Louis Gregory and the Advancement of Racial Unity in America.*

158 Bahá'u'lláh, *The Kitáb-i-Aqdas*, para. 64, p. 42. The word 'mischief' or 'corruption' (*fasad*) alludes to a profound corruption of one's nature that results in public disorder or, more generically, unrest. It is a broad category that may combine features of moral outrage, social alarm, etc. For a comparative study of the term see Iqbal and Lewis, 'Governance and Corruption: Can Islamic Societies and the West Learn from Each Other?', in *American Journal of Islamic Social Sciences*, vol. 19, no. 2 (2002), pp. 1–33.

159 'Abdu'l-Bahá's talks with Laura Clifford Barney were published in 1908 under the title *Some Answered Questions.* In this work 'Abdu'l-Bahá, while upholding the right of the community

to defend itself from criminals, strongly advises non-retaliation in cases of one-to-one personal aggression, and the deployment of educational and preventive measures as means of curtailing crime (Chs. 76 and 77, pp. 306–14).

160 See Pokorny, 'Bahá'ís and American Peace Movements', p. 319.

161 As stated by Charles Chatfield: 'The meaning of the word pacifist changed under pressures for patriotic conformity in 1917–1918. Having had the benign connotation of one who advocated international cooperation for peace, it narrowed to mean one who would not support even a "war to end war"' (Chatfield, 'World War I and the Liberal Pacifist in the United States', in *The American Historical Review*, vol. 75, no. 7 (1970), pp. 1920–1937.

162 'Abdu'l-Bahá had emphasized the importance of the two ('Abdu'l-Bahá, *Will and Testament*, quoted in Shoghi Effendi, *Bahá'í Administration*, pp. 10–11), and Shoghi Effendi called repeatedly on Bahá'ís to dispel any doubts on their compatibility (ibid. p. 197).

163 See *Directives from the Guardian*, no. 144, p. 53. The Universal House of Justice has restated this guideline, adding: 'Bahá'ís cannot voluntarily enlist in any branch of the Armed Forces where they would be subject to engage in the taking of human life' (*Lights of Guidance*, no. 826.). In the United States Bahá'ís applying for exemption were required by law to prove their membership in the Bahá'í community. This in turn made it advisable for the American Bahá'ís to restate their faith at the age of fifteen (ibid. no. 224, p. 71).

164 Shoghi Effendi, *Directives from the Guardian*, no. 132, p. 48.

165 Shoghi Effendi, *Citadel of Faith*, p. 90.

166 Shoghi Effendi, *Directives from the Guardian*, no. 144, p. 53.

167 ibid. no. 145, p. 54.

168 The Universal House of Justice maintains this recommendation even in cases of civil unrest.

169 'Regarding your question about children fighting: the statement of the Master, not to strike back, should not be taken so extremely literally that Bahá'í children must accept to be bullied and thrashed. If they can manage to show a better way of settling disputes than by active self-defence, they should naturally do so' (*The Compilation of Compilations*, vol. 1, p. 306).

170 See Karlberg, 'Constructive Resilience: The Bahá'í Response to Oppression'. One may be tempted to establish a link between this notion and the traditional concept of fortitude in Christian theology, which includes a profound sense of what Craig Titus calls 'theological flourishing' (see Titus, *Resilience and Christian Virtues: What the Psychosocial Sciences Offer for the Renewal of Thomas Aquinas' Moral Theology of Fortitude and Its Related Virtues*, p. 397).

171 Shoghi Effendi refers to the Kitáb-i-Aqdas as 'the Mother Book of His Dispensation, and the Charter of His [Bahá'u'lláh's] New World Order' (*God Passes By*, p. 213). Similarly, the *Will and Testament of 'Abdu'l-Bahá* is also described as the 'Charter of a future world civilization' (ibid. p. 328). 'Abdu'l-Bahá's *Tablets of the Divine Plan* are also referred as the 'Charter of the Master Plan of the appointed Centre of Bahá'u'lláh's Covenant' (Shoghi Effendi, *Citadel of Faith*, p. 113).

172 ibid. p. 58: '. . . and the wings of yet another conflict, destined to contribute a distinct, and perhaps a decisive, share to the birth of the new Order which must signalize the advent of the Lesser Peace . . .'

173 See Shoghi Effendi, *The World Order of Bahá'u'lláh*, pp. 19 and 65.

174 ibid. p. 79.

4 The Nature of Man in the Bahá'í Writings

1 'Abdu'l-Bahá, *The Secret of Divine Civilization*, p. 66.

2 'Abdu'l-Bahá, *Selections from the Writings of 'Abdu'l-Bahá*, no. 15, p. 32.

3 'Abdu'l-Bahá, quoted in *Star of the West*, vol. 17, p. 238.

4 Bahá'u'lláh, *The Kitáb-i-Aqdas*, para. 75, p. 47.
5 'Abdu'l-Bahá, *Selections from the Writings of 'Abdu'l-Bahá*, no. 201, p. 246.
6 In dealing with this underlying theoretical problem past thinkers have developed what Waltz has termed 'images' of war, i.e. representations that locate violent conflicts in either the nature of individual human beings, the State, or in the kind of conflictive relationships obtaining between States (see Waltz, *Man, the State and War: A Theoretical Analysis*).
7 See Bahá'u'lláh, *The Summons of the Lord of Hosts*, pp. 66–7.
8 Bahá'u'lláh, *Gleanings from the Writings of Bahá'u'lláh*, LXXVIII, p. 151.
9 Bahá'u'lláh, *Hidden Words*, Arabic no. 24: 'Transgress not thy limits (*ḥadd),* nor claim that which beseemeth thee not. Prostrate thyself before the countenance of thy God, the Lord of might and power.'
10 See Eliade, *The Myth of the Eternal Return: Or, Cosmos and History.*
11 Bahá'u'lláh, *Tablets of Bahá'u'lláh*, p. 142.
12 ibid. p. 141.
13 ibid.
14 ibid. p. 142.
15 ibid. p. 140.
16 Bahá'u'lláh frequently attests to the creative power of the Word of God: 'Every event must needs have an origin and every building a builder. Verily, the Word of God is the cause which hath preceded the contingent world . . .' (ibid. p. 141).
17 ibid. p. 144. The Arabic word *ṭabí'a* (nature) means 'to provide with an imprint, impress or impression', 'to impress with a stamp, seal or signet'.
18 'Abdu'l-Bahá, *The Promulgation of Universal Peace*, p. 270.
19 Bahá'u'lláh, *Gleanings from the Writings of Bahá'u'lláh,* XCIII, p. 189.
20 Most Bahá'í prayers express this relationship, but nowhere is this truer than in the case of the obligatory prayers.
21 'Abdu'l-Bahá, *Muntakhabátí az Makátíb-i-Ḥaḍrat-i-'Abdu'l-Bahá*, p. 151.
22 Bahá'u'lláh, *Gleanings from the Writings of Bahá'u'lláh,* XCIV, pp. 193–4.
23 ibid. XCV, p. 194.
24 'Abdu'l-Bahá, *The Secret of Divine Civilization,* p. 33.
25 Bahá'u'lláh, *Gleanings from the Writings of Bahá'u'lláh,* CXXIV, p. 262. For a parallel text see also ibid. XCIII: 'Know thou that every created thing is a sign (*áyat*) of the revelation of God. Each, according to its capacity (*qadr-i-marátibhá),* is, and will ever remain, a token of the Almighty' (p. 184).
26 Bahá'u'lláh, *Kitáb-i-Íqán*, para. 107, p. 101.
27 Bahá'u'lláh, *Gleanings from the Writings of Bahá'u'lláh,* XCIII, p. 186.
28 Bahá'u'lláh, *Kitáb-i-Íqán*, para. 109, p. 102..
29 'All things are living', thus runs the Qur'ánic verse quoted by 'Abdu'l-Bahá in his 'Tablet to Dr Auguste Henri Forel', in *Bahá'í World*, vol. 15, p. 38.
30 See 'Abdu'l-Bahá, quoted in *Star of the West,* vol. XIII, no. 5 (August 1922), p. 99: 'Religion must be moving and day by day must grow and evolve. If it remains motionless it becomes decadent and declines, for the bounties of God are continuous. Inasmuch as the bounties of God are continuous religion must be growing and evolving.'
31 See 'Abdu'l-Bahá, quoted in *Star of the West*, vol. 11, no. 19 (2 March 1921), p. 317: 'Cremation suppresses it speedily from attainment to these transformations, the elements becoming so quickly decomposed that transformation to these various stages is checked.'
32 For a comprehensive treatment of the subject see Lovejoy, *Great Chain of Being*, pp. 56–9; also Guenon's *Symbolism of the Cross* and *The Multiple States of Being*. The key element in this conception is that existence embraces a succession of degrees or stations which progresses

or rather perfects itself through integration, in such a way that a higher degree of existence contains in embedded form all previous degrees, and for that very reason similarities, analogies and parallels of great symbolic value between various realities are bound to be found: 'The noblest of all earthly beings is man. In him are realized the animal, the vegetable and the mineral kingdoms, that is, all these degrees are contained in him in such wise that he is endowed with them all. And, being endowed with all these degrees and stations (*maqámáat, marátib*), he is informed of their mysteries and aware of the secrets of their existence' ('Abdu'l-Bahá, *Some Answered Questions*, ch. 40, p. 180). For a comprehensive discussion and reconciliation of the 'chain of being' perspective (logic of resemblance) and modern historical epistemologies (historical logic, logic of difference) see the various studies devoted to various aspects of this question by Nader Saiedi: *'Aql, Dín va Jam'ih dar Andíshiy-e Bahá'í* [Intellect, Religion and Society in Bahá'í Thought], *Insán dar 'Irfán-i-Bahá'í* [*Man in Bahá'í Gnosis*], *Risáliy-i-Madaniyyih, Mas'aliy-i-Taŷaddod dar Khávarmiánih* (English expanded version titled *An Introduction to 'Abdu'l-Bahá's The Secret of Divine Civilization*, Converging Realities 1, 1, Landegg Academy, 2000), and *Maẓharíyyát, Shálúdiy-i-Illaháyyát-Bahá'í* (*Theophany, Foundations of Bahá'í Theology*, pp. 5–31). Some of these questions are revisited by Saiedi in his introduction to the Báb's writings in *Gate of the Heart*, pp. 1–25, *passim*.

33 See 'Abdu'l-Bahá, quoted in *Star of the West*, vol. XIII, no. 5 (August 1922) p. 99.

34 Quoted by Zarqání, *Maḥmúd's Diary*, p. 66 (for a variant of this text see *Star of the West*, vol. 14, no. 7 (October 1923), p. 209); see also Zarqání, *Maḥmud's Diary*, p. 139: 'The chain of creation is interwoven in a natural law and divine order. Everything is interlinked. A link cannot be broken without affecting that natural order. Everything that happens is in conformity with this order and is based on consummate wisdom.'

35 See 'Abdu'l-Bahá, 'Tablet to Dr Auguste Henri Forel', in *Bahá'í World*, vol. 15, pp. 42.

36 ibid.

37 Bahá'u'lláh, *Gleanings from the Writings of Bahá'u'lláh*, XCIII, p. 188.

38 ibid. The Persian text is much more concise and synthetic than the English rendering by Shoghi Effendi. The English version brings to relief aspects which in a literal translation would have sounded obscure or in any case liable to be interpreted in the opposite way to the intended one. For instance, the last phrase 'it hath been ordained to occupy' is a gloss of the word *khud* ('its'). A literal rendering of the sentence would have read 'and each [existent] thing should be viewed in its [own] station'. Shoghi Effendi, however, implicitly establishes a contrast between God and the station of his creatures, thus underlining that no station has a standing on its own. This is quite in harmony with a previous statement by Bahá'u'lláh: 'His relationship to His creation knoweth no degrees' (ibid. p. 185).

39 Bahá'u'lláh describes, for instance, the 'station of distinction' as pertaining 'to the world of creation and to the limitations thereof'(See Bahá'u'lláh, *Kitáb-i-Íqán*, para. 191, p. 176).

40 Bahá'u'lláh, quoted in a letter from the Universal House of Justice to all National Spiritual Assemblies, 27 March 1978; also quoted in Hatcher and Martin, *The Bahá'í Faith: The Emerging Global Religion*, p. 92.

41 Bahá'u'lláh, 'The Four Valleys', para. 36, in Bahá'u'lláh, *The Call of the Divine Beloved*, p. 98.

42 Bahá'u'lláh, *Gleanings from the Writings of* Bahá'u'lláh, CXXIV, p. 262.

43 ibid. LXXXII, p. 162.

44 'Abdu'l-Bahá, *Some Answered Questions*, ch. 52, p. 231.

45 'Abdu'l-Bahá, *Paris Talks*, no. 23, p. 68.

46 'Abdu'l-Bahá, *Some Answered Questions*, ch. 51, p. 229.

47 '. . . but the reality of man is an all-encompassing (*ḥaqíqat-i-jámi'ih*) and universal reality (*ḥaqíqat-i-kullíyih*) which is the seat of the revelation of all the divine perfections. That is, a

sign of each one of the names, attributes, and perfections that we ascribe to God exists in man." (ibid. ch. 50, p. 226).

48 Letter written on behalf of Shoghi Effendi to an individual, 20 November 1937, in *Lights of Guidance*, no. 392.
49 'Abdu'l-Bahá, *Some Answered Questions*, ch. 64, p. 271.
50 See for instance 'Abdu'l-Bahá, *The Promulgation of Universal Peace*, p. 465: 'From this standpoint his nature is threefold: animal, human and divine. The animal nature is darkness; the heavenly is light in light.'
51 'Abdu'l-Bahá, *Foundations of World Unity*, p. 51.
52 'Abdu'l-Bahá, *Some Answered Questions*, ch. 55, p. 241.
53 Quoted in Zarqání, *Maḥmúd's Diary*, p. 27.
54 Abdu'l-Bahá, *Some Answered Questions*, ch. 81, p. 327.
55 'Abdu'l-Bahá, *The Promulgation of Universal Peace*, p. 69; see also pp. 69–70: 'The tree, so to speak, is the greater world, and the seed in its relation to the tree is the lesser world . . . Likewise, the greater world, the macrocosm, is latent and miniatured in the lesser world, or microcosm, of man. This constitutes the universality or perfection of virtues potential in mankind. Therefore, it is said that man has been created in the image and likeness of God.' See also 'Abdu'l-Bahá, *Some Answered Questions*, ch. 3, p. 11.
56 'Abdu'l-Bahá, 'Tablet to Dr Auguste Henri Forel', in *Bahá'í World*, vol. 15, p. 38..
57 'Abdu'l-Bahá, *Some Answered Questions*, no. 40, p. 179).
58 'Abdu'l-Bahá, *The Promulgation of Universal Peace*, p. 21.
59 ibid. p. 141.
60 Words attributed by Anna Kunz to 'Abdu'l-Bahá, in *Star of the West*, vol. 13, no. 6 (September 1922), p. 143.
61 'Abdu'l-Bahá, *The Promulgation of Universal Peace*, p. 288.
62 'Abdu'l-Bahá, *Paris Talks*, no. 20, p. 62.
63 ibid. no. 29, p. See also *Tablets of Abdul-Baha Abbas*, vol. 1, p. 116: 'The laws governing them [the vegetable, animal and human spirit] are as the laws which govern all phenomenal being (i.e., all existences belonging to the phenomenal or material universe, called "the world of generation and corruption"), in respect to generation, corruption, production, change and reversion . . .'
64 'Abdu'l-Bahá, *Some Answered Questions*, no. 32, p. 148.
65 Words attributed to 'Abdu'l-Bahá by Anna Kunz, quoted in *Star of the West*, vol. XIII, no. 6 (September 1922), p. 143.
66 *Tablets of Abdul-Baha Abbas*, vol. 1, p. 115.
67 'Abdu'l-Bahá, *The Promulgation of Universal Peace*, p. 286. The Persian term to render the concept of pantheism is the Arabic borrowing *waḥdat'ul wujúd,* that is, 'unity of existence' or 'existential monism'. 'Abdu'l-Bahá makes important qualifications, stressing that pantheism is 'true' in the sense that even a single atom may reflect 'all the virtues of life', but not in the sense that all things *are* God. Moreover, 'Abdu'l-Bahá states: 'There is neither reality nor the manifestation of reality without the instrumentality of God.'
68 See 'Abdu'l-Bahá, *Some Answered Questions*, ch. 36.
69 ibid. ch. 67, p. 281.
70 'Abdu'l-Bahá, *Selections from the Writings of 'Abdu'l-Bahá*, no. 103, p. 130.
71 Quoted in *Ḥuqúqu'lláh, The Right of God*, p. 8.
72 Bahá'u'lláh, 'The Seven Valleys', para. 14, in Bahá'u'lláh, *The Call of the Divine Beloved*, p. 18.
73 ibid. para. 8 (p. 16). Interestingly, the term *taqlíd* (plural *taqálid*) appears translated sometimes as 'dogmas'. See 'Abdu'l-Bahá, *Tablets of the Divine Plan*, p. 32. See also ibid. pp. 93–4,

where the word *taqlíd* appears three times and is translated as 'imitations', 'dogmas' and 'superstitions' respectively.

74 ibid. para. 13 (p. 17).

75 See ibid. para. 5 (p. 15): 'The steed of this valley is patience (*ṣabr);* without patience the wayfarer on this journey will reach nowhere and attain no goal.'

76 'Abdu'l-Bahá, *The Promulgation of Universal Peace*, p. 148.

77 ibid. p. 160.

78 See Bahá'u'lláh, *Kitáb-i-Íqán*, para. 2, p. 3.

79 'Abdu'l-Bahá, *The Promulgation of Universal Peace*, p. 195.

80 See 'Abdu'l-Bahá, *Some Answered Questions*, ch. 40, p. 179.

81 'Abdu'l-Bahá, *Paris Talks*, no. 31, p. 98.

82 ibid. no. 28, p. 84. See also Weil, *Closer than your Life-Vein: An Insight Into the Wonders of Spiritual Fulfillment.*

83 'Abdu'l-Bahá, *Some Answered Questions*, ch. 58, p. 251.

84 Bahá'u'lláh, *Kitáb-i-Íqán*, para. 76, p. 69.

85 Bahá'u'lláh, *Gleanings from the Writings of Bahá'u'lláh,* CLX, p. 338.

86 'Abdu'l-Bahá, *Paris Talks*, no. 9, p. 28.

87 ibid. no. 22, pp. 65–6.

88 'Abdu'l-Bahá, *Some Answered Questions*, ch. 71, p. 292.

89 ibid. ch. 3, pp. 10–11.

90 ibid. p. 11.

91 'Abdu'l-Bahá, *Selections from the Writings of 'Abdu'l-Bahá*, no. 25, p. 54.

92 'Abdu'l-Bahá, *Some Answered Questions*, ch. 67, p. 281.

93 'Abdu'l-Bahá, *Selections from the Writings of 'Abdu'l-Bahá*, no. 68, p. 105.

94 Bahá'u'lláh, *Gleanings from the Writings of Bahá'u'lláh,* LXXXII, pp. 165–6.

95 Bahá'u'lláh decries the attempt by Ḥájí Mírzá Karím K͟hán Kirmání to consider a number of esoteric sciences as indispensable to the attainment of a proper understanding of the mysteries of the *mi'ráj*. (Bahá'u'lláh, *Kitáb-i-Íqán*, para. 203, p. 185).

96 ibid. para. 201, p. 182.

97 Bahá'u'lláh, *Tablets of Bahá'u'lláh*, p. 144.

98 See 'Abdu'l-Bahá, *The Promulgation of Universal Peace*, p. 253: 'Every subject presented to a thoughtful audience must be supported by rational proofs and logical arguments. Proofs are of four kinds: first, through sense perception; second, through the reasoning faculty; third, from traditional or scriptural authority; fourth, through the medium of inspiration.'

99 'Abdu'l-Bahá sees the fourth method exemplified in the school of the Illuminati (*is͟hráqíyyún, ḥikmat-i-is͟hráq*), also known as followers of the inner light, that is, the post-Avicennian Islamic Neo-platonists, whom he describes as a Society of Friends whose meetings were held in silence (*Paris Talks*, no. 54, p. 185; needless to say, not to be confounded with the Quakers, despite the similarities). On the *Is͟hraqíya* see Corbin, *History of Islamic Philosophy*, and *En Islam iranien*, 4 vols., especially vol. 2, pp. 40–80.

100 'Abdu'l-Bahá, *Some Answered Questions*, no. 83, p. 345.

101 'Inspirations are the prompting or susceptibilities of the human heart. The promptings of the heart are sometimes satanic' ('Abdu'l-Bahá, *The Promulgation of Universal Peace*, p. 254).

102 ibid. p. 255. The addition of an inspirational or mystical dimension to knowledge is suggestive of a wider inclusion of the insights gained through the mystical path. If this understanding is correct, the obvious tension that in the past has characterized the relationship between the mystical streams and the more scholastically-minded currents may happily be resolved in a creative interplay of both.

103 'Abdu'l-Bahá, *Selections from the Writings of 'Abdu'l-Bahá*, no. 1, p. 3.

104 'Abdu'l-Bahá, *The Promulgation of Universal Peace*, p. 229.
105 Bahá'u'lláh, *Hidden Words*, Arabic no. 36: 'Rejoice in the gladness of thine heart, that thou mayest be worthy to meet Me and to mirror forth My beauty.'
106 Shoghi Effendi refers to this point as a 'promise': 'A race of men – is His written promise – incomparable in character, shall be raised up which, with the feet of detachment, will tread under all who are in heaven and on earth, and will cast the sleeve of holiness over all that hath been created from water and clay (*The Advent of Divine Justice*, para. 48, p. 31, quoting Bahá'u'lláh).
107 Bahá'u'lláh, *Gleanings from the Writings of Bahá'u'lláh,* CLXII, p. 340.
108 ibid. XLIII, p. 95.
109 Bahá'u'lláh, *Tablets of Bahá'u'lláh*, pp. 161–2.
110 Bahá'u'lláh, *Gleanings from the Writings of Bahá'u'lláh,* CX, p. 216.
111 ibid. CLXIV, pp. 342–3.
112 See Bahá'u'lláh, *Hidden Words*, Arabic no. 13: 'I created thee rich, why dost thou bring thyself down to poverty? Noble I made thee, wherewith dost thou abase thyself?'
113 Bahá'u'lláh, *Gleanings from the Writings of Bahá'u'lláh,* CXIII, p. 260.
114 'Abdu'l-Bahá's exegesis of the story of Adam and Eve provides additional insights that, from a Bahá'í perspective, correct the traditional Christian view of mankind and, in the process, the related doctrines of atonement, salvation through Jesus Christ, final judgement and life after death, all of which are coloured by the theological implications of the original sin. 'Abdu'l-Bahá's interpretation of the story of Adam and Eve eliminates the objectification of Satan, looking at the enthronization of evil, together with all the attending maladies of the *humana conditio* (sin, pride, violence, war) from a perspective incompatible with the notion of the transmission of sin. The fact that 'Abdu'l-Bahá seemed to reserve very little place for the doctrine of original sin and man's fallen nature was not lost on many of his Christian hearers. Some of them saw in this one of the main reasons to consider the doctrine taught by 'Abdu'l-Bahá fully at variance with Christianity. See Khurshid, *The Seven Candles of Unity*, pp. 138–40.
115 'Abdu'l-Bahá, *Selections from the Writings of 'Abdu'l-Bahá*, no. 227, p. 302.
116 ibid. no. 220, p. 275.
117 See Bahá'u'lláh, *The Kitáb-i-Aqdas*, para. 148, p. 72: 'Ye have been forbidden in the Book of God to engage in contention and conflict, to strike another, or to commit similar acts whereby hearts and souls may be saddened'; see also *Gleanings from the Writings of Bahá'u'lláh*, C, p. 205: 'Amity and rectitude of conduct, rather than dissension and mischief, are the marks of true faith.'
118 'Abdu'l-Bahá, *The Promulgation of Universal Peace*, p. 117.
119 In Bahá'u'lláh's words: 'The religion of God is for love and unity; make it not the cause of enmity or dissension' (*Tablets of Bahá'u'lláh*, p. 220).
120 See Hourani, 'The Basis of Authority of Consensus in Sunnite Islam', in *Studia Islamica*, vol. 21 (1964), pp. 13–60. Hourani quotes the following medieval definition of consensus: 'The agreement of independent scholars of Muhammad's Community in a particular period upon a legal decision.'
121 See Momen, *Introduction to Shi'i Islam,* pp. 175–6.
122 See Abu Bakr Siraj, 'The Spiritual Function of Civilization', p. 106.
123 For a discussion of *taqlíd* and *ijtihád* see Lambton, *State and Government in Medieval Islam*, pp. 12 and 113.
124 Peters, 'Idjtihád and taqlíd, in 18th and 19th Century Islam', in *Die Welt des Islams*, vol. 20, no. 3–4 (1980), pp. 131–45.
125 A *fatwa* is a reasoned opinion issued by a *mujtahid* or a *muftí* on a point of law.
126 See Pareja, *La religiosidad musulmana*, pp. 45–6.
127 Peters, 'Idjtihád and taqlíd, in 18th and 19th Century Islam', pp. 131–2.

128 See note 194 in Bahá'u'lláh, *The Kitáb-i-Aqdas*, pp. 250–51.

129 Bahá'u'lláh, 'The Seven Valleys', in Bahá'u'lláh, *The Call of the Divine Beloved*, pp. 15–16 (emphasis added). The definition of *taqlíd* implicit in Bahá'u'lláh's comment is based on Qur'án 43:23, where the rejection of God's Prophet is made excusable by charging him with deviating from the ways of the ancestors.

130 For all practical purposes ordinary Sunni Muslims had no other recourse but to follow any of the four canonical schools of jurisprudence. Direct access to the qur'ánic sources or a personal interpretation of the Revelation, in the Christian sense, is not possible except within these confines.

131 Bahá'u'lláh, *The Tabernacle of Unity*, p. 27; Persian version available in Sifídvash, *Pishgaman-i-Parsí Nizhad*, p. 36.

132 See *The Tabernacle of Unity*, ibid. Yet some subsidiary principles of jurisprudence might need to be derived if some of the regulations of the Aqdas are to find application, as suggested by Udo Schaefer, *Bahá'í Ethics*, vol. 1.

133 See Saeidi, *Gate of the Heart*, pp. 18–19, and Bayat, *Mysticism and Dissent: Socioreligious Thought in Qajar Iran*, p. 105.

134 Bahá'u'lláh, *Kitáb-i-Íqán*, para. 48, p. 46.

135 See Cole, 'Imami Jurisprudence and the Role of the 'Ulama: Mortiza Ansari on Emulating the Supreme Exemplar'.Without implying that 'Abdu'l-Bahá's position was wholly conditioned by the Persian politico-religious context, there is no doubt that in assessing the novelty and relevancy of his ideas particular attention must be paid to their Islamic context.

136 'Abdu'l-Bahá, *The Promulgation of Universal Peace*, p. 153.

137 ibid. p. 294.

138 See Shoghi Effendi's elaboration in *The World Order of Bahá'u'lláh,* p. 22: 'Its [the Bahá'í Faith's] excellence lies also in the fact that those elements which in past Dispensations have, without the least authority from their Founders, been a source of corruption and of incalculable harm to the Faith of God, have been strictly excluded by the clear text of Bahá'u'lláh's writings. Those unwarranted practices, in connection with the sacrament of baptism, of communion, of confession of sins, of asceticism, of priestly domination, of elaborate ceremonials, of holy war and of polygamy, have one and all been rigidly suppressed by the Pen of Bahá'u'lláh; whilst the rigidity and rigour of certain observances, such as fasting, which are necessary to the devotional life of the individual, have been considerably abated.'

139 Bahá'u'lláh, *Tablets of Bahá'u'lláh*, p. 39.

140 Abdu'l-Bahá, *'Abdu'l-Bahá in London*, p. 120: 'To me prison is freedom, troubles rest me, death is life, and to be despised is honour. Therefore, I was happy all that time in prison. When one is released from the prison of self, that is indeed release, for that is the greater prison.'

141 'Abdu'l-Bahá, *Paris Talks*, no. 49, p. 166.

142 ibid. no. 18, p. 55.

143 Words attributed to 'Abdu'l-Bahá by Mírzá Ahmad Sohrab, quoted in *Star of the West*, vol. 13, no. 10 (January 1923), p. 270.

144 See Bahá'u'lláh, *Hidden Words*, Arabic nos. 52–3.

145 ibid. nos. 48–51.

146 'Abdu'l-Bahá, *'Abdu'l-Bahá in London*, p. 120.

147 Quoted by Zarqání, *Maḥmúd's Diary*, p. 414.

148 Bahá'u'lláh, *Tablets of Bahá'u'lláh*, p. 70.

149 ibid. p. 93.

150 See 'Abdu'l-Bahá, *Some Answered Questions*, ch. 78. On the subject of industrial disputes see also *Star of the West*, vol. VIII, no. 1 (21 March 1917), p. 7.

151 Bahá'u'lláh, *Tablets of Bahá'u'lláh*, p. 155: 'The essence of wisdom is the fear of God, the dread of His scourge and punishment, and the apprehension of His justice and decree.'
152 ibid. p. 63.
153 Bahá'u'lláh, *Epistle to the Son of the Wolf*, para. 49, p. 27.
154 Bahá'u'lláh, in *The Compilation of Compilations*, no. 565, p. 248: 'Lacking the fear of God an infinity of odious and abominable actions will spring up, and sentiments will be uttered that transgress all bounds.'
155 Bahá'u'lláh, *Tablets of Bahá'u'lláh*, pp. 184–5. See also 'Abdu'l-Bahá, *Paris Talks*, no. 41, p. 139: 'We should, therefore, detach ourselves from the external forms and practices of religion. We must realize that these forms and practices, however beautiful, are but garments clothing the warm heart and living limbs of Divine truth.'
156 Bahá'u'lláh, *Gleanings from the Writings of Bahá'u'lláh*, CXXVIII, p. 277–8.
157 Bahá'u'lláh, *Tablets of Bahá'u'lláh*, p. 238.
158 Bahá'u'lláh, *Kitáb-i-Íqán*, para. 214, p. 193.
159 'Do not go to extremes. Even in thinking do not go to excess but be moderate. If there is too much thinking you will be unable to control your thoughts' (words attributed to 'Abdu'l-Bahá by Anna Kunz, *Star of the West*, vol. 13, no. 6 (September 1922), p. 143).
160 Shoghi Effendi, in *The Compilation of Compilations*, no. 1768, p. 240.
161 Bahá'u'lláh, *Tablets of Bahá'u'lláh*, p. 117.
162 Bahá'u'lláh, *Kitáb-i-Íqán*, para. 28, p. 30.
163 Grundy, *Ten Days in the Light of 'Akká*, p. 30.
164 Bahá'u'lláh, *Tablets of Bahá'u'lláh*, p. 231.
165 See 'Abdu'l-Bahá, *Some Answered Questions*, no. 37, p. 169.
166 'Abdu'l-Bahá, *Selections from the Writings of 'Abdu'l-Bahá*, no. 36, p. 76.
167 Bahá'u'lláh, *Kitáb-i-Íqán*, para. 199, p. 182.
168 See ibid. paras. 253–4, p. 228.
169 19:81 (translation by Muhammad Assad).
170 ibid. 45:23.
171 Bahá'u'lláh, *Kitáb-i-Íqán*, para. 202, p. 184.
172 For an illustration see Bahá'u'lláh, *Tablets of Bahá'u'lláh*, p. 104.
173 Bahá'u'lláh, *Gleanings from the Writings of Bahá'u'lláh,*, III, p. 6.
174 'Abdu'l-Bahá, *Selections from the Writings of 'Abdu'l-Bahá*, no. 206, p. 259.
175 Bahá'u'lláh, *Gleanings from the Writings of Bahá'u'lláh*, CIII, p. 209.
176 'Abdu'l-Bahá, *The Promulgation of Universal Peace*, p. 300.
177 See 'Abdu'l-Bahá, *Selections from the Writings of 'Abdu'l-Bahá*, no. 202, p. 247: "Ye observe how the world is divided against itself, how many a land is red with blood and its very dust is caked with human gore. The fires of conflict have blazed so high that never in early times, not in the Middle Ages, not in recent centuries hath there ever been such a hideous war . . .'
178 ibid.
179 'Abdu'l-Bahá, *The Secret of Divine Civilization*, p. 104.
180 'Abdu'l-Bahá, *The Promulgation of Universal Peace*, p. 158.
181 'Abdu'l-Bahá, *Paris Talks*, no. 13, p. 37.
182 In his Tablet to Auguste Forel 'Abdu'l-Bahá quotes the Qur'án ('All things are living') in support of his assertion that all beings are endowed with life.
183 As 'Abdu'l-Bahá points out: 'The attainment of any object is conditioned upon knowledge, volition and action' (*The Promulgation of Universal Peace*, p. 157).
184 This integration of the middle world of mankind into the higher world of spirituality is made through a conscious directing of human thought, will and action in the direction of the Sun of Reality. Instances of this way of reasoning are plentiful in the Bahá'í writings. The following

is a case in point: 'Nevertheless some thoughts are useless to man; they are like waves moving in the sea without result. But if the faculty of meditation is bathed in the inner light and characterized with divine attributes, the results will be confirmed' ('Abdu'l-Bahá, *Paris Talks*, no. 54, p. 188).

185 'Abdu'l-Bahá, *Paris Talks*, ibid. no. 20, p. 60. For a typical depiction of physical things as captive of nature: 'If a man looks around at the world around him, he will see how all created things are dependent and captive to the laws of Nature. Man alone, by his spiritual power, has been able to free himself, to soar above the world of matter and to make it his servant' (ibid. no. 3, p. 7).

186 See the following quotation attributed to 'Abdu'l-Bahá (Grundy, *Ten Days in the Light of 'Akká,* p. 60): 'We need to be strongly tested in order to prove our Faith to ourselves and to the world. Tests are always surrounding us. They are according to the greatness of the Cause, just as the size of a wave is according to the sea upon which it rises.'

187 Bahá'u'lláh, *Hidden Words*, Arabic nos. 52, 53.

188 'Abdu'l-Bahá, *Paris Talks*, no. 57, p. 191: 'Man is, so to speak, unripe: the heat of the fire of suffering will mature him.'

189 'Abdu'l-Bahá, *The Promulgation of Universal Peace*, p. 142: 'Spiritual progress is through the breaths of the Holy Spirit and is the awakening of the conscious soul of man to perceive the reality of Divinity.'

190 Bahá'u'lláh, *Hidden Words,* Arabic no. 16.

191 'Abdu'l-Bahá, *Some Answered Questions*, no. 52, p. 232.

192 'Abdu'l-Bahá, *The Promulgation of Universal Peace*, p. 154.

193 Bahá'u'lláh, *Gleanings from the Writings of Bahá'u'lláh*, CI, p. 206.

5 A Framework for Peace: The Bahá'í Ethos

1 Bahá'u'lláh, *The Tabernacle of Unity*, p. 7.

2 Shoghi Effendi, *The Advent of Divine Justice*, p. 16.

3 Rev. 21:1.

4 Bahá'u'lláh, *The Kitáb-i-Aqdas*, para. 143, p. 71.

5 'Abdu'l-Bahá, *Some Answered Questions*, no.48, p. 217.

6 The same is true of their counterparts (prejudices, fanaticism, rather than 'vices'). Shoghi Effendi has left some pungent descriptions of the behaviours to avoid, some reminiscent of Saint Paul's letters, but no systematized elaborations on them.

7 Bahá'u'lláh, *Gleanings from the Writings of Bahá'u'lláh,* XVI, p. 39: 'Say: O men! This is a matchless Day. Matchless must, likewise, be the tongue that celebrateth the praise of the Desire of all nations, and matchless the deed that aspireth to be acceptable in His sight.'

8 See Bahá'u'lláh, *Hidden Words*, Persian no. 35: 'For ere long the assayers of mankind shall, in the holy presence of the Adored, accept naught but purest virtue and deeds of stainless holiness.'

9 Bahá'u'lláh, *Kitáb-i-Íqán*, para. 216, p. 196. The text goes on to say: 'He [the seeker] will contemplate the manifest signs of the universe, and will penetrate the hidden mysteries of the soul. Gazing with the eye of God, he will perceive within every atom a door that leadeth him to the stations of absolute certitude. He will discover in all things the mysteries of divine Revelation and the evidences of an everlasting manifestation.'

10 'Abdu'l-Bahá, *Some Answered Questions*, ch. 29, p. 132.

11 Keck, 'On the Ethos of Early Christians', in *Journal of the American Academy of Religion*, vol. 42, no. 3 (September 1974), p. 440.

12 See Gil Santesteban, *Hacia un discurso bahá'í*, pp. 48–9.

13 Quoted by Grundy, *Ten Days in the Light of 'Akká,* p. 5.

14 See Saiedi, *Logos and Civilization*, pp. 53–110.
15 'Abdu'l-Bahá explains that the believer 'must come to know and acknowledge the precepts of God and realize for a certainty that the ethical development of humanity is dependent upon religion' (*The Promulgation of Universal Peace*, p. 403).
16 Bahá'u'lláh, 'The Seven Valleys', in *The Call of the Divine Beloved*, p. 27.
17 'Abdu'l-Bahá, *Some Answered Questions*, ch. 57, pp. 247–8.
18 Bahá'u'lláh, *Tablets of Bahá'u'lláh*, p. 189.
19 See Bahá'u'lláh, 'The Four Valleys', in *The Call of the Divine Beloved*, pp. 92–3: 'The dwellers of this abode know not the destination, yet they spur on their chargers. They see naught in the Beloved but His very Self. They find all words of sense to be meaningless, and senseless words to be full of meaning'; also *Tablets of Bahá'u'lláh*, p. 156: 'The essence of true safety is to observe silence, to look at the end of things and to renounce the world.'
20 Bahá'u'lláh, *Gleanings from the Writings of Bahá'u'lláh*, LXXXII, p. 159.
21 Bahá'u'lláh, *The Kitáb-i-Aqdas*, para. 36, pp. 31–2.
22 'Abdu'l-Bahá, *Some Answered Questions*, ch. 65, p. 275.
23 ibid. ch. 84, p. 349.
24 See 'Abdu'l-Bahá, *Paris Talks*, no. 27; *Some Answered Questions*, ch. 19; *The Promulgation of Universal Peace*, p. 147.
25 'Abdu'l-Bahá, *Some Answered Questions*, ch. 48, p. 217.
26 'Abdu'l-Bahá, *Selections from the Writings of 'Abdu'l-Bahá*, no. p. 299.
27 Shoghi Effendi, quoted in *Lights of Guidance*, no. 1845, p. 543.
28 Shoghi Effendi, *Directives from the Guardian*, p. 86.
29 The following is a representative statement of this idea: 'If the heart of the people become devoid of the Divine Grace – the Love of God – they wander in the desert of ignorance, descend to the depths of ruin, and fall into the abyss of despair where there is no refuge' (*The Pattern of Bahá'í Life*, p. 53).
30 Bahá'u'lláh, *Tablets of Bahá'u'lláh*, pp. 34–5.
31 Bahá'u'lláh, *Hidden Words*, Arabic no. 2.
32 'Abdu'l-Bahá, *Khiṭábát*, p. 783.
33 See *Lights of Guidance*, no. 318, p. 92. Bahá'u'lláh restates this same idea in terms which contrast with the Muslim understanding of the moral duty to 'enjoin the good': 'Thus, whoso seeketh to assist God must, before all else, conquer, with the sword of inner meaning and explanation, the city of his own heart and guard it from the remembrance of all save God, and only then set out to subdue the cities of the hearts of others' (*The Summons of the Lord of Hosts*, pp. 109–10).
34 Bahá'u'lláh, *Tablets of Bahá'u'lláh*, p. 157. See also Bahá'u'lláh, *The Tabernacle of Unity*, p. 54: 'Verily, justice is a lamp that guideth man aright amidst the darkness of the world and shieldeth him from every danger. It is indeed a shining lamp. God grant that the rulers of the earth may be illumined by its light. This servant further imploreth God to graciously aid all men to do His will and pleasure.'
35 Bahá'u'lláh, *Gleanings from the Writings of Bahá'u'lláh*, CXXIII, p. 261.
36 'Abdu'l-Bahá, *The Promulgation of Universal Peace*, p. 91.
37 Shoghi Effendi, *Directives from the Guardian*, p. 86.
38 Shoghi Effendi, *The Advent of Divine Justice*, pp. 21–2.
39 ibid. p. 18.
40 ibid. p. 19.
41 ibid. p. 36.
42 Bahá'u'lláh, quoted ibid. p. 19.
43 *The Compilation of Compilations*, vol. 2, p. 20.

44 See Bahá'u'lláh, *The Summons of the Lord of Hosts,* p. 115: 'every claim requireth a proof, not mere words and displays of outward piety.'
45 A point made repeatedly by 'Abdu'l-Bahá and usually underlined by Shoghi Effendi by contrasting the emerging Bahá'í Faith, devoid of priesthood and rituals, with the established orthodoxies, and ecclesiasticism (see his summary statement of 1947 addressed to a UN Commission).
46 See Shoghi Effendi, *Unfolding Destiny*, p. 445: 'Philosophy, as you will study it and later teach it, is certainly not one of the sciences that begins and ends in words. Fruitless excursions into metaphysical hair-splitting is meant, not a sound branch of learning like philosophy.'
47 Bahá'u'lláh, *Tablets of Bahá'u'lláh*, p. 240.
48 'Abdu'l-Bahá, *Some Answered Questions*, ch. 22.
49 Bahá'u'lláh, *The Kitáb-i-Aqdas*, para. 36, p. 31.
50 Bahá'u'lláh, *Tablets of Bahá'u'lláh*, p. 26.
51 See Bahá'u'lláh, quoted in *The Compilation of Compilations* ('The Importance of Prayer and Meditation'), vol. 2., no. 1723, p. 225.
52 Bahá'u'lláh, *Kitáb-i-Íqán*, para. 213, p. 193.
53 Bahá'u'lláh, *Hidden Words*, Persian no. 76.
54 Bahá'u'lláh, quoted in *The Compilation of Compilations* ('Trustworthiness'), vol. 2, no. 2032, p. 332.
55 Bahá'u'lláh, *Tablets of Bahá'u'lláh*, pp. 172–3: 'Every word is endowed with a spirit, therefore the speaker or expounder should carefully deliver his words at the appropriate time and place, for the impression which each word maketh is clearly evident and perceptible. The Great Being saith: One word may be likened unto fire, another unto light, and the influence which both exert is manifest in the world.'
56 ibid. p. 172.
57 See Shoghi Effendi, *God Passes By*, p. 253; also the Báb, *Selections from the Writings of the Báb*, p. 56.
58 See Nabíl-i-Zarandí, *The Dawn-Breakers,* pp. 92–3.
59 Bahá'u'lláh, *Gleanings from the Writings of Bahá'u'lláh,* V, p. 8.
60 ibid. CXXXIX, p. 303.
61 ibid. CXXXVI, p. 296.
62 ibid. XLIII, p. 92.
63 ibid. CXXVIII, p. 277.
64 ibid. CLVIII, p. 335: 'God hath prescribed unto every one the duty of teaching His Cause. Whoever ariseth to discharge this duty, must needs, ere he proclaimeth His Message, adorn himself with the ornament of an upright and praiseworthy character, so that his words may attract the hearts of such as are receptive to his call. Without it, he can never hope to influence his hearers.'
65 ibid. XLIII, pp. 93–94.
66 Words attributed to Bahá'u'lláh by Ḥájí Mírzá Ḥaydar-'Alí, *Stories from the Delight of Hearts*, p. 109.
67 Bahá'u'lláh, *Tablets of Bahá'u'lláh*, p. 173.
68 Bahá'u'lláh, *Gleanings from the Writings of Bahá'u'lláh,* CLIV, p. 329.
69 See *Bahá'í World*, vol. XV, pp. 37–42.
70 'Abdu'l-Bahá, *Some Answered Questions*, ch. 65.
71 Bahá'u'lláh, *Hidden Words*, Persian no. 5.
72 Bahá'u'lláh, *Gleanings from the Writings of Bahá'u'lláh,* CXXXVII, p. 299.
73 Bahá'u'lláh, *Hidden Words*, Persian no. 80.
74 Bahá'u'lláh, quoted in Shoghi Effendi, *The Advent of Divine Justice*, p. 20.

75 ibid. pp. 20–35.
76 'Abdu'l-Bahá, *The Secret of Divine Civilization,* p. 21.
77 Bahá'u'lláh, 'The Seven Valleys', in *The Call of the Divine Beloved*, pp. 15–16; 'Abdu'l-Bahá, *Some Answered Questions*, ch. 10, pp. 44–5.
78 Shoghi Effendi, *The Advent of Divine Justice*, pp. 48–50.
79 'Abdu'l-Bahá, *The Secret of Divine Civilization,* pp. 20–21.
80 See *The Compilation of Compilations* ('Family Life'), vol. 2, pp. 386–419.
81 ibid. ('Trustworthiness'), vol. 2, pp. 327–55.
82 Bahá'u'lláh, *The Kitáb-i-Aqdas*, para. 4, p. 20.
83 'Abdu'l-Bahá, *Selections from the Writings of 'Abdu'l-Bahá,* no. 48, p. 91.
84 'Abdu'l-Bahá, *'Abdu'l-Bahá in London*, p. 87.
85 'Abdu'l-Bahá, *The Promulgation of Universal Peace*, p. 93.
86 'Abdu'l-Bahá, describing the Bahá'ís in Iran, states: 'They not only promulgate principles; they are people of action' (ibid. p. 120). The emphasis on action as a guarantor of the sincerity of one's intentions constitutes a reiterated theme in the Bahá'í writings: 'It is incumbent upon every man of insight and understanding to strive to translate that which hath been written into reality and action' (Bahá'u'lláh, *Gleanings from the Writings of Bahá'u'lláh,* CXVII, p. 250).
87 'Abdu'l-Bahá, *Selections from the Writings of 'Abdu'l-Bahá,* no. 41, p. 84.
88 Bahá'u'lláh, *The Summons of the Lord of Hosts*, pp. 66–7.
89 See Shoghi Effendi, *The Promised Day Is Come*, p. 110.
90 Bahá'u'lláh, *The Summons of the Lord of Hosts*, p. 66.
91 Bahá'u'lláh, *Gleanings from the Writings of Bahá'u'lláh*, CXII, pp. 218–19.
92 ibid. CXVII, p. 250.
93 See Lewis, *The Political Language of Islam*, pp. 40–41.
94 'Abdu'l-Bahá, *The Secret of Divine Civilization,* pp. 2–3.
95 Bahá'u'lláh, *The Tabernacle of Unity*, p. 10.
96 'Abdu'l-Bahá, *The Secret of Divine Civilization,* p. 96.
97 'Abdu'l-Bahá, *Khiṭábát*, p. 779. For the quotation from Imam Ali, see Bausani, *Religion in Iran*, p. 399.
98 'Abdu'l-Bahá, *Abdul Baha on Divine Philosophy*, p. 27.
99 Webster's *Ninth Collegiate Dictionary* defines 'ethos' as 'the distinguishing character, sentiment, moral nature, or guiding beliefs of a person, group, or institution'.
100 'Abdu'l-Bahá, *The Promulgation of Universal Peace*, p. 31. The original not being extant, we can only presume that the term 'divine philosophy' translates *ḥikmat-i-ilahí.*
101 ibid. p. 59.
102 ibid. pp. 326–7.
103 ibid. p. 326.
104 ibid. p. 327.
105 ibid.
106 ibid. pp. 59–60.
107 ibid. p. 60.
108 ibid. p. 328.
109 'Abdu'l-Bahá, *The Secret of Divine Civilization,* p. 46.
110 Bahá'u'lláh, *Gleanings from the Writings of Bahá'u'lláh*, CX, p. 216.
111 'Abdu'l-Bahá, *The Promulgation of Universal Peace*, p. 158.
112 ibid. p. 97.
113 ibid. p. 41.
114 ibid. p. 32.
115 ibid. p. 126, and also p. 151: 'The sun is one, but the dawning points of the sun are numerous

and changing. The ocean is one body of water, but different parts of it have particular designations – Atlantic, Pacific, Mediterranean, Antarctic, etc. If we consider the names, there is differentiation; but the water, the ocean itself, is one reality.'

116 ibid. p. 42.

117 ibid. p. 140.

118 'Abdu'l-Bahá, *Paris Talks,* no. 13, p. 41.

119 Speaking of the unity of existing religions 'Abdu'l-Bahá emphasizes the fact that this claim is a characteristically Bahá'í tenet: 'Bahá'u'lláh has announced that the foundation of all the religions of God is one, that oneness is truth and truth is oneness which does not admit of plurality. This teaching is new and specialized to this Manifestation' ('Abdu'l-Bahá, *The Promulgation of Universal Peace*, p. 454).

120 Bahá'u'lláh, *Gleanings from the Writings of Bahá'u'lláh,* CXI, p. 217.

121 For the complete text of the conversation between 'Abdu'l-Bahá and Pasteur Monnier see Sours, *Without Syllable or Sound: The World Sacred Scriptures in the Bahá'í Faith*, pp. 142–53. The text is taken from *Star of the West*, vol. 4, no. 3 (28 April 1913), pp. 51–5. On the Trinity, see also *Tablets of Abdul-Baha Abbas*, vol.1, p. 117, and 'Abdu'l-Bahá, *Some Answered Questions*, ch. 27.

122 Bahá'u'lláh, *Kitáb-i-Íqán*, para. 93, p. 86.

123 ibid. para. 42, p. 41.

124 Quoted in Nabíl-i-Zarandí, *The Dawn-Breakers*, note p. 38 (translation taken from https://bahai.works/Translation_of_French_Foot-Notes_of_the_Dawn-Breakers/Chapter_II).

125 Bahá'u'lláh, *The Tabernacle of Unity*, p. 25.

126 ibid. p. 26.

127 'Abdu'l-Bahá, *Selections from the Writings of 'Abdu'l-Bahá,* no. 15, p. 32.

128 Bahá'u'lláh, *Epistle to the Son of the Wolf*, p. 62: "That which God hath ordained as the sovereign remedy and mightiest instrument for the healing of the world is the union of all its peoples in one universal Cause, one common Faith".

129 Shoghi Effendi, *The World Order of Bahá'u'lláh*, pp. 57–8.

130 Bahá'u'lláh, *Gleanings from the Writings of Bahá'u'lláh,* XXXVIII, pp. 87–8.

131 'Abdu'l-Bahá, *Abdul-Baha on Divine Philosophy*, p. 35.

132 ibid. p. 69.

133 'Abdu'l-Bahá, quoted in *Star of the West*, vol. 24, p. 382.

134 'Abdu'l-Bahá, *Abdul Baha on Divine Philosophy*, p. 42.

135 Shoghi Effendi, Summary Statement, 1947, Special UN Committee on Palestine. See also Shoghi Effendi, *The World Order of Bahá'u'lláh*, p. 58 for a similar statement dated in 1932.

136 Shoghi Effendi, *The World Order of Bahá'u'lláh*, p. 114.

137 See ibid. pp. 21–2.

138 ibid.

139 Shoghi Effendi, *Bahá'í Administration*, p. 96.

140 Shoghi Effendi, *The World Order of Bahá'u'lláh*, p. 148: 'Their common, their fundamental object is to insure the continuity of that divinely-appointed authority which flows from the Source of our Faith, to safeguard the unity of its followers and to maintain the integrity and flexibility of its teachings.'

141 ibid. p. 23.

142 See Lakoff and Johnson, *Metaphors We Live By*.

143 Bahá'u'lláh and 'Abdu'l-Bahá, quoted by Shoghi Effendi in *The Promised Day Is Come*, para. 287, p. 116.

144 See 'Abdu'l-Bahá, *'Abdu'l-Bahá in London*, p. 80.

145 For an overview of the use of imagery in Bahá'u'lláh's writings see Hatcher, *The Ocean of His*

Words, pp. 202–31.

146 See also McGlinn, *Church and State: A Post-modern Political Theology*, pp. 249–57, particularly p. 252 describing Shoghi Effendi's preference for pairing and binaries. While McGlinn's examination of the concept of organic unity is given in connection with the main topic of his book, his description of the duet pattern within and without the Bahá'í system as a 'love affair' that resists ultimate confusion seems very apt.

147 The expressions 'organic unity' and 'unity in diversity' cannot be found as such in the original writings of Bahá'u'lláh and 'Abdu'l-Bahá, although their implied meaning is conveyed through a number of expressions. When retranslated into Persian, 'organic unity' is conveyed through the phrase *vaḥdat-i-dh̲átí* (lit. 'essential unity'; see Bahá'í International Community, *Haḍrat-i-Bahá'u'lláh*, p. 40).

148 Both unities can be construed as modalities of related problems, such as the reconciliation of the One and the Multiple, the individual and the collective, nature and culture, simplicity and complexity, problems, which although variously studied in philosophy, sociology, and anthropology, have a clear counterpart in the theological question of monism.

149 Shoghi Effendi usually pairs the term 'organic' with the words 'life', 'unity', 'union', 'structure', 'community', 'evolution', 'institutions', 'change'. Thus, the notion of 'life' is tied up with 'organic' in the following passage written on his behalf: 'The formation of a new National Body in any case is an organic thing, and a new and lively flow of life will go out into all the members of the Community from this Assembly.' (Shoghi Effendi, *Arohanui: Letters to New Zealand*, p. 73). 'Embryonic' is used overwhelmingly by Shoghi Effendi to qualify the word 'Order', followed at some distance by 'Faith' and 'institutions'.

150 For a treatment of the political implications of Bahá'í organic imagery see McGlinn, *Church and State*, pp. 249–57.

151 A prime instance of this was 'Abdu'l-Bahá's Tablet to Auguste Forel.

152 On Bushnell's organicism see Cherry, 'The Structure of Organic Thinking: Horace Bushnell's Approach to Language, Nature, and Nation', in *Journal of the Academy of Religion*, vol. 40, no. 1 (1972), pp. 3–20.

153 For a literary approach to organic imagery and its role in Romantic theory see Abrams, *The Mirror and the Lamp: Romantic Theory and the Critical Tradition*, pp. 167–77 and 184–225.

154 See Spengler, *The Decline of the West*, p. 3.

155 See Opler, 'Cultural and Organic Conceptions in Contemporary World History', in *American Anthropologist*, vol. 46, no. 4 (December 1944), pp. 448–60.

156 ibid. p. 366, where Opler lists a number of American and European writers with organicist leanings.

157 Opler explains the essence of organicist thinking as the grounding of supremacist ideas in biology, conveniently described and theorized as an elementary struggle where only the strongest and the fittest deserve to rule. Opler's organicity is a category that usually embraces, though not necessarily, racism. This conception flies straight in the face of 'Abdu'l-Bahá's vision of nature and biology as God's harmonious handiwork, ruled by the laws of reciprocity.

158 Shoghi Effendi, *The World Order of Bahá'u'lláh*, p. 43.

159 See for instance 'Abdu'l-Bahá, *The Promulgation of Universal Peace*, p. 420.

160 Shoghi Effendi, *Messages to the Indian Subcontinent*, p. 108.

161 See Shoghi Effendi: 'When a person becomes a Bahá'í, he gives up the past only in the sense that he is a part of this new and living Faith of God, and must seek to pattern himself, in act and thought, along the lines laid down by Bahá'u'lláh. The fact that he is by origin a Jew or a Christian, a black man or a white man, is not important anymore, but, as you say, lends colour and charm to the Bahá'í community in that it demonstrates unity in diversity' (*Lights of Guidance*, no. 239, p. 68).

162 *The Compilation of Compilations,* vol. 1, p. 71. See also 'Abdu'l-Bahá, *Selections from the Writings of 'Abdu'l-Bahá,* no. 139, p. 160: 'All the members and parts of the universe are very strongly linked together in that limitless space, and this connection produceth a reciprocity of material effects.'

163 'Abdu'l-Bahá, *The Promulgation of Universal Peace*, p. 338.

164 Shoghi Effendi, quoted in *Lights of Guidance*, no. 213, p. 60.

165 See for example Shoghi Effendi, *God Passes By*, pp. 58–9 and 389–90.

166 'Abdu'l-Bahá, *Some Answered Questions*, ch. 13.

167 Bahá'u'lláh, *Gleanings from the Writings of Bahá'u'lláh,* LXXII, p. 140.

168 Shoghi Effendi, *Principles of Bahá'í Administration*, p. 2.

169 This view correlates with 'Abdu'l-Bahá's definition of progress as 'the expression of spirit in the world of matter' ('Abdu'l-Bahá, *Paris Talks,* no. 29, p. 88).

170 See Shoghi Effendi, *Bahá'í Administration*, p. 103; also *The World Order of Bahá'u'lláh*, p. 9: . . . 'the whole machinery of assemblies, of committees and conventions is to be regarded as a means, and not an end in itself . . .'

171 The Universal House of Justice, 'The Promise of World Peace', in *Messages from the Universal House of Justice, 1963–1986, The Third Epoch of the Formative Age*, p. 695.

172 While still a student at the American University in Beirut, in 1915, Shoghi Effendi had penned a sketch entitled 'Parliamentary Discipline' (the article can be accessed at http://bahai-library.com/file.php?file=shoghieffendi_rules_parliamentary_discipline&language=), drawing on the popular *Robert's Rules of Order for Deliberative Assemblies* (Chicago: Scott, Foresman, rev. ed, 1915). Granted that 'any deliberative assembly or organization should devise and adopt for itself a constitution and bye-laws which shall be subordinate to the general parliamentary rules of order', Shoghi Effendi goes on to stress that: 'What is necessary and important is that the members of that organization should master those laws and items in their constitution. They should before anything else acquaint themselves with parliamentary discipline and should practice on them and apply them whenever they find a chance to do so.' One can see here the germ of Shoghi Effendi's future preoccupation with laying down the 'constitutional basis of Bahá'í communities in every land' and the infusing of spiritual values into its machinery (see his comments in 1927 regarding the Declaration of Trust drafted by the National Assembly of the United States and Canada, in *Bahá'í Administration*, pp. 135–6). A result of this operation was the considerable simplification of procedural matters all along the various levels in Bahá'í administration compared to established democratic practices at the time. This was also marked by a clear reluctance to codify hard and fast rules, if anything enhanced by an abhorrence of opinionatedness. Cases were to be treated in general on a case by case basis and on their own merits (see *Dawn of a New Day*, p. 90: 'Every case coming before the Assembly should be judged on its own merits, and be decided individually without any recourse to new rulings'). Beyond the existing By-Laws everything else was of secondary importance: 'He [Shoghi Effendi] is everywhere urging the believers . . . to not add *procedures* and *rulings* to the Cause. He considers that what he has laid down in Bahá'í Administration is essential, but that practically everything else is secondary and he wishes the Assemblies, your own included, to deal with things with elasticity, as they come up, case by case, and not by continually passing new rulings to cover all similar cases' (*Letters from the Guardian to Australia and New Zealand, 1923–1957*, p. 74).

173 Shoghi Effendi, quoted in US *Bahá'í News*, vol. 85 (July 1934), p. 13.

174 *The Compilation of Compilations,* vol. 1, p. 98.

175 See Bahá'u'lláh, *The Kitáb-i-Aqdas*, note 52, p. 190.

176 See Bahá'í International Community, *The Bahá'ís: A Profile of the Bahá'í Faith and its Worldwide Community,* p. 43.

177 Bahá'u'lláh, *The Summons of the Lord of Hosts*, p. 90.
178 'Abdu'l-Bahá, *The Secret of Divine Civilization*, p. 17.
179 *The Compilation of Compilations*, vol.1, pp. 97–8.
180 ibid. p. 103 (emphasis added).
181 ibid.
182 Bahá'u'lláh, quoted in Shoghi Effendi, *The Promised Day Is Come*, para. 37, p. 20.
183 'Abdu'l-Bahá, quoted in *The Compilation of Compilations*, vol. 1, p. 93.
184 ibid.
185 Bahá'u'lláh, quoted in Bahá'í International Community, *The Prosperity of Humankind*, pp. 7–8.
186 'Abdu'l-Bahá, quoted in *The Compilation of Compilations*, vol. 1, p. 93.
187 The selection of an international language is regarded in fact as one of the appointed signs of mankind's coming of age (see Bahá'u'lláh, *The Kitáb-i-Aqdas*, para. 189, p. 88, and note 194, p. 250).
188 ibid. para. 30, p. 29.
189 Bahá'u'lláh, 'The Seven Valleys', in *The Call of the Divine Beloved*, pp. 15–17.
190 See Bahá'u'lláh, *Gleanings from the Writings of Bahá'u'lláh,* CVI, p. 213: 'Be anxiously concerned with the needs of the age ye live in, and centre your deliberations on its exigencies and requirements.'
191 Shoghi Effendi, *Bahá'í Administration*, p. 64.
192 'Abdu'l-Bahá, *Selections from the Writings of 'Abdu'l-Bahá*, no. 43, p. 87.
193 Bahá'u'lláh, *Gleanings from the Writings of Bahá'u'lláh,* CXXXVI, p. 297: 'Beautify your tongues, O people, with truthfulness, and adorn your souls with the ornament of honesty.'
194 ibid. CXXXVII, p. 299.
195 ibid. CXXXIV, p. 290.
196 ibid. CXXXIX, p. 305.
197 'Abdu'l-Bahá, *Selections from the Writings of 'Abdu'l-Bahá,* no. 227, p. 298.
198 Bahá'u'lláh, *The Kitáb-i-Aqdas*, para. 19, p. 26; 'Abdu'l-Bahá, *Selections from the Writings of 'Abdu'l-Bahá,* no. 193, p. 231: 'For backbiting is divisive, it is the leading cause among the friends of a disposition to withdraw.'
199 Bahá'u'lláh, *Tablets of Bahá'u'lláh*, pp. 27, 38.
200 'Abdu'l-Bahá, *Selections from the Writings of 'Abdu'l-Bahá,* no. 15, p. 30: 'The teacher should not see in himself any superiority; he should speak with the utmost kindliness, lowliness and humility, for such speech exerteth influence and educateth the souls.'
201 Bahá'u'lláh, *Tablets of Bahá'u'lláh*, p. 219: '. . . the tongue is for mentioning what is good, defile it not with unseemly talk.'
202 Bahá'u'lláh, *Kitáb-i-Íqán*, para. 214, p. 193: 'For the tongue is a smouldering fire, and excess of speech a deadly poison.'
203 Bahá'u'lláh, *Epistle to the Son of the Wolf*, para. 41, p. 24.
204 'Abdu'l-Bahá, *The Promulgation of Universal Peace*, p. 197: 'Under an autocratic government the opinions of men are not free, and development is stifled, whereas in democracy, because thought and speech are not restricted, the greatest progress is witnessed. It is likewise true in the world of religion. When freedom of conscience, liberty of thought and right of speech prevail . . . development and growth are inevitable.'
205 *Lights of Guidance,* no. 218, p. 62.
206 Bahá'u'lláh, *Tablets of Bahá'u'lláh*, p. 40: 'They should enquire into situations as much as possible and ascertain the facts, then set them down in writing.'
207 Shoghi Effendi, *Dawn of a New Day*, p. 201: 'Electioneering and all forms of propaganda are against the spirit of Bahá'í elections.'

208 ibid. p. 61: 'There can and should be no liberals or conservatives, no moderates or extremes in the Cause. For they are all subject to the one and the same law which is the Law of God. This law transcends all differences, all personal or local tendencies, moods and aspirations.'
209 ibid. p. 129: 'The Guardian feels very strongly that everywhere, throughout the entire Bahá'í world, the believers have got to master and follow the principles of their divinely laid down Administrative Order. They will never solve their problems by departing from the correct procedure . . .'; see also p. 194.
210 'Abdu'l-Bahá, *Selections from the Writings of 'Abdu'l-Bahá,* no. 44, p. 87.
211 ibid.
212 Shoghi Effendi, *Bahá'í Administration,* p. 63.
213 When referring to those consulting 'Abdu'l-Bahá avers: 'They must be wholly free from estrangement and must manifest in themselves the Unity of God' (quoted by Shoghi Effendi in *The Compilation of Compilations,* vol. 1, p. 95).
214 Shoghi Effendi, *Principles of Bahá'í Administration,* p. 47.
215 See *The Compilation of Compilations,* vol. 1, p. 316.
216 *Lights of Guidance,* no. 860, p. 255.
217 ibid. no. 882 ff., p. 262.
218 'Abdu'l-Bahá, *Selections from the Writings of 'Abdu'l-Bahá,* no. 44, p. 87.
219 See Bahá'u'lláh, *The Kitáb-i-Aqdas,* para. 148, p. 72: 'Ye have been forbidden in the Book of God to engage in contention and conflict . . .'
220 *The Compilation of Compilations,* vol. 2, p. 58; see also 'Abdu'l-Bahá, *The Promulgation of Universal Peace,* p. 183.
221 See National Spiritual Assembly of the Bahá'ís of the United States (comp.), *Developing Distinctive Baha'i Communities,* p. 16: 'The Guardian would advise you to give up the method of asking other members to voice your opinion and suggestions. This indirect way of expressing your views to the Assembly not only creates an atmosphere of secrecy which is most alien to the spirit of the Cause, but would also lead to many misunderstandings and complications.'
222 See Shoghi Effendi, *Bahá'í Administration,* p. 64: 'They must, at all times, avoid the spirit of exclusiveness, the atmosphere of secrecy, free themselves from a domineering attitude, and banish all forms of prejudice and passion from their deliberations.'
223 See 'Abdu'l-Bahá, *Some Answered Questions,* no. 3, p. 8: 'rational arguments . . . are what the people of the world require in this day'; see also *The Promulgation of Universal Peace*: 'Every subject presented to a thoughtful audience must be supported by rational proofs and logical arguments', p. 253.
224 'Abdu'l-Bahá, *Selections from the Writings of 'Abdu'l-Bahá,* no. 44, p. 87.
225 *The Compilation of Compilations,* vol. 1, p. 93.
226 Bahá'u'lláh, *Tablets of Bahá'u'lláh,* p. 168.
227 Any miscarriage of due process or any gross violation of Bahá'í law on the part of an elected member may result in serious sanctions.
228 'Abdu'l-Bahá, *'Abdu'l-Bahá in London,* p. 120.
229 This approach clearly characterizes all the major statements submitted by the Bahá'í International Community to the United Nations.
230 Bahá'í International Community, *The Prosperity of Humankind,* p. 11.
231 See Bahá'u'lláh, *Hidden Words,* Arabic no. 2.
232 *The Compilation of Compilations,* vol.1, p. 93.
233 Bahá'í International Community, *The Prosperity of Humankind,* p. 20.
234 This is in sharp contrast with what happens in most democratic systems, where substantial dialogue is reserved to representatives at the various levels of organized life. People at the

grass-roots level of society, however, lack direct access to decision-making bodies. Their rights to being heard and making representations are seriously mediated by a mass of bureaucratic hurdles.

235 This point is also made by Winters, 'Communicative Interaction: Notes on Relating Habermasian Universalism to Bahá'í Consultation.'

236 In this regard, the Bahá'í administrative system is post-conventional. See Cortina, 'Ética discursiva', in Camps (ed.): *Historia de la ética*, pp. 541–2.

237 ibid.

238 Seena Fazel explains that the phrase '"progressive revelation" is often used to summarize the Bahá'í position in relation to other religions, and is based on Baha'u'llah's statement "*fa-lammá balagha al-amr*"', which Shoghi Effendi translated as "this process of progressive revelation". Literally this means the "maturation" of religion, capturing within it a sense of both commonality and progression, analogous to the maturation of an individual' ('Baha'i Approaches to Christianity and Islam: Further Thoughts on Developing an Inter-Religious Dialogue', in *Bahá'í Studies Review* vol. 14, pp. 39–51).

239 The essential part of religion, as opposed to the non-essential refers to 'morals', 'realities and meanings', and the 'knowledge of God' (See 'Abdu'l-Bahá, Khiṭábát, p. 738). 'Abdu'l-Bahá elaborates further the moral aspect by stating that it includes: 'faith, knowledge, certitude, justice, piety, high-mindedness, trustworthiness, love of God, and charity. It is mercy to the poor, assistance to the oppressed, generosity to the needy, and upliftment of the fallen. It is purity, detachment, humility, forbearance, patience, and constancy. benevolence, purity, detachment, humility, meekness, patience and constancy' ('Abdu'l-Bahá, *Some Answered Questions*, ch. 11, p. 54).

240 See Küng et al., *Christianity and World Religions: Paths to Dialogue, with Islam, Hinduism, and Buddhism*, pp. xiii; and Küng and Kuschel, *Global Ethic: The Declaration of the Parliament of the World's Religions*. Hans Küng and Karl-Josef Kuschel have been careful to find an ethical common ground (the Golden Rule) for secular ideologies and religions to work together, leaving the study of other commonalities or differences (symbolical, metaphysical) for background discussion (in Küng and Kuschel, *Global Ethic*). 'Abdu'l-Bahá's approach coincides with Küng in stressing the ethical factor as the surest common ground bridging differences; but He also points to the fundamental convergence in most of the other respects, including the eschatological aspect, which is not seriously considered in most discussions despite the importance that eschatology plays in most traditions. Küng sees the differences between the Christian confessions (Orthodox, Catholic and Evangelical) as already collapsing into one of 'attitudes' (see his *The Catholic Church*). 'Abdu'l-Bahá would argue that differences among all the great religions would also collapse when seen from the horizon of God's Plan for humanity. The statement by the Universal House of Justice *One Common Faith* and its predecessor *Letter to the World's Religious Leaders* broach the subject from the Bahá'í perspective of continuance of the revealed Word.

241 The concept of the eternal Covenant of God is often reiterated in the notion of a God Who is the God of 'the living', forefathers and future generations included ('thy God and the God of thy fathers' (Bahá'u'lláh, Tablet of Aḥmad, in most Bahá'í prayer books)). The expression 'creative Word' appears first in the writings of Shoghi Effendi.

242 Gouldner compares the metaphorical base of ecology and systems theory in ways that are applicable to our theme: 'Like the new ecology, systems theory embodies a new vision of unity. But if ecology is grounded in organismic metaphor and has romantic antecedents, systems theory resonates a mechanical metaphor more continuous with the technocratic consciousness and, unlike ecology, embodies a humanistic imperialism centered on the impulse to manage (dominate) the environment. If ecology has a strong populistic tinge, systems theory is imbued with a stronger elitism, being the "natural" ideology of bureaucratic planners and centralizers' (*The Future of Intellectuals and the Rise of the New Class*, p. 43.

243 Quoted in Research Department of the Universal House of Justice, *Conservation of the Earth's Resources*.

244 The 'rediscovery' of the fact that democracies can be also war-prone, ancient Athens being the ready-made example, shows how other commonplaces such as the 'democratic peace' principle can take a second place in polemological studies if need be.

Summary and Conclusions

1 See Bausani, *Religion in Iran: From Zoroaster to Bahá'u'lláh*, pp. 379–80.

2 Bahá'u'lláh, *Kitáb-i-Íqán*, para. 57, p. 55.

3 'Abdu'l-Bahá, Tablet to Andrew Carnegie, in *Star of the West*, vol. 6, no. 11 (27 September 1915), p. 83.

4 See for example 'Abdu'l-Bahá, *Some Answered Questions*, ch. 40, p. 181.

5 'Abdu'l-Bahá, *The Promulgation of Universal Peace*, p. 438.

6 Bahá'u'lláh, *Gleanings from the Writings of Bahá'u'lláh*, CVI, p. 213.

7 'Abdu'l-Bahá, *The Promulgation of Universal Peace*, p. 124.

8 See Hudson, *Defenseless America*, p. v.

9 Words of 'Abdu'l-Bahá conveyed to President Bliss of the American College of Beirut, Syria, at Haifa, Palestine, quoted in *Star of the West*, vol. 18, p. 181.

10 'Abdu'l-Bahá, *Selections from the Writings of 'Abdu'l-Bahá*, no. 206, p. 256.

11 Shoghi Effendi, *Messages to America, 1932–1946*, p. 32.

12 Worthy of note also is the fact that neither 'Abdu'l-Bahá nor Shoghi Effendi singled out Great Britain for that leading role.

13 See Shoghi Effendi, *Bahá'í Administration*, p. 186.

14 Regarding this institution Shoghi Effendi explains: 'Divorced from the social, humanitarian, educational and scientific pursuits centering around the Dependencies of the Mashriqu'l-Adhkár, Bahá'í worship, however exalted in its conception, however passionate in fervour, can never hope to achieve beyond the meagre and often transitory results produced by the contemplations of the ascetic or the communion of the passive worshiper. It cannot afford lasting satisfaction and benefit to the worshipper himself, much less to humanity in general, unless and until translated and transfused into that dynamic and disinterested service to the cause of humanity which it is the supreme privilege of the Dependencies of the Mashriqu'l-Adhkár to facilitate and promote' (ibid.).

15 Bausani, *Religion in Iran: From Zoroaster to Bahá'u'lláh*, pp. 398–9, 401, 404.

16 Bahá'u'lláh, *Gleanings from the Writings of Bahá'u'lláh*, LXX, p. 136.

17 ibid. XIV, p. 27: 'Bestir thyself, and magnify, before the entire creation, the name of God, and celebrate His praise, in such wise that all created things may be regenerated and made new.'

18 'Abdu'l-Bahá's psychological dissection with reference to the *'ulamá* is trenchant: '. . . some, on the contrary, whose reason has been corrupted by personal motives and the clarity of whose perception has been clouded by self interest and conceit; whose energies are devoted to the service of their passions, whose sense of pride is perverted to the love of leadership, have raised the standard of opposition and waxed loud in their complaints' (*The Secret of Divine Civilization*, pp. 11–12).

19 Bausani refers to Bahá'í eschatological fulfilment as fundamental to an understanding of religious unity and unity between religions (*Saggi sulla Fede Bahá'í*, pp. 332–3. Psychologically, seeing the eschatological convergence of all religions in the light of a new Revelation (the Bahá'í Faith) provides a strong sense of reconciliation with 'previous' dispensations, whatever their historical limitations: '"Converting to Bahaism" does not mean, therefore, to accept a different religious tradition . . . bur rather to find in one´s original tradition "reasons" allowing us to better understand that this given tradition is not final' (ibid. p. 332, my translation).

20 This understanding permits Bahá'í believers to refine their own approaches to established religions, seeing more positively what other religions have been contributing to the well-being of humanity. Common elements in the Abrahamic religions (the notion of the Covenant, for instance) have the obvious ring of the familiar, but the mystical element of apophatic Bahá'í theology also connects with most of the traditions of the farthest East.

21 See Bredsdorff, 'Lovejoy's Idea of "Idea"', in *New Literary History*, vol. 8, no. 2 (1977), pp. 195–211.

22 See Rassekh, 'Haft Gúniy-i-vaḥdat'.

23 For the purposes of a general comparison, I take Tim Dunne's summary of liberal positions as a reference point; see Dunne, 'Liberalism', in Baylis and Smith (eds): *The Globalization of World Politics: An Introduction to International Relations*, pp. 163–181.

24 Alternating waves and simultaneous paroxystic expressions of optimism, self-confidence and pessimism can be found running deep, as well as on the surface, of most of nineteenth and twentieth century 'thought' in both Europe and the Americas. A systematic study of these waves could also help us to better understand the limits as well as possibilities of the reception accorded to 'Abdu'l-Bahá in the West. Analysis of such states of mind and public opinion could pay special attention to the dual and hybrid nature of public moods, and to their increasing subservience to ideologically driven agendas.

25 For a discussion of international relations theories in connection with Bahá'í articulations, see Saiedi in 'Replacing the Sword with the Word: Bahá'u'lláh's Concept of Peace', *Bahá'í World Website* (2019), and 'Az demukrásíy-i-farhangí bih demukrásíy-i-síyásí', in *Payám-i-Bahá'í*, nos. 489–490 (August–September 2020), pp. 5–9. Saiedi has also provided lengthy discussions on this same subject in both Persian and English podcasts, available at https://youtu.be/uMqU-dT-RMw and https://youtu.be/uMqU-dT-RMw. A historically contextualized summary of 'Abdu'l-Bahá's views on peace is also given by Egea, who contrasts the premises and prevailing thinking on peace at the turn of the century with the views put forward by 'Abdu'l-Bahá ('Reading Reality in Times of Crisis: 'Abdu'l-Bahá and the Great War' (2021), in *The Bahá'í World*, online at https://bahaiworld.bahai.org/library/the-cause-of-universal-peace/; likewise Hogenson, 'The Cause of Universal Peace: 'Abdu'l-Bahá's Enduring Impact' (2021), in *The Bahá'í World*, online at https://bahaiworld.bahai.org/library/the-cause-of-universal-peace. For a comprehensive treatment of 'Abdu'l-Bahá's North American tour see Stockman, *'Abdu'l-Bahá in America*.

26 For a comprehensive report on the way religious NGOs relate to the UN see Knox, *Religion and Public Policy at the UN*. As the authors of the report point out, observer status (general, special consultative, roster status) is not in itself indicative of the level of commitment to UN goals: 'We asked our interviewees to identify the key religious actors at the UN today. After the Holy See (whose status as Permanent Observer is unique), two groups stood above the rest: Quakers and Baha'is. These faiths share some common traits that may explain their high regard in UN circles. Both hold basic tenets consistent with UN ideals – for Quakers an end to war and conflict, for Baha'is the establishment of a peaceful and equitable world. Both seek to build consensus on issues by engaging all concerned parties. Perhaps most important, both operate as facilitators rather than partisan advocates' (p. 39).

27 Properties which liberal and socialist conceptions of excellence and self-improvement tended to reinforce in different ways though sharing a common belief in 'progress' and the 'perfectibility' of human beings and their society. Positive reevaluations of global history and their common enterprises can be found in recent works aimed precisely to cover the bright side of the story, exemplified by historians such as David Cannadine, *The Undivided Past: Humanity beyond Our Differences*, and Paul Kennedy, *The Parliament of Man: The United Nations and the Quest for World Government*. From a Bahá'í perspective, works of a similar nature and intent are John Huddleston's *The Search for a Just Society*, and all the statements produced by the Bahá'í

International Community, but most notably *The Prosperity of Humankind* (1994), *Turning Point for All Nations* (1995), and *Who is Writing the Future?* (1999).

28 'Abdu'l-Bahá, *Selections from the Writings of 'Abdu'l-Bahá*, no. 227, p. 297.

29 'Abdu'l-Bahá, *The Secret of Divine Civilization*, p. 43.

30 And epitomized in 'Abdu'l-Bahá's encounter with Maxim Hudson, the inventor of explosives, whose brother was the inventor of the eponymous machine gun. There is some *déjà-vu* irony in the fact that Muhammad Reza Shah, self-styled as Reza Khan, would consider fitting to have the frontispiece of one of his palaces decorated with a mosaic depicting a machine gun (see Abrahamian, *A History of Modern Iran*, p. 63).

31 The Institute approach helps to overcome the problem of acculturation in a community devoid of clergy or missionaries by empowering individuals through an intensive learning and re-socializing experience reflective of a conception of knowledge as shared situated knowledge. Previous emphases on a learning of Bahá'í administration, including procedural and historical knowledge, have been redirected towards a prompt assimilation of the 'fundamental verities' of the Faith in a context of service and social action. Adult education principles and systematizing efforts have been developed extensively in Latin America, partly supported by a Freirian conception of education that seeks and profits from the transformative value of systematized personal and collective 'awareness'. Key Bahá'í contributions in this field are Farzam Arbab´s and Paul Lample's works, most of them available at https://bahai-library.com. On systematization, the most comprehensive work is Holliday, *La sistematización de experiencias práctica y teoría para otros mundos posibles*. An interesting aspect of this is the democratization (as opposed to demoticization) of knowledge these processes entail both in terms of access and production: observations, perceptions, insights, data gathering, documentation, reflection and consultation can for the most part be easily consolidated into real advances in shared knowledge.

32 Instances of which include:

- the substantive streamlining of administrative work, currently centred around a limited number of 'core activities' . . . serviced by a limited number of agencies, many of which have been reabsorbed into both the Institute and 'cluster area' dynamics, or redefined within contained ad hoc specialist advisory bodies;
- the channelling of the energies of the community towards establishing a welcoming 'culture of growth' characterized by a conscious blurring of the boundaries between the Bahá'í community and the wider community. This is complemented by an emphasis on a 'humble posture of learning', and a willingness to embrace change. The overall process is expressly conceived as one of experimentation through informed trial and error.
- the setting of new operational boundaries around cluster areas, as distinct from the demarcations of Local Spiritual Assemblies. Cluster areas draw on human resources for the purposes of propagation and promotion of community service activities and usually comprise two or more municipalities;
- the enhancement of the role of Continental Counsellors and Auxiliary Board Members in terms of their own involvement in the devising of teaching plans, follow-up activities and advisory capacities vis-à-vis the elected arm;
- the introduction of the Law of Ḥuqúqu'lláh on a firmer footing together with the availability of the Kitáb-i-Aqdas in major world languages;
- the establishment of Regional Councils, a third intermediate administrative level aimed at devolving National Assembly functions to the regional level;
- the increased concentration on transformation through education of the new generations of believers, an area where the Bahá'í community has gathered considerable experience; and
- the refinement of electoral and representational processes.

33 See Australian Bahá'í Community, *Creating an Inclusive Narrative.*

34 'Abdu'l-Bahá, *Tablets of Abdul-Baha Abbas*, vol. 1, p. 39; see also Abizadeh, 'Politics beyond War: Ulrich Gollmer's Contribution to Bahá'í Political Thought'; also Schaefer et al., *Making the Crooked Straight*, pp. 466–8.

35 Examples of this are the assumption of the G-20 of its role as the international economic forum, and the push for a world currency, two important factors in the emergence of a global polity.

Index

'Abdu'l-Bahá 51-3, 111
in 'Akká and Haifa 290, 291
journeys to the West 32, 62-4, 66, 69-73, 86, 121, 134, 282, 293-8 *passim*, 303, 332
Will and Testament 106, 208, 238, 305, 309, 313
and World War I 65, 85, 105, 134
see also The Secret of Divine Civilization, Seven Candles of Unity, Tablets of the Divine Plan, Tablet to the Hague
for writings and talks of 'Abdu'l-Bahá on the various themes in this book, see separate entries
Abú-Ḥanífih 165
action 73, 88, 93, 96, 116, 145, 155, 163, 167, 175-6, 181-2, 184-5, 190, 195, 196, 214, 218, 224, 226-7, 229, 246, 302, 307-8, 320, 324
collective 127, 250, 289
see also deeds
Adam 109, 162
and Eve 177, 318
Addams, Jane 70, 296
Administrative Order, Bahá'í 6, 88, 109, 116-20, 134, 137-8, 212, 218-22, 244, 252, 308, 312, 329
Africa 21, 27, 306, 311
Afroukhteh, Youness 68
Akbar, Emperor 4, 34
'Akká 25, 28, 38, 52, 59, 65, 94, 105, 113, 285, 291
Alamein, Battle of 129
Ali, Imam 198
Alkan, Necati 4, 51, 280
altruism 94
Amanat, Abbas 3, 25
America, Americans 61, 69-73, 100-01, 115-16, 125, 131-5, 137-8, 141, 235, 237-40, 295-7, 300, 304, 312, 326
Bahá'í community 7, 112, 122, 306, 309, 312, 313
Latin 333
North 52, 62, 64, 70-71, 79, 91, 112, 130-32, 134, 137, 239-40, 295-6, 300, 309, 312
Republics of 21, 41, 292
system of government (United States) 72, 132-3, 216
see also United States
American Civil War 58
American continent 29, 41, 132, 332
American Peace Society 70
American Society of International Law 70
American University, Beirut 105, 327
amity meetings (race amity) 7, 312
Anglo-Persian War (1856–57) 25
animals 79, 149, 150, 213
anthropology vii, 2, 8-10, 143, 229, 240, 244, 248, 250, 298, 326
spiritual 143, 240, 281
apocalypse, apocalyptical 21, 28, 122-3, 128, 137, 162, 231, 282, 307
Arakawa, Viscount 55
arbitration, international arbitration vii, 6, 36, 38, 52, 59-60, 69, 76, 101, 126, 234, 245, 296
Aristotle 146, 200
arms, armaments 3, 39, 41, 56, 65-6, 70-71, 191, 251
carrying of 134, 136, 138, 240
arms race 37-8, 65, 67, 169
reductions 3, 33, 40-41, 47, 56-7, 101, 234, 245, 247, 293
see also disarmament
atheism 152

Atlantic Charter 130
Auxiliary Board 213, 219, 333
awham (vain imaginings) 7, 9, 11, 12, 82, 242, 281
Ayoub, Mahmoud 22
Azalis 23, 28, 94, 287

Báb, the 3, 5, 18-19, 21-3, 27-8, 46, 105, 108-9, 113, 165, 191, 286, 291, 303-7
  Shrine of 113, 206
Bábí Faith, Bábís 2-3, 5, 11, 18-20, 21-9, 74, 111, 283-7, 305
Badasht, Conference of 18, 22, 74, 216
Badí' 27, 286
Baghdad, Iraq 19-20, 283, 311
Bahá'í Administrative Order 6, 88, 109, 116-20, 134, 137-8, 212, 218-22, 244, 252, 308, 312, 329
Bahá'í Faith, the 2, 41, 88, 107, 109, 111, 113, 117, 129, 187, 189, 199, 205, 207, 250-52, 279, 293-4, 301, 304, 308, 309, 319, 323, 331
  emancipation of 119-20
  'fundamental verities' of 106, 238, 305, 333
Bahá'í Holy Places 113, 129, 137, 238, 239
Bahá'í International Community 77, 128, 224-6, 247, 250.55, 309, 310, 311, 329
Bahá'í 'principles' (lists of) 11, 77, 82-3, 86-92, 182, 199, 234-6, 247, 251-2, 282, 300-01
Bahá'í World Centre 117, 306, 308, 311
Bahá'í World Commonwealth 117, 123, 128, 138, 308
Bahá'í Year Book 112
Bahá'u'lláh
  life of 16-27, 28, 31-2, 37-8, 43, 282-3, 284-5
  Shrine of 113, 309
  Will and Testament (Kitáb-i-'Ahd) 51, 287
  for writings of Bahá'u'lláh on the various themes in this book, see separate entries
Bahíyyih Khánum 17, 19, 305
balance of power 36-8, 41, 43
Balkans 37, 65, 80, 85, 295
Balyuzi, Hasan M. 3, 16, 25, 51, 299
Banú Qurayzah 17, 19, 282
Barney, Laura Clifford 51, 192
Bausani, Alessandro 5, 30, 241, 286, 331
Bayán, the 22, 24, 29, 46, 285
behaviour, human 6, 8-9, 23, 30, 42, 66, 94, 98, 134, 142, 161-2, 165, 168-9, 181-2, 187, 190-95, 207, 222, 225, 242, 321
Bentham, Jeremy 36
Berger, Peter 2
Bible 28, 64, 108, 210, 286, 300, 305
Bishárat (Glad-Tidings) 24, 33, 284, 289, 290
Bloch, Marc 7
Britain 44, 72, 299, 331
Browne, Edward Granville 31-2, 37, 43, 232, 287, 290
Brunner, Constantin 210
Burckhardt, Jacob 7
Burgel, Johan Christoph 34
Bushnell, Horace 210

calamity, catastrophe 63, 110, 118, 120-23
Calduch, Rafael 38, 289
California 73, 80, 297
Canada 80, 301
Carlyle, Thomas 210, 305
Carnegie, Andrew 69, 234
Caucasia 25
Central Organization for a Durable Peace 77-8, 84, 299
century of light 63
Chatfield, Charles 313
children 42, 66, 76, 80, 83, 93, 136, 169, 205, 223, 305, 313
Christ (Jesus) 15, 28, 96, 105, 117, 174, 203-4, 294, 302, 308, 318
Christianity, Christians 36, 52, 64, 108, 110, 116, 120, 135, 177, 186, 196, 203, 206-7, 288, 294, 300, 308, 310, 313, 318, 319, 326, 330
civilization vii, 54-6, 72, 75, 97, 99, 101, 195-6, 227, 241, 243, 253, 292, 294, 297, 308
  divine, spiritual 7, 55, 67, 78, 83, 87, 106, 118, 142, 152, 159, 188, 201, 228, 239, 241
  evolution of 109, 121-2
  excess of 161
  new 236
  and peace 249
  technical 64
and war 51, 70, 116, 235
world 31, 114, 118, 120-22, 313
class struggle 58, 89, 101, 294
Cobden, Richard 36, 245
Cole, Juan Ricardo 3-5, 16, 30, 34-5, 37, 40, 51, 280, 282, 289
collective centres 124-5, 174, 177, 181, 188, 201, 236

collective security vii, 5-7, 15, 26, 33, 35-47, 52, 58, 64, 68, 91, 99, 100-101, 127, 136, 141, 197, 232-3, 236, 239, 244-9, 251-2, 289, 292
colonialism 4, 57, 72, 280, 297, 310
Columbia University 200
Comenius, Jon Amos 35, 287
commerce 36, 66, 67, 69, 70, 72, 101, 218, 246, 288 *see also* trade
communication 36, 182, 187, 194, 216, 217, 227, 229, 246, 252 *see also* dialogue
communism 94, 237
community 97-8, 169, 193, 195, 214, 224-5, 227, 229, 242-3, 252, 312-13, 326
  Bábí 18-20, 22-4, 28, 283
  Bahá'í 2, 3, 5-6, 11, 15, 23, 25, 28-9, 52, 71, 94-5, 105-8, 111-12, 115-17, 119, 128-9, 136, 137-8, 165, 194, 210-11, 215, 216, 218-26, 238, 244, 246, 250-53, 303, 309, 326, 333
    Australian 251
    Canadian 301
    Iranian 78, 240, 309
    North American 7, 122, 130-31, 134, 137, 240, 300, 306, 310, 312, 313
  international 40, 61
  Muslim 18, 163, 231, 218
  of nations 132
  world 6, 118, 239, 306, 308
  see also Bahá'í International Community
compassion 97, 203, 223-4
Congress of Vienna 37, 43, 288
conquest
  spiritual 160, 182, 188, 239, 322
  territorial 30, 36, 60, 66
conscience 6, 10, 25, 29-30, 100, 105, 134-5, 165, 166, 168-9, 195, 218, 222, 224, 227, 240, 288
  false 163
  freedom of 4, 328
  global 197
  unity of 2, 52, 77, 80-81, 86, 90-91, 93, 100, 217, 223-4, 236, 247
conscientious objection 134
consciousness, human 23, 34, 44, 80, 90, 118, 145, 149-50, 161, 176, 183, 190, 194, 219, 224, 226, 242-3, 321
consultation vii, 9, 33, 40, 42, 47, 56, 92, 158, 162, 166, 182-3, 195, 215, 216-26, 227, 229, 232-3, 244, 247, 329
contamination of earth 54
cooperation 38, 52, 79, 83, 146, 212-13, 223, 234
  international 57, 296, 313
Counsellors, Bahá'í 213, 219, 233
courtesy 192, 221, 228
covenant 6, 35, 56-7, 228, 233, 239, 243, 330, 332
  of Bahá'u'lláh 6, 15, 29, 46, 51, 56, 57, 141
  International 245
creation, existence, world of 143-4, 156, 209, 303, 315 *see also* Nature
cremation 314
crime, criminals 57, 66, 83, 97-8, 101, 134, 167-8, 237, 313
Crimean War 5, 37
Crucé, Emeric 35, 287
culture 8-10, 43, 54, 92, 99, 101, 167, 182, 188, 195, 203, 227, 241, 247, 249, 252, 326, 333
  world c. 118, 308

Daniel, prophecy of 119, 239, 308
Darwinism 52, 79, 162, 235, 299
Day, Michael 51
death 25, 66, 71, 79, 98, 185-6, 211, 286, 295, 319
  life after 212, 242, 318
decentralization 217, 229, 246
decision-making 35, 40, 158, 166, 218, 223, 226, 229, 330 *see also* consultation
deeds 19, 23, 75, 94-5, 96, 108, 168-70, 182, 185-6, 190, 192-3, 321 *see also* action
demilitarization vii, 43, 91, 245, 288
democracy 4, 40, 44, 52, 56, 69, 72, 129, 226, 227, 229, 240-41, 246, 327, 328, 329, 331, 333
Despard, Charlotte 74
dialogue 2, 3, 182, 191-2, 204, 221, 225-6, 229, 244, 250-51, 282 *see also* communication
dignity, human vii, 9, 10, 12, 96-7, 142, 159-60, 163-4, 167, 172, 176, 241, 284
Dilthey, Wilhelm 7
diplomacy 36, 38, 40, 69, 81, 297, 299
disarmament 47, 67-8, 91, 232, 245, 251, 295, 297
Dispensation(s) 46, 109, 118, 141, 156, 209, 228, 285
  of Bahá'u'lláh 6, 11, 21, 24, 28, 51, 63, 74, 109, 111-12, 118, 131, 159, 174, 181, 205, 228, 252, 291, 313

previous 46, 110, 124, 125, 167, 181, 205, 319, 331
divine philosophy 2, 90, 199-200, 243
Dror, Yehezkel 246

ecclesiastics 219, 307, 323
economics 77, 82, 83, 87, 91, 92, 95, 98-9, 105, 233-4, 251, 298, 306, 334
economy, divine 11, 14-15, 203, 213, 220, 238
Edirne, Turkey (Adrianople) 25, 28, 283, 285
education 78-9, 87, 98, 122, 147, 153, 160-62, 169, 188, 195, 201, 222, 229, 236, 247, 250, 333
of children 76, 83, 223
and crime 313
compulsory 87
female 55, 75-6, 83, 297, 298
moral 247
and peace 237, 252
spiritual 156, 160, 188-9, 247, 328
universal 35, 87, 89-90, 91, 100, 141, 234, 236, 247, 249
Egea, Amin 51, 332
Egypt 52, 71, 197, 234, 289, 309
Eliade, Mircea 143
Emerson, Ralph Waldo 210
Enfantin, Barthélemy-Prosper 4, 37
England 105, 126, 297, 298
English language 51, 59, 105-6, 281, 315
Enlightenment, the 4, 11, 43, 184, 242, 247-8, 288, 307
environment 194, 229, 330
equality 67, 83, 84, 94, 147, 161, 164, 217, 229, 301, 310
before the law 29, 300
gender 74, 75, 87, 89, 91, 222, 234, 236, 240, 298
eschatology 7, 11, 15-16, 21-2, 43, 46, 108, 141-2, 159, 162, 181, 204-5, 231-2, 238-9, 241, 243, 244-5, 248, 250, 285, 286, 330, 331
Esslemont, John 58, 292-3, 310
ethics 9-10, 38-9, 43, 54, 89, 91-3, 95, 96, 134, 136, 147, 182-3, 190, 193, 195-6, 201-2, 205, 207, 213, 225-6, 227, 229, 242, 245-8, 322, 330
ethos 9, 43-4, 183, 250, 324
Bahá'í vii, 7, 10, 12, 16, 43, 142, Part V (entire), 236, 242-3, 250
Europe, European 3, 15, 35-8, 40-41, 45, 52, 55, 62, 64-5, 69, 80, 100, 105, 116, 125-9, 233, 237, 245, 281, 287-8, 294-5, 297, 300, 310, 332
evolution 9 148, 244
of civilization 109
of concepts, ideas 11, 111, 244
of institutions 117, 308, 312, 326
of mankind 118, 124-5, 200, 212-13, 240, 243, 247
of religion 2, 5, 112, 114, 124-5, 207
spiritual vii, 148, 207, 267
existentialism 101, 249

fairmindedness 187, 189, 228, 229, 244
faith 3, 6, 10, 30, 70, 92-3, 125, 152-3, 165, 168, 197, 286, 318, 321, 330
one common 31, 47, 209, 325
spirit of 152-3, 156, 201
fanaticism vii, 12, 100, 167, 173, 228, 232, 242, 249, 281, 321
Fascism 211
Fatḥ 'Alí Sháh 25
Fazel, Seena 2-3, 330
Faydí, Muḥammad-'Alí 51
Febvre, Lucien 7
federalism 69, 131-2, 138, 216, 237
Fiore, Pasquale 70, 296
force
servant of justice 292
use of 19, 21 24, 26, 38, 45, 54, 57-9, 64, 75, 136, 192, 197, 229, 232, 247, 289, 292, 294, 298, 299
forces (energies, powers) 55, 110, 113, 115-16, 123, 131, 168-9, 201, 236, 242, 246, 249, 252, 305, 306, 307, 309
active, the 144
constructive 54
of evil 21, 233, 307
human 56, 80, 186-7
Forel, August(e) 192, 246
forgiveness 97, 176, 194, 279
Formative Age 111, 116, 118, 119, 305
France 72, 126, 288 *see also* Paris
Francis Joseph, Emperor of Austria 29, 116, 308
Franco-Prussian War 37
freedom 29, 40, 46, 57-9, 72, 82, 84, 89, 95, 96, 100, 141, 151, 156, 161, 162, 165, 168, 175, 177, 188-9, 194, 201, 217, 242, 319
of conscience 4, 222, 224, 328

from desire 170-71
of expression 221-2, 224, 328
political 141
religious 15, 120
unity in 90, 92, 93
from violence 15, 159, 242
from war 7, 39, 59, 233
from the world of nature (material) 78, 83, 87, 92, 248, 321
free will 160
free trade 37, 245, 288, 297
fundamentalism 23, 164

Galtung, Johan 52
gender equality 234, 240 *see also* women
Germany, Germans 37, 65-6, 116, 126-7, 295, 309
Gibbon, Edward 110, 305
globalization 3, 279, 288
spiritual 142
God 143-5
fear of 41, 168-9, 320
kingdom of 7, 12, 15, 43, 62-3, 90-91, 149, 156, 161, 181, 186, 233, 241, 248, 250, 299
oneness (unity) of 91-5, 145, 177, 195, 199, 301, 302, 329
plan of 6, 11, 217, 239, 330
remembrance of 29, 155, 170, 176, 322
will of 24, 113-15, 143-4, 159-60, 182, 184-5, 193, 206, 216
Word of 23, 45, 46, 68, 108, 119, 141, 144, 165, 171, 195, 210, 285, 294, 305, 314
God Passes By 51, 106-7, 109, 130, 238, 305
Golden Age (Bahá'í) 111, 117-19, 131, 137, 211, 308
Gospels 193, 204 *see also* Bible
governance, global, world system of 34, 43, 56, 64, 80, 131, 229, 246, 251, 303
government(s) 34-5, 39, 41, 47, 56-7, 60-61, 65, 67, 226, 309
American 72, 132-3, 216
autocratic 328
democratic 4, 44, 328 *see also* democracy
federal 69, 131-2, 138, 216, 237
monarchic 44, 290
parliamentary 44, 61, 126
representative 40
republican 44, 290
world 131, 303
government, obedience to 134-5
Greater Peace 32, 46, 115

Habermas, Jürgen 226, 229
Hague, The
Conferences 56, 60, 61, 68
Tablet to 6, 11, 51, 60, 77-85, 86, 90-92, 94, 99-100, 233-4, 237, 246-8, 282, 298
Tribunal 60, 299
Haifa 65, 105-6, 113, 290, 291, 297, 305
Hands of the Cause 123, 219, 309
heart, human 1, 6, 11, 41, 44, 59, 75, 85, 97, 101, 131, 142, 144, 146, 143-5, 158, 160-61, 164, 168, 175, 177, 182, 187-8, 191-2, 194, 200, 206, 229, 238, 317, 318, 322, 323
Hegel, Hegelian 115, 297, 307
hermeneutics 5, 89, 202, 204, 229
Heroic Age 111, 306
Hidden Words 193, 284
Him Whom God shall make manifest 5, 18-19, 22, 283
Hindus 34
history 2-3, 7-8, 72, 75, 88, 97, 105-19, 124, 127, 131-2, 137, 142, 144, 183, 215, 227, 238-9, 253, 284, 305, 332
sacred, spiritual 10-11, 108, 113, 115, 117, 137, 205, 207, 228, 239
Hogenson, Kathryn Jewett 51
Hollinger, Richard 51, 69
Holsti, Kalevi J. 37
Holy Alliance 36
Holy Spirit 62, 87, 149, 151, 153, 156-7, 182, 200-01, 224, 242, 301, 321
House of Worship (Akbar) 34 *see also* Ma<u>sh</u>riqu'l-A<u>dh</u>kár
Hudson, Maxim 70-71, 235, 333
Hugo, Victor 35
Huizinga, Johan 7
humanity, human race *see* mankind
human body 147, 153, 214, 218
human nature 2, 7, 9, 36, 38, 42-3, 101, 142, 149, 162, 166-7, 175, 200, 223, 281
animal 149, 176, 316
spiritual 147, 149-50, 167, 182, 192, 231
see also consciousness; heart; mind; understanding
human rights 128, 226, 251, 290301
and obligations 128
ḥuqúqu'lláh 95, 333

Ibn-i-Aṣdaq 77
idealism 6, 11, 60, 64, 133, 211, 225, 246
idolatry 66, 95, 171-2, 176, 181, 242, 309
ijmá (consensus) 163-4
imagination 151, 170-72
 vain vii, 12, 82,142, 154, 166, 167-76, 181, 192, 249, 281
Imams 22, 26-7, 198
 Twelfth, Hidden 108, 286
imitation 62, 82-3, 84, 89, 142, 154, 163-6, 172-4, 176-7, 188, 200, 202, 217, 220, 249, 317
 see also taqlid
immortality 101, 152, 184-6
imperfections 96, 149, 167, 186, 194-5
imperialism 4, 25, 38, 57, 101, 197, 237, 280, 330
industrial disputes 169, 237, 319
industrial sciences 298
industry, industrialists 37, 67, 69, 70, 290
Inis, Claude 38
international agreements 37, 52, 56
International Court of Justice 129, 289-90
internationalism 69, 85, 132, 246, 280, 309
international law 36, 57, 60, 70, 99, 101, 296
international relations 2, 36-7, 41, 58, 125, 131, 237, 246, 332
international solidarity 58, 294
Iran, Iranians 18, 21, 51, 54, 55, 101, 120, 128, 134, 136, 137, 238, 240, 248, 251, 284, 285, 291, 304, 309, 324
Iranian Constitutional Revolution 240, 284
Iraq 19-20, 25, 46, 283
Isaiah, prophet 131
Islam, Islamic 5, 11, 17-18, 21-6, 28-30, 45, 74, 110, 112, 123, 125, 162-5, 207, 231-3, 282, 285, 286, 305, 310, 317, 319 *see also* Muslim
Israel 129, 238, 309, 311
Istanbul 20, 21, 25
Italy, Italians 37, 58, 70, 127, 303

Jamal (Cemal) Pasha 105, 303
Japan 55, 68, 70, 71, 127, 293, 302, 303
Jehovah's Witnesses 135
jiḥad
 abrogation of vii, 5-7, 11, 15, 21-6, 29-32, 39, 45-6, 231-3, 238, 245, 251- 292
 defensive 3, 22
 in Islam 45, 233
 in Sufism 5
 offensive 21
Job, prophet 21
Jordan, David Starr 70, 296
Judaism, Jews 17, 52, 64, 100, 108, 110, 129, 203, 282, 294, 326
Jünger, Ernst 116
jurisprudence 29, 163-5, 319
justice, injustice 1, 11, 15, 26, 39, 41, 42, 57, 68, 72, 78, 83, 85, 87, 94, 97, 113, 152, 159, 166, 167, 182, 186-9, 196, 202, 220, 223, 225, 228, 229, 239, 244, 248, 279, 292, 320, 322, 330
 force to be servant of justice 64, 292
 trilogy with peace and unity 1, 15, 114
just war 6, 45, 57, 59, 232, 245, 251, 292

Kant, Immanuel 10, 36, 40, 42-3, 163, 245, 289, 303
Karbila, Iraq 20, 22, 283
Karlberg, Michael 136
Keck, L. E. 183
Keynes, John Maynard 299
kings 15, 26-8, 39-41, 54, 81, 111, 196, 219, 231, 285, 286, 290
Kitáb-i-Aqdas 26, 28-9, 41, 46, 119-20, 134, 213, 220, 232, 282, 285, 292, 313, 319, 333
Kitáb-i-Íqán 22, 146, 184, 204, 231, 282, 321
knowledge 10, 30, 34, 87, 90, 97, 109, 112, 141, 144-7, 151-2, 156-7, 163, 165, 170-72, 175, 177, 184, 187, 190, 195, 197, 199-200, 201, 216-17, 221-9, 237, 247-50, 252, 305, 6- 320, 333
 four means of acquiring 157, 166
 of God 24, 96, 145-6, 155, 186, 200, 203, 238, 322, 330
 human, limited 143, 151-2, 157, 165, 244
 intuitive 151, 154, 317
 of oneself 187
 Satanic 155
 spiritual 151, 156-7
Küng, Hans 228, 330
Kuschel, Karl-Josef 330
Kurdistan 19, 293

Lake Mohonk Conference 69, 134, 296
Lakoff, George 209
Lambden, Stephen 28
language
 international auxiliary, universal 3, 32, 35, 37,

40, 42, 47, 52, 78, 83, 87, 89, 91-2, 100, 220, 233-4, 236, 245, 249, 289-90, 328
organic 210 *see also* organic analogy
symbolic 204, 210
unity of 91-3
law(s) 42, 76, 78, 83, 87, 96, 98, 134, 150-52, 159, 168, 207, 228
of the Báb 4-5, 22, 24, 46
of Bahá'u'lláh 6, 24, 26, 29, 41, 46, 55, 59, 67, 88, 95, 107, 113, 119, 120, 184, 194, 208, 211, 213, 216, 218, 223, 232, 233, 240, 248, 282, 290, 327, 329, 333 *see also* Kitáb-i-Aqdas
of change 151
divine 46, 55, 148, 184, 214, 282, 305
enforcement 5, 29, 36, 40, 42, 57, 83, 99, 127, 208, 240, 295
equality before the 29, 300
international 36, 57, 60, 70, 99, 101, 296
of Islam 11, 24, 30, 74, 163-5, 284, 285, 318
abrogation *see* war, holy; *jihád*
of nations 36
of nature 36, 150, 156, 175, 235, 315, 316, 321
private 193
of reciprocity 212, 214, 252-3, 326
religious, purpose of 201, 204, 228
rule of 4, 70, 246
Lawḥ-i-Karmil (Tablet of Carmel) 238, 287
Lawḥ-i-Dunyá (Tablet of the World) 23
Lawḥ-i-Ittihád (Tablet of Unity) 90, 93-5, 248
Lawḥ-i-Maqsúd 38, 39, 54, 289, 290
League of Nations 60-61, 78, 84, 99, 123, 126-7, 130, 132, 239, 245, 290, 297, 299, 310, 311, 312
Lesser Peace 3, 6, 10, 15, 31-5, 38, 42, 46-7, 115-17, 119-22, 124, 130-31, 137-8, 233, 238, 245, 249, 251, 289, 313
Lewis, Bernard 35
liberalism 4, 36, 78, 100, 115, 162, 246, 280, 329, 332
light 75-6, 90, 97, 124, 149, 152, 155-6, 160-61, 176, 182, 196, 206, 243, 311, 316, 317, 321, 322, 323
century of 63
limits, limitations 8-9, 24, 37, 40, 43, 56, 59, 70, 81-2, 88, 143, 146, 150-57, 165, 169, 176, 194, 205, 207, 213, 224, 237, 240, 247, 289, 308, 314, 315, 327, 331-2
Locarno, spirit of 126, 310
London, England 37, 79, 121, 294
love 15, 44, 51, 62-4, 71, 75, 80, 85, 87, 152-6, 161, 182, 184, 191-2, 194-5, 200, 202-3, 213, 228, 236, 279, 294, 295-6, 299, 318
of God 96, 154, 156, 171, 173, 181, 186, 188, 194, 238, 322, 330
of one's country 125 197, 290
of transcendence 181, 186-7
Lovejoy, Arthur 7-9, 183, 244, 280-81

MacEoin, Denis 5, 16, 283, 304
MacNutt, Howard 70, 297
Mahdi 46, 232
Malinovskii 36
man vii, 7, 10-11, 15, 44, 55, 63, 66-8, 71, 75, 96, 100, 142-62, 166-8, 172-7, 185-9, 193-7, 200-01, 211, 213-14, 217, 220, 225, 229, 301, 302, 308, 318, 321
dignity of vii, 12, 96, 142, 159-60, 163, 176, 241
mine rich in gems 160
inherent nobility of 147, 149, 159-61, 176, 181-2, 201, 242, 248, 315, 318
natures in 149-51, 157, 167-8, 176
perfectibility of 90, 142, 176
reality of vii, 80, 145, 148, 153, 159-60, 162, 315-16
Manifestation (of God) 1, 5, 23, 27-8, 46, 68, 95, 114, 115, 151, 155, 160-61, 165, 171, 177, 182, 189, 202, 205, 211, 214, 283, 291, 304, 307, 325
Supreme 27, 109
Universal 63
mankind, humanity, human race 10, 15, 31, 41-2, 47, 51, 56-7, 64-5, 66, 68, 81, 162, 196, 200, 240, 242, 246, 318, 321
coming of age 31, 44, 47, 105, 118, 164, 209, 212, 216, 232, 328
Covenant with God 15, 29, 35, 46, 56, 115, 142, 167, 177, 237, 330
destiny of 115, 119, 122
education of 87, 90, 156, 160, 169
evolution of 109, 124, 125, 141, 200, 213, 233, 240, 243
happiness of 15, 56, 67, 84
history, spiritual history, of 108, 115, 117, 127, 141
impact of Bahá'u'lláh's teachings on 107, 110-11, 187, 211

interests, welfare, well-being of 6, 43, 67, 75, 79, 84, 86, 90, 133, 192, 196, 218, 226-7, 246, 252
love for 161, 202
maturity of 47, 109-10, 118-19, 132, 137, 164, 204, 220, 226-8, 233, 290, 305
needs of 60, 101, 212, 229, 237, 246
oneness of 43-4, 78, 82, 87, 89, 91-3, 97, 99-100, 125-6, 137, 153, 164, 174, 197, 199-200, 203, 216, 228-9, 236-7, 248, 252, 279, 290
peace, goal of 77, 80-81, 84, 87, 112, 117, 141
potential of 11, 181, 201, 235, 241
and religion, role of 55, 78, 87, 202, 322, 332
representatives of 60, 64, 99, 233
salvation of 142, 227, 243
service to 44, 78, 145, 192, 195, 197, 200, 216, 219, 227, 229, 241, 242, 298, 331
spiritualization of 15, 156, 159, 320, 322
suffering of 52, 63, 65, 67, 71, 85, 122, 124, 127, 131, 162, 173, 224, 239, 310, 311
unification of 1, 31, 35, 112, 114, 124, 131-2, 138, 186, 202-3, 247-8, 252, 279, 283, 302
martyrdom, martyrs 3, 21, 24-5, 46, 111, 134, 205
Marxism 115, 246, 310
Mashriqu'l-Adhkár (House of Worship, Bahá'í temple) 95, 123, 241, 331
material civilization 54.5, 78, 83, 87, 96, 99, 292, 294
materialism 83, 115, 249, 294, 307
material world, materiality, vii, 6, 52, 56, 100, 101, 146, 149-50, 152, 157, 167-8, 169, 176, 186, 192, 200-01, 214, 238, 246-8, 316, 327
Messiah, Messianic 21, 28, 52, 232-3, 283, 307
metaphysics 2, 89-90, 100, 128, 156, 161-2, 169, 232, 241, 244, 281, 330
hair-splitting 157, 190, 323
Middle East 5, 52, 136
militarism 4, 39, 55, 116
military, the 40, 42-3, 56-8, 63, 66, 71, 81, 129, 290, 303, 308
military service 134-5, 234, 240
mind, human 11, 41, 54-5, 75, 80, 89, 101, 115, 141, 144, 149-51, 153, 155-8, 160, 162, 168, 170-71, 176, 182, 200-01, 210, 247, 249
Mírzá Buzurg 17-18
Mírzá Yaḥyá 19, 28, 283
moderation 46, 54, 74, 161, 183, 191, 193, 201, 284
modernity 3-5
Momen, Moojan 51
Monnier, Pasteur 204
monoanthropism 15, 43
moral, morality 2, 7, 9-10, 25-6, 45, 54-5, 66, 82, 89, 92, 96, 99-100, 150, 161, 169, 177, 181-3, 184-98, 200, 204, 216, 219, 225-33, 236-43, 247-50, 288, 292, 297, 305, 322, 330
in Bábí religion 21-2
m. choice 96, 167, 175, 187, 202
degradation of 66-7, 98, 176, 307
m. imperative 68, 93, 246-7
Kantian 40-42
rational 96-8
and taking of life 135
and use of force 57-8
Most Great Peace 3, 6, 10, 15, 31-5, 38, 44, 46, 59, 68, 72, 114-17, 120-21, 131, 138, 216, 227, 233, 238, 250-51, 279
motifs 2-3, 8, 25, 95
Movement of the Left 86
Muhammad, Prophet 17, 27, 28, 29, 125, 169, 233, 285, 318
Muhammad Shah 18
Mullá Ḥusayn 108
multilateralism 40, 58, 68
Muslims 18, 21, 23, 29-30, 35, 52, 55, 99. 108, 163-4, 170, 204, 207, 231, 249, 282, 284, 285, 286, 287, 303, 307, 319, 322 *see also* Islam

Nabíl's Narrative (*The Dawn-Breakers*) 16, 109, 304
Najaf, iraq 20, 283
Nakhjavání, 'Alí 33
Napoleon (Bonaparte) 66, 308
Napoleon III 116
Napoleonic wars 35
Naṣir-i-Dín Sháh 25
nationalism 4, 38, 66, 81, 89, 94, 125-6, 131, 197, 237, 284, 296, 307, 309, 310
nationality 10, 30, 125, 290, 308
National Spiritual Assemblies 112, 208, 213, 333
nation-building 124-5, 310
nation state 43, 125, 196, 243, 294
nations, unity of 90, 93, 120-21,
Nature (world of, law of) 42, 78-9, 82-3, 87, 92, 143-4, 146, 150, 159, 175, 200, 209, 211, 235, 294, 298, 299, 321, 326

Nazi regime 94, 211, 311
Nayríz, Iran 21, 22, 284
New York 66, 130, 132, 294, 297, 312
New York Peace Society 69, 296
Nicholas II, Tsar of Russia 56, 60, 84, 293
Nicolas, A.L.M. 204
Nineteen Day Feast 194, 218, 226, 241, 244
Nobel Prize 70, 86, 299
nobility, of man 17, 19, 72, 78, 105, 122, 132, 147, 149, 159-62, 167, 176, 181-2, 193, 201, 242, 248, 315, 318
non-aggression pact 126
non-confrontation 2, 221

Opler, Edward Morris 8-9, 211, 228, 240, 242, 326
oneness of religion vii, 91-2, 199, 205, 215-16, 228, 243, 302
oppression 41, 58, 96, 136, 292, 313, 330
organic
  analogy 109, 114, 124, 128, 146, 204, 208, 209-16, 228-9, 243, 250, 252, 326
  unity 9, 12, 93, 183, 209-15, 216, 228, 243-4, 248, 326
Ottomans, Ottoman Empire 3-5, 30, 34, 43, 52, 108, 285, 288, 297, 303

pacifism 5, 36, 134-6, 138, 240, 294, 299, 313
Paine, Thomas 43, 245
Palestine, Palestinians 129, 311
Pankhurst, Emmeline 74
pantheism 145, 153, 302, 316
Paris, France 55, 206, 294, 300
  Treaty of 43, 288
patriotism 125, 155, 177, 313
  and prejudice 66, 70, 82, 87, 92
  and war 51, 66, 70, 323
peace
  Bahá'í concept of, approach to1-12, 15-16, 45, 52, 84, 8-9-90, 112, 123, 134-6, 182-9, 228, 231, 244-53, 310
    in teachings of 'Abdu'l-Bahá 32, 47, 52, 55, 56, 62-4, 78-85, 99-101, 121, 224, 233-8, 245, 247-8, 251
    in teachings of Bahá'u'lláh 15-16, 31-2, 38-40, 43-6, 81, 220, 231-2, 245
    in writings of Shoghi Effendi 15, 106, 112, 114-18, 119-20, 1330-31, 136, 137-8, 238-40, 252
  conference (advocated by Bahá'ú'lláh and 'Abdu'l-Bahá) 40-41, 56, 99, 219–20
  foundations of 229, 240, 244, 247
  Greater 32, 46, 115
  inner, spiritual 154, 161, 167-8, 170, 175, 197, 231
  international 72, 78, 80, 235, 302
  Lesser 3, 6, 10, 15, 31-5, 38, 42, 46-7, 115-17, 119-22, 124, 130-31, 137-8, 233, 238, 245, 249, 251, 289, 313
  Most Great 3, 6, 10, 15, 31-5, 38, 44, 46, 59, 68, 72, 114-17, 120-21, 131, 138, 216, 227, 233, 238, 250-51, 279
  political 35-40, 52, 56-9, 68, 73-81, 88, 119-20, 121, 126, 236, 244, 251-2, 288-9
  as process 119, 141, 215
  religion, role of in 174, 201-3, 228, 279
  scope of 78-81, 86, 90, 99-101, 142, 151, 181, 224, 227, 234, 240, 243, 247-9, 251-2, 332
  social, general 67, 81, 161, 197, 244
  trilogy with justice and unity
  and unity 24, 52, 58, 62, 118, 120-21, 215, 243
  universal 1-2, 32, 55-9, 68, 72, 74, 76, 77-8, 80-84, 86-7, 91, 96, 99, 132, 141, 202, 217, 233, 236-7, 247
  women and 74-6, 108, 298
Peace Conference
  in Bahá'í writings 40-41, 56, 99, 219-20
  at The Hague 293
  at Lake Mohonk 69
peace organizations 62, 69, 101
peace treaties 287
  binding 56, 99
  of Paris 43, 288
  Turkomanchy 25
  of Versailles 65, 77, 85, 126
  of Vienna 43
people of Bahá 6, 29, 181, 239
perfectibility (of man) vii, 90, 142, 167, 176, 195, 229, 242, 247-8, 332
perfections 9, 83, 96, 110, 142, 145, 148-50, 152, 155, 176, 181-2, 186, 188, 243, 315-16 *see also* imperfections
Peters, Rudolph 164
philanthropy 69, 70, 94, 114, 192
philosophy, philosophers 16, 40, 42, 45, 89, 101, 136, 151, 199-200, 226, 229, 281, 289, 323, 326
  divine 2, 90, 199-200, 243, 324

natural 200
Plato, Platonism 160, 200, 317
policing 136
internal 36, 40, 57, 297
international 70, 135
politics, politicians 3, 8, 17, 28, 42-3, 51-2, 69, 74-8, 82, 84, 98, 99, 105, 110, 125, 133, 134, 237, 252-3, 308
international 289
national 66
new form of 252
(non)-participation of Bahá'ís in 135, 240
and peace 35, 77, 81, 120, 224, 236, 244, 252
and religion 55, 231, 285, 287, 300
and war 51, 70, 246, 252
political
corruption 307
freedom 141
prejudice 78, 82-3, 87, 92
reform 100
revolution 37, 123, 240, 246, 284, 294
unity 90, 92, 93, 109, 120-22, 124, 131, 173, 233
poverty 87, 98, 156, 168, 175, 187, 302, 318
power
of words (utterance) 19, 23, 63, 160, 191, 223, 229, 323
powerlessness 67, 156
prayer 136, 170, 220, 314
prejudice vii, 10, 12, 66, 78-83, 87, 89-93, 100, 115, 133, 142, 166, 172-7, 181, 189, 194, 220, 228, 234-6, 242-3, 247-9, 281, 321, 329
press, the 52, 62
prison 18-19, 43, 52, 66, 98, 167-8, 311, 319
of ego, self 194, 319
of limitations 224
progress 54, 66, 97-8, 109, 115, 117, 151-2, 175, 201, 215, 236-7, 249, 288, 308, 314-5, 321, 327, 328, 332
progressive movement 89, 205, 251
progessive revelation 124, 203, 206-7, 209, 228, 239, 330
Promised Day Is Come, The 106, 128, 238, 287, 204, 205
prophecy 21, 29, 64, 11, 119, 225, 239, 300, 308
public opinion 47, 62, 91-2, 127, 135, 166, 217, 229, 233, 234, 245, 248, 299, 302, 332
punishment 17, 21, 83, 96-8, 173, 320
capital 66
Qá'im 21, 27, 46, 205, 232
Qayyumu'l-Asmá' 21, 28, 191
Quadruple Alliance 36
Quakers 69, 135, 317, 332
quietism 5
Qur'án 28, 29, 108, 125, 164, 172, 210, 218, 285, 302, 305, 314, 319, 320

race, racial 94, 121, 127, 203, 236-7, 243
discrimination 128
diversity of 212
human 15, 31, 44, 56-7, 87, 92, 105, 109, 118, 197, 200, 226
new race of men 159, 181, 241, 318
prejudice 10, 66, 87, 92, 94, 133, 173, 189, 197, 236-7, 242, 299
segregation 239
unity of 33, 87, 91-2, 112, 114, 125, 127-8, 160, 162, 164, 174, 201, 209, 295
war 51, 70
racialism 94, 101, 211, 299, 302
Radhakrishnan, S. 16
ranks and stations 18, 29, 93, 94, 145-7, 153, 219
rational, rationality 2, 38, 149-51, 156-7, 162, 176, 203, 217, 219, 223, 250, 317, 329
rational morality 96-8
rational soul 150, 155-6
reciprocity 35, 44, 45, 52, 112, 154, 182, 212-14, 223, 242, 253, 326, 327
Redman, Earl 51
realism, realistic 4, 6, 11, 42, 45, 68, 116, 162, 171, 211, 246, 280, 290
utopian 4, 280
reason, reasoning 16, 34, 36, 42-3, 54, 82, 86, 87, 96, 97, 151-2, 154, 157-8, 163-4, 171, 183, 199, 201, 242, 281, 295, 317, 318, 320, 331
reconciliation 52, 59, 119, 141, 182-4, 205, 223, 243, 284,315, 326
international 35, 39, 41, 72, 89
of religious differences 52, 141, 182, 205, 243, 331
refinement 9, 55, 156, 181, 188, 189, 191, 201, 228-9, 243, 332, 333
regime change 57
religion
civilizing role of 97, 99, 187-8, 322, 330
love, cause of 51, 78, 279, 318
oneness, unity of vii, 15, 31, 33, 62, 87,

90-94, 199, 202-3, 205, 209, 215-16, 228, 243, 302, 325
peace, cause of 1, 24, 68, 78, 79-81, 87, 168, 174, 201-2, 228
reconciliation of 52, 141, 182, 205, 243, 331
and science 55, 78, 87, 89, 91, 100, 141, 199, 217-18, 234, 236, 247, 249
unity, cause of 1, 24, 78, 87, 100, 201-2, 318
Remey, Mason 86-7
renewal 26, 63, 142-4, 174, 187, 233, 241, 243, 294
revelation
of the Báb 5, 26, 305
of Bahá'u'lláh (Bahá'í r.) 6, 24-5, 29, 46-7, 74, 109, 111, 117, 119, 137, 181, 188, 190, 204-6, 218, 231, 233, 241, 279, 285, 304-6, 331
in previous religions 95, 124, 137, 284, 319
progressive 124, 174, 204, 207, 209, 228, 239, 241, 243, 306, 330
role of 97, 106, 141, 158, 160, 200, 237, 321
universal 6
Revelation, Book of (in New Testament) 63, 181, 213
revolution 37, 123, 240, 246, 284, 294
Reza Shah 240, 333
Riḍván
Declaration of Bahá'u'lláh 21, 22, 25, 141
Garden of, Baghdad 20, 22, 24, 160
ritual impurity 6, 29, 30-31, 46, 231
Roman Empire 45, 71, 110, 123
romanticism 281, 330
Rousseau, Charles 289
Rousseau, Jean-Jacques 36, 245, 288
rule of law 4, 70, 246
rulers (and kings) 3, 15, 26-8, 33, 39, 41-4, 46-7, 57-8, 111, 115-16, 196, 213, 245, 288, 322
of America 41
European 15, 116
Muslim 35
Russia, Russians 18, 25, 60, 68, 71-2, 288, 293, 294, 309
Russo-Japanese war 68

Saiedi, Nader 5, 16, 22, 332
Saint-Pierre, Abbé 36, 288
Saint Simon 4, 37, 245, 280
salvation 30, 119, 142, 175, 186, 196, 207, 227, 243, 277, 318
sanctions 41, 57, 126-7, 289, 299, 329
San Francisco Chronicle 72
San Francisco Conference 130, 297
Satan, satanic 80, 155, 162, 317, 318
Scharbrodt, Oliver 4, 51
science 151-2, 157, 161, 177, 190, 235, 298, 323, 331
education in 83, 90, 98, 298
esoteric 317
of peace 71
pseudo- 235
and religion 55, 78, 87, 89, 91, 100, 141, 199, 217-18, 234, 236, 247, 249
of war 65-6, 71, 80, 159, 235
script, one common 40
second birth 181, 186
Secret of Divine Civilization, The 24, 39, 51, 54-8, 91, 99, 128, 165, 217, 218-19, 231, 233-4, 248-9, 285, 286, 291
security
collective *see* collective security
concept of 89
international 36-8, 59, 234, 251
national 39-40, 41, 57, 91, 132
and peace 42, 44, 58, 81, 86, 100, 162, 247, 251
and penalties 168
personal 291
sedition 15, 22-3, 25-6, 231-2
self-defence 30, 134, 136, 138, 289, 313
self-interest 66-7, 72, 171, 242, 288, 331
service 75, 87, 132, 147, 160, 167, 182-3, 214, 226-8, 333
to humanity 44, 67, 78, 190-203, 216, 219, 237, 241-2, 331
military 134-5, 234, 240
servitude (to God) 145, 184, 221
Seven Candles of Unity 90-97, 120-21, 205, 248
Seven Valleys 164, 184
Sharia 29, 163
Shaykhism 18
Shí'ism 3, 18, 284
Shoghi Effendi
life of 105-6, 303, 311
writings and translations 32-3, 106-7, 109, 210, 238, 294 *see also God Passes By*, *The Promised Day Is Come*, 'The Unfoldment of World Civilization', *The World Order of Bahá'u'lláh*

for writings by Shoghi Effendi on the various themes in this book, see separate entries
Short, W. H. 70
sincerity 96, 166, 186, 193, 197, 235, 324
Siyáh-Chál 18-19, 284
Siyyid Káẓim-i-Rashtí 108. 109, 204, 304
slavery 101, 233, 280
Smiley, Albert 69, 296
Smith, Peter 2-3, 123, 279-80, 310
socialism 78, 84, 197, 294, 332
social reformism 3
sociology 2-3, 8, 15, 218, 280, 299, 306, 326
Socrates 200, 247-8
Some Answered Questions 51, 312-13
Sorel, George 116
soul, human 148-51, 154-6, 160, 168, 171, 175-6, 184-5, 188-9, 192, 194-5, 201, 211, 227, 331, 304, 306, 318, 321, 328
immortality of 101, 184-5, 249
sovereignty
of God 35, 46, 63, 142, 232
national 43, 61, 94, 120, 124-6, 133, 137, 231, 239, 244, 286, 305
Spengler, Oswald 210-11
spirit 143-56, 167-9, 176, 182, 190-91, 200-01, 204, 214, 238, 252, 305, 327
animal 153, 316
divine 151, 153-6
of faith 152-3, 156, 201
Holy 62, 87, 149, 151, 153, 156-7, 182, 200-01, 224, 242, 301, 321
human 148-56, 167, 175-6, 182, 192, 214, 242, 305, 316
of service 87, 219
vegetable 153, 316
spiritual
attributes 23, 75, 148, 159, 169, 187-9, 190-95
behaviour 187, 189, 190-93
peace 154, 168
perspective 54, 91, 109, 154, 243
powers 63, 67, 201, 321
reality of man 149, 167, 175, 182, 206, 214
transformation 220, 240-41
spirituality vii, 116, 146, 148, 167, 171, 182, 185-8, 190, 207, 227, 299, 320
spiritualization 15, 25, 45, 138, 153, 176, 193, 211, 227, 245, 327
standardization 37
Stanford University 70, 73
Stockman, Robert 51, 300
struggle for existence 52, 79, 83, 99, 101, 162, 235, 299
Suez Canal 37
suffering 21-3, 66, 80, 85, 97, 123, 124, 127, 234, 321
redemptive 22, 26
Sufism 5, 45, 287, 306-7
suffrage, universal 76
Sulaymaniyyih 20
Sultan (of Ottoman Empire) 25, 27, 28
super-state 125-6, 245, 303, 311

ta 'áṣṣub (prejudice, fanaticism) 7, 9, 11, 12, 82, 242, 281 *see also* prejudice
Ṭabarsí, Shaykh 5, 22, 23, 284
Tablet to the Hague 6, 11, 51, 60, 77-85, 86, 90-92, 94, 99-100, 233-4, 237, 246-8, 282, 298
Tablet to Queen Victoria 38, 42, 44, 218
Tablets of the Divine Plan 130, 238, 313
Taft, President 73
Tagore, Rabindranath 16, 69, 72, 296, 297, 302
Ṭáhirih 22, 74, 284, 297
taqlíd (imitation) 7, 9-12, 25, 29, 154, 162-5, 173-4, 177, 181, 188, 195, 220, 227, 249, 286, 316, 319
taxation 34, 67
technology 10, 70, 100
Tehran, Iran 17
Ten Year Crusade, Plan 123, 129, 240, 307, 308, 310
themes, sub-themes 7-9, 242, 281, 307
Titanic, the 294
tolerance, intolerance 203, 205, 223, 232, 252, 280
toleration 34, 36, 205, 236
Torah 204
trade 36, 190, 218, 246, 290, 293, 296, 297 *see also* commerce
free 37, 245, 288, 297
Training Institute, Bahá'í 213, 250, 333
transcendence 143, 147-8, 153, 164, 172, 181, 186-7, 239, 243
transition 15, 34-5, 58, 109, 111, 115, 120, 138, 184, 305
treaties *see* peace treaties
tribunal(s) 36, 288

Hague 60, 299
Supreme, universal, world 60-61, 78, 84, 87, 89, 91, 126, 233, 236, 245, 300
Tripoli 60, 295
truth 1, 24, 30, 34, 43, 82, 106, 128, 151, 158, 172, 175-6, 191-2, 195, 199, 202, 204-7, 211, 220, 222-3, 234-6, 238, 242-4, 248, 290, 297, 302, 320, 325
independent, unfettered, investigation of 78, 82, 87, 89-90, 91, 100, 162, 165-6, 182-3, 199, 217, 221, 227, 229, 236, 244, 249, 301
truthfulness 63, 166, 189, 193, 221, 228, 328
Twelfth Imám 108
twelve principles 86-92, 301
twentieth century 63, 120, 141, 233, 294, 303, 332

ulamá 10, 29, 54-5, 163, 229, 285, 331
ummah 22, 29, 231, 233, 310
understanding, human (gift of) 42, 54, 145, 157, 161, 168, 172, 185-6, 192-3, 220, 244, 324
spiritual 156
UNESCO 290
'Unfoldment of World Civilization, The' 106, 109, 120, 238, 294
United Nations 128-30, 207, 247, 289, 297, 303, 309, 310, 311
Charter 129-30, 297
Security Council 129, 288
United States 69, 72, 80, 101, 126-8, 130-32, 216, 235, 237, 297, 301, 313
of Europe 310
see also America
unit ideas 8-9, 244-5, 251, 281
unity
of conscience 2, 52, 77, 80-81, 86, 90-91, 93, 100, 217, 223-4, 236, 247
in diversity 93, 183, 210-12, 215, 228, 244, 248, 326
organic 9, 12, 93, 183, 209-15, 216, 228, 243-4, 248, 326
political 90, 92, 93, 109, 120-22, 124, 131, 173, 233
trilogy with justice and peace 1
see also freedom, God, language, nations, peace, political, race, religion, Seven Candles of Unity
Universal House of Justice 33-4, 47, 106, 111, 113, 117, 119-20, 137, 208, 215, 218, 239, 244, 279, 290, 293, 303, 309, 311, 313, 330
universality 126, 205, 245, 316
utopia, utopian 4, 37, 39, 69, 73, 88, 244, 280
utopian realism 4, 280
utterance, power of 191, 229 *see also* words

Vaḥíd 21
vain imaginings vii, 12, 82,142, 154, 166, 167-76, 181, 192, 249, 281
Versailles, Treaty of 65, 77, 85, 126
Victoria, Queen 38, 42, 44, 218
Vienna, Treaty of 43
violence 15, 17, 19, 23, 26, 30, 43, 45-6, 76, 96-101, 134, 136, 142, 159, 160, 162, 166, 167-73, 176-7, 182, 191, 231-4, 237, 240-46, 249-52, 294, 307, 314, 318
state-led 11, 36, 116
virtues 83, 97-8, 128, 137, 142, 147, 150, 152-3, 166, 181-3, 187-9, 192-3, 200, 220, 223, 227-8, 242, 316, 321
Voll, John 164
voluntary sharing 29, 78, 83, 87, 92, 95

Waltz, Kenneth N. 142, 314
war 1, 6-7, 15, 26, 31, 35-8, 42-6, 116, 121, 122, 128, 131-2, 134-5, 142, 162, 167, 231-5, 243, 251-2, 187-8, 292-3, 298, 307-8, 313, 314, 320, 331
holy 3, 5, 6, 23-6, 29, 30, 45, 232, 287, 319 *see also jihad*
just 6, 45, 57, 59, 232, 245, 251, 292
Warburg, Margit 3
wealth 17, 67, 87, 94, 147, 170-71, 187, 193, 243
unity of 95
western
Bahá'ís 86, 109-10, 112, 293, 300
civilization 72, 99
governments, powers 54, 72, 197, 303
imperialism 25
press 52
traditions, systems 4-5, 10, 31, 57, 68, 86, 94, 157, 244, 297
women 74, 298
Wilhelm I, of Prussia 29
William II, Kaiser 116
Wilson, Woodrow 72-3, 101, 115, 130, 132, 239, 297, 317
fourteen principles 73, 130, 297

wisdom, wise 2, 54, 64, 80, 112, 144-6, 148, 157, 169, 191, 193, 200, 219, 223-4, 229, 247, 252, 286, 315, 320
women 30, 74, 80, 90, 100, 159, 167, 197, 236, 251, 297-8
equality with men 74-5, 78, 83, 87, 89, 91, 222, 234, 240
and peace 52, 74-6, 100, 141, 237, 298
words, power of 19, 23, 63, 160, 191, 223, 229, 323
creative 10, 108, 144, 228, 330
see also God, Word of
world citizenship 43-4, 91, 118, 132, 197, 246, 290, 308
world civilization 31, 114, 118, 120-22, 313
world government 131, 303
world undertakings, unity in 90-91, 93, 100, 141, 217, 236, 247
World War I 38, 65, 68, 79, 85, 130-31, 135, 233, 294, 297, 302, 312
World War II 100, 110, 116, 118, 120, 128-9, 130-31, 302
World Order of Bahá'u'lláh 47, 107-8, 117-18, 122, 136, 189, 241
World Order of Bahá'u'lláh, The 109, 237-8

Yazdání, Aḥmad 77
Young Ottomans (Turks) Revolution 4-5, 52

Zanján 22, 23, 284

About the Author

Born in Pamplona, Spain, Miguel Gil studied History at the University of Navarre, and subsequently obtained an MA in modern European studies (Monash University), a Postgraduate Diploma in Translating (Victoria College of the Arts), and a PhD at La Trobe University in Australia. Miguel has translated over seventy titles of Bahá'í literature into Spanish and has also served in various capacities on different Bahá'í bodies both in Spain and Australia. He is the author of *Diálogo de Religions: Camino de Paz*, and *Hacia un Discurso Bahá'í* (*Dialogue of Religions: A Pathway to Peace*, and *Towards a Bahá'í Discourse*). He is currently finishing working on two bilingual dictionaries, Spanish–Persian, and a Persian–Spanish reader. He currently resides in greater Melbourne with his wife, Elham Sami.

www.ingramcontent.com/pod-product-compliance
Lightning Source LLC
Chambersburg PA
CBHW081757300426
44116CB00014B/2156
* 9 7 8 0 8 5 3 9 8 6 5 0 8 *